IN
ENDLESS
WRATH

IN ENDLESS WRATH

Unraveling the Congo Genocide Inside
Africa's Longest War

XEBO

ARPress
ILLUMINATING IDEAS.
EMPOWERING VOICES

ARPress
45 Dan Road Suite 5
Canton MA 02021

Hotline: (888) 821-0229
Fax: 1(508) 545-7580

Ordering Information:
Quantity sales. Special discounts are available on quantity purchases by corporations, associations, and others. For details, contact the publisher at the address above.

Printed in the United States of America.
ISBN-13:   Paperback   979-8-89356-809-7
               eBook   979-8-89356-810-3

Library of Congress Control Number: 2024904470

TABLE OF CONTENTS

TO THE X MILLIONS
SLAUGHTERED IN ENDLESS WRATH
IN EASTERN DRC
Unraveling the Congo Genocide Inside
Africa's Longest War

CHAPTER 1
THE UNEXPECTED ENCOUNTER

On that sunny Saturday at the end of the month of May, the vast landscape, in front the Bass Lake Retreat Center in Wake County, was adorned by a thick resplendent green grass lawn. Tall white oak trees provided, every twenty square yard or so, a magnificent shadow under the cool wind breeze of late Spring. For guests arriving to celebrate a wedding, the center offered a gorgeous setting. On the right-hand side of the big house, tall red maple trees stood in captivating contrast against the shining green lawn where the landscape washed into the expansive lake. In the back of the building there was a two stories annex building where the wedding party including the bride, the maid of honor and the bridesmaids occupy the top floor, while the groom, the best man and the groomsmen occupy the first floor.

On this Saturday of May 25, 2013, the weather in the Raleigh area was balmy. This was a descent, pleasing and warm temperature during the long Memorial Day weekend, overing between sixty-five and eighty degrees. It was rather dry, not cold, or hot, perfect weather for a wedding event and for the guests who came from many regions of the US.

On the top floor of the Center building, Mado Chibere, the bride, was quietly pondering over the incredible trifecta that has jolted her life this latter part of Spring. She has just graduated from Duke University with a combined degree of Bachelor of Science and Master of Science in Chemistry with Hight Distinction. She has completed all phases of her matrimonial steps including the civil, the traditional and in about two hours or so, she would conclude the religious step. Finally, after a week of planned honeymoon in the island of Martinique, she would be joining her husband, the very sweet Kolokay Boda in their new house in Dallas, Texas, metropolitan area where she has already locked in a

1

job of assistant lecturer in Chemistry at a local college.

From the huge window of the annex top floor, looking outside to the long line of festive and noisy guests arriving to honor her wedding, Mado had a sudden strange sense of both panic attach and overwhelming joy for the tremendous achievement of the trifecta. She attributed all that to being resilient, studious, patient and above all for following assiduously every counsel that her parents provided. That was essentially the case from her loving and dotting father, Reverend Patrick Chibere, affectionally called "Pa Chi" in the Congolese community. A God-fearing man, now a towering elder pastor at the Raleigh Metropolitan Church of Our Savior. Mado said a quiet prayer to thank her parents for sustaining her all along.

Mado closed her eyes and remembered her family odyssey to get to the glorious event they were about to enjoy. She remembered how the family abandoned their village escaping the endless wars that visited the Eastern region of her native Democratic Republic of Congo, arriving in the US as a political exile at the age of eight years old by way of countless refugee's camps in place she could not remember in Uganda and Tanzania. They luckily arrived in the US as the same family unit which left DRC with the same parents, three sisters and a brother. Mado could not remember the atrocities, the depravations, the acts of humiliation that her parents faced throughout the odyssey. Yet she knew that her parents never lost faith and always managed to look ahead and to strive for a better hopeful future that the awesome God they trust and pray for daily reserved for them and their children.

With her eyes still closed, Mado whispered to herself: "God is great! And it is certainly Not Bad, Not Bad indeed for a cringy girl from Walikale"! Walikale being the Eastern territory of the North Kivu province of DRC.

While still in deep thoughts with her eyes closed, Mado was shaken up to the festive mondain reality of the day. She was brought back to the happening of the wedding. The maid of honor and the bridesmaids were engaged in a naughty loud conversation about what would happen to Mado after the wedding hoopla. In a high pitch laughter, they wanted to know if Mado has thought or dreamed about the libidinous invasion that would occur when everybody would be gone after the wedding party, and she would be left alone naked to deal with the invasion. They asked and insisted on knowing how Mado

2

would react when confronted with the presumed big member of her husband when he would try to penetrate her presumed virgin lower part. Mado stayed quiet for a second and did not answer. Childishly she ran up to the bathroom and closed it quickly to relieve herself of another anxiety attack she did not want to think about. The naughty gang raised another laughing uproar behind.

The joyous party continued further that afternoon, when Mado's elder pastor father presided over the religious wedding ceremony for his daughter, assisted by the entire pastoral body of the church. The father could not restrain himself from crying throughout the entire ceremony until his deputy pastor had to relieve him from officiating. The wedding party continued with guest being serenaded with Congolese gospel music during the dinner and the mix of Congolese gospel and secular music when the dinner was winding down.

It was during that party intermission that a lady by the name Charlotte Keregi, a longtime friend of Mado's mother, Mrs. Suzanne Chibere noticed something astray. Charlotte was helping to serve food for about two hours. A very beautiful lady in her late forty, Charlotte claimed to be a window from the time she arrived in the US in the same group as the Chibere's family. She managed to make a new life for herself in the US when she arrived and quickly entered the health care field. Despite her limited English currency, she struggled to take nursing academic studies for a long time to graduate as a Registered Nurse. She maintained a very private life, keeping to herself. She devoted most of her free time to Church functions under the leadership of "Pa Chi". But she avoided any social entanglements, helping as much as she can her good friend Mrs. Chibere.

While she was serving food to the guests, she noticed a very well-dressed gentleman being served. She thought that she recognized him from the time of sad war events in Walikale. She was surprised and shocked to see the man talking and laughing loudly, eagerly, and publicly with no trace of any concern of being recognized in the middle of the Congolese community. Charlotte rushed to the bathroom to collect herself. While in the bathroom she became convinced that she was hallucinating, she made a mistake. But she started sweating profusely as if she was sick or something. She came out of the stool and wiped her face with cold water. At that instant, her longtime friend Mrs. Chibere, who was looking for her help walking in and was also surprised about

3

her state of mind.

"What is going on Charlotte, I saw you rushing out of the helping line and coming here. It was not like you, cool Charlotte. I waited to see you come back but you did not. That is why I came to check on you. And you are looking even far worse than when I saw you a while ago. What is going on?"

"My very dear Suzanne, maybe I am hallucinating. But I saw him right here, I almost served him food. But when I saw him advancing through the food line I ran out. I came her."

"Please, Charlotte, you did you see whom. I don't understand. Who is he?"

"Major Adamas Kagita!"

"Who?"

"I am telling you I saw Major Adamas Kagita!"

"Who is Major Ada... Adamas Karuga, Kagita?"

"I am sorry, Suzanne, I am not here to spoil your daughter's wedding party. I don't want to stir any trouble, a terrible past, terrible memories I have never shared with you or anybody, Suzanne. Let me collect myself. I don't want to step out and see that man again. He reminds me of the worse day of my life. I told you, maybe I am mistaken. My God, I just cannot believe that he would come in middle of us and prance as nothing has happened... I beg you, Suzanne. It is your daughter's wedding, and I love Mado as a daughter I never had. Please go back to attend your daughter's wedding. I would be OK. Just give a time to recover. I would quietly get to my car and go home. I would be all right!"

"Charlotte, I cannot leave you in that stage you are in. No way. There is nobody here in Raleigh I can depend on as a sister. You have always been there for me. The wedding is almost done with it. But you Charlotte, you have always been for me and for my family. When Mado moves on with her husband, we will be left here in the Raleigh area. We will continue to depend on each other. I cannot leave you now. No way. You and I will be stepping out to get to the bottom of this as quietly as possible. Come on sister! Wait, put back a bit of your make-up you know how. I am waiting for you. You know what we need to do. We

4

will take a cell picture of him. We will check him around and see if you are mistaken. If he was a criminal you knew back home, then well we will take care of him today. The nerve of him to come to my daughter's wedding, he is the one spoiling things, not you! Let us go!"

The ladies finally came out of the bathroom. People were now dancing to the latest secular tune by Koffi Olomide, a Congolese super star. And it did not take long for Charlotte to identify the Major. He was dancing with a lady she did not recognize. She took a frontal picture of the Major and his dancing partner. Her friend Suzanne also did the same. That provoked the Major to go back to where he was seated. To Mrs. Chibere's horror, he was seated on the VIP side of the wedding party. Suzanne was now curious to find out who he was seated with. Again, another horror, he was in an animated conversation with the Church second in command pastor who relieved her husband during the tearful wedding ceremony. Suzanne resolved to change their strategy.

Mrs. Chibere dragged Charlotte back to the bathroom for consultation.

"Charlotte, things do not look good at all. This man came in as invited by the church deputy pastor. I noticed he was a bit unsettled when I took his frontal picture. He did not appreciate it and went to seat. Now I would like to ask you to wait for me here. I am going to talk my husband who would check the man out. If possible, he would invite him in a secure place where you can come and out the man. Would that work for you?"

"Yes!"

"Now before I leave, tell me briefly what is the deal with this man, what has he done to you back then? I must tell my husband the gravity of the problem."

"It is a grave sad issue. Well, do you remember the gold mine carrier in Walikale? He was the butcher of Kwazimu mines. He was responsible for my husband murder, both my parents' murder, two of my uncles' murder, my older sister killing, and my younger brother killing. Major Adamas Kagita hacked all of them to death because he could not have me, and he claimed that he was double timed by my two uncles about a gold convoy. I managed to run away to distant relatives in Rutshuru territory while he was searching for me, and I joined your fleeing group

5

to Uganda. It was a nightmare I swore never to relive until today and I never told that story until I saw him today."

"OK, all right, and you don't want me to help you out! Hell no! It is my nightmare too! Just hang tight here, I am going to have a serious talk with my husband!"

It took about forty-five minutes for Suzanne to come back.

"My husband told me that from everything he saw and heard, he is also convinced that you are telling the truth. He has decided to drag the man to a center office in the back and will call us to join them. Stay put! Jesus, the nerve of him. We will get to the bottom of this. I will come back soon."

As soon as Suzanne left, Charlotte reached out to her cell phone and dialed 911.

"Yes, maam, my name is Charlotte Keregi, I want report that I have on sight a gentleman that has been researched to have killed six of my relatives. He is right here at this party enjoying himself."

"Maam, if this is this a prank or a crank call, I am going to send cops to arrest you, you hear me. Now what kind of help do you want or get out of this 911 call."

"No, maam, this is not a crank call, I am telling you that the man who has murdered my six relatives is here at this wedding. If you do not send police, he would disappear and probably go on murdering more people. Do want this on you head and record."

"No, where are you, I am sending a bunch of cops to arrest this murderer."

"Thank you, I am waiting for you outside the Bass Lake Center building. They must ask for Charlotte Keregi. Thank Your!"

As soon she hanged, Suzanne came in and gave the room number where her husband was guiding the man.

"I need to advise and warn my daughter of the probable disturbance that may happen. But my husband assured me that the whole thing will be dealt with as much as possible as we can. We must get to the bottom of this. Hang tight, I will see you later."

6

Charlotte packed her stuff and went in front of the building to wait for the cops. It did not take long for the cops to come in three cars sirens blazing loudly. Charlotte run up to them to shut off the sirens. She took them to the back of building not to disturb the wedding party and found the room where the Major was seated talking with the Elder Pastor.

The cops did not wait to engage in the conversation and put handcuffs on the major who looked completely bewildered. After he was secured, the lead cop asked Charlotte to identify the man.

"Yes, sir, that is Major Adamas Kagita who killed six members of my family in Kwazimu Mines in Walikale in the North Kivu Province of DRC.":

The arresting officers were completely shocked to hear Charlotte's accusation.

"Maam, can you repeat your accusations against this man."

"Yes, sir, that is Major Adamas Kagita who killed six members of my family in Kwazimu Mines in Walikale in the North Kivu Province of DRC.":

"But maam, we do not recognize any US jurisdiction in your statement. We don't know if we can arrest this man."

"Six people hacked to death and you don't want to arrest him, six people of my family killed, you want to release the murderer. I don't understand. Are we in North Carolina?"

"I understand what you are saying but I am afraid we do not have ground to arrest this gentleman. If he had murdered your relatives in the US, I would be glad to arrest him but we cannot proceed about murders in jurisdictions we do not and cannot police. Do you understand maam?"

"No, if you would let him go and he would come to kill me. Is that what you want to happen? Please, arrest this man. I cannot believe that I have to argue about this. He is a criminal. That is ridiculous."

"Sir, what is your name?"

"My name is Okito Jefferson.'

"Where do you live?"

"In Barco Corolla area!"

"Oh, that is by the sea!"

"Yes, it is beautiful area!"

"What do you do there?"

'I am retired."

"Well, maam, we have a problem here. First of all, the man is not the Major you have identified, and he lives in a very nice area of North Carolina. This must be a mistaken identity."

"No, I know this man and I can assure you that he killed my family relatives."

"What about you, Sir, do you know this man?"

"No, I never met him until today. I am Reverend Patrick Chibere, I am the father of the bride. I trust the lady here for identifying this man. I believe her. In my country a lot of people have committed despicable crimes, you have no idea. Letting him go would be a grave mistake."

"I am sorry Sir. I did not say that we are going to let him go. We will book him at the precinct, we have already registered all the accusations that the lady provided us. After booking the gentleman then we would let him go after notifying all levels of state and federal legal jurisdictions about the lady accusations. I would advise the lady to bring her accusations appropriately starting at the district court and that will be properly adjudicated all the way up to the right jurisdiction. That is the best thing we could do now. Don't worry, the man would come with us to the precinct. The march to justice is a bit long and complicated in the US, but if the accusations from the Lady are correct and stand, the man would pay the price for his crimes at the end. Bye!"

Major Adamas Kagita was led in handcuffs by the back of the building and straight into one of the police cars that was brought very close to the back entrance. The cops left. Very few of the guests inside the Center were aware of what had happened in the background of the wedding party which continued without disturbances. The Elder Pastor and his wife tried in vain to console and hold a very perturbed Charlotte to enjoy the waning hours of the wedding party. At about five forty-five in the evening, the bride's parents decided to let Charlotte go home. Still, they secured a niece to follow Charlotte Keregi to her house around Clayton suburb.

CHAPTER 2

LEGAL REMEDIES

As soon as Charlotte reached home, she quickly removed the wedding beautiful dress she wore and cried to herself to sleep. She was extremely upset and remorseful for the disturbance she thought she caused during the wedding ceremony that her best friends, the mother and the father of the bride held that day.

Charlotte felt bad to have spoiled the wedding party despite all the consolation and the support the couple provided for her. No matter what the couple told her that they have managed to keep the incident very private, Charlotte kept repeating that she should not have called 911 to alert the cops to arrest Major Adamas. The couple insisted that they were duty bound to assist her and that they were equally victims of the same atrocities that she has suffered back home. The Chibere repeated many times that these atrocities have visited most of the wedding guests and there was nothing Charlotte needed to be excused about and they would have reacted the same way and reached the same decision to involve the police if they have met any of their former executioners in the US or anywhere else in the world. Charlotte pushed back telling the couple that she was more concerned about how their daughter Mado felt about the disturbance that could have wrecked the most important day of her life. The couple dismissed that chain of thought and tried to convince Charlotte that their children shared their feelings about all these events in the Eastern region of DRC. But they did not reveal that they have not talked nor discussed about the same events with their kids since they came to the US, In fact, the couple had decided then to spare their children the difficult exchange about these atrocities. The couple decided to trust God to guide their children to find for themselves the painful odyssey of the family coming to the US. The conversation with the couple went nowhere when Charlotte, in the end, requested to go home. The couple finally obliged.

10

Charlotte awoke after about three hours of sleep. She realized that she needed to sleep after the huge headache she suffered seeing the Major Adamas after about fifteen years from the massacre her family suffered in the hand of that executioner in 1998, at the height of heinous atrocities that she lived in DRC. It was only about nine twenty pm when she awoke. It was still early on Saturday evening, and she was not scheduled to go back to work on Tuesday. She has taken three days off to help her friend in the variety of the long weekend wedding festivities. But now, she would be immobilized at home, not willing to disturb the Chibere family with another distress. Charlotte was going to spend the long weekend cooked up at home.

Home was a beautiful two stories townhouse that Charlotte has purchased about two years ago in a very quiet section of Clayton suburb. The townhouse was more than modest. It had a large master bedroom with a sumptuous bathroom on the second floor along with two gracious bedrooms with their own separate bathroom for visitors. A loner single lady, Charlotte lived by herself in the townhouse. In the past two years she had no more than three passing visitors, two ambulant nurses she took in and a very distant relative lady who visited from Montreal, Quebec in Canada. Charlotte preferred that very lonely life since she came to the US. Except for assisting Suzanne Chibere in her husband's church functions when she could, Charlotte had no social life. She declined and discouraged every attempt that the Chibere couple made to open her to strictly Christian base social interactions. She advised the couple by repeating and saying this:

" I intend to honor God's will to have given me a husband for two years of my life. God decided to take my husband away and I decided to honor my husband's memory in a lifetime widowhood and celibacy."

This ominous declaration raised a threshold bar that her friend Suzanne Chibere and her husband, the Pastor Papa Chibere found too high to bridge. With time they left Charlotte alone and abstained from attempting to raise any other attempts at social interactions. That suited Charlotte fine. She dedicated herself to her medical professional job twenty-four hour seven days. Her dedication afforded her rapid promotion to become chief registered nurse manager of close to six Dialysis medical unit centers in the area. The promotion brought along increased salary compensation and benefits. Charlotte used her increased income to adorn her townhouse with high end household

11

items. She also bought top line cars and invested the rest in a variety of stock market investments and real-estate. Still, Charlotte lived rather frugally, avoiding at all cost any social interactions. She was not obligated to financially support relatives back in her native areas of DRC. Most of her surviving family members have run away from her native dangerous areas. They managed to leave the country. They were dispersed in Kenya, Tanzania, South Africa and throughout Europe. Like herself, they also kept a very low profile about their life, not willing to talk about their background. The women, specifically, avoided all references to what they lived or experienced back home. They were afraid to be tagged with the stigma of rape and other atrocious sexual violences that have been or not visited upon their body. Most also distinctively avoided social interactions which can lead to unexpected dramatic sexual intimacies. After so many years, just as in the case of Charlotte, they experienced no sexual feelings or desire, they felt no sexual attraction for anyone. They became virtual asexual.

After she awakened that Saturday, Charlotte knew that it would take her a long time to go back to sleep. For the first time in about five or so years, she went downstairs to her bar next to her high-grade living room. She thought that she needed something to match her confused state of mind, so she helped herself with the Johnny Walker Black reclining big bottle. She poured a bit of it in a small glass to stall her confused state of mind. But her mind did not agree with the rough taste of the whisky she has not tasted for so long. She emptied the small glass quickly in the kitchen sink. She thought that maybe a red wine smooth taste would do. A few sips confirmed her inclination. She poured the red wine in a tall wide glass and went back upstairs. At that instant her phone rang.

"Hello, Charlotte, I called three times, there was no answer. Are you alright?" Suzanne was at the other hand with the background noise of the wedding party.

"Oh, dear Suzanne, I am alright. Given my very disturbed state of mind, I could not help but I went to sleep when I got home. I slept for about three hours. And now I am awakened trying to figure out how I am going to stayed occupied for the next two days, until Tuesday, to go back to work."

"Well, I told you to hang around with us. The wending party is still going on and your daughter, Mado, is very upset you are not around. She wanted to see you before she leaves for her honeymoon in la Martinique. But Charlotte, I did not tell her anything about honeymoon practices. I wonder what counsels you can provide her about honeymoon when you have abandoned that territory long time ago. "

"You are always very funny, Suzanne. I wonder sometimes, how you manage being married to a Pastor."

"Please, Charlotte, I have not made any vow of celibacy as you have done. And Mado never wants to have intimate talks with her mother. So, you are the only grown adult person she enjoyed talking about everything else. I trust you would engage her decently in that area."

"Now, Suzanne, you must remember that I was married for two full years. That time was devoted to a full sexual interaction with my departed husband. I don't want to expand on that experience. Maybe, just maybe and for your information, my husband and I have covered during these two years enough to fill twenty, thirty, forty years of lifetime experience of sexual intimacies for a married couple."

"Excuse me, Charlotte, I beg your mercy. In that case, you must see my inexperienced, and I must assume, virgin Mado before she departs for Martinique for what you know I am talking about."

"Oh, I see! So, your most urgent issue today is about her inexperience and virginity in that territory. Don't you think that it is a bit too late to worry about it currently. Furthermore, let me see, in about two or three hours Mado would join her husband in that hotel wedding suite that has been reserved somewhere in downtown Raleigh, the deed will be done, it is too late now."

"All right, you can mock me as much as you want, Mrs. Sexology Expert! That is the worry every mother experience about their daughter on their wedding night. My mother did. I am certain your mother did too. Unless you had reassured her that night that you were ready and willing."

"Nonsense, my mother, and I had a regular talk about that territory way before my wedding night. I know that you did not, and you would be better off to leave Mado alone and please do not traumatize my beautiful Mado today with your nonsense. Mrs. Chibere, Mado and I have covered all these subjects. I would be more than happy to call her to wish a happy honeymoon."

"Ah, that would not do. Yours truly may benefit of the same counsels, have you ever thought about that?"

"Of course not! I know you are trying to trick me to come back. I know that you want to see me to help you out of your unnecessary hangups. I will not be able to come. You are just using some other means to get me out. Really, after that shock I had today, I want to take a little bit of time away by myself. I will call Mado, I promise."

"Charlotte, you are right, I want to meet with you and to talk if I can be of any assistance as a friend. Just let me know, I am very relieved to hear you are recovering. But again, anytime you want me to come let me know and soon. Take your time. I just want to advise you to keep your line of communication. If not with me, but with anybody, family, acquaintances, lovers, partners, anybody. Sorry, specifically family, talk with them! What about that lady from Montreal, who came to visit with you one or two years ago. Call her!"

"I am glad to remove lovers and partners I don't have. That lady in Canada returned to North Kivu. She is married now. You know how married women avoid widows."

"Not me, you know that. Please search for family members so you can talk about this incident. It will help."

"You are right. I will check. Thank you. Will Talk.'

"Charlotte, we love you so very much."

"I love you all too."

Charlotte can hear the loud noise from the guests dancing and responding, as in a choir, to another Congolese hot tune. She felt that she was in the right place at home. She was very happy to hear the merry ambiance that the Chibere family and all the guests were having for Mado's wedding. She remembered the year around preparations that took to get to this Memorial Day weekend. She assisted the family every step of the way. And the family was extremely grateful that she kept Mado away from Mrs. Chibere's nagging intrusions. Charlotte literally adopted Mado as a daughter she never had. Charlotte was most thankful over the engagement that the entire church congregation provided to ensure that the Elder Pastor "Pa Chi" gave a graceful wedding ceremony to his daughter. The minute it was announced

14

that the wedding was going to take place in about six months, church members threw endless events to raise funds for their adored elder pastor major undertaking. They did this to honor Pastor "Pa Chi" for all he has tirelessly done for the congregation members in all manners and events. Pastor "Pa Chi" spared nothing to assist church members for funerals, weddings, school fees, graduations, new house down deposits, hospital care and so on. And as he never stopped to tell the church community:

"We came into this foreign land with nothing but the bags of our sorrow. So, to thrive in the Grace of Almighty God, we have no choice but to stay united and help each other in the small ways as well as in the large ways. "

That sermon resonated in every church member's mind. When the news of his own daughter's came about, Pastor "Pa Chi" received more than he has bargained for. Different church groups managed to raise enough funding for each major expense item for the wedding. The Ladies group took care of the wedding dresses and the honeymoon trip to Martinique. The Youth group rented the Center facilities. The Choir Group engaged the D.J. and the musical instruments. The Elder council took care of foods, drinks, and everything else. Charlotte knew the church full engagement because she oversaw the entire treasury of the wedding event. Whenever the funding of a wedding expense came out short, she did not hesitate to utilize her own money to close the shortfall. She was more than happy to assist the Chibere family which stood by her for so long from the time she decided to run away from the Walikale region of the North Kivu province. The wedding became her silent drive to pay back all that she has received from that family and more.

Charlotte was rather relieved that her shocking encounter that day did not disturb the event the entire church community had worked to bring about tirelessly for so many months. The resolution of the shocking encounter could wait. Yet after pondering about what her friend Suzanne had suggested, Charlotte decided to reach out to relatives who had experienced the same trauma as she did in the past. There was one relative she exchanged news about the country on a regular basis. Reverend Stanislas Keregi, a distant cousin on her father side, now a Lutheran Church Pastor based in the city of Uppsala in Sweden, came in mind. Reverend Stanislas, now above sixty-five years, was a respected pastor attending to the Congolese community spread around the Sweden capital of Stockholm. Reverend Stanislas was very close to Charlotte's father. He mentioned many times that they grew up together in the same compound of Charlotte's grandfather, the elder Keregi. He parted company from her father when he was recruited into the Walikale Luther Church equivalent of the diocese. He was being groomed to become a pastor back then. The last time Charlotte saw him was when she stopped with her refugees' group in Kampala, Uganda, on their way to Tanzania and further on to the US. Charlotte shared with the Reverend the painful atrocities that visited the family. Reverend Stanislas cried for two days. He informed Charlotte that he was also being rescued as a refugee from Walikale to go to Sweden. He gave Charlotte his main contacts in Sweden. As soon as she settled in Raleigh, North Caroline, she reached out to Reverend Stanislas. They have regularly exchanged family news since then. The next day on Sunday, Charlotte called the Reverend around nine am, it was about three pm in Uppsala.

"Uncle Stanis, you won't believe who I run into yesterday at a wedding party of the daughter of my very dear friend Suzanne, the wife of our pastor, "Pa Chi" I have talked about quite often."

"Yes, you mentioned that pastor, and I believe from the Chibere family."

"Exactly, their daughter Mado married to a fine Congolese gentleman from Dallas."

"God be blessed and praised! So, you ran into somebody, a fine gentleman and you are calling dear uncle Reverend Stanislas to come bless your union! I would be more than honored. Charlotte, can you imagine how long the entire family has been waiting for this news. God be blessed and praised! Tell me mere!"

"No, no, no, uncle Stanis. This was rather a very painful encounter. I crossed the awful Major Adamas Kagita!"

There was this loud noise on the other end of the call, as if Reverend Stanislas dropped his phone set and was trying to recuperate it. Then he came back with a tense respiration.

"Did you say Major Adamas Kagita!"

"Yes Sir, the very awful Major Adamas Kagita!"

Another twenty seconds of silence followed from the Reverend. He then resumed in a very stingy voice.

"Well, I have been telling you for a long time, you can go anywhere in the world with your American passport. Why do you insist on staying in that country. Come and join us here in Sweden, you would never meet this garbage of killers. We have provided all their names to make sure that they are not welcome here. Can you imagine? Each one of these murderers is registered here as "persona non grata". We got them listed. Well, I am not surprised. At least the Swede were never hypocritical about this. They analyzed Congo story very well, from 1960 through now. They know who was, who is, who will be pulling the strings about all that has happened in the Eastern region of Congo. They know the roles of every stakeholder in this endless drama from Mobutu to all the jokesters in Kinshasa, Kigali, and Kampala. They can tell you all the intermediaries and mercenaries in North and South Kivu. And above all, they know how the big high-tech companies pushed jokesters like President Clinton and Premier Minister Blair to upset the politics of Central Africa to get strategic minerals like Coltan no matter what. They brought in whom they called "New Generation Leaders: Kagame in Rwanda, Museveni in Uganda, Meles Zenawi in Ethiopia, Afewerki in Eritrea. In the process, they got Mobutu kicked out in a war they funded, a war that is going on with more than twelve millions of dead people, fifteen years later. They gave carte blanche to Museveni and Kagame to plunder strategic minerals in the Eastern Congo to cart them to Rwanda and Uganda, killing indigenous Congolese without restraint. Do you know that Rwanda is now the world first exporter of Coltan without no mines to point at ..."

"Uncle Stanis, please I am talking about Major Adamas Kagita, and you got me all over the world. I saw him and I reported him to the police."

"And!"

"They took him away!"

"And!"

"They said they are going to get back to me."

"And!"

17

"I don't know what happened and will happen afterward. I am just reporting to you what has happened."

"My very dear niece, let me tell you what has happened since then and I must tell you this without abusing your common sense about you reporting Major Adamas Kagita. Nothing! Absolutely Nothing, my very precious dear Charlotte! As we speak, I can tell you that Major Adamas Kagita has already been released after they booked him at the police station on Saturday night. They probably made a few calls to the North Caroline Attorney Office and were told to release him because what you have accused him of does not come under their jurisdiction. They will raise the matter with higher federal authorities, the FBI, the CIA, the Attorney General, the Secretary of State, and so on. And that will take time!"

"I know that!"

"That is better, that is wonderful. What I was trying to say was this, your reporting of Major Adamas Kagita is an insignificant act in a much greater and bigger scheme of thing way above you and I, you and Major Adamas Kagita."

"I don't care, insignificant or not, I will make him pay as long as he is here in the US."

"I am saying this, at the end of the day, it would be a bit hard and difficult for the very system that drove the murder of your husband and your family members to indict itself and Major Adamas Kagita who acted as the system agent. Do you see where I am going?"

"Reverend Stanislas Keregi, are you suggesting that I drop my complaint?"

"Yes, as long as you live under that system, it will be hopeless, nothing will be done."

"I am sorry, I cannot abandon my complaint. I would carry it until I cannot carry it for the sake of my husband and my family members and everything I have sacrificed in my life. Thank you so very much Uncle Stanis for your advice. Thank you!"

"Please, Charlotte, don't hang up, we need to talk more about this …"

Charlotte closed her cellphone; she did not wait to hear what the

Reverend pleaded at the end. She felt a bit disabused. Her reaching out to the Reverend was a fiasco. She was not surprised. Uncle Stanis has maintained the same posture when talking about the US position toward DRC. Charlotte did not dwell over the high-level politics between the US and DRC as he did. She tried to listen and understand what the Reverend was saying but she was basically practical. Her world was defined by her busy work and her restricted environment outside work. In addition, there was also the most important goal in her life, something she has never shared with anybody and that was about to bear revenge against what Major Adamas Kagita has done to her and her family. From the time she joined the refugees' group, trekking dangerously through Eastern Congo territories, going through Uganda, reaching Tanzania, boarding the plane at Dar-Es-Salam to come to the US, that goal gnawed at her inner soul continuously. The Saturday painful encounter was just a mental link in the long chain of Charlotte's goal of her life. There was no way she was going to let that goal go unattended. She also knew that to be effective, she would need to raise her goal a bit higher in the realm of big politics, as suggested by the Reverend. The only difference was that she was not going to raise it in vain, with no action. She would raise it as part of a successful reach of her goal. As a matter of fact, she gained even more resolve when she interrupted the conversation with the dear Reverend Stanislas. Charlotte would carry it on.

19

CHAPTER 3

KAGITA IN THE POLICE PRECINT

The sergeant, who commanded the police team to investigate Charlotte's 911 call, was not pleased about the outcome of the investigation. He was very irritated and more at loss to show that the incident he was led to investigated was way above his status, skills, aptitude and understanding. The sergeant, named Sidney "Sid" Osbury, was a nonsense cop, more inclined to basic police functions of "cops and robbers" in the relatively peaceful suburb areas surrounding Raleigh urban agglomeration. His summer weekend occupation consisted of directing hot cop car chase of delinquent drunk teenagers along narrow alleys between small water flows and lakes outside Raleigh. These car chases were usually concluded with prompt arrest of teenagers who did not cause major car accident or transferring to ambulances to local hospitals teenagers who were seriously harmed by car collisions. In both cases, Sergeant "Sid" spent the late night at the precinct booking the sorry teenagers, holding them until their parents showed up to post their bail the next day on Sunday morning.

In his cop background, Sergeant "Sid" would count not more than five serious homicides annually in the area under his jurisdiction. In these rare occasions, Sergeant "Sid" was relieved when the North Carolina State police detectives and the regional FBI center took over the investigation of these homicide cases. The sergeant was happy to return to his casual low level disturbance cases in the community he knew very well with folks he was the most familiar. Charlotte's 911 call was very unusual and uncanny for the sergeant. His first inclination was to gather a team of well-armed cops to go the Center and arrest this perpetrator, who has killed six people, was having fun in a wedding party. He thought of leading a SWAT team to the Center. But after talking to the Center manager, he was persuaded not to come in with unnecessary frightening charge. He was told that wedding party was evolving so smoothly and there was no sign of violent people around. The Center Manager insisted that the wedding party was made of Church going people led by a very peaceful Elder Pastor he knew very well, "Pa Chi" from many prior Church engagements, He added that these people were not in habit of carrying guns. The Center manager strongly advised a low key unintrusive approach.

Sergeant "Sid" was still a bit irritated when he arrived at the Center and became a bit suspicious about the Center Manager's advice when he saw that the wedding attendees were all black. He restrained himself only to find out the investigation went on as smoothly as it was proposed at the beginning. Sergeant "Sid" was surprised by the investigation session that took place when a Black lady named Charlotte accused, in even tone, a very well-dressed black gentleman, with many names, of killing six of her relatives ten or fifteen years ago. Listening to the two antagonists, Sergeant "Sid" quickly surmised that there was a serious case of mistaken identity. He was ready to get out of the center and dismiss the 911 call as a waste of his precious weekend time. But the insistence of Charlotte's plea and the grave intervention of the so-called wise man named "Pa Chi" persuaded him to hold on to the purported criminal named Major Adamas Kagita who went now by another confusing name of Okito Jefferson. For the sergeant, the issue was at best confusing. He was not about to start an investigation of crimes committed in a faraway country named Democratic Republic of Congo, deep in a jungle in Africa ten to fifteen years ago. Given the grave accusation, Sergeant "Sid" tried forcefully not to look incompetent. He decided to hold Major Adamas Kagita for booking in the precinct. He put the major in handcuffs to show the Elder Pastor and Charlotte how seriously he regarded the accusation. He still wondered whether he was exceeded his jurisdiction, his authority or both.

On the way to the precinct, he even apologized to the man named Major Adamas Kagita.

"Sir, I hope you understand my position. I don't know you from Adam nor Eve. But these accusations are so grave I could not let you go without a little investigation. I have no choice but to book you at minimum. Don't worry, your car will be brought to the precinct, and you would be out there after we have booked you and get some clearance from higher up in our chain of command. Do you understand?"

"Believe me, Sir, I understand. But it is still a big shame that somebody would come out of nowhere and accuse somebody else of such monstrosities ten to fifteen years ago. I am a peaceful businessman as you are going to learn very soon with relationships higher up in the State department and many high-level authorities in this country. As you said it: you don't find serial murderers in Barco Corolla area where I live with my family in a big property of about three hectares there along the river. It is a terrible shame to be invited to a wedding and to leave in handcuffs in a police car. All I can say and repeat again and again is that lady had a sad case of mistaken identity. Well, I would say no more. I would just let the course of justice follows its natural path. I just hope that you would give me a chance to reach out to my big-time partners to hear this unjust cabal."

"As soon as we are done with the booking, you will be given all the venues to make these calls. By the way we are getting to the precinct."

Sergeant "Sid" led the Major, still handcuffed, out of the back seat. He personally took charge of booking him as politely and diligently as possible to prevent any excessive outburst that he knew his crew had usually reserved to local black people most of time. Sergeant "Sid' had found himself responding in the past to Police brutalities against people of color in detention in his precinct. He was not about to take any chance in this case. He was more perplexed by the Major's case coming from faraway places overseas. He knew that he was going to answer a lot of investigation calls from higher up jurisdictions. He did not trust his crew members to fill these big shoes.

He managed to assign the Major to a cell regularly reserved for local VIP people and their children. He excused himself to summarize the incident in a draft police report and to share that preliminary report by making calls to high judicial figures leading the State Police, the FBI, the District Attorney in the County. At each instance he was met by a deafening silence of about three to five seconds before the person at the other end responded. In each instance, Sergeant "Sid" was asked to update his report with a complete reference about all the parties and exchanges that took place during the incident. In each case, Sergeant "Sid" was asked to proceed with the booking the Major and to signify to him that he will be released on his own reconnaissance and from then on he could not leave the state of North Carolina, must make himself available for questioning about the accusations. At the same he was free to consult with lawyers to assist him around the accusations.

All the judicial contacts advised Sergeant "Sid" that they will pay him a visit the next day on Monday. After spending about forty minutes talking with the county judicial leaders, Sergeant "Sid' felt that he was in a higher judicial purpose, he went to see his precinct Chief who congratulated him on a proficient job done and to carry on as instructed and added:

"Sid, this could well be your 15 minutes of fame and lead you to bigger things. Carry on!"

Sergeant "Sid" booked the Major and shared the instructions that came down from higher up. He told the Major that he was free to go home and advised him to stick around his house when the various judicial folks would come to ask him a lot of questions. Major Kagita agreed and responded:

"I have nothing to hide. I would make myself available to any of these folks. I must also tell you that I would reach out to my business partners to assist him against these accusations."

As soon as Major Kagita was outside the Police Precinct, he started looking for a gas station before taking highway 64 toward the North Carolina Outer Banks region where his house is located. When he came to the weekend party, Major Kagita was planning to spend Saturday in one of the five-star hotels in Raleigh. He was hoping to be lucky enough to win the nightly favors of one of middle age single ladies during the party. As a matter of fact, one of the church elder pastors had invited him to the wedding party without really knowing him when he impressed the pastor with increasing sizable church donations during a few remote Bible exchange conferences. But during the wedding party, the pastor engaged him very suspiciously as soon as he sat him with a group of church middle-aged ladies. His conversations were rather coarse, putting the ladies very ill at ease. The pastor evaded talking with him until the incident. It was about one thirty in the morning when he was finally released. He was not about to honor the reservation at the five-star hotel. He wanted to be as far away the town of Raleigh as possible, as far away from the Congolese community as possible.

As soon as Major Kagita loaded his Lexus sedan car with gas, he asked the gas attendant about the best way to reach highway 64. He proceeded to park the car as far away from the next car as possible. He opened the middle deep pocked where he retrieved a box containing a small

23

cell telephone provided to him by his American intelligence service contact. The cell phone was permanently fully charged and had only one contact number which he pressed to dial. A strange verification responded.

"Contact Pin!"

Major Kagita entered a number on the back of the cell phone:

"2327-243"

The verification continued:

"You are near Raleigh, North Caroline, Purpose!"

Major Kagita enter another:

"95-243" which meant "Entertainment."

There was a pause then a male voice took over speaking in French:

"2327, this is Chief Campos, what can I do for you?"

"Oh, thank you so very much! I did not want to talk to nobody else but you!"

"OK, what can I do for you?"

"I am in a very big trouble!"

"How bad?"

"Reconnaissance, cover broken!"

"Well, you are in Raleigh area, you were warned to avoid that area. I wanted you to stay in North Texas or New Mexico. You insisted on North Carolina. I am not surprised that your cover is broken in Raleigh. Are you leaving the area?"

"Yes, but I am very tired after being uncovered, accused of killing six peoples in DRC, arrested, and booked in a police precinct, I want to stay overnight in a hotel on my way to Barco Corolla. Can you help me with a hotel reservation past 95 on 64"?

"I will but I want you to help me with your own version of being uncovered as you remember it including the people, the conversations and places where all this happen. Now, I could call tomorrow morning and you will get me the entire written version of the incident. I must be ready to counter what the folks who, on the civil side, would come after you, starting Monday morning! Do this promptly, Bye!"

The cell phone shut off. Major Kagita drove the car in the direction the gas attendant has provided. It took him about fifteen minutes to take 64 West. After about an hour of driving, Major Kagita received on his regular cell phone an express reservation at around 64 West and 95 South intersection at Holyday In hotel at Rocky Mount. He rested at the hotel and woke up at ten in the morning. He tried to remember the incident including the people, the conversations, and the places. He did his best writing all down. Soon after he got a reminder from Chief Campos with a request to fax the written report to a fax machine number. Major Kagita faxed the report. But he was certain that the report has captured the essential parts of the incident. He felt that his anger at having been uncovered was preventing him from remembering every aspect of the incident. He had a sumptuous lunch before taking the road again to Barco Corolla. After more than two hours of driving, the sight of a beautiful sunset over the large water expanses of the outer banks of North Carolina gave Major Kagita a better mental vision of his standing.

The sight reminded him of his life multiple churns from the abrupt termination of student life at the University of Kisangani to the vagrancy and the abandon he suffered at the hands of his own family in the Butembo areas to the rescue that war lords afforded him as a military enforcer in Walikale mines supervision. This was where and when he earned the much-feared nickname of Adamas or Danger of Death. Major Adamas Kagita used the last churn in his life to promote himself slowly and efficiently as the main military General enforcer to move large quantities of Grand Kivu minerals to the neighboring countries of Uganda, Rwanda, and Burundi, to be exported to the world. With the total collapse of the state authority in the Eastern provinces of the country, the likes of Major Adamas and more than two hundred war lords became the real conduits of the systematic looting of DRC minerals in the Great Kivu region. This was accomplished on the pile of unaccounted lives of maimed, murdered, raped, dismembered people. Major Kagita rose easily to the rank of the extremely efficient manager of minerals logistics throughout the Great Kivu region. He went as far as to establish himself as the reliable provider of these minerals. When the coltan mineral gained in higher technological stature in the manufacturing of cell phones, Major Kagita became the go to man to ensure that large quantities of coltan could leave DRC to transit through Rwanda warehouses on their way to all the major manufacturers of cell phones in the world. When the DRC central government started to gradually recover its state authority over the mine's region, Major Adamas became so important, he had to be protected by major western country intelligence services to cover his past bloody minerals looting activities which have provided an incredibly large financial bonanza spread in hundreds of billions between Hong Kong, Seoul, London, Paris, New York, Helsinki and Berlin. The decision was made to evacuate Major Adamas Kagita to the USA under the new name of Okito Jefferson in the remote outer banks of North Carolina. The idea was that Mr. Okito Jefferson would continue to enjoy his financial bounty quietly with his small family along the outer banks of North Carolina. The idea was that he must stay away from being uncovered as Major Adamas at all costs and mainly from Congolese communities dispersed in the US. Mr. Okito Jefferson followed that prescription for a long time until that fateful Saturday of May 25, 2013, at the wedding party near Raleigh. And this was about more or less eight years since he left DRC. This unbelievable churn in the life of Major Adamas was no different from the life of many underworld figures in US, who have decided, for one reason or another, to betray major figures of underworld families in the US, in their murderous racketeering engagement in major urban centers. They were provided with new identities and new occupations away from their original locations of criminal life.

The slow approach to the vast estate Mr. Okito Jefferson had managed to acquire in Barco Corolla reminded him of the life he could stand to lose if the uncovering of his previous life is not properly pushed back under the sanctuary the American intelligence service has worked so hard to build. His eyes started swelling with tears when he crossed the huge electric portals of the estate that opened. He wondered how he had stupidly managed, in a dumb flick of his mind, to lose it all. When he walked into the beautiful big house, his obedient wife was standing in the living room with a small wet towel to wipe his brow and slowly remove his jacket. From a strict set of instructions, he had given her from the beginning of their union, the young wife was never to question his whereabouts inside or outside their home. For the very purpose of his newly arranged life in US, the young lady was very quickly betrothed to him from an impoverished family outside

Butembo. Her substantial dowry was no different from her being sanctioned from human trafficking into slavery bondage. She was about eighteen years old trying precariously to advance and complete her secondary studies. The quickly arranged traditional marriage to an apparently rich man she never met or saw before was a tremendous relief from the uncertainty of her life in a region consumed by the ravages of endless war and brigandage and worse of women rape. She had no idea where this man was taking her as they left Butembo and went through Uganda and some distant areas only to board a plane to come to US she never heard of. She quietly settled into the role of a wife, successively bearing three children to Adamas. It was a bit difficult to determine whether she was happy in this new role. But she kept her part of the bargain by attending to every whim from her husband.

CHAPTER 4

THE WAIT

The conversation with Uncle Stanis left Charlotte more resolute to pursue some legal remedies. But she was completely confused about how to do it, how to go about it. She had no ideas how to start or push it. She remembered the cop who led the instruction of her complaint. She got him figured out. His conversation did not make sense at all. He looked completely lost. She was disappointed to hear him wondering whether he had any authority to arrest Major Adamas Kagita who had killed so many people back home. That hesitation rang hollow in Charlotte's mind. As far Charlotte was concerned, a murder was a murder, in Raleigh as well in New York City, in Paris, Brussels or Johannesburg, in Kinshasa, Lubumbashi, Kigali or Butembo. And certainly, in her village of Kwazimu. She could not believe that this man, this cop, was hesitating about arresting this murderer of Major Adamas Kagita. Does it matter where the murder took place. Charlotte remembered seeing people being arrested in his neighborhood for far less. She remembered the last time she was in the area Walmart; the cops came roaring with four cars to pursuit and arrest two young kids. They were so driven to arrest them. And this cops supervisor or whatever he pretended to be, was there wondering if he had authority to do anything. Charlotte was wondering now whether Major Adamas Kagita has been released right around the corner from the wedding party. She was told that his expensive car was not in the parking lot. People have seen the cops driving it away. So, she assumed the police gave him back his car to go back to where he lived. Charlotte, for the first time, opened the big bottle of "Glenfiddich" whisky she bought four years ago when she was expecting visitors from Congo, and who did not care for hard liquor. She poured a good size of whisky to calm herself to sleep.

The next day she awakened at around seven thirty in the morning. But her work shift was due to start at around two in the afternoon. She went back to sleep. She was awakened by a call at about nine forty-five. She was about to cancel the call until she read that the call was coming from the same number the cop's supervisor gave her. She picked it up.

"Good morning, this is Sergeant "Sid" who led the investigation of your 911 call, do you remember me?"

'Oh yes, so you arrested Major Adamas Kagita, right, is he still in jail?"

"Well, that is not the way we do business here in the US. Maam, I booked him and then I released him on his own reconnaissance. Don't you worry, we are investigating all that you have accused him of having done. Remember you accused me of very serious crimes, of murdering your parents and a lot of people in your village in Congo right. Well, that is a very serious charge we must investigate. That is why I am calling you. I gave you a lot of references for you to touch basis today. Have you called anybody yet? Did you call the Raleigh County District Attorney, the FBI Field Office, the North Caroline Police Center in Raleigh?"

"No, I did not! I was waiting to hear from you."

"Well, my police report raised a lot of alarms all over. I really want to help you to provide a good report for all these people. My Boss wants me to assist you to collect and to present a good story to these people. Do you want to work me?"

"I don't know. Did you say that you are Sergeant "Sid"?"

"Yes1"

"I must be frank with you. I was disappointed with your reaction when I shared what Major Adamas Kagita has done to members of my family and so many other people back home in DRC. I got the impression that you did not believe me and did not take me seriously. To tell the truth, I was hurt. I could not believe that you could not take me seriously at my age. That was the first time I shared that terrible family story. If you see me in this country, it was very much because of that horror story…."

"Well, Maam, I am terribly sorry if I left that impression. I prayed that you do not share that impression with anybody else. I was trying to tell you then that the horrible story you were sharing happened outside

United States and I probably would not have jurisdiction or authority to investigate it. I am very sorry if I left the impression that I would not bring serious consideration over murders or one murder that happened anywhere in the world. Never! I raised my hand to uphold the law on the Bible anytime and anywhere, Maam! I have never failed that duty from the time I swore to uphold the law, I am not about to fail now. Are you with me, Maam?"

"Yes, Sir, I am! That is much better! This is the language I expected from you from the start. I am relieved that I am hearing it now. I believe that we are talking the same language now. Thank you. Now what do you want me to do?"

"Now you are talking, Lady! As I said before, there are a lot of people who want to talk to you. They all share one major abiding concern. They don't want any criminal named Major Adamas Kagita walking around the streets of North Caroline with a terrible past of having murdered a bunch of people somewhere in the world. No, Si, they don't want that, and do you know why, well it is that simple: a murderer, like a thief, remains a murderer. What a murderer has done in one place, he or she would be tempted to do it again and again and again in another place. Are you following me, and all these people in the law enforcement including yours truly won't like to see that happen. That is the reason they want to talk to you to investigate your story to prevent Major Adamas Kagita to act funny, to go around in our peaceful Raleigh County, in our peaceful state of North Carolina murdering people all over again. They would not like it!"

"I see, I would not like it either. So where would I start?"

"Well Maam, I deeply share your pain and I want you to provide these people a credible story about that Major Adamas. I want you to collect your thoughts as far back as you can, put them down in writing in an outstanding sequence with some memorable pictures or facts you can get. After you have done this, I can review and find ways to strengthen your story and present it to these people. You see, I sincerely believe that if you start talking to these people as you did last Saturday, they will dismiss your story as hearsay, not serious, just as you accused me to do. Let me share a secret. After I left the party center with Major Adamas as you call him, I start wondering the same way you said it today. I say to myself, why would this very sensible lady come up with this horrific story about this gentleman looking person. I convinced myself that there must be a serious angle to your story. From that time, my criminal investigator antennas were raised over Major Adamas. I started treating him as somebody with a hidden criminal past. I treated him as if he was hiding something. I don't know anything about you or Major Adamas, but when he said that he lived in that part of North Carolina Outer banks where big houses start listing at above five hundred thousand dollars and he could not mention any business he is involved in, I knew that the man was in the run hiding from some terrible past. I wrote this in my police report to these higher people in law enforcement. That is why they are all agitating to talk to you. That is why you must help yourself in presenting a very credible story. Do you understand?"

"I got it Sir! I must lay out a credible story. But are they going to wait for my collection of a decent story?"

"They will! They are agitating for a credible story, the more concise and credible the better! Hold on I am getting a call from the District Attorney office! Wait for ...! Sergeant "Sid" stepped outside Charlotte's house and was engaged in a very animated conversation for about ten minutes.

"Maam, my instincts were right. You must really work hard to bring about a credible story for presentation. You won't believe what the call was all about. My contact at the District Attorney called and wanted me to rush to their office. Apparently, they got inquiries from Washington, precisely from the Justice Department around your encounter with this Major Adamas. It sounds very serious. As I said, please get your story straight and concise. I am going to Raleigh downtown office. Please work on this story. I will get back to you. We need to get it straight and concise. Take as much time as possible to get it right. Will be in touch."

It was about time for Charlotte to start getting ready for work. She had a huge migraine trying to choose whether to get to work or to start getting her story straight for all these people who wanted it. She called Sergeant "Sid" trying to determine how many days the law enforcement people were willing to wait. The answer was swift, no more than three days. Charlotte decided to take two days off to finish the report and resume her routine work late on the third. Her supervisor granted her request. Her request was the first in about four years for a very dedicated worker Charlotte has always been. Charlotte started writing her story.

Charlotte vividly remembered the sequences of events that happened when his brothers worked in Kwazimu coltan mines around the summer of 2005. Their maternal uncles invited them to join the afternoon shift when they were usually done with the various farming works that occupied them in the vegetables extensive family plantations that have been the staples of the family from the past thirty or so years. Charlotte was exempt from mining work. She stayed closer to her mother and sisters busy tending to vegetables plots closer to the family home. The sisters were also in charge of a vast array of poultry, goats, and lambs that the family had. Charlotte was the last of four sisters who had managed to be betrothed right after they completed their secondary schools. They married local boys they grew up with. Charlotte, the studious one and more beautiful than her older sisters, was not particularly interested in following her sisters' path. For some strange reasons, she thought and believed that she was destined for greater things far from the family village. Still a persistent younger man won her heart and married her. The man was in medical field. He was a medical assistant in the area. Charlotte lived with the man for about two years. At the end, she told her mother of their family plans. She wanted to get higher education in one of the big towns of the North Kivu, while her husband would remain behind attending to a growing medical practice. Charlotte mentioned that she would go to either Goma, Beni or Butembo. She said that she wanted to become either a nurse or a teacher. Her husband supported her plans. It should also be noted that Charlotte remained a stunning married beauty in the area. She repeatedly declined the most powerful suitors in the area while dreaming to build a solid marriage with her husband and to move on the bigger things. It was in that vein that she came across one of the Kwazimu mines supervisors when she took a bus that took her to Butembo to pay a visit to a distant maternal relative associated with a nursing school in town. Charlotte's mother sent her to this relative to learn more about the medical field she had vague interest in. The mining supervisor who sat not far from the beautiful Charlotte turned out to be the awfully celebrated Adamas Kagita on his way to Butembo to visit with his own family at the time. Adamas tried unsuccessfully to get Charlotte's attention during the long nine-hour trip. At every stop, he insisted on buying stuffs for the beautiful Charlotte who declined the attention. Adamas tried every lover's disguise to interest the lady but in vain. He gave up when they arrived in Butembo. But he still managed to find out where she stayed and showed up uninvited to the distant relative's compound at Charlotte's great discomfort. This went nowhere. By the time she came back to the village after about three weeks in Butembo, Charlotte was surprised to learn the exaggerated interest over her that the big mining supervisor Adamas has revealed to his brothers who worked under in his command. Adamas went as far as to tell anybody from her family working in the mines that he must marry Charlotte, a married woman. That was worse than an affront for the beautiful Charlotte who responded with a categoric No!

At that time Charlotte did not realize the increasing powerful and murderous tentacles that Adamas Kagita was exerting in the mines. She did not know how much power of life and death this man nicknamed Adamas or "Danger of Death" in the Swahili slang of the region. She did not know that Adamas started harassing all known members of her family in mines supervision. He intimidated them to do all in their power to get Charlotte to accept his crazy relationship proposal. At the beginning this looked like a childish pursuit for his uncles and brothers until that fateful day when he forced the oldest uncle to venture through an area of mines known for multiple dangerous and fateful landslides. When the uncle did not come back from his trek and could not be found, Adamas approached a family member and explicitly warned him that if the family continues to deny his proposal, he will be next to venture in the same area. The whole family got the message and stopped going to work to the mines. Three days later, the body of the oldest uncle was unearthed, and his funerals services turned into a virtual strike that paralyzed Kwazimu mines for a week. From that time Adamas swore to teach the family harsh lessons by firing all known family members from mining work. Charlotte's brothers left the village area and went to a boarding school very far from the village. About three months, Adamas set up a roadblock against a light truck that was bringing Charlotte's three brothers back to the village for a long holiday. With some hard-core vigilantes, Adamas sprayed bullets against the truck killing the 3 brothers, the driver and five other people from the village. Still covered with blood, Adamas proudly came to the huge family compound, he continued the mayhem, killing Charlotte's husband, parents, and every living person, Adamas and his wild cohorts could find. Altogether close to fifteen family members were slaughtered in the compound. Luckily, Charlotte was away at the time, still looking for her next nursing school, this time in Goma where the sad news reached her. The massacre prompted another work stoppage in Kwazimu mines for three weeks. Adamas was quickly

33

evacuated to an unknown mine supervisory in Rutshuru area for the next seven months. With a help of a major protestant church in the area, Charlotte came back to quickly collect her belongings and to start the refugee trek that would bring her to the US. She never had a chance to attend the graceful huge funerals service for her husband and family members.

With tearful eyes, Charlotte struggled to write, by long hand, all the details of that fateful episode in the afternoon, specifying all the people's names, places, times as she remembered them. By seven pm, she had accumulated more than fifteen pages of the harrowing story. She took a break for about an hour and half. She came back reviewing and editing the story. Then she added various testimonies from countless people who corroborated the story. By about midnight she had more than thirty-seven pages of the story. She was hungry, she fixed a cold fresh dinner for herself and went to sleep. She jumped out from her bed at about three am in the morning, sweating profusely as in a nightmare. She rushed into the bathroom and washed her face with cold water. She remembered the terrible fright she had when the trek was crossing the Congo-Uganda border, and her group was told that it was not going to go through the closed immigration services until the next day morning. The group set up tents that night near the border. Sometime before going to sleep, Charlotte went to relieve herself alone in the nature nearby. She rushed very quickly to her tent thinking to have seen Adamas, armed to teeth with his vigilantes, looking for her. Once inside the tent in company of two other ladies, on the run like herself, she cried while shaking to no end, was comforted through prayers and sad religious songs for a long time. Finally, she tried to recline her whole body to sleep but stayed awake all night. Charlotte was repeatedly revisited by the same nightmare after the fateful wedding party encounter with Adamas. She added that nightmare to her story. She went to sleep at about five in the morning when the first morning sun flickers were invading her bedroom.

Sergeant "Sid" called around ten thirty. Charlotte was very delighted to share all that she had put down, amounting close to forty five pages of her frightful episode.

"Woooah, I was expecting no more than twenty pages. You did pretty good. But tell me, was that all type written in a PC?"

"Oh, no, I am sorry, I wrote on a long hand. Is that bad?"

"Absolutely not, you can now retype it using a typewriter or a PC. I always find handwriting a story gets you to bring more reality to it when you are in live contact of your true feelings. Some people can translate any story using a machine, a typewriter, or a PC. In my case, handwriting is the best. Listen you have done the essential job. Now anybody who can read your handwriting can retype it. And guess what, if you are like some of us, common mortal, that is the time to clean up your orthograph or other silly mistakes. So, what is going to be, do you want to do it yourself or I can get somebody to type it?"

"Thank you, Sergeant "Sid", I want to do it myself. This is so personal; I want to finish it myself. How was your meeting in Raleigh? You said that there were some inquiries from Washington D.C., what was that all about?"

"Maam, I would not lie to you, my contact at the District Attorney office told me that his boss had a long conversation with somebody in DC about your encounter with Adamas. His boss was very tight lipped about what DC wanted only to say that we must handle your statement very carefully. That is all. That is why I want you to lay it as clearly, carefully, and as truthfully as possible. I am very relieved and happy that you followed my advice. Coming up with forty-five handwritten pages was just awesome. Don't you worry, by the time you type it all, we might have got between twenty-five to thirty-five pages. That is still an awesome and slam-dunk story. It is all in the preparation, it is all in a well detailed preparation if you want Justice served from your story. I would not keep you distracted anymore, try to finish typewriting the story. Edit it pretty good to render your story the way you want it. Hopefully tomorrow we will print it, don't forget to page number the text. Then we can set up an appointment to deliver the story to the big shots. Very soon."

"Then what would happen?"

"Well, you would be called for interview, that is when you would be asked a lot of questions about the story. At this stage you are miles ahead with all that you have written."

"And what about Adamas?"

"Oh, he was told to stay put, cannot leave the area until he is invited for questioning over all that you put in writing. If his responses are not satisfactory, if his responses do not remove his presumed culpability, then he will be indicted and there will be criminal proceedings against him in a court of law. This is a long process, Maam, this is what I have been trying to explain to you from the beginning. If these murders have happened here in the US, the process would go faster. The truth is this, these murders must be proven from abroad, and that is not easy, do you understand?"

"I am learning this as fast as I can. I am now willing to see that process through."

"My God, this is what I have been waiting to hear from you, thank God! The rows of justice in US are unfortunately slow, but they move until, for better or worse, Justice is served. That is hard to believe for a lot of people, a lot of American citizens. Many have given up on these rows, they do not believe in them. Imagine if it is hard for American citizens, how would it be for those who became American citizen from abroad. It is even harder. But I do, I would do everything in my power to bring you along to believe and trust in the rows of Justice in this country."

'Sergeant, that is a tall bargain even for me. But in this case, it is too personal, I don't have a choice. I am already fully engaged."

"Time would tell, time would tell. Bye!"

In the Eastern outer banks of North Caroline where Major Adamas Kagita, alias Okito Jefferson, resides, a different and brand of the rows of Justice was earnestly being activated. Adamas was incessantly on the phone with various contacts along the long supply chain of blood minerals. The chain extended from the Kwazimu mines in Walikale, through Beni-Butembo, through makeshift plane speedways in the jungle, through Uganda and Rwanda mines warehouses along the borders with DRC, through Kigali and Kampala minerals drop shipment centers, through multinational strategic supply chain centers, through major financial centers which fund the technological transformation of the strategic minerals to their advanced very expansive and profitable usage. The chain virtually includes the intelligence services and political officers which support and enable the hidden supply chain in these various countries. Adamas started with the main contacts in Kwazimu mines to strengthen his powerful profitable purpose. The next in line were the main contacts in Uganda and Rwanda who have provided him the protection and safe passage to US. And finally, his contacts in Langley or wherever they were posted in US for the moment. This time he reached a "Colonel Laurens" who could be reached in Phoenix, Arizona or Fort Lauderdale, Florida. The same "Colonel Laurens" responded to calls as Ramos, Vice President of Marketing in a company at Charleston port in South Caroline.

"Jeff, what the hell were you doing at a wedding party in Raleigh, full of Congolese who came from the Big Kivu? That was the most stupid thing you have done to date. You broke every rule we have set for you. Has it ever occurred to you that you may encountered the very people you have brutalized all that time back in DRC. Remember I insisted that you join me in Phoenix, Arizona. You declined and I was overruled then. Look where we are now. Please, don't give that nonsense excuse to pray with some old friends. Jeff, you had no friend back then, how in the world did you get friends now. In your case prayer amounts to banging some ladies, and no other lady, it got to be Congolese. What is it with you? A pussy is a pussy for me. Asian, black, Latino, white, Chinese, a pussy is a pussy! I know you told me one time that in your case, fucking without Swahili moaning is no fuck at all. Well, you got your Swahili moaning and now you are going straight back to Walikale where you have a line of old friends waiting for you with machetes. Jeff, you know very well you are a dead person back home. You owe so much blood to so many people, nobody wants to run the risk to protect you back home. And nobody wants to see you in Uganda or Rwanda. What are we going to do now? Do you know that Human Watch and Amnesty International have a thoroughly documented dossier about what that lady was talking about. We will try to suppress as much as we can with our contact, but it won't be easy."

"So, I am screwed ready to be put in jail!"

"Just about! I guess it all depends on how your friends in Uganda and Rwanda will push to bury stuff in DRC. That is your only saving grace!"

"Well, I will take my chance there!"

"How, you cannot leave now! Please lay low, please and leave the powers that be to act. And stop calling the entire chain. You never know who is listening now on the Internet! Stay away from international calls! Please, I will call, OK!!!"

Adamas was completely defeated. Colonel Laurens, or whatever his name is, did not help. It looks like he has always been under surveillance since he moved to North Carolina. The contacts in the US are fully aware of his every move. He did not believe that they would throw him back in the Congolese lion's den. Maybe, just maybe he has underestimated what the trio Kagame-Kabila-Museveni have plotted to lower the bloodletting in the Great Kivu for the sake of multinational business. Adamas realizes now that he was a bad apple they dumped in the US. So, he was screwed alone in the US. Still the trio did not know that he had few cards he could use to force them to support him no matter what. It is the Jungle law. He would use it to the maximum. Come to think of it, he never told the Colonel about Swahili moaning. Who in the world told him such a failing? So, for the American contacts, it came down to a sexual pursuit of Swahili moaning. Unbelievable! Adamas got up and called up his younger wife to verify. When she showed up, Adamas noticed she was bland as ever. In fact, she never uttered a sound during any of their intimacies. Now he remembered that among many of his many rules of bed manners she was not to look at him in the eyes in bed, she always gave him the back and she was forbidden to enjoy sex during intercourse. By consequences, she was not about to moan in Swahili, never. How in the world Colonel Laurens found out about this? Have the contacts interviewed his wife? Or have they planted microphones in the house to spy on him? Adamas dismissed his wife to take care of the children, and she disappeared obediently as usual. Adamas observed her departing and laughed to himself. He thought that Colonel Laurens' observation was so true! No Swahili moaning there! Maybe he was really in search of missing Swahili moaning when he went to that wedding party. He was making good progress with two ladies until the disaster that the crazy broad brought along. His contact in the Pastor's Church has arranged heavily drinking forays before but it occurred in some isolated housing. It always ended in a company of two Swahili speaking ladies in one of Raleigh five-star hotel VIP room. He cavorted all night with them until he let them go the next morning after rewarding them handsomely. Colonel Laurens probably was well informed of these forays   He poured a good shot of Bourbon he could find and went upstairs to sleep.

CHAPTER 5

FIRST INTERVIEW

The following day, Sergeant "Sid" picked up Charlotte at around nine in the morning and drove to the largest public library in the county where they rented a private working room with a decent professional printer. They printed, read and re-edited Charlotte's story of about thirty-five pages. They took no break and were done with thirty-seven well written pages of Charlotte's story at about three in the afternoon. Sergeant "Sid" then called the District Attorney office to set an appointment to deliver the story. They were surprised when they were told that the reading of the story will be shared with representatives from the FBI's office and the North Caroline State Police. The appointment was set for the following week on Tuesday at 10:30am.

"I thought that the so-called law enforcement folks were eager to get my story, why the delay?" Charlotte asked,

"Maam, this tells me that your story was a big deal for a lot higher up. It sounds as though you are being considered a star witness of some sort. Maam, I am starving, let's continue this conversation at my favorite restaurant, my treat. Are you working today?"

"No, I have requested two days an half days to complete this writing. I am scheduled to go back to work tomorrow evening. I am also starving."

The restaurant was just around the corner from the public library. It took less than ten minutes to get there.

"Now that you got your story down pat, you just have to re-read it to make it stand as whole." Sergeant "Sid" was advising Charlotte as soon as they were seated.

"Don't you worry, this is a very personal story. I could have come up with hundred pages to tell it all."

"Well, Maam, I am telling you this, because I have seen how these law enforcement folks think. It is like second nature for them to look for holes in any story they hear. I am no different. These folks believe nothing from anybody but their own. That is how they think and are made of. Now why do you think they have such a high rate of divorce in their marriage. They trust nobody but their own. I trust and pray that they are not going to harass or second guess your story. That is how they work. You took a serious crack at this, I saw how animated you were reading and re-reading what you wrote, I am confident it is solid. In fact, it is a good thing they gave you five days to calm down, to cool off until next week on Tuesday. As I say, concentrate on reading and re-reading your story."

"Thank you, Sir, I must thank you for trusting me to close a very important event in my life. I don't know what will happen, but Adamas must pay for what he has done to me and my family. If he does not pay it here on earth, he will certainly pay in hell!"

"Definitely, he will pay somehow, Maam, I must bring you back home. We will stay in touch until next week. If there is anything I need to share. I will call you. You have made our work much better; I can assure you."

Charlotte was dropped home. She had almost a day to fill until his work scheduled the next day. She checked her food stock, it was obvious she was so busy, she forgot to replenish her food provision for the week. She rushed out to go to her usual food store. As she was stepping out, her longtime friend, Mrs. Suzanne Chibere was at her door just about to knock.

"What is going on with you, Charlotte, I have called more than twenty times in two days. You are not picking your phone. Hold on where are you rushing out to now. What is going?"

"Come on lady, come with me to the food store. I will tell you all, come on, we will take my car, come this way."

"I was very busy the last two days." Charlotte started the car and moved it out of the garage.

"Busy, doing what!"

40

"Well, I have been spending a lot of time with that police Sergeant or Captain who arrested Adamas!"

"Adamas, who is Adamas, oh I am sorry, that man at the wedding, whatever they did to him, was he arrested?"

"Yes, he was arrested, fingerprinted, mug shot and finally released on his own recognizance. He is under surveillance, he cannot leave his house, cannot leave the state until the law enforcement people start interrogating him."

"Wooooah, that is big, that is good news after he murdered your entire family. God is alive. He is getting his due. I must tell the Pastor about this!"

"Please, not yet, we will get there. You see the way it will go is like this. I was asked to write my story, which I have been doing for the past three days. I excused myself from work, closed my phones, wrote by hand about fifty pages of the story, I typed in my PC. I reviewed with that Sergeant all day today. We just finished cleaning the story. We will deliver it next week on Tuesday to law enforcement people. That would be the basis to indict Adamas and judge him. I am being told that Justice is very slow here in US for murder cases. They must make sure that my story sticks. This is what I have been doing. I am sorry you could not get in touch with me. This is very important to me."

"So, what about me, what about our community, what about all these other people who have suffered the same calamities. Did you think of them? I strongly believe that you need to pursue this not as a lone victim. I heard that million people have suffered the same calamities back home and abroad. Let us unite to stand tall!"

"Of course, I know that Suzanne, but the accusation must start somewhere. I want to start the ball rolling. The more the better of course. Believe me, it was not easy putting down the terrible story. It was gut wrenching with a lot of tears for two days in the row. You know what, I was going to talk with the Pastor to set a meeting where I will share the entire legal process. I want to do it in an orderly way after I am done with the first meeting with the law enforcement people and they are from the District Attorney, the FBI, the North Caroline Police Department."

"Wooooah, Adamas is done, he is screwed. Good for you!"

41

"Suzanne, you see, I felt the same way as you are saying it. But I realized the past three days, it is a long shot, a long process. And as the Sergeant kept telling me, the story did not happen here in US, it happened abroad, in Congo. So, the burden of proving these murders, these calamities, is very high. It literally falls on me, or whoever in our community is willing to tell similar stories. You know me, my all life has been defined by these events. I am driven to see it through. I don't know if the next person will be willing to carry this burden as much as I am. I know my cross, I can only guess the other people's crosses. I would not want to put that burden on every person out there. Do you read me, Suzanne? That is why we must be careful talking about my case. When I will be ready, I owe it to you and your husband, to share it with both of you. Then we will decide what to do. Fair enough?"

"Fair enough, I agree. But that still does not excuse you to keep me without news from you. You are my eyes and ears, never leave me so desperate like that. I guess you had no news from my poor baby daughter in her honeymoon. You know what girls go through honeymoon. My God! I cannot bear to think what that man is doing to my poor girl!"

"Jesus is that all you can come up with, while I am in the mist of grave remembrance. You must be crazy, Suzanne, wondering about your daughter honeymoon activities. Tell me how different was it for you back home when my good man, the Pastor visited your lower parts the first time? How was it, painful?"

"No, I welcomed it? I begged him to hurt me … five times five times more. I enjoyed it thoroughly, thank you!"

The ladies erupted in strident loud laughter. Charlotte almost lost control of her car and managed to move the car to the side and stopped it. They laugh again so loud people outside the airconditioned sealed car can hear their commotion.

"Poor Pastor Chi with such shameless wife!"

"We were both shameless for two days in a row. He enjoyed it just as much as I did! Our families were relieved when we came out of our room the third day and my daughter came out on the dot exactly nine months after."

"Enough, enough, we are in the store now, can you change the conversation?"

"I won't, did you talk to my daughter?"

"No, I did not! I will talk to her sometime by the end of this week."

"That will be too long. She will lose very important details."

"What a crazy mother!"

"What a crazy lovely friend!"

Charlotte had a hard time completing her food shopping in company with her best joking friend. After they parted company, Charlotte realized what her best friend was trying to do. Suzanne pushed that light and merry conversation to ease her friend into her mundane self after three days of difficult remembrance. Charlotte needed a good laugh after all. She was grateful for Suzanne's visit. She was also grateful that Suzanne would respect her timeline about her legal activities regarding the unexpected encounter during her daughter's wedding. To date very few people in the community were aware of this, she absolutely wanted to keep that way.

Charlotte also worked hard to maintain a mundane appearance for the next few leading to the Tuesday appointment. She kept to her routine life, routine work, routine activities while reading and re-reading the thirty-seven pages she worked on with the Sergeant who strangely did not call. She suspected that he was also trying to give her a mundane space the same way her best Suzanne has done. She appreciated both just the same way. But on the night before the appointment, she was awakened again by the same nightmare that bothered her before. She could not go back to sleep from three-thirty on. The difference this time, she was not inclined to use hard liquor to calm herself. She repeated the "Lord is My Shepherd" Psalm 23 more than thirty times to sleep. She was awakened by a phone call about eight am by no other Sergeant "Sid" who was literally singing:

"This is the day, this is the day that the Lord has made!"

They greeted each other as old friends.

"I am glad you are awake. I will pick you up outside at ten o'clock!"

"Yes, Sir!"

Charlotte dressed as conservatively as if she was going to a wake.

Sergeant "Sid" made a remark about it and approved it all heartly. When they arrive at the District Attorney office, they were surprised to be greeted by the Boss himself, Timothy O'Grady, a tall avuncular man, with a booming voice. He greeted Charlotte with all the charms of a Southern aristocrat, pronounced her full name with full French accent for Charlotte and unmistakably for Keregi. Charlotte was made at ease. Mr. O'Grady directed them to a big conference room where all attendees rose to greet the important witness guest. Mr. O'Grady introduced her gracefully:

"Ladies and Gentlemen, before you introduce yourself, I have the great honor of introducing Mrs. Charlotte Keregi along with our own, Sergeant "Sid". Please take your seats. The purpose of this meeting is to take a presentation prepared by Mrs. Charlotte Keregi regarding the various statements she made on the day of May 25th, 2013, when she encountered a gentleman, she recognized as a "Major Adamas Kagita" who later identified himself as "Mr. Okito Jefferson". Through statements Mrs. Charlotte Keregi made that day, she accused "Major Adamas Kagita" of having murdered members of her family in the Eastern area of Democratic Republic of Congo in 2008. Mrs. Charlotte Keregi made these statements spontaneously in a state of shock and anger. These were grave accusations that law enforcement authorities take very seriously, much so that "Major Adamas Kagita" alias "Okito Jefferson" was arrested, fingerprinted, booked, and released on his own recognizance. He has also been advised at this time not to leave the state of North Caroline, while we start instructing these accusations. Now, Mrs. Charlotte Keregi, have I stated correctly why we are here and the purpose of your visit."

"Yes, Sir!"

"Thank you, now each of here in this conference needs to tell Mrs., Charlotte Keregi, which law enforcement agency you are representing and your name and title."

"My name is Frederic St Clair, First Agent of Raleigh County FBI Office, representing the FBI."

"My name is Sergeant Jennifer Barrow, from the North Carolina State Police, representing the State Police."

"My name is Johnson Mattheson, Third Deputy District Attorney in the Raleigh County, I will represent the District Attorney Office in this matter."

For your information, these three people represent the three concerned agencies and they have brought their own crews to faithfully register issues specific to their agencies. That is the reason why the conference room is so well attended. I can assure you during various meetings we will have with you, these agencies will be involved, they will be introduced to you.

"Did I miss anybody?"

"I assume not. Now let us give Mrs. Charlotte the chance to share the presentation she has prepared, Mrs. Charlotte Keregi, please share your presentation."

Charlotte, seated next to Sergeant "Sid", approached the microphone, lined up upward and started reading her thirty-seven pages story after having distributed the full text to every attendee. It took her about forty-five minutes. She read it all in a monotonous voice with tearful eyes. Her voice rose only two or three times specifically when she recounted the nightmare of having seen armed Adamas over the Uganda border. She wiped her brow and tears and sat for about two minutes holding her head to compose a bit. The conference room was equally deafening silent for a while. Mr. O'Grady finally broke the stalemate, he took to the mike and asked if there were any question. But before anyone responded, he also added that it would be most appropriate for attendees to prepare their questions during a twenty-minute break. This will give Mrs. Charlotte time to recover from the difficult reading of her story. Sergeant "Sid" took the opportunity to comfort Charlotte.

"You did excellent. I was not sure if you would finish your presentation. It was a very difficult one. Believe me, we all share your sympathy." Sergeant "Sid' got up to get a cup of tea for Charlotte who was quickly approached by a younger District Attorney staff member. She looked about twenty to twenty-five years of age. She also recomforted her. They shared a small talk about their origins. The lady introduced herself as Ludmila Garrov. She said that she was from Serbia. She came to the US as a refugee after the partition of the greater Yugoslavia. She added she was aware of what she was talking about. She claimed to have witnessed similar stories she had no strength to share or to revisit. She

45

assured Charlotte that she admired her courage and strength. Charlotte answered that she did not think she was any different to anybody else. She added that from the time she arrived in the US she had sworn to share these calamities somehow, but running into hat murderer made her more than determined to act to tell her story.

Sergeant "Sid' brought back a warm cup of tea with some cake pieces. Mr. O'Grady recalled the attendees and asked them to ask them direct questions to Charlotte.

The first to raise a question was no other but Johnson Mattheson from the District Attorney staff.

"Thank you, Charlotte, for your presentation if you don't mind calling you by your first name. Listening to your presentation, I must point out a few things that we will need to clear up to advance the purpose of our meeting today. The first thing my esteemed boss, Mr. O'Grady, alluded to from the beginning. We need to make sure that we reconcile the identity of the man you are accusing of murdering members of your family. He mentioned "Major Adamas Kagita" you said you recognized, and the same person claimed to be "Okito Jefferson". We will need to dispel that confusion very quickly. Mrs. Charlotte Keregi, you will agree with me that we don't want to waste time on any mistaken identity. You must help us very quickly to establish that "Major Adamas Kagita" and "Okito Jefferson" are not two different persons but the same person. You must help us to show that the same person is hiding his murderous identity. The sooner, the better. And that issue of identity is very important not just for the purpose of this meeting but also for what my colleague from FBI, Agent Frederic St Clair can talk about."

"Thank you for the introduction, Mr. Mattheson. I might add to the same request. While Mr. O'Grady mentioned two names, we are also interested in the third person responding to the same identity by the name of "Okito Jalabi Jefferson". We need to clear this identity for a different reason. This individual is being monitored for suspicion of distributing drugs along the Interstate Highway 85 from Atlanta to Richmond. We are not certain if he is the same person you were talking about. We want to make sure that he is not involved in criminal enterprise of receiving drugs from overseas from Colombia by way of Mexico. Our interest is straightforward. Once a criminal, always a criminal. If he has been engaged profitably in criminal activities in

Congo, the attraction would be the same, to engage in criminal activities in the US. So, we will need help there too. Back to you Johnson."

"Mrs. Charlotte Keregi, the same way you were able to provide us with thirty-seven pages of presentation, we want to urge you to provide us with testimonies about this man from back home. We believe you have more reliable sources than we can come up with. Believe me we also have our conduits. But we want you to work with us to generate as many reliable facts as possible and that will stand the verification in the court of law. We are talking about friends, relatives, churches, schools, work locations, communities of interest, newspapers who can provide pictures, videos, statements, stories, articles, internet blogs in web sites that are available. In this business, the more the better. You never know where the truth would come up. This is plea, a request we have for you to make your story presentation stick. Do you think you can help us?"

"Yes, Sir, I will shake down my community for everything. And I can assure you, they will shake down their contacts back home for the same thing. That is possible. As you can see, I am entirely new at this venue. I am a nurse specializing in Anesthesiology. I am very familiar with investigations in the medical field as you well know. Every person that walks into the medical premises needs to be examined, in other words investigated for sickness or things that are not working well in the body. It is practically the same thing. Though we use different methods and tools, we tend to the same activity, investigation."

"Exactly, Mrs. Charlotte Keregi. You say it better. As we say, you help us to help you."

Mr. O'Grady moved again to ask if there were any other questions. There were none.

"As Mr. Mattheson put it so eloquently, we have got a lot of work ahead of us, dispel the many identities this individual is wearing will help and your input in this matter would be much appreciated. We will examine your presentation for further reviews and or interviews as we move along. If there is no other request or question for Mr. Charlotte Keregi, we want to thank her for her presentation and we will be in touch, thank you."

Mr. O'Grady closed the first interview meeting with Charlotte. He invited Charlotte and Sergeant "Sid" to his office. Strangely enough the younger Staff member, Ludmilla Garrov preceded them. When they were seated Mr. O'Grady introduced Ludmilla Garrov to them as his trusted, most dynamic, and highly intelligent Staff member. He said that he was very proud to have recruited her out of the prestigious Law school of the University of North Carolina in Chapel Hill, his own alma mater. He added that he had followed her anonymously and from a strong recommendation of a dear friend, a professor at the school. Her legal academic ascent for the past three years to her graduation Magnum Cum Laude and Exceptional Valedictorian speaks volume of her potential. He told them that he hired her the same day as her graduation. He did not want to take a chance to compete with the vultures, the vampires from the big money law firms in Charlotte. He said that he wanted to ensure that Ludmilla entered the legal profession uncompromised, from the side of people, the true bearers of the levers of Justice. He wanted Ludmilla to consider deepening her legal learning from the prosecution side to the highest academic level. He closed his introduction by telling Charlotte that Ludmilla would be her main contact in his office and asked her to provide Charlotte with her business card. He then turned to Sergeant "Sid" with strong professional advice.

"My good man "Sid", I want to thank you for guiding Charlotte to build that strong presentation. Now don't be modest, I can tell, read, and detect a lot of input and presentation construction. Charlotte was at least honest about it when she said that she had no legal background, that she is an expert in examining people, investigating their sickness. A very smart analogy. The truth will set me free if I reveal that I have been bugging your boss to release you to our office to be our main interface with the police investigators, the detectives and so on. Your boss has always declined. Now I know why. But I would continue pushing my request all the way to the state Governor if I can. It is about time that your boss stands on his own criminal referrals and reports. You have been doing your job loyally a bit for too long. Believe me I am working on it. Please join us."

"It would be an honor sir!"

"An honor, no, you deserve it!"

"Again, thank you both for honoring us today."

Charlotte and Sergeant "Sid" left the District Attorney Office very pleased and satisfied with one another and left for lunch at their designated restaurant.

CHAPTER 6

NATIONAL SECURITY CONCERNS

As soon as Mr. O'Grady took leave of Charlotte and Sergeant "Sid", he rushed to his office where a confidential telephone device was rigging endlessly. He picked it up very quickly before it was to be routed to his secretary. He knew exactly who his correspondent at the other end was. He barked at his telephone set.

"Gwendolyn, can you give me at least enough time to compose myself after the long meeting we had about your latest spoiler from Langley. I don't know how you can manage to survive in that office of yours, pretending to manage the levers of justice of the US. If you ask me, I will say that your agency works twenty-four hours seven to degrade those levers with your overseas hoodlums in the name of national security."

"Please, I don't need another lecture from you currently. We all have assigned work to do, all right. Yours to keep the people of North Caroline safe from criminals, mine to protect the US national security from adverse acts and people from abroad. You know and I know that my function is not as clear cut as yours. You know and I know that sometimes we make short cuts that are not taught in our academic law schools to advance our national security. Now let us keep our work and function distinct but work together ok."

"Rubbish, what do you want?"

"Well, how did the famous lady presentation go?"

"Very bad for your client if you want to know. We are dealing with a very smart lady who is very much driven to reach her goal of bringing your client to justice in the American soil. It is not going to be pretty. And don't ask me to stop her because I won't."

"Who is asking you to stop, nobody is asking you to stop her! We are asking to proceed within the framework of protecting …"

"The US interests at home and abroad! I heard that before."

"And what is wrong about it?"

"Gwendolyn, if you were not a relative and a long-time friend, I would have terminated this conversation a long time ago. I always wonder why you went to law school, was it to raise the levers of justice like most naïve law school students, or you study law to screw every tenet of justice. My God, you did well! And your father, my dear uncle, an esteemed Federal Judge at the Fifth Circuit Appellate Court must be turning many times over in his coffin, watching you making a mockery of the US law system. You did well rise in that bull shit office expressly dedicated to the legal defense of our national security. What is your title there?"

"I am happy you ask, it is Associate Deputy Attorney General, National Security Division, thank you. Please spare me further insults. Last time, I told you to concentrate on the multiple identities of that individual. The idea was to throw a bit of monkey wrench in forms of more time delays in the legal pursuit while our friends in Langley are devising a good way out of this legal mess. What happened?"

"Oh, that one was also taken care of at the meeting. I left it to my Deputy to lay the groundwork for that instruction. Funny thing, he was joined by our friends from FBI who added a third identity confusion. I was sitting there thinking that that was another of your silly game. So obvious that you talk with the FBI on a daily working basis. What a joke! Anyway, our client was very happy to, in her own words, shake down her people to clear the identity confusion with a lot of references. It will take a while, give, or take four to six months, before we have clarified his identity. But I am telling you right now, the District Attorney Office in Raleigh is proceeding with the instruction. As soon as I get about twenty percent of those references, I am looking for a judge to start squeezing your individual. And I am not going to wait four to six months. Two to three max! Tell you friends at Langley, we don't like their garbage in our backyard. Is Florida full? What about Arizona? National security, my ass! When is it going to end after Vietnam, Iran, Afghanistan, Iraq? And now Congo! And you are always associated with the worst of them? We never learn!"

"Two to three months will be a bit short for them. It took them more than a year and half to bring him in, give them some time to resolve their multiple agency problems. The US national security issues are not dealt in Vatican!!"

"But Gwendolyn, tell me why bring such an individual here in the US. He was bad enough out there in that part of DRC. Any way you look at it, he has been no good all along. Why bring him here! What kind of national security concerns were solved or resolved by bringing him in? Help me educate me!"

"Now you are talking. Our powers that be got themselves in a deep shit for a long time in that part of the world all the way back ten years ago, in fact 1993. Remember 1993, that is Clinton administration. We are already out of Vietnam, rebuilding US as the No1 premier power in the world. We can do anything we want; the Soviet Union is gone. We got young new blood cooking at the top, it is time to change the world. Now we have young blood cooking at the top not only in the US but also in the UK. Big academic minds are flourishing all over. Remember that the time Information Industrial Revolution was at hand. The big Dot.com is boiling over. AT&T is being broken up into many incredible outfits. Internet came in emblazoning force. Information technology is embarking on new designs, new inventions, new electronic device resizing. That is the time cell phone technology required new resizing, new superconductivity that will manage in one small place, bigger memory, new applications, bigger space. That is the time also a new strategic mineral is found to effectively integrate these new features. Unfortunately, this new mineral is only found in the worst part of the world. It is found in the eastern region of Zaire which was at that time tired of the long dictatorship under Marechal Mobutu Sesse Seko of more than thirty years. This country was so mismanaged, it was decided to simply change the country's leadership. The decision was made to impose political leadership that answered only to multinational companies interested in extracting that mineral. The decision was made to topple our own old friend, Marechal Mobutu, and put in place a regime that would fulfill the multinational companies' goals. The new administration in DC decided with the British PM administration to bring about a new political leadership, English speaking in that region to enable the new strategy. Overnight, new political leaders emerged in that region of Africa, in Rwanda, Uganda, Ethiopia, Kenya and Tanzania. The only miscalculation in that push was the inability of Washington to prevent the genocide that resulted from the new strategy., the killing of about eight hundred people from the Tutsi tribe. That remains the major guilt of Washington to abide by anything that the new emerging political leadership wanted in the region, including to the takeover, the invasion of DRC to topple the President Marechal. To tell the truth, the grave miscalculation from the brightest new Washington leadership was underestimating the tribal political allegiance in Africa. That miscalculation translated into the Far West plunder of the strategic mineral resources in the Eastern Region of DRC by the new political leadership in Rwanda for the benefits of multinational companies. This miscalculation has become the actual US strategy for some time. Now. That miscalculation had generated a much bigger genocide of Congolese people in the region on top of the plunder of the mineral resources including the much-coveted Coltan. That miscalculation had generated a terrible American strategy that tends to stifle the broadcasting of the terrible mess we have made there including now as you are witnessing the protection of awful people like our famous individual in our own soil. Now tell me, cousin, what should I do when that strategy lands on my desk. Should I resign or suffer through it and push it on some other desks. You can say all you want, my goal in this issue is to get the management of that messed up strategy to land on somebody else's desk. And you must help me."

"I see, what a mess! You are right. I don't want my cousin and the O'Grady name to become the laughing stock over the Potomac River, especially since I am being actively solicited to run for the Senate seat that the other side is about to relinquish. I will see how I will manage that hot potato. Still, I can assure you that it won't be easy."

"I never say it would be easy. But it is up to you to play the factor time. That is all I am asking you to do. Hold that bag as long as you can. Hear me! Don't release the instruction phase until I have made progress in moving it away."

"But, Gwendolyn, you are dealing with ruthless people in Langley, don't you think they may be thinking the same way, where to dump that SOB. What about the famous individual, he must be also thinking the same way. In his case, it would be how to make his case a threat to all of you back in DC. What I am saying, he knows where the dead bodies are buried. You had already helped him to a good deal of dead bodies, casquets, cemeteries and God only know what else. He can come up with or resurrect blackmails against you folks in DC or a lot of people in place back in these countries in Africa. Have you thought about that?"

"I am, an all the time. But I can sit here devising one thousand schemes to move my plan. Believe in the hidden world, everyone is working hard to get to the top. I can only play my cards the best way I can and leave the rest well to chance. I am very relieved you are now appreciating the mess I got myself into and how I need to get out of it!"

"My deep sympathies! And yes, it won't be easy, not easy ... and bye!"

Mr. O'Grady hung the phone and said to himself, "DC can be rough!"

CHAPTER 7
WITNESS TESTIMONY

When Charlotte left the restaurant in company with Sergeant "Sid", she was dropped by home to get ready for her evening shift scheduled to start around six-thirty. She was very pleased and satisfied with the first interview she had with the law enforcement people. She was treated very well, she thought, much better than she expected indeed. She was given all the respect and the sympathy she wanted. She was grateful to Sergeant "Sid' who has prepared her very well with the presentation she made and that was also well received. She was also grateful for all the advices she received from these people to enhance her presentation with reliable witness testimony. While she was changing into her medical uniform, she received a call from no other but the young District Attorney Staff member, Ludmilla Garrov.

"Hello, this is Ludmilla from the District Attorney Staff office!"

"Yes, I remember you very well, I was happy that Mr. O'Grady designated you as my point of contact in the office. I hope that you will assist me to the best of your ability."

"I would try. This is in fact a follow-up to my introduction. I want us to work together with the least amount of formality as possible. To start with, please, I would appreciate that you address me as Ludy when we are conversing."

"I like that, and me Charlotte would be fine, thank you!"

"That is better. After you were gone, Mr. O'Grady wanted me to share more advices about enhancing your presentation. He wants to warn you that you will be in front of you a powerful defense team for that individual with multiple aliases. Remember that people who managed to bring him in to the US had serious motives to do that and have powerful financial interests to protect. They would use every legal tool to protect that individual in the court of law. He added that he does not have to tell you that they have powerful political connections. He said that you have on your side the public District Attorney Office ready to carry your accusation in the court of law. This does not mean that you are in a disadvantaged position, absolutely not. This means that you must arm the District Attorney Office with the best legal testimonies that would overwhelm that defense team in every aspect of the law. Do you understand?"

"Yes, I understand, and I am following you clearly."

"That means that the testimony we will bring must be above reproach, it must not be compromised by errors, mistakes, omissions, or untruth. That testimony must be clear and overwhelming as the drop of clear water. That testimony must be reliable from reliable people, uncompromised people, preferably family members who have a strong stake in seeing that that individual is punished to the full extent of the law. That means you and I must be in the front of cleaning the bult of that testimony ensuring that it does not come from people we are not convinced or certain of their intention. Is that clear?"

"Yes, I understand what you are saying. I understand that even in our own community there are people ready to sell their soul for a ridiculous drop of money they don't even need or want. Unfortunately, where I came from, the corruption is so widespread I must be careful about everything I will do in this project. I am relieved that your boss is thinking about that theme. Believe me, I would not let any shortcoming enter that testimony, so help me God. I trust that with your capable and skilled involvement we will sanitize these testimonies."

"Thank you, Charlotte, that is the message my boss wanted you to carry around all the time as we work in this legal project."

"Thank you, Ludy!"

"I don't want to hold you any longer, I believe you have a long night work schedule today, so long."

The enthusiasm that Charlotte had carried a while ago dropped a bit at the end of the call. Yet she shared what Ludy, and her boss were advancing. That was the reason she had been extremely private about her life from the time she left DRC. She prayed that one day she was going to rise to make Adamas pay for his murderous acts. She never spoke about this overwhelming goal to anybody. She kept quiet about it. Karma had it that Adamas fell into that trap. She certainly surprised the Chibere couple by the intensity of her reaction during the implausible encounter. They had never seen her in such a violent and loud riposte. That was the reason she avoided getting in touch with them. Charlotte was also guilty about it all. The Chibere family was the closest she could call family from the start of her separation from DRC. They had supported her throughout the painful trek from Walikale region through Uganda through landing in Raleigh. They never asked anything in return. She also paid back in return attending to assisting them to raise their children and doing so many other family tasks. She could not possibly cut that family cord now. Charlotte decided that she had no choice but suffer the Chibere involvement in her witness testimony project. She would try to clean up any shortcoming coming from the Chibere as fast as quickly as possible.

On the other hand, she knew that there was only one person who could honestly assist her in the cleaning up of the collection of witness testimony. Uncle Stanislas Keregi was the one. Charlotte knew that Uncle Stanis, as she enjoyed calling him, enjoyed an incredible progressive network within Congolese diaspora and back home. That network was generally formed of people dedicated to move the country to a legitimate and democratic direction of rule of law, nationalist progressist economic expansion, implementation of genuine democratic infrastructures free of sectarian, tribal, regional inequities. Although Charlotte was most time tired of his endless political lectures, she knew that Uncle Stanis meant and lived by his political credo and conviction. He would be able to dig and provide the most reliable witness testimony about Major Adamas Kagita in every aspect of the accusation that would be raised against him in any local, national, international court anywhere in this world. All she had to do was ask.

Charlotte reached out to Uncle Stanis.

"Hello young lady, I missed hearing from you. How are you? Whatever happened about the encounter with Adamas? Have you managed to put him in an American jail? Did the American allowed you to jail him?"

"Please don't start that nonsense again. I am calling you for a serious talk. I know everyone did not have the chance to go and land in the utopia Sweden like you did. I did not choose the country to go to as a refugee. The UN decided that for me and I came along when my life was in danger. I was glad to go anywhere. I did not know where they were taking me. After about a week of trekking through places I had no idea of, I was put in a plane, a cargo plane where we all camped on the floor. They transferred us to some military base where we were collected into a civilian no name plane to another military base in US where we stayed for a week, and they decided to bring our group to Raleigh which I never heard of and did not know. And here I had lived for the past eight years or so, changed my life for the better, survived as best as I could until the same Adamas surfaced. Uncle Stanis, I cannot run from where I am. I must deal with this matter right here in the US whether I like it or not. I must use their law enforcement structure whether I like it or not if I want to get some legal remedial that the American Court, not the Swedish, not the Congolese, not any other country would provide. Am I clear on that? So, it is up to you to assist me if you want. It is up to you to use your substantial network in the Congolese diaspora and back home to help me to help yourself too. Because all the family members that Adamas killed are also your brothers, sisters, nephews and nieces. Are you ready to help or not?"

"Of course, I will help you, even if I don't trust the system that brought about the calamities."

"Uncle Stanis, I know where you are coming from, you don't need to repeat it. I need you for a very particular reason. Let me tell you as simply as I can. Yesterday, I was invited to make a presentation of about thirty-seven pages summarizing the accusation I made against Adamas. The presentation was made in front of people from the District Attorney Office of the Raleigh Count, the Raleigh County FBI Office, and the State of North Caroline Police Department. The conference room was packed for the presentation. It went very well, I believe. I was asked to strengthen my presentation by adding witness testimonies of the events covering how Adamas murdered our family members. They want me to add reliable facts to my presentation. To quote them, they want us "to generate as many reliable facts as possible and that will stand the verification in the court of law. We are talking about friends, relatives, churches, schools, work locations, communities of interest, newspapers who can provide pictures, videos, statements, stories, articles, internet blogs in web sites that are available". There is nobody I can depend on to generate these reliable facts and sources as broadly as you, my Uncle

Stanis. That is why I am coming back to you. "

"I hear you and I would do it. As a matter of fact, I have already collected a good portion of these facts and sources, I would love to start sharing right away. Provide me the right email ids, databases, post office boxes to send what I have."

"By the way, the first issue we must clear up is his identity. The man has three different identities currently. Two from Uganda against the one we know in DRC. The urgent process now is to dispel the Uganda ones and bring him back to his location of murders in DRC. We must do everything to establish his Congolese identity and background from birth until today."

"Don't worry, we got all that and more. Some Congolese Diaspora groups have already created a voluminous case implicating Adamas in so many massacres in the Eastern area up to the time he was evacuated to the US. They have already dropped it at the International Criminal Court at the Hague, Netherlands. The case is gathering dust there because as you know accusing Adamas at the ICC is equivalent to accusing the current government in place in DRC. This government stands as a prime accomplice with the government of Rwanda in those crimes. Now only the sitting government in Kinshasa can initiate such a case. That is where lies the dilemma. This government will never accuse itself in the ICC. Now you see where I am going. We will be very happy to share all that we have with any court in the world including that one in Raleigh and we will see what they will do with it."

"As I said, my task is to enhance my presentation. Whatever the American Court does with it will be out of my hands. But at least, I have kept my bargain, at least I have kept my own promise to bring Adamas to answer for the crimes he committed wherever I will be in my life. I swore to that goal, I am fulfilling it."

"So, God help us! I told you and I am repeating you will get more than you expected. I am about to shake down every path to satisfy your request. I also have to tell you that our people are thoroughly compromised and corrupted to betray anybody for two pieces of green or dollar. I hope you are not going to rely on anybody but family collecting these testimonies. I must say this because I have participated in many of these processes cleaning out the compromised input from the reliable. I am not certain you would be able to do that."

"I was already warned about this. I would rely entirely on you when it would come to cleaning the set. "

"That is much better. I have a lot of work ahead of me. I must go at this time."

"Thank you, Uncle Stanis, thank you so very much."

Charlotte knew that her dear Uncle Stanis was going to be the one to deliver the most reliable documentation to come. She raised her hands to thank God. She sat down and struggled to find how she was going to approach the Chibere couple to make the same request. She knew that Pastor Chi was going to become aware of it, sooner or later. About her presentation to the law enforcement team. Pastor Chi has always been regarded as the main contact around legal matters concerning countless people in the Congolese community in Raleigh. Charlotte was nervous to let the very Pastor Chi down to learn about her involvement with legal authorities from a third party. Pastor Chi was going to be very disappointed more so because he was a prime witness with his wife Suzanne of the encounter with Major Adamas Kagita. Overwhelmed with guilty, Charlotte called her good friend Suzanne to tell her that she was going to pay her and the Pastor a visit the upcoming Saturday evening. She mentioned that she was going to share important news around what has happened after the police involvement in that matter. Suzanne was delighted to welcome her friend. She claimed that she was going to cook her best dishes.

"Our delightful and beautiful lady has arrived", so Pastor Chi announced to his wife, that Saturday eight pm in the evening. It was raining hard that day, Charlotte struggled to enter the house with packs of dessert she always brings on similar occasions.

"Please, Charlotte, why did you not call me to help you half-way with all these bags. Besides, it has been raining all day. We could have postponed this meeting until tomorrow after the main noon service. This is too much work."

"Postpone what, I have been busy cooking for my good friend all afternoon. I have been looking forward to a good evening of merry talk and you want to postpone it. Forget it. She is here for me if you want to know. We will talk until tomorrow morning."

"So sorry, ladies, for butting in your get together. I am retiring to my little office to prepare for my sermon tomorrow Sunday. Let me know if you need me for anything."

"Come on, Pastor Chi, I came to talk to both of you. You have been married to your crazy wife for so long. You must be used by now to her corny talk. Have you not?"

"I have been trying, I can assure you, Charlotte. Whenever I think that I have succeeded, she would throw me a new curve to push me back to start all over again. You know that every other week, I am out there calling on a Man and a Woman and I quote "Join in holy matrimony for Better and Worse". I say it sometime without thinking. And when I am done, I go back to my car and in a moment of meditation I say to myself "Is it real and serious what I told these people, do they realize what is in that Better or Worse statement." Then I reach home, and what does your good friend, my dear wife, the one I have been married for Better and Worse, do you know what she asks me before I remove my hat and coat, well she said, "Did you forget to buy so and so I asked you to buy this morning?" My good lady Charlotte, I did not remember such a request."

At that moment the ladies looked at each other and blurted in a loud laughter that puzzled poor Pastor Chi.

"Did I say something funny, what did I say?"

The ladies expanded their laughter, falling on each side of the big sofa in the living room in face of the aggravated Pastor Chi. Finally, Charlotte intervened.

"Pastor Chi, that request is what makes and brings marriage alive. It got nothing to do with Better or Worse. It has got to do only with the better side of marriage to test the man's will to take the least he does not know. It is for the Better. Don't you know that, Pastor Chi?"

"Oh, I see, do you want to say that what have been missing is that one ingredient all these years. It is bad enough I am struggling to try, now I have been tested, thank you ladies. I must go and pray for the Lord to increase my tolerance and wisdom."

"Please, don't go. I came here for an important talk with both of you. Please, take this nice glass of red one I bought for you. You will like it.

Sergeant "Sid" I have been working with, invited me to this restaurant where it was offered. I tried it and I really enjoyed it. It is a new genre named Macbeth from Argentina."

"Suzanne, did you hear this, Charlotte is having dinner with a Sergeant "Sid", who is this man?"

"Now are you going to sit down and hear me, this is very serious?"

"Charlotte, I am sitting, you have my full attention, I am hearing you. Can you wait to start talking after we have the meal that Suzanne has been cooking so she said all afternoon?"

"Yes, I can wait. I just did not want you to leave us alone."

"Suzanne, bring the food. I am hungry and in hurry to listen to the story that Charlotte wants to share involving a Sergeant "Sid". I pray that I will be the one to bless for Better and Worse what we have be dreaming all these years. God is alive and so gracious, Amen!"

"You two always must bring anything concerning me overboard. You always have a multiple-choice selection. It could be: "A man gives a bouquet of flower" or "I am pregnant" or "A man sends me a card" or "When is the wedding date" or "I went to Miami for vacation" or "It must be a secret Catholic wedding" or "I am visiting a cousin in New York" or "A green card union". Do you want anymore?"

"Yes, you forgot "The week vacation at the rented Outer Banks Bungalow by yourself" or "A honeymoon with the just divorced deacon", Suzanne added for another chain of loud laughter.

When the dinner was completed, Pastor Chi rushed to clear the dining table of all. And very quickly filled the glasses for Charlotte, Suzanne, and himself with the Macbeth red wine from the second of the three bottles that Charlotte had brought.

"Thank you, Charlotte, I love this red wine. We are not going to touch the third bottle unless you want me to rush to the wine and spirit store in this raining time. I will keep the third bottle one for myself until I replenish it with another set of three or four bottles. Thank you. Now Charlotte you have got the floor. What do you have for us. "

"Suzanne and Pastor Chi, you have known me from the beginning when you traversed that region of our North Kivu in terrible conditions you remember, and I don't have to talk about. You have supported me all along and I thank you from the bottom of our heart. I must apologize for one thing. I was very private about until that Saturday of your daughter's wedding when I encountered Major Adamas Karuga. I may have mentioned that he was responsible for the murder of many members of my family. But I never told you that I have dedicated my entire life to one thing, and one thing only, to bring this man to justice by all means necessary. I kept that from everybody, even from you two and your family. I am sure that you have noticed that I have given up everything in my life. I am not attached to anybody, I hardly socialize, I deliberately avoid any social entanglement or marriage prospects. Look at me and ask me why a fairly young lady does not want any social mixing. I am sure you wondered what was or is wrong with me. Let me say it here and as loudly as I can. There is nothing wrong with me. I am not sick or anything like that. I was and am preserving myself for that battle, I know that it will come. I did not know when or how. I only knew that one day if God preserves me, I will wage that battle. I want it to preserve myself because I strongly believe that I owe it to my entire family to bring this man to justice for the injustice he had brought to us, to my family who had never knew him, never interreacted with him, never armed him, never had anything to do to or with him. For him to start casually and deliberately killing anyone associated with my family was well wrong. And later I learn that he did it because he wanted to force me to be his slave wife or something to that effect. But even if that was the case, it was up to me to accept or to reject his advance. Why did he have to take it on every member of my family and kill them so wantonly. Why did he have to take it on my dearest husband family and kill him so wantonly. That became a personal goal that I did not want to indispose anybody else with. I could not pursue that goal in the mist of marriage commitments. That would not have been fair for my partner or the children who would come. That is why I maintain a celibate life. I also know that the minute I start any legal proceeding, I will not have life for anybody else but myself fully dedicated to that goal. I sincerely apologize for having kept you to out of that goal. You were the only family I had known the minute I joined that trek from Walikale to Raleigh. Please forgive me!"

"Charlotte, and I speak for both of us here and if I may, my entire family; you don't have to apologize for what you just shared at this moment. We knew, observing you through what you call the difficult

63

trek we went through, you had like most of us difficult past. We heard about the massacre of your family from many sources. We also decided to respect your privacy leaving to Almighty God the grace and the wisdom to guide you to conquer your past while setting you in the right path of survival. Charlotte, as a Pastor, I have been called by God to do this not only for you but for the entire community of our people who probably went through the same calamities you have been through and do no want to talk about them and are not as courageous as you are to do something about it. For better or worse, I am not to judge whether they are ready or not willing to do something about it. My call as a Pastor to guide them one way or another and with prayer. Charlotte don't have a doubt about it for a second, Suzanne and I will stand by you and will support you one way or another and always with prayers from and for the Almighty God who after all is the only path to guide us in the past, in the present and in the future. Now what do you want us to do."

"I had no doubt about your support one way or another. That is why I came here today to ask again for your support. After my encounter with Adamas, a lot of things have happened. I have been in contact with Sergeant "Sid", the police leader who came to arrest Adamas. The policeman who was leading the interrogation, you remember. From my little involvement with police, I did not know what would happen. To tell the truth, I was initially disappointed by the way this Sergeant conducted the interrogation. I noticed he gave Adamas more deferment than I expected. He was extremely polite to a man I consider as a monster, a man that I know killed so many members of my family. I went on crying for four days about that. I judged this Sergeant harshly when he said from the beginning that he was not comfortable about exercising any jurisdiction over matters that happened in faraway places like DRC. I could not believe how he dealt with the situation so matter-of-factly. But I missed one important point. He was doing his job according to the precepts of law that are the norms here in the US. Remember "Everyone is innocent until proven guilty". That is one of the primary elements of the rule of law. Since I have not been privy to the mechanism of the rule of law, be it here or where I came from, I had zero reference of what should have taken place. I became very disappointed about what the man was doing back then. I was disappointed that while God did everything to put in presence of the very man I swore to put in jail, I screwed it up. I let Adamas go free, so I thought. I did not appreciate what the police did after they took him to the precinct. I did not realize that he was booked, fingerprinted, interrogated to give his whereabouts, his identity, his family. his residence, what does he do to live, his job, his acquaintances and so on. So, when Sergeant "Sid' came back calling me and instructing me about the process, I dismissed him entirely. But he was not to let me get away with my ignorance. He insisted and kept calling. Then finally when I realized he wanted me to improve my accusation during the encounter, I decided to test him. That is when he convinced me about the best way to proceed with my accusation. He suggested writing a long expose about what I know about Adamas, what he did to my family and my trek from Walikale to Raleigh. I joined Sergeant "Sid". I wrote about fifty pages of a presentation that we edited down to thirty-seven pages. Sergeant "Sid" arranged for me to make a presentation to three agencies including the District Attorney Raleigh Office, the FBI Raleigh Office, and the State Police Raleigh Center. I made the presentation to a packed conference center with the Raleigh County District Attorney himself presiding. I have a copy of my presentation here. It was well received."

"That is wonderful, Charlotte and congratulations, we are very proud of you. Now and unequivocally, I must say that we are going to support you in that endeavor, am I right Suzanne?"

"Of course, Pastor Chi, now I know why my only friend has been missing from action the two weeks. No words from Charlotte. Of course, I must and will support her."

"By the way, for your information, I got a call from people who always consult with me when a Congolese in Raleigh County has a serious issue with police. These contacts have progressed from the time a huge number of Congolese started migrating and coming to Raleigh from Zaire during the 1990. These contacts opened the way for the county law enforcement to diffuse matters that can be quickly settled as minor infractions instead of allowing them to move from petty infractions to a major criminal case. It was obvious that most of these situations were misunderstandings about translation. Most of these Congolese understood and spoke elementary French. They struggled to understand and speak English. So, a lot of us Pastors became translators for people in the community when they were involved in legal matters. I have helped a lot of our folks in that regard. So, one these contacts asked me if I knew about a presentation that a Congolese was going to make about a murder of her family. I told him I did not hear such a story in the community. Now I know what he wanted to share with me. I told him that no Congolese was involved in killing his family in Raleigh area. He said that he was sorry and added that maybe he did not understand the story. He said that he was surprised that I was not aware of that story. You know that he called me twice. I repeated that I did not hear anything like that. I owe him an apology. He was probably at that presentation of yours wondering why I was so categoric denying the story. Well now I know, and it was no other but our own Charlotte!"

"Well Pastor Chi, now you see why I insisted on coming to see you today. I suspected that sooner or later, you would be made aware of my presentation."

"Come on, Charlotte, no more excuses. I support your decision entirely. Now when I come to think of it, I should have been more involved trying to follow up with that Sergeant "Sid" after he took Adamas. I should have followed up to find out whatever happened with the accusation. I did not and I failed you our very esteemed friend. So, the shortcoming rests more on us. Of course, we can say that we were caught up with our daughter's wedding. A good excuse but not a plausible one when we were witnessing the encounter right there at the wedding party. My God, I failed you Charlotte, of all people."

Pastor Chi had a bit of tears coming down his eyes. Suzanne joined her husband in the lament. Charlotte became mortified by the overwhelming scene of guilt that she did not expect, and she was deeply touched.

"Pastor Chi AND Suzanne, I did not come here to accuse nobody. I told you that this has been a personal odyssey, a cross I did want to lay on anybody. I came here to explain why I gave up all my life to carry that cross. Now you are confounding me with this lamentation. Please stop!"

"Charlotte, I hate to hear you saying that it is your cross to carry alone. We came from the same area of DRC. Have you ever thought that we may have suffered the same calamities? The difference being that you chose to do something about it and we have moved on to other life concerns, maintaining our marriage, raising our children, doing everything except standing for our large family and all those we left behind back in DRC, while they are being beaten down, harmed all day long, left sick, tortured, starving without food, killed deliberately, days in and days out, those becoming strangers in their own villages, territories, province and country of DRC. And while they are living with those calamites, we are here in Raleigh County worrying about our own mundane life concerns. Now tell me who should feel guilty. The one who chose to forget what is going on back home or the one who chose to do something about it, the one who stood up against Adamas and the other Adamas's of this world. Charlotte, please just let us know how you want us to support you now?"

"All right, well after I finished giving my presentation, the law enforcement people warned me that the details in my presentation must enhanced by reliable facts that will stand the stringent verification of the court of law. For instance, remember I told them that when I had an encounter with a Major Adamas Kagita, he identified himself as an Okito Jefferson from Uganda. Therefore, we had one person with two identities. In addition, the representative from FBI said that they have been monitoring a certain Okito Jalabi Jefferson for drugs trade from over Interstate 85 from Atlanta to Richmond. Meaning that we now have three identities for the same person. As far as the law enforcement agencies are concerned, the first legal priority is to reconcile these three identities into one and same person that we know as Major Adamas Kagita. Remember the American don't know Adamas from Okito or Jefferson or Jalabi. All these are aliases this man had worn during his criminal career. We must reconcile all to Major Adamas Kagita. Reliable facts must be made available to the Court to dispel these multiple identities as quickly as possible. They suggest as I explained to my Uncle Stanis who is also willing to help, "to generate reliable facts from friends, relatives, churches, schools, work locations, communities of interest, newspapers who can provide pictures, videos, statements, stories, articles, internet blogs in web sites that are factual and available." I want you Pastor Chi to call up your church members to assist us to generate these reliable facts from as many people here and from home. A District Attorney Staff member has been assigned to work with to sort these facts, to clean to reliable standing. I know it is a huge undertaking. But it is possible and necessary to reach the goal we must nail Major Adamas Kagita and put him away to jail for a long time. I was also advised not to underestimate the dark forces that made it possible to get such a criminal from the criminal ground of Walikale to a space of Outer Banks of North Carolina where he lives savoring the deeds of plunder of natural resources of DRC on the back of many dead people. They said we must be vigilant in collecting these reliable facts ensuring that they are reliable at all the time from reliable people right here in Raleigh County and in DRC. "

"I see! I can assure you Charlotte that we will do our part to support you in this collection. It is not going to be easy but God helping we will reach our goal. We will."

"Thank you so very much."

CHAPTER 8

CHURCH AGENDA

When Charlotte decided to take her leave, the rain that was falling all the time that evening changed into a thunderous pouring rain. The Chibere couple restrained Charlotte from venturing outside in the pouring rain. They insisted on continuing the difficult conversation about devising the most effective courses and strategies to engage the church members to assist in building a solid case against the murderous Adamas. But the more they talked, Charlotte could not help but read the couple's terrible confusing mental state about her case. As soon as she noticed a small break in the pouring rain, she got up.

"My very dear friends, I must rush home to accept some early Sunday calls from my uncle from Sweden. I will appreciate that you understand that he will be sharing very painful legal episodes that he had started collecting. Besides, I have kept Pastor Chi from preparing his Sunday sermon. I am sorry I must take my leave now."

"Rubbish, Charlotte, this will be the whole church engagement to support and to stand by you. Keep in mind that there is no one, I repeat, no one in our church who has not been affected by the same stories you will be collecting. By the way, you are right, the rain is almost over, we will walk you to your car. Let me and your friend carry your bags so that all you will do is to jump on the driver's side while we quickly load stuffs in your car. Charlotte, I will make sure that the Raleigh Metropolitan Church of Our Savior will be fully engaged in this endeavor, God is my witness."

However, the rain restarted pouring with increased intensity. And the Chibere couple struggled mightily to fill the back seat with bags while Charlotte started the car. They quickly rushed back to the house when the car was already disengaged. When the couple were back in the living room, it became difficult to tell whether the running drips from Mrs. Chibere face were from the rain or were unrestrained tears after listening to painful episode her dear friend was living. The couple was now seated quietly in the living trying to recuperate from the difficult discourse.

"As you said, Darling, each member in our church had lived a variant of what Charlotte had lived. However, most of us have been trying to live and let live. We are far away from our country and trying to forget what we saw and lived there in DRC. Most of us have very deep scars we refuse to confront. We wake up every day to bury those scars. In fact, we don't know which one of us, like Charlotte, is being eaten by those scars. I was always very afraid of and concerned about my friend Charlotte. I tried many times to tease her to resume, what I was kidding myself to be, a normal life. I observed her for a long time. I became scarred that she was going to be driven crazy about whatever she kept buried in her soul. She never shared it as she did today. She made me feel so small, so irrelevant, about what should have mattered in priority. Now I am wondering whether I went too far ahead taking care of matters at hand, maintaining a household, raising our kids, keeping our marriage whole, supporting you in your church functions. Did I miss something? Did I turn my back on those left behind in DRC? I don't know, it is so confusing. Charlotte is going to challenge a lot of us, a lot of our life, Pa Chi! At the end, I can assure you, It is not going to be easy for nobody."

Pastor Chibere absorbed all that his wife was saying. He also wiped a few tears from his face.

"Indeed, Charlotte is going to challenge a lot of our lives here in Raleigh. Remember in Luke 9:23, Jesus looks at his disciples and tells them,

"Whoever wants to be my disciple must deny themselves and take their cross and follow me. For whoever wants to save their life will lose it, but whoever loses their life for me will find it".

Charlotte has been carrying her cross for as long as we have known her. It is a challenge she has fully accepted at the exclusion of everything else. You see to carry your cross means to fully put your trust in God amid the storms and battles in your life. It always saddens me when I see the symbol of cross being defiled left and right by people who would not and could not be able to spell "cross" anyway. The cross is the ultimate station in any human. I must confess it is not given to anybody to carry the cross. We can hope and try, but it is not always obvious. Human life is usually a chain of storms and battles, it is impossible to go through that chain without putting your trust in Almighty God. That is the true meaning of carrying one's cross. And I must say you also each person is given his or her symbol of a cross to carry. And Ma Chi, I must tell you have valiantly carried your cross through your chain of storms and battles while you had our children, raised them to a successful maturity, maintained your household and marriage whole and God is my witness, supported your husband in his call of pastor. And we must not forget that each member of our church is also struggling to carry his or her own symbol of the cross in his or her respective life. I can say it because I am honored to see that every day. God strongly advised each of us never to judge how, when or where anybody is carrying his or her cross. Only God is the last arbiter of the way the cross is carried. We need to pray abundantly for Charlotte, for ourselves and for the church to devise effective ways to assist on the collection of as many as possible testimonies from the church members. I need to put in place a credible process for this. I really need to get a lot of input from my contacts in the legal enforcement agencies."

During the next two weeks, Pa Chi consulted first his primary contacts in the North Carolina State Police in Raleigh about the best course to take. He was referred to the same District Attorney Office that organized Charlotte briefings. The young District Attorney staff member, Ludmilla Garrov was sent to talk to the Pastor Chibere. In a full professional circle, she invited Charlotte to meet with the Pastor. Charlotte surprised Pa Chi when she showed up with the younger Ludmilla at the meeting. The Pastor was quickly brought to speed around the protocols Charlotte and Ludmilla have devised to drive the process. It was very elaborate. The pastor was greatly relieved for not to have to create a new set of protocols and specifically affidavit forms to collect testimonies. He was impressed by the depth and the length of legal expertise that Charlotte had developed and accumulated in the short time of her involvement in the presentation. The younger Ludmilla impressed him equally with her legal advanced expertise. He was shocked to learn that she had accumulated legal academic expertise to the level of a Ph. D at such a young age. On the other hand, Charlotte fully appreciated the fact that the meeting took place with no other church elder member. This sent a strong signal that Pa

Chi was not going to let the collection of testimonies dispersed among people with no clear stake in the legal proceedings. With Ludmilla unrelenting support, Charlotte drove this significant point at the end of the meeting. So much so that Pa Chi decided the ladies will control the process of collecting the testimonies at the church premises starting with the selection of witness made by the Pastor who introduced them to the collections panel composed of Charlotte and Ludmilla. The ladies took over the process at this point, scheduling first the preliminary interview where they decided whether the witness input was worthwhile pursuing. They moved on to schedule the main legal interview, preferably after work for about three to four hours. If relevant materials emerged from the main interview, additional interviews were scheduled until the collection was exhausted. They edited the testimonies into the prescribed legal affidavit format. They scheduled a reading of the testimony affidavit with the witness for edition and concurrence. The witness signed the affidavit to close it.

The pastor introduced close to fifty-seven witnesses. A solid thirty-eight witnesses completed the entire process within the next two months and half. The very well controlled process was successful, delivering extensive documentations and media back-up way beyond Charlotte's and Ludmilla's expectations. The affidavits documented sixteen additional multiple criminal and murderous incidents and cases involving Major Adamas Kagita. The man was cited in more than hundred twenty-one murders and fifty-eight rapes.

At the end of the process, Pastor Chibere held a special prayer service one Friday to thank all those who have participated in the collection of testimonies. According to specific instructions from the District Attorney Office, there was no mention of what was collected. Dinner was also offered for the participants. Charlotte and Ludmilla thanked each participant personally.

The church affidavits collection was very small compared to what Uncle Reverent Stanislas Keregi's collection drive has put in motion from Sweden. It should be clearly stated at this time that Charlotte expected that his Uncle Stanis collection drive will take on many fronts. Some will be extremely helpful, strictly legal focusing like a laser beam on Major Adam dubious past as Charlotte wished, but the other fronts will be essentially political and strategic expounding on Uncle Stanis major themes around Major Adamas's involvement. Uncle Stanis considered Major Adamas as a sad tool of Western economic strategy about DRC. His repeated telephone call sermons have made this clear for a long time. Charlotte had no choice but to receive both sets of his collection drive.

Uncle Stanis' collection dump was voluminous and impressive. It spanned a long list of countries including DRC, Uganda, Rwanda, Burundi, Kenya, Tanzania, South Africa, Belgium, France, Germany, Italy, Switzerland, Sweden, Denmark, Holland, Hong Kong, Thailand, Dubai, Australia, and US. Documentations from legal, judicial, economic, and political international institutions were inserted in the collection. The affidavits were sourced from various United Nations agencies including the International Criminal Court and major public and private Human Right organizations. Uncle Stanis left no stone unturned. As a matter of fact, his collection evolved into a distinct voluminous political indictment of the entire vicious plunder of DRC mineral resources from 1997 through present, cleverly narrated on the marge of Major Adamas growing criminal record. The affidavits collection reconstructed Major Adamas's biography from birth in 1975 at Butembo, a city in the North Kivu province, his elementary and secondary education progress in the same city. The collection continued with his on and off academic education at the University of Kisangani around 1997 and his still unexplained expulsion from the same college, marking the beginning of his descent into hell, into a depraved life of hardened murderous criminal. His return to Kisangani was also thoroughly documented. Major Adamas was then enrolled in the Uganda army during the murderous confrontation with the Rwanda Army during the six-day June war of 2000. Afterwards, he switched side joining the Rwanda deepening its involvement in illegally and savagely occupying huge swaths of DRC territories in the North Kivu province. The illegal mining and trafficking of Coltan became an extensive armed undertaking for the Rwanda army with the resulting widespread massacre of native population which resisted the forced displacement imposed on them to exploit the Coltan mines. This is the time Major Adamas excelled in insuring that the process of digging and shipping various mineral resources, including Coltan, from the North Kivu province to Rwanda and Uganda borders went on unimpeded, killing or terrorizing native people who stood against the traffic. Along the way, Major Adamas settled his own scores against people who prevented him from imposing his own will in social or business matters he happened to be engaged in. To make a name for himself, Adamas was never satisfied to punish these people, he will go after their entire family or entire village, killing their relatives after raping their women. This was the reason he earned the nickname of Adamas, a convoluted version of his first name of Damien. "Adamas" in Swahili translates into "Man". "Adamas Hatari" in Swahili translates into "Dangerous Man". For a very strange mutation, Major Kagita enjoyed being addressed as "Adamas", while his mean streak implied, he was "Adamas Hatari". This was extended in French as "Danger de Mort" or "Danger of Death". He took pride in the implication, and everybody understood it His subsequent rise in the plundering business was established against various militias fighting for the control of mineral mines of North Kivu. He emerged as a hardcore war lord in the territories of Lubero, Walikale, Masisi, Rutshuru and Beni. These biographical affidavits will be crucial to keep his life presence and chain of criminal acts right there in DRC. They will become necessary to nullify his fake Uganda biography cleverly mounted by his Uganda and Rwanda protectors.

Charlotte had no choice but to accept this entire collection package from his beloved Uncle Stanis. She was also grateful to notice that Ludmilla Garrov, her principal contac6t at the District Attorney Office, was more than pleased by the extensive coverage that the collection of affidavits provided by Uncle Stanis provided.

"Charlotte, from my background of support to the legal works we need to prosecute at the District Attorney Office, I have never seen or enjoyed the depth, the logic, the follow-up that these affidavits are bringing. Don't get me wrong, the folks at the pastor's church have done an excellent job, their affidavits were personal accounts of what happened in DRC, a far way country in Africa. Remember this, for the prosecution team, that is the District Attorney Office, that is me and of course you, the main witness must make the case, must convince people who probably have never heard of North Kivu, never heard of Walikale territory, never realized that the main component of the cell phone they use all the time is refined coltan which is found in that part of world, and for which your life has been put in danger forcing you to come to US as a political refugee, for which people like Major Adamas killed, raped and committed all sorts of despicable crimes to terrorize people in order to control the extraction and the traffic of the same coltan from that region to the manufacturing centers where cell phones are finally made. Your Uncle Stanis collection of affidavits tied all that presentation together so much so that, if for instance, I could make the presentation of how horrible and devilish a person Major Adamas was and is, these affidavits would come in handy. If I can spend an hour navigating these affidavits, the fate of Major Adamas will be effectively sealed. He will be condemned in any court of law in the US. He would probably spend the rest of his life in a federal prison. What I am seeing here, Charlotte, is not different from when I have seen my own very dear Uncle did back home in Yugoslavia after the Second World War. He was a lawyer by trade and inspired me greatly to pursue my studies of law. My Uncle was Lead Prosecutor of Nazi Collaborators. He shared a lot of what he needed to prosecute these people. First, he used the Nazi motivation to eradicate Jew people from earth. From there he described to the jury all sorts of criminal offenses the Nazi collaborators committed against the Jewish people. No Nazi collaborator came out innocent from these presentations. You are the second person I am sharing my background with. The other one is Mr. Timothy O'Grady, the Boss, the Raleigh Country District Attorney. It is not by accident that Mr. O'Grady appointed me as your main control. It is squarely based on my background.'

Listening to Ludmilla, Charlotte was relieved. She was deeply concerned that her uncle's collection was going to appear too political. Although she was aware that the collection content was necessary, she was still concerned that the District Attorney Office would shy away from its political orientation. As Ludmilla's observation concurred with hers, she was still restrained from showing her delight. Ludmilla's concurrence was only a step to what she wanted and expected, above all, Mr. O'Grady, the boss's full adhesion to her uncle's theme. Until such a time she would read, hear and seek that adhesion, she would dread very carefully while in the District Attorney team and remain reserved in her opinion and behavior.

Charlotte's position was not misplaced. After about two months of affidavits collection, she was invited by Mr. O'Grady into his office conference room to get the status of the evolution of her case. Ludmilla sat next to her. The original law enforcement members were also present. Mr. Johnson Mattheson, Third Deputy District Attorney in Raleigh County, led the presentation of the status, while Mr. O'Grady led the meeting with a stoning silence. Mr. Mattheson briefly congratulated the affidavits collection team without mentioning the members of the team. Charlotte was surprised and disappointed by the lapse. Ludmilla won't even look at her from that time. However, Mr. Mattheson continued his presentation and spent a good part of his presentation warning the assembled team about the high caliber of Mr. Okito Jefferson's defense team recruited among the best and brightest National Security Agency private defense lawyers in Washington D.C. He insisted on sharing the fact that all of them were either Harvard or Yale graduates. He closed his presentation by admonishing the assembled team to raise their legal skills in prosecuting the case as he put it, the so-called National Security Agency lawyers are coming to bury the lowly Raleigh District Attorney Team completely unprepared in matter of National Security. For a few seconds, Mr. Matheson's defeatist posture put a damp on the assembled team conviction to prosecute the case in their best of each member's ability. Mr. O'Grady stoning silence accentuated the defeated atmosphere when he got up and walked to the large conference window and stood there looking absently at the distant gathering of dark clouds about to dump a pouring rain on Raleigh in about twenty minutes or so. When he turned around and looked at Ludmilla, he flashed a distinct demeanor as to direct Ludmilla to challenge Mr. Mattheson presentation.

"Mr. Mattheson, I heard your presentation, I heard about the high caliber of the defense team highly skilled in defending individuals compromised in National Security matters. I must disagree profoundly with your discomfort. Gathered here are people dedicated in law enforcement which they have sworn to upload against all criminal offenses that put at risk our national peace, our national civil order anywhere in this United Stated of American, be at Denver in Colorado, Key West in Florida, New Orleans in Louisiana, Detroit in Michigan or yes Raleigh in North Carolina. The case here has everything to do with murders perpetrated outside of the US by an individual who wants to live among us. The question is simple: should we accept a known criminal, a murderer, to live among us. Is this a matter of National Security, you bet it is. It is at the elementary junction of our life. If Mr. Mattheson would not accept an American murderer to go free from murdering American citizens and live in his backyard, would he accept a foreigner who is a murderer of people in his country to come and live next to him in his backyard. I don't think so. Believe me that law enforcement will proceed whether the defense team is full of Ivy League lawyers or not. This District Attorney Office will prosecute such an individual here in Raleigh County."

"Thank you, Ludmilla, thank you Johnson. As far as this case goes, these two points of view are pretty much eloquent in their own merits. We would be signing off our own legal peril if we neglect one of these views in favor of another. We must, I insist we must remain vigilant not to neglect these two points of view.as we proceed in prosecuting this case. These two members of my staff have presented here honestly what we are going to face as we go forward prosecuting this case. Mr. Mattheson and Ms. Garrov have expressed the ambivalence that we will face. These two almost opposite points of view will challenge us seriously. As Mattheson has stated, we will be seriously tackled by the defense team. I would not raise them as highly skilled in National Security matters. I know that they come highly moneyed with strong references with the powers that be. We, on the hand, are the law enforcement team highly skilled in enforcing the laws of our land. Let us not forget it. I want this team to steep yourself in matters of National Security, that the other elephant that will crowd the proceedings. We must raise our National Security profile in this case. I urge you to do like me. I went to school every week in these matters. I must abuse you now. I did not go to University of North Carolina Law School, Duke University Law School nor any other major Law Academic institution in the state. No, I certainly would like to, but I read, read and read. Yes, I read the affidavits that Ludmilla from my staff and our witness Charlotte have assembled. After you have read the voluminous collection of more than eight hundred sixty-three affidavits, you will build a tremendous background of our case respective to all features including National Security matters. I must call on you to congratulate the ladies on a super outstanding job. By the way I must also tell you that within two weeks, a federal judge will be selected to start preliminary hearing. And I don't have to announce our first order of work is to squash the super high moneyed defense team request to dismiss the case on the ground of … you got it, National Security.! We got our work cut out for us. Ludmilla and Charlotte will always be available for any input or explanation around the affidavits. Thank you."

The twists, churns and turns of the status meeting left Charlotte a bit dizzy. Charlotte received a strong dose of the tribulations of the wheels of justice. This went on in the space of about an hour, from being upset about the initial lapse expressed at the beginning of the meeting to being a bit confused by the praise from the Boss at the end of the meeting. Worse, she just could not get any visual support from her legal partner, Ludmilla, who was avoiding her angry stare throughout.

She was now smiling at Charlotte. She simply made a cross sign on her lips to signify to Charlotte that she understood her seesaw trip. She invited her to an early dinner.

"What do you think of the status meeting?" Ludmilla started the conversation when they were seated at her favorite restaurant a mile from the office. It was a steak house restaurant.

"What do I think, I would say it was crazy! First that Mr. Mattheson would not even mention our names and was lauding the defense team. Then you came to give him a lecture about law enforcement. And your Boss closes the conversation reconciling your opposing interventions. What else can I say? It was a learning experience. When it was over, it brought me back to how I evolved appreciating Sergeant "Sid'. He also brought me along to appreciate what you call the wheels of justice. Now I started suspecting that most of you folks in law enforcement share the same DNA. It takes a genre to absorb it. It is very different from what people outside the law enforcement think of dealing with Justice. It is different. You know what, as we evolved in collecting the affidavits, I was of the mind that they were not enough, they were not going to make the case. Especially after the collection from the church folks. But I became very pleased with the dump that my Uncle Stanis provided. I saw also how you were delighted about it. But before the status meeting, I fell back to my precious suspicion that the overall collection was not enough. I could not put my finger over what was enough, and I waited. After this status session, I came out even more puzzled. Tell me Ludmilla, when would you say that what you have is enough in a case in Justice?"

"I don't know about other countries. I learned about the nuances and meanders of law right here in the US. If you want my answer, there is no such thing, in prosecuting or defending a case, that makes the case for guilty or not guilty. I am not talking about those "Ah Perry Mason" moments that we see in movies or TV. These "Ah Perry Mason" moments do not exist. When justice is being dispensed in terms of what is or is not permissible according to the law, the range is vast from innocent to guilty. If somebody comes to you and says that he or she knows the range perfectly, then he or she is lying. Always remember that Justice is dispensed by Human Beings reading laws and laws are always evolving as human beings are evolving. I am sure throughout your life you have noticed that acts that were taboos became permissible, and those that were permissible became taboos. At the end Justice is continuously evolving like human beings. I am not saying that laws are always evolving, not at all. Some laws have remained permanent from one generation to another. Laws around murder have remained the same since the time of laws that Moise came down with from the mountain. But that has not prevented some people to get away with murder specially the powerful people, and remember, always for a time."

"Charlotte, I must apologize that you are being thrown into the legal process and discourse such as the conversation we had today without warning or preparation. I understand that you may, at times, feel out of place and overwhelmed about what is being discussed. Some of us who have been trained in the legal process forget that not everybody knows about the legal process practiced in the court, particularly the parties, the language and the logic involved. For instance, the debate or the conversation we had today focused on what is defined in court as "Discovery" or the legal exchange between the prosecution team in this case, the District Attorney Office and the Defense Team which will defend Adamas. Here again, I am making the same mistake by going ahead of myself. Without confusing you further, let me just say that after you made your accusation about Adamas that fateful Sunday, you had in fact triggered a whole new legal process which included yourself as a plaintiff and Adamas as the accused. Remember you made, or should I have said, you developed a lengthy accusation statement that was registered by the District Attorney Office accusing Adamas of grave criminal offenses. From that time, Adamas was advised to get a legal defense party to counter your accusation in a court of law. In other words, unless we heard otherwise, Adamas has countered that he is innocent of your accusation, and he will defend himself in the Court of law. He went on to hire a Defense Team. Now in preparation of a trial where your accusation and Adamas's counterclaim will be aired, we have spent two months collecting proofs of your accusation. I must assume that Adamas and his defense team are also gathering proofs of his innocence. The legal process will soon move to the time when a Judge will be selected to conduct the trial about your accusation and Adamas's counterclaim. Are with me so far?"

"Yes, I am!"

"Thank you, Charlotte. We are getting very close to the time when a

Judge will call this trial. Let me be clear about the role of the Judge. He or she will preside over the trial according to five basic tasks:

-preside over the trial proceedings including jury selection and see that the order is maintained throughout the trial,

-determine whether any evidence that the parties want to use is illegal or improper,

-before the jury begins its deliberations about the facts in the case, the judge gives the jury instructions about the law that applies to the case and the standards it must use in deciding the case,

-in bench trials (trials that do not involve jury and conducted by the judge alone), the judge must determine the facts and decide the case, sentence convicted criminal defendants. In criminal courts, the Prosecution team works to prove guilt beyond a Reasonable Doubt while the Defense team attempts to create Reasonable Doubt so that its client is found innocent. As you can see, the entire legal process hinges on those crucial two words "Reasonable Doubt" which the Prosecution works hard to overcome and the Defense pushes equally very hard.

-To achieve a final balance between these two drives, the Court system has provided a key step called "Discovery". According to the American Bar Association, Discovery is the formal process of exchanging information (documents) between the trial opposing parties (Prosecution and Defense) about the witnesses and the evidence that they will present at the trial. In other words, Charlotte, all the documents we have collected the past two months or so will be shared with the Defense Team defending Adamas. This Defense Team is also under legal obligation to share whatever evidence documentation they will present at the trial. Of course, the Judge will preside over the exchange insuring that it is executed legally. Both parties, the Prosecution, and the Defense, are bound to share all legal evidence documentation including exculpatory evidence for the accused. As you can see, Charlotte, Discovery is a powerful tool to ensure that Justice is rendered legally, properly, and fairly.

I hope I have clarified the conversation we had today. What do you th ink?"

"Wooooah, thank you, Ludmilla, I am learning every day. I sincerely appreciate it. Thank you so very much."

CHAPTER 9

BIG SHOES LAWYERS

While Mr. O'Grady dispensed modesty and humility around the tribulations of the wheels of justice at the District Attorney Office status meeting, Okito Jefferson's defense team was flying high in its self-congratulatory march to vanquish the lowly provincial unsophisticated legal gang that was pushing papers in Raleigh. The team elected residency not far from Mr. Okito mansion. The defense team rented the most expensive bungalow on the Outer Banks. The bungalow was built right there on the beach. Its owner, Mr. Gary Offarel from a landed family in North Carolina, was another big time lawyer in the prominent legal partnership of Dunstreet and Fishbowl in Washington, D.C. Mr. Offarel had built the bungalow initially at about three hundred yards from the sea water. Now the three-story bungalow stood at less than sixty yards from the sea water. Renting the bungalow to the defense team was the last attempt to recoup the real-estate investment gone sour before the invading sea. The bungalow was a twenty-minute ride to Mr. Okito mansion on the other safe side of the Outer Banks.

The defense team was led by an ambitious young lawyer named Miles Everett, fresh from Yale Law School about five years ago. Miles came to Dunstreet and Fishbowl with an impeccable background. The Yale Law School credit came at the top of an academic journey that included London School of Business, Paris Sorbonne Sciences-Po, Georgetown University International Studies. three years prime legal assignment at the National Security Office of the US Attorney General during the second Bush mandate solidified his National Security credentials. At forty-one, Miles was the right person in the law offices of Dunstreet and Fishbowl to preside over this legal assignment involving a lot of murky intelligence services contacts. Miles knew that, after five years at the law offices, this assignment was intended either to raise him to partnership level or to let him go. He has clearly studied the case before accepting it. His many contacts in intelligence services have guarantee him a slam dunk easy victory given the status of the US's standing around the national security issues in the case. He was assured that no matter what will come out of Raleigh, the government higher up will not change the status quo that has worked efficiently well for the US since 1997 through five different administrations, two Republican and three Democrat. You don't get as much consensus as that. The intelligence services' contacts have counselled him to keep Mr. Okito very low key, returning him to the primary national security agreements that allowed him to come to the US in the first place. Miles was assisted by two younger lawyers and a staff secretary. They all occupied the bungalow premises with six rooms, a huge dining room that was converted into an office Miles staff was comfortable in the bungalow with large windows giving into an ocean splendid view.

During the many conversations Miles had with Mr. Okito, alias Major Adamas Kagita, he advised Okito of the same strategy. He assured him that his first order of defense was to hold firmly his legal identity entering the US. He stated that Mr. Okito should not worry about that line of defense because the prosecutor had no means or ways to establish any other identity. Whatever that lady will bring will be hearsay and mistaken identity. Miles repeated many times that he was Mr. Okito and nobody, nothing would change that circumstance. When Mr. Okito asked whether the US government will testify on his behalf. Miles frantically said no. He reminded Mr. Okito that the primary national security agreements cannot be debated in the court of law. He assured him that the US government is funding his defense and that is good enough and cannot be dragged in the court of law in the matter of national security. Miles literally screamed at Mr. Okito stating that if he had not broken and violated the agreements by exposing himself, there was not going to be any need to defend him at this time in the first place. Miles added that he was there to defend him and the government of the US he represents. Miles also revealed that his objective was to get him quickly resettle somewhere in the US where there will be absolutely no chance of the types of encounters he had. Mr. Okito was shaken by these revelations.

Every time Adamas came back from the meetings with the lawyers, he brought down half of his preferred scotch bottle of Johnny Walker Black. As time went by, he virtually lost confidence in the defense team. He did not have a strong conviction that these lawyers knew what was going on in the areas of DRC he knew very well. He got the distinct impression that his defense team was grossly underestimating the prosecution. He called his intelligence services contact, Colonel Laurens.

"My good man Colonel Laurens, are you sure that these lawyers, you got for me, can tell the difference between Kinshasa and Brazzaville, or Butembo and Masisi. I don't think so. You sent me law students who still believe that "President Mobutu Sesse Seko is still in power" in Kinshasa fifteen years after his death. They cannot even spell Coltan. My God, this will be a legal fiasco. I can feel it in my bones. I should just walk in that court in Raleigh and proclaim that I have killed that lady fifteen times and go to jail. It is awful, really…"

"Come on, Mr. Okito, you are exaggerating. We have done all we could to extract you from virtual assassination in Walikale and brought you here to live a quiet life. You screwed it up. Yes, you know you did it. We are trying to get a better venue. Everything that lawyer Miles told you is true. He is well trained. I don't have to tell his real background but believe me he is very good. Let me tell you, some of us who live in the Shadow, don't go out there bragging about things. But we work hard for what we do. You cannot understand it because you screw things for all to see. That is not how we operate. Believe me, we do our best. Now finish your scotch, lie down, and call me tomorrow. It looks like every time you come back from the Outer banks, you get so agitated. Please call me tomorrow. Now I want to tell you something you need to do when in contact with lawyers: get yourself a good powerful cell phone to tape all conversations you are having with your lawyers to avoid who said what, when, and where. One day you would thank for this advice."

Colonel Laurens was of no help. Adamas started believing that he was being thrown into the lion's den. He had no idea what was being transacted at this time between all these people who had decided that he would leave DRC and come to the US. He was told that the three Presidents from DRC, Rwanda, and Uganda, have concurred that he has become a major liability and was to leave the business area or be killed. He also knew that three Presidents were concerned about the financial blackmail he was prepared to mount against them if ever they tried anything against him. In fact, that financial blackmail was mounted by Langley for its own purposes to keep the three presidents on constant leash and he was simply the designated fake initiator. That worked to his advantage. The rules of engagement are very sordid in the misplaced governance of Eastern DRC. He never understood why he was selected. That was irrelevant as long as he was kept alive. And now he needs to find whatever happened to the blackmail. Is it about to change. Adamas debated alone whether he needed to call Colonel Laurens to get a bit of clarification around the blackmail. The more he thought about it, he realized that he was not going to get anything from the famous Colonel Laurens he had never seen but who knew every one of his steps from the time he arrived in the US with his wife and kids. In times, Adamas felt that he was in a bubble, worse, a golden jail without bars, that can close on him anytime. He resigned himself to pouring a half pint of scotch while looking outside the expansive window from his mansion living room giving into the extended backyard. He was also puzzling over the Colonel's advice about taping lawyers. He decided he would get that cell phone to tape all his important conversations. He sat down and tried to doze a bit. He suddenly remembered a key contact in Kinshasa. This man has been in various governments that the President Joseph Kabila, otherwise named President KD in Eastern DRC or "Kiungo Dhaifu" in Swahili meaning "Weak Link", has mounted. He was the main representative of Kagame in Kinshasa, a survivor of many civil wars in the Eastern provinces of DRC. He wore many covers. Adamas preferred to address him with his most cynical cover of "Reverend Drago". He could reach him anytime and anyhow. Their calls always started by the reading of Revelation 12:11:

"And they overcame him by the blood of the Lamb, and by the word of their testimony; and they loved not their lives unto the death."

For a person who had lived all his life through the exercise of swords and various guns violence against thousands of people, the reading of this verse before exchanging news with Reverend Drago, was surrealist. Adamas was at times confused hearing his correspondent screaming the verse so matter-of-factly. He became accustomed to the ritual after a while. He stopped trying to question the motive and the intent of the Reverend. Adamas decided that the Reverend Drago must have found a spiritual mantra despite all the murderous events he had engineered at different levels of responsibility he assumed to direct the endless mayhem he has personally driven in the Eastern region of DRC. At the end of their calls, Adamas was often shocked to hear the same Reverend close the conversation with the same citation of Revelation 12:11. And he did this after providing Adamas with specific instructions to kill so many people and to make the murderous mineral traffic from Eastern Congo to Rwanda as efficient as profitable for Kagame's regime. There was never a merciful account of the hecatomb that was being waged. Adamas tried in vain to close these calls with his own spiritual invocation. He went for a big glass of scotch. He decided that Reverend Drago operated at another level of spiritual denial.

"Hello, son, the Leadership has indicated that you are under a lot of cloud in your beautiful domain in North Carolina. How did you wind up in such a mess, after all that we have established for you there in North Carolina by the Grace of Our Lord. I must tell you that the Enterprise is very disappointed."

"My sincere regards to the entire Enterprise and to the Leadership. I am personally disappointed as well, just to let you know. Still, I am not certain that our guests are helping the way I expected. They are not listening to any suggestion I am providing them. I cannot believe that they are trembling in face of that lady. This is ridiculous. We have overcome worse than this. Back then, remember it!"

"Son, back then was in our Enterprise terrain, in our domain. I am sure you understand that it is a bit different now. We are doing all we can with our guests to help you. But it is not going to be easy. Do you understand? I heard that you are getting excited there. That is not the way to be grateful. Leadership has many ways with your guests, remember that. So, you must do your part by staying still until there is an otherwise instruction. Remember what we have fought for, what we are fighting for, it is and remains for the blood of the lamb that was shed a while ago and we never stopped redressing that offense everywhere we must. Your guests have stood by our credo. We have, you must stand still not to disturb the commitments of our guests. That was also your commitment when you signed up to be in the grace of your guests. Always remember that is a two-way street. We keep our commitment as well as your guests will keep theirs without any aggravation any noise from our parts nor your part. The small inconvenience you are suffering today comes because of not respecting your commitment and you know it. The Leadership is working hard to keep the guests in tune with our credo. That task becomes difficult when bad noise and bad press start disturbing our mutual commitments. That is why you must stand still. Do you understand?!"

"Certainly, I do! But what about Lemera?"

"Nothing and don't go there! I repeat stay still!"

"When are you coming over?"

"Not any time soon. I was there for the National Prayer Day, remember! I carried all these Kinshasa compromised fools with me. I am trying to come up with a good strong excuse to be invited by our dear guest Senator. I will let you know. Be still."

"What about the Potomac's deal, still holding?"

"Forget it, and please don't go there or all bets will be off. Be still and quiet!"

Before he knew it, the Reverend was screaming the same old Revelation 12.11verse, and the call went dead. Adamas poured scotch in a tall glass. The message that Reverend Drago gave him was the least comforting. He was being told to keep quiet, to follow the directives that his defense team was providing him. Directives he has found generally stupid and not helpful. He was being told not to disturb the guests, his guests, in other words the power that bee, the power that extracted him from a potential assassination if he had stayed one more day in that part of Africa Great lakes, be it in DRC, Rwanda or Uganda. He was being reminded to be grateful for what the guests had done for him. He was being reminded to stop abusing the guest's patience and tolerance.

However, if there was one thing Adamas was very scared of, he had no idea how this judicial action that this crazy lady has initiated, would end. He could not see any positive outcome at the end of this upcoming judicial action. He wondered aloud about his perspectives, his chances. Would he be sent back to be killed in the Great Lakes region or would he be sent to another part of world of the US carrying another brand-new identity? Every time he raised that issue, the defense team drew a blank. The defense team could not answer his question. The younger lawyer associate told him bluntly that he was losing his mind, that the case would not venture to such wild outcomes, that his question was irrelevant That is when he realized that the defense team that was provided for him had no idea who the hell he was, and all the circumstances that led him to be in North Carolina. The fact that his defense team was operating in complete ignorance and vacuum irritated him to no end. He then surmised that he was probably being sacrificed at the so-called altar of the blood of the lamb that Reverend Drago kept alluding to.

But Adamas thought that he had never signed up to such a credo. He knew that he was not a fool, he had lived the life of a dangerous, fearful, and mediocre war lord only for the power and the wealth that the plundering of Eastern DRC provided. He could not care less what Kagame, Museveni or Kabila had in mind around the plundering that went on. In fact, the plundering made him more powerful, wealthier than he would not have thought he would become when he started working for that Army Major who set up a high sexual patronage in the town of Kisangani. Precisely, when he started compromising and corrupting first year student girls at the campus of the University of Kisangani to become expensive call girls for wealthy people in town. That was his first taste of landing into a criminal enterprise. After about six months of involvement, he paid dearly for that adventure by being expelled from the university, being locked in jail for about four months. The debacle came down when one of the girls turned out to be the niece of the Governor of the Oriental Province. When Adamas came back to his native town of Butembo, he had a hard time explaining why he was expelled from the university and why he did four months of jail time. But Adamas was hooked to the easy money that crime provided. He never looked back and started his long criminal journey to become later a major war lord.

If Adamas decided that he had not signed up to Reverend Drago's credo, he also decided that he needed to determine his best recourse to protect himself against any adverse venue from the judicial action. After a lot of reflection, he determined that his best course was to get to the bottom of the mysterious motivations that the power that be had created to get him out of the lions' den in the Great Lakes region. To date, Adamas had no idea what was invented behind his back to extract him from the claws of very dangerous political leaders in the region including Kagame, Museveni, and Kabila. He knew that one must be very lucky to be spared by one of them, but to be spared by three of them at the same time was next to impossible. He was convinced that only a much higher power, probably external higher power must have intervened to accomplish such a feat. Only an external higher power, the American power, was involved. That much he logically concluded.

But his speculation, however grandiose, missed one key element: what was the definite motivation. Adamas had no clue. He was back at square one of discovery with no direction and no content. It was turning out the price of working for so long in the dark sides of major political drives in an area of world where reality is always absent, where night is day and day is night. It is where every political event takes so many shades to a point where the event can easily be nullified as if it never happened. One major example of such events was the catalyst for the eruption of the 1994 genocide in Rwanda. If the catalyst was the assassination of President Habyarimana when his jet plane was blown up, the responsibility of that assassination has never been resolved.

As the sole beneficiary of the mysterious motivations, Adamas has never bothered to know what was concocted on his behalf to get him out. But the strange appearance has remained that the three Presidents have struggled to keep friendly contacts with him from afar. They separately acted as if he was holding Damocles' Sword over their respective heads. Time and again their emissaries probed him over a variety of political, financial, social, military events and acts he has or has not been associated while being a very dangerous war lord in the active function of leading the mineral plundering across the three states. Many times, he had no idea what the emissaries were talking about. In case where he remembered having played an active part, Adamas was still no sure if the event or act was so determinant to lead the American side to engineer his extraction. Now that he was comfortably settled in the US, Adamas kept remembering one financial event where financial venues were presented to him by a so called Malaysian financial consultant he met in Nairobi, Kenya. The man proposed to Adamas to set up an offshore banking account in Mauritius Island for the purpose of hiding his financial looting which at times amounted to more than hundred sixty-eight millions of American dollars under covered names. The financial consultant mentioned, while laughing very loud, that the three Presidents he works for had already set up similar accounts around the world. Adamas listened to the proposal and did not understand at the time what the man was proposing. It took about a year and half for Adamas to set up the account after an Australian financial consultant he met in Johannesburg convinced him to do the same. This Australian also reminded him of the conversation he had with his boss the Malaysian. That was the last time he saw the Australian financial consultant. He never heard of the Malaysian boss. From that time, he became accustomed to paper communication with folks in Mauritius Island where he never set foot. His guests in the US alluded briefly to his offshore banking revenue stream when he was being extracted from Africa. They thanked him that he did all right to ease his entry into the US because they insisted that he was never going to be helped by the US Treasury for financial support, he was never going to be a burden to US taxpayers. Adamas did not understand the irony of that statement. Thinking back of this exchange, Adamas thought that this financial event was probably significant, but he did not see any relation to the three Presidents. He thought that it was not a secret that the current African Presidents have learned of better ways to stash their financial looting trophies since the past silly way of bringing trunks full of bank notes and depositing them in coded numbered bank accounts in Geneva in Switzerland. Besides, his financial bonanza could not compare to their mountains of billions of dollars. He dismissed that course of appeal. He needed to search further. He was back to square one. He was back in the care of his famous, high priced but ignorant defense team and there was nothing he could do to change his posture. He realized that he must wait to see the evolution of judicial action and maybe something will happen to offer a clear strategy to confront what he now concluded to be a final chapter of his stay in the US. Adamas started resigning to the fact that he has been sacrificed at the altar of the blood of lamb.

CHAPTER 10

TRIAL PRELIMINARIES

On September 23, Charlotte, as the main plaintiff in the case. received a letter from the District Attorney Office Staff advising her that a District Court Judge for Case No. 56397, "US vs Jefferson Okito" has been selected. The Judge turned out to be an African American, appointed recently by President Obama. She was very young, about thirty-seven, after a stellar legal academic background from Yale University and professional legal apprenticeship in Wall Street, Atlanta, and Dallas big law firms. Judge Patricia Leighton-Garver came from a prominent Atlanta family completely immersed in Southern various civil right campaigns. Judge Leighton-Garver was in a hurry to -process her first trial. The letter stated that she was going to introduce herself to the Prosecution and Defense teams as early as Monday October 7, 2013, and start Jury selection a week later on October 14, if possible, provide instructions over National Security protocols and other legal issues around the case and if possible, start the trial around November 4, 2013.

Charlotte made a sign of the cross after reading the letter. She said a prayer thanking the Lord for advancing the legal adjudication of a personal matter that she had held dearly from the day she came to the US. Extending both hands high to the ceiling, she called upon spirits of family members who passed away killed by Adamas and those who have suffered the cruelty of the Death Danger. She raised her voice advising them that she had now brought their murderer to account for their untimely death and their suffering in a court of law. She raised her hands again to implore God to guide the court proceeding in the name of Justice for all. Charlotte then read John1:29 where John the Baptist sees Jesus and exclaims, "Behold the Lamb of God who takes away the sin of the world." She went on to exclaim loudly in French that "Jesus chose to suffer crucifixion at Calvary as a sign of his full obedience to the will of his divine Father in carrying away the sins of the world ... The same will be for Jesus, a lion-like lamb that rose to deliver victory after being slain on the cross, the same will be for Jesus who will lead all of us to victory in this upcoming trial, Amen! The same will be for all of us dispersed lambs of Christ, Our Lord Shepherd, whose blood has been shed and continued to be shed from the mountain volcan of Nyiragongo to the fertile plains of Walikale, from the lake Edward to Butembo, through murderous cavernous trunks of Masisi and Rutshuru! The same will be for all us lambs of God, now refugees in distant land, begging for mercy and justice for the same blood of Lamb, blood of our Lord! May our almighty Yahweh guide us, protect us in this venue to reclaim justice for the blood of our lambs, Amen!".

Charlotte went on her knees and meditated silently for about five minutes and finally kissed the closed Bible on the floor. Charlotte stayed on her knees, had tears streaming down her face. She then remembered a song in Swahili. The song was made popular by a local group in the area. The song title was "In Endless Wrath" summarizing the awful conditions people in the area have endured for the past twenty or so years. The song had become a rallying cry for people throughout Eastern DRC. Still on her knees with hands raised to the ceiling Charlotte belted it in a steep voice:

"The Day never rises In Walikale

As In Endless Wrath

Paths are strewn with overnight mayhem

Blood is spread all over
Deafening Silence blankets the horizon
Frown faces cross the venues
Not knowing where they are going
Where they are coming from
Abandoned infants are screaming
Of Hunger and Desolation
Next to Dead Mother Corpses
The Day never rises In Walikale
As In Endless Wrath."

On this momentous day, with that song touching cry, Charlotte felt that she had really renewed her long kept vows to herself and her family members. Charlotte wiped out her face and got up. She was also

91

pleased that the letter arrived on her day off, allowing her to celebrate a momentous event in her life without the shackles and commitment to be at work attending to absent minded patients not aware of what has happened to her that particular day.

She got up and placed the first a call to Sergeant "Sid" to inform him of the news. The cop was delighted and told her that she would be sailing to a great victory over evil. She reached out to Ludmilla who repeated the same best wishes expressed by Sergeant "Sid". Ludmilla added that she was going to prepare her over court appearances and demeanors when the trial date gets closer. But before hanging up, she asked Charlotte a pertinent question:

"I want to make sure that you understood what you read in that letter. After that last meeting at the office, when legal terms were flying about, I decided to assist you anyway I can every step of way in the journey of legal procedures we will go through, including the upcoming trial. That is my function. So, about that letter, are you comfortable to have understood everything, are there areas you want me to expand or explain, please ask me now."

"Oh Ludmilla, let me say that you are more than an angel that came to me in what you just called the journey of legal procedures we are going through. Remember I started this legal motion. I did not know what I was getting into. I thought that all I needed was to make the accusation and the court system will take care of the rest. My Awesome God! Was I so wrong and misplaced! I am not a lawyer; I don't have any legal training. But I landed in very capable legal hands, starting with Sergeant "Sid" that I openly distrusted at first only to thank my awesome God for the help he provided me in developing that plaintiff accusation note. Then you came to the scene continuing the same awesome legal help including your boss, Mr. O'Grady. You two have carried that legal endeavor to where I have dreamed of getting for more than ten years from the time I came to the US. Ludmilla, I must tell you that the letter is the fulfilment of a dream. Of course, there are a few legal technicalities I want you to explain but there will be such a time later. Today, let me celebrate this accomplishment and thank you and your team for making it possible. Will get to those technicalities later. Today is a celebration day. Thank you!'

"You are most welcome!" Ludmilla was shaken to the core of her soul by the exchange. Charlotte was in a celebratory mood, not really inclined to ask questions over a few things that raised her attention while reading the letter: first the title of the case "US vs Jefferson Okito". That should have been "Us vs Major Adamas Kagita". She wanted to know why the change. And the second question mark was about the allusion to the Judge providing instructions over National Security protocols and other legal issues around the case. That one was a big question mark for Charlotte. She needed further explanation around this one. But not today. Today will be a celebration day.

When Charlotte started calling his Uncle Stanis, she cancelled the call. She wanted to indulge him in a long lazy weekend call he expected, not a short unfamiliar announcement. She would wait for their usual Saturday morning calls.

"Very good news, mama Pastor!", Charlotte reached out at her dear friend Suzanne, the Pastor's wife.

"Finally a marriage proposal, Charlotte, I am bringing a big Champagne bottle we will drink it now starting at about 11:30am until .."

"You must go there with your crooked mind. How do you happen to marry a Pastor of all people!"

"Let me tell you, his member rises to glorious vigorous attention every morning before our first prayer. And I oblige always. I have never heard him complain as a Pastor. Thank you very much! Now what are the very good news you have for me!"

"I am sorry for the indiscretion. I must thank God to have blessed the pastor and you on your daily matrimonial ritual! Hallelujah! Hum, I just call to let you and the Pastor know that a Judge has been selected for the trial of Adamas and it should start sometime in the beginning of November. I just got a letter advising me to get ready to testify. Very sorry that I must share such a mondain news far from the exciting news around your matrimonial plan. Please share the news with the Pastor."

"You would not dare hang up on me, Ms. Keregi. You would not. Come on, you are so high on your legal horses, you cannot take any joke. Of course, it is wonderful news. Who do you take me for, Charlotte, a teenager trembling on a hot date, ambivalent about losing her virginity, not clear how she feels when she will lose it. Who else should I talk to about my libido? You are the only person I must indulge in that conversation. I don't have any other friend but you. Charlotte, really, I don't know how you manage. I mean compared to myself. Tell me, not even a masturbation, I want to know."

"What do you want to know if I masturbate, yes, I do! Yes, I look at myself when naked and I get excited! Yes, I long to be invaded sexually by a man of my choice! I told you time and again, the temptation comes and dies quickly with me when I think of my lifetime vow, all sexual dies! Now you know. I don't expect you to understand it, but this is what I am!"

"Sincerely speaking, and if I may, you have carried your vow to its major accomplishment so far. Then what, are you going to remain as you put it, dead?"

"I don't know, Suzanne, maybe I will awaken. Hopefully it won't happen after my menopause. Then it will be bye-bye!"

"God forbid, if I can help it!"

"This is very funny, as a Mama Pastor, you should be encouraging me to temper my libido, not the reverse. Let me ask you, as a Mama Pastor, how do you manage with the Church ladies when they come to ask you intimate questions as what we are talking about now?"

"Let me answer your question honestly, I don't say anything, I tell them I am very limited in advices in that field. I know a few expert ladies in the Church, who can help, I direct them to them. I directed my own daughter to you, remember. You did an excellent job, remember?"

"True, but I shared regular common knowledge I have picked up as a medical professional with a Master Degree. I must attend various gyn seminar to keep my certification. Your daughter has benefited from my medical training, not personal involvement. These trainings come in an avalanche of papers, lectures, talks, speculations, and innuendos which, when compiled together, form the basis for a good source of various conversations which I share with your daughter. If you want to know if these conversations covered the most intimate involvement of a couple. Your daughter appreciated the sharing of so much. Whenever I could not answer a question, I left it for further input from the medical staff at work. I may be wrong, but I can say that your daughter married with as much information as any bride needs the first night of her matrimonial sexual life."

"Was she tempted to indulge her future husband sexually before the marriage blessing?"

"I did not ask that question; you should ask her?"

"I was so afraid that she did. I mean I, myself, was so hot, anticipating the first time, I begged the Pastor to get on with it before the marriage blessing. He refused. I was so afraid of myself; I took four to five showers every day to cool my libido the week before the wedding. I was projecting the same over my daughter. She is my daughter after all. Thank God all went well for her out there in Texas. "

"As I said, I did not ask that question. Besides, what is the problem now, they have been married for three or four months, creating babies by now?"

"Really, they are having twin, she told you that. That depraved man, he was abusing my poor girl before the marriage, I knew and suspected it! Rascal he was! My poor daughter!"

"Hold it right there, I did not say that she is pregnant. I have not talked with your daughter since she got married. I know nothing about their matrimonial status, all right. For God's sake, they are married now anyway, they are entitled to their own privacy. Just because you were a hot pussy back then, you should not go out there assuming that your daughter was doing the same. That is not fair."

"I was a hot pussy back then! Is that what you called me, a hot pussy back then! What about now?"

"Suzanne, this conversation is going nowhere, I am going to close it!"

"Got you again! Darling Charlotte, your loving HP or hot pussy on the line. Don't hang up, just say you love me before you drop me."

"You are crazy, and I still love you."

"Better, I will tell the Pastor the great news. Remember we are praying for you every day and forget all the stupid things I said today, bye."

"Bye!"

As soon as Charlotte hung up the phone, she heard a doorbell ring. There was a visitor at the front door. She was not expecting anybody.

When she opened the door, there was a tall young Latin looking gentleman with a set of tools that telephone technicians walk around with fixing telephone lines.

"Good morning, lady, my name is Oswego, Donaldo Oswego. I was sent by the Home Security System company named "HOSE LLC". You have applied on the internet to get a discounted installation of a wired and wireless system installation for $375.00 and a monthly service of $38.99. That is an unheard discount. Well, I came today to install the system if you don't mind. If you want to verify everything, here are my business card, my installation authorization to sign and our service agreement. I can also reschedule the installation if you want too giving you a chance to review the authorization and sign it with the service agreement."

Charlotte moved from the front door to a clear area where there was a wooden bank. This was to signify to the interloper that she was not ready to let him in. She asked the man to sit down then said:

"Mr. Oswego, I have no idea of what you are proposing to me now. To date, I live with my partner for so long with no need of home security system service. I never applied for such a service. I will check with my partner if he has requested such a service. I would not authorize you to install any system today. I would not sign up for such a service. I will ask you now to vacate my premises before I call my friend who is a Sergeant in the Police force. Please don't ever show up in my premises again." She returned the service installation and agreement papers but kept the business card for further verification. "

"I am very sorry, Lady. Our company is a legal legitimate enterprise, you can call us and verify this any time. It looks like I caught you at a very bad day or a bad time. Have a very pleasant day."

The man left and got in a parked gray van with no indication of the "HOSE LLC" anywhere. He left abruptly. Charlotte had a cold sweat while dismissing the man. She wondered if this was not the beginning of harassment, she would be subject to because of the upcoming trial. It dawned on her that Adamas must have very powerful connections in the USA and what she had achieved to date was not going to be left without retribution. She must be protected somehow but how? She will share this aggravating episode with Ludmilla and Sergeant "Sid".

If Charlotte thought that she was being harassed by mysterious powers, the Raleigh County District Attorney, Mr. O'Grady, was confronted with the actual powers that be from Washington D.C. in the person of his own niece Gwendolyn. Mr. Grady loved to ironically address her as the Assistant to the Assistant to the Assistant to the Assistant Secretary in the National Security Office of the US Attorney General. He was never clear about what the hell Gwendolyn did in that office nor in what capacity. The only thing he knew was that she called him now and then sharing inside stories she collected in that office about National Security matters. Before this crazy story, Gwendolyn was the only person to whisper to him matters of US National Security he should keep to himself if he wants to run for the coveted junior seat of Senator from the State of North Carolina. Gwendolyn shared for your ears and eyes-only stories. So, she said. Her uncle wondered sometimes if they were just her own speculations. Mr. O'Grady discounted about 35% of these stories. But all changed when a National Security matter landed in his own office. Mr. O'Grady had no choice but to mount a higher guard now.

"Uncle O'Grady, I am hearing that the legal business that your Office is transacting is getting very complicated!"

"In what way?"

"Well, we thought that it was not going to spiral into a full-blown legal proceeding, a public trial for God's sake!"

"So, what is a problem, or an issue about bringing the matter to a public trial. Tell me, what I should do when an individual makes a public accusation against another individual. The District Attorney Office receives the accusation, collects voluminous testimony from the wide world, decides to move the matter to court where a Judge is selected and set the timetable for a jury trial. Tell me what I was supposed to do?"

"Squash it, my dear Uncle, squash it! You see, you are not thinking about your political future then. I thought that you wanted to become the Honorable Senator from the State of North Carolina. Don't you realize that sitting there in Raleigh, leading a jury trial against your own Government in obscure matters of National Security, do you think that will win you political support from your friends in Congress, Senate, Corporate world, or the government?"

"Gwendolyn, repeat what you just said! Squash it! I am afraid that you did not learn your dear Uncle political orientation well. To your attention, I must advise that I did not enter politics to follow the dictates of any political party or friends in Congress, Senate, Corporate world, or the government. I entered politics to follow my conscience first and the so-called dictates mentioned above if and only if they are in accord with my conscience. It has never been the other way around. For that reason, I believe at the age of sixty-four years old, I am still in political purgatory here in North Carolina waiting to be anointed to higher offices, all that because of statements and acts made all along my political life. Believe me, I am not going to retract a single past act or statement to please the political guards in any party. If I am going to remain and die in North Carolina back waters because of my political conscience so, be it."

"I guess you are not going to play political ball in this upcoming trial?"

"In my District Attorney functions, I don't play political ball. I call it the way it comes, transparent and straight up. Besides what is there to play political ball with. My dear niece, I read the voluminous testimony that came down about that man. It is awful. You would not share a dry piece of bread with the man in the desert. Unless all the collected testimony is fake and made up, he is a rogue. Now you must tell me what law the US is fulfilling dealing with this kind of scum of earth? Gwendolyn, you sit there in your air-conditioned office room shuffling papers while the strategy these papers are advancing is just plain inhuman. And you and your colleagues proudly stand out there pontificating that according to the Presidential Executive Paper number 289288, we need to accommodate this murderer to advance our National Security interests. What national interest but that of the Kentucky two-bit Mining Consortium that extracts the 3T's in that war torn part of the world. Is that what you call American interest! Please don't start that misplaced joke with me."

"I guess you will not listen to me."

"Only if you make sense and there is no bull shit."

"Listening to you, I surmise that we are going to fight two fronts. The District Attorney Office and the Judge who has been selected to conduct the trial. You know and I know that Judge Patricia Leighton-Garver is in a hurry, young and ambitious, on the run to make a loud name for herself. I don't have to give you her background to show where she will go, how she will lead her bench."

"Oh, you don't have to tell me that she is an African American appointed by your boss's boss, another African American with a specific agenda for National Security matters in that part of the world, and I forgot to mention, of the Republic of Kenya descent, sponsored and got passed the Bill 109S2125 "Democratic Republic of Congo Relief, Security, and Democracy Promotion Act of 2005 or another one in the Section 1502 of the Dodd-Frank Act, are you ready, around Conflict Minerals when we found out that Apple, Intel and Motorola were buying conflict minerals to make products such as smartphones, and laptop computers. Is not what we are talking about now? Was this scum of earth involved in that conflict? So are you going to be surprised that Judge Leighton-Garver would take her legal leaning not from your National Security Legal Office, but from her, I should say, legal Mentor, the President of the US."

"I see!"

"Gwendolyn, sometimes you scare the hell out of me. I am amazed that you cannot tell when you are, as you were saying, playing politics or upholding your conscience. I would appreciate it when you talk to me to make the difference between these two conditions. Try my method, raise your voice in the first case and lower your voice in the latter. You tend to do this backward. You must leave an awful impression after you leave the scene. Do you know what people would say about you: "My God, the lady really believes in the bull shit!" And that is fair advice from your dear Uncle."

"Sir, thank you so very much!"

"Any time, any time indeed!"

When Mr. O'Grady closed the call, he requested to see Ludmilla. She came to his office at once.

"Are you getting thoroughly informed about the Classified Information Procedures Act, or CIPA?"

"Yes, I am, Sir!"

"Well, you know that Judge Leighton-Garver has advised she wants the Prosecution and the Defense teams to be well appraised of these

99

procedures. You should know that the Defense will lean entirely their defense around CIPA. They will try as hell to squash the entire trial proceedings based on their reading of CIPA. We will not let them get away with it. From what I am hearing, CIPA established ways for judges, prosecutors, and defense lawyers to frame classified information so that it could be used in public without compromising protected information like sources, methods, and sometime contents. Do not be surprised that the defense team tried this vigorously. It is obvious that the defense would lean on this because the litigation involving the statute will be waged behind closed doors ensuring that any proposed use of CIPA does not infringe on the rights of the accused to a fair trial. I want to review specific cases that allow the court to block, censor, or create substitutions for classified evidence under certain circumstances. I am talking specifically about all the legal documentations that opened the way for the defendant to leave the Eastern area of conflict in DRC and to come here to the US. Believe me from what I see, this will determine the difference between the success or the defeat of the prosecution in this case. If we can overcome this stage, we will be sailing home free. Your review of this matter will be extremely crucial, Ludmilla!"

"I agree with you, Sir!"

"Thank you and get on with it!"

That evening, Charlotte still in celebratory mood, received a call at about eight pm from the Pastor who was in fact singing praises to the Lord to have answer the calls not just from Charlotte from those who have participated in the collection of testimonies. But strangely, using the same Lamb of God reference that Charlotte started the day with, the Pastor, borrowing from John 1:29 sang his version of Agnus Dei:

"Lamb of God, you take away the sin of the world, grant us peace.

O Lamb of God, that takes away the sins of the world, have mercy upon us.

O lamb of God, that takes away the sins of the world, have mercy upon us.

O lamb of God, that takes away the sins of the world, grant us thy peace."

Charlotte was even more blessed when she heard her friend Suzanne answering the last call to the lamb of God to grant us thy peace. Yet the Pastor was not finished in joining on the day celebration. He begged Charlotte to schedule a whole weekend of prayers before the beginning of the trial. He insisted that he needed to associate the church with this monumental event irrespective of the outcome. He reminded Charlotte that the upcoming trial was not Charlotte's calvary alone. The community must share in this. Charlotte agreed reluctantly. Suzanne surprised her by saying that she would chair the weekend prayers event for the church ladies' group. She has never offered to lead any church event. Her agreement went up tenfold. The Pastor closed the surprising praise session with a long prayer. Charlotte went to sleep in the same glorified celebratory mood she started with.

Her scheduled Saturday conversation call with Uncle Stanis went a bit shaky from the start.

"After all that all the people have worked very hard to build the case with that District Attorney Office Staff, you must pay them with complete neglect, Charlotte. We must learn from a third party that the trial has finally been scheduled. I was shocked to learn this. And you waited four days, four days to call. What is the matter with you. Are you going insane or overwhelmed by this legal venue. Let me know if it is getting too much for you. We can always get somebody else to carry that torch."

"I am very sorry, Uncle Stanis. I wanted us to go over this great news in our regulated uninterrupted Saturday time. What third party are you talking about to have shared this news?"

"Well, your friend Ludmilla Garrov, I think! She sent us an email to inform us of the great news!"

"Wooooah, that is a surprise. She did not say anything about that. I guess she had to abide by some office protocol. She kept reminding me that your submission was more than excellent. She said that she learned more about the case thanks to your input. She claimed that you covered the case from every possible angle to make the prosecution team so effective throughout. Her boss, Mr. O'Grady, the District Attorney, had repeated the same observation many times. I don't know if I should be upset or relieved that Ludmilla stole my thunder. Well, the bottom line is that we made extraordinary advance. What do you think?"

"Charlotte, I am delighted for you to have carried this process to this point. But there is a reservation from my part! You know I must hold my celebration music. If the trial was taking place in any other place but the US, I would tell you that we are going to sail home free in this trial. I must express my reservation for one major raison and listen to me very carefully. Adamas was extracted by the American Government for a very good reason from the zone of murderous, criminal behavior, only to be posted safely where you saw him. And I bet this has happened under some obscure US National Security reasons. Now you have accused him of murderous and criminal behavior perpetrated in Congo while he is pretending to be a model citizen in North Carolina, covered by the American Government. Now listen to me carefully again. Bringing Adamas to court is equivalent to bringing the American government to court. The funny thing is this, the prosecution team is the District Attorney Office. And this office is called in the title labeling the case as "US" that is the government of US against or vs Jefferson Okito, the new Adamas extracted from DRC under a funny name to the US. In other words, you have one branch of government against another branch of government under the guise of National Security matter we have no idea of. Charlotte, this is why I will maintain my reservation about this trial. Believe me, I am not saying it could be a gross scam. Absolutely not. When it comes to matters of National Security, that country can sometimes be funny. We saw it when their New York Times revealed so many hidden secrets about the Vietnam War. Well, you can say that politically, people were exhausted supporting a war that brought them nothing but body bags. People got tired of it. Is it the same condition we have here. I don't know. Time will tell. In the meantime, I will maintain my reservation."

"This is the reason I did not want to share my celebration so soon. I wanted to thank God to have, as you said it, carried the process this far. What would happen after is out of my hands? As you Pastors love to proclaim it, I believe that as in 2 Timothy 4:7 "I have fought the good fight …. I have kept the faith". I would not say that "I have finished the race …" That is still to be verified. But and again, I will certainly rely on Paul again at this time as the trial is about to unfold; "I will Rejoice in Hope, be patient in tribulation, be constant in prayer!"

"Very well said, my niece, I loved your faith. I pray that it will be rubbed to my soul!"

"Uncle it is. Still, if you read that letter, I also had question marks about two things. The first is the name of Jefferson Okito that Adamas has been using since he came to the US. They know it is a fake, yet it is posted for all to see on the case title. Well, you have already mentioned it. I want to get further clarifications of this from Ludmilla. The second question mark has to do with the reference to National Security issues or matters. That really blew my mind. I had no idea what was being talked about then. But Listening to your reservation, it is becoming clear now. I don't want to claim that I understand it. But should I raise it with Ludmilla? Because I have told her that I would do this later."

If you ask me, you should rather not. The reason being that they are certainly debating this among themselves. Coming from you, a major witness will be discouraging for them. Please leave it alone unless they raise it themselves."

"I see, I would not bring it up then. It will nag me anyway. Uncle Stanis, let me thank you from the bottom of our heart for your extraordinary contribution. I am here predilecting what we will happen in the trial, but we came from too far we gave up now God willing!"

"Remember, Charlotte, it is a battle for all of us. It is not just for you, our family only. We represent a whole region if not a whole nation. Remember that. God willing, we will overcome it."

"Thank you, Uncle Stanis."

That night, for the first time in a long time, Charlotte had a restful night of sleep. She was not awakened by the usual mood swings which had always troubled her from the time she came to the US, preventing her to enjoy a full five to six straight hours of sleep.

CHAPTER 11

LEGAL IDENTITIES

When Judge Leighton-Garver convened the prosecution and defense team to provide them with her instructions about the trial procedures, the first major issue to surface was, as expected, the legal identity of Adamas Kagita alias Jefferson Okito. The District Attorney, strong with the voluminous testimony about the accused, provocatively suggested that the case be relabeled as "US vs Kagita". The defense team strongly objected to this move.

"The accused entered his legal identity as Jefferson Okito," wondered the Judge, "why would the prosecution want the court to entertain the unusual motion to change the case labeling to a different name at this time. Am I missing something, please help me!"

"The prosecution would rather address the accused as Adamas Kagita, better yet as Major Adamas Kagita with a long series of murderous acts spanning decades."

"Come on, that is exactly what the trial intends to establish whether the accused is Jefferson Okito or what the accusation has named Adamas Kagita. Is the prosecution already closing the trial proceedings. This is sounds to me a bit backward, starting the trial by a closing statement."

"Thank you, your Honor, this is exactly our point. If the prosecution does not want to argue the whereabout of Jefferson Okito and jump the whole trial proceedings to a closing statement to declare Mr. Okito what he is not, then this trial should be dismissed now and be declared as void."

"Not so fast, counsel, our motion must be viewed as a request to the defense team to establish the legal identity of Jefferson Okito as soon as possible. The prosecution does not want to waste the valuable time of our Honorable Judge to guide the trial proceedings over a person who never existed but in the fictive imagination of the defense team.

"Well, I am completely lost now. I must assume that the defense team is ready to establish the identity of Mr. Jefferson Okito as part of the proceedings, is that correct?"

"Yes, your Honor, please disregard the prosecution early tantrums. We have all we need to establish Mr. Jefferson Okito as a legal person."

"Hopefully through regular legal identity papers, none of those mysterious National Security papers that allowed Mr. Jefferson Okito to enter the US," shouted the District Attorney.

"Please, ladies and gentlemen, I am the appointed Judge to guide the trial proceedings here. I am the only party here to authorize what should or should not be produced as evidence papers. Is that clear? I am amazed that the prosecution team is jumping the gun to decide what I would allow or not allow. I have already advised both teams of the purpose of the meeting. I remembered that it was to provide instructions about how we would manage the introduction of National Security papers in these proceedings and only if we must. I believe that I reserve the right to scrupulously guide this process legally and fairly no matter how the prosecution or the defense feels about it. I also noted that we will be dealing with an individual considered by law as of "Alien of Foreign Descent". I heard the prosecution mentioning mysterious National Security papers. I don't know what he is talking about. I am presuming that he is making references to Classified Information pertaining to this case. Just in case where the trial proceedings lead to Classified Information, I must instruct you to review and to follow carefully all the legal guidelines contained in the Classified Information Procedures Act of November 1988 and its pertinent modifications and updates. I have reviewed them and will remain the sole interpreter of these guidelines. I hope I am making myself clear over this subject. I am a bit disappointed to notice that the prosecution and the defense teams have come to this meeting not to absorb my instructions but to argue your points. This is a warning. I would not tolerate any wayward behavior in my court regarding these guidelines. Good luck to your teams to prepare your interventions reviewing all discovery documentations now. I will call you for another meeting if I have other preliminary trial procedures of interest. Thank you.'

The acrimonious turn of the meeting did not please the Judge who walked out of the meeting room without extending greetings to both teams. She was followed by the defense team. But the District Attorney Office team remained seated.

"Don't you worry," Mr. O'Grady said to his team. "I poked the defense team on purpose to find out to what extend they will rely of National Security papers. Have you noticed that they were very reluctant to mention National Security papers. Of course, the Judge was displeased. She should be, she called what she thought to be a civil meeting. I shook her and the defense team deliberately and for a reason. I was sending her a strong piece of advice letting her know that these National Security identity papers are usually fake made-up papers. She wanted to be civil about it, but she knows, she wanted to try to be fair about it, that is not my problem. It will be on her. She read exactly my move and became upset. Believe me, this was a great move. Let's get out of here and bone up on CIPA guidelines."

When Ludmilla Garrov got home, after attending Judge Leighton-Garver the prosecution and defense teams meeting, she received a call from Charlotte.

"Hello Ludmilla, I am finally getting back to you to clarify two things that I read in the letter that your office had sent. I don't know if you have time to talk at this time."

"Of course, I do. I am just coming from a meeting that the Judge called for the prosecution and the defense team. It was interesting.!"

"Interesting indeed. Well, as I said there were two things. The first had to do with the way the case was called, "US vs Jefferson Okito". I did not understand why that man was not being addressed as I know, "Adamas Kagita". I don't know this Jefferson Okito. Can you explain how that strange name got there?"

"This is funny you are asking this. The meeting that the Judge called started exactly with that issue. The meeting got very loud and tense between us, the prosecution team, and the defense team for that man. The Judge got very upset when the prosecution team, that is us, challenged the defense team about that name. Charlotte, let me explain something. The accused that you called or are calling Adamas Kagita must be called whatever he wants to be called for the purposes of the trial. That is his basic right until the prosecution, that is us, can demonstrate without any legal reservation or doubt that that name is a fake or wrong name, and he is without any doubt Adamas Kagita. If we cannot demonstrate that we are dealing with Adamas Kagita in this trial, then the whole accusation will be dismissed and thrown away. That is the burden of the prosecution to bear. That is why we needed all that voluminous documentation to establish who the hell is Adamas Kagita from the time he was born until the time you met him at that wedding party. Your Uncle Stanis and your church have provided everything we need to prove that that man is Adamas Kagita. I am sure of this. On the other end, remember that that man entered legally into the US using a different name, that Jefferson Okiro's name. We, the prosecution team, don't how and why he had entered the US using that name. to cover his criminal Adamas Kagita identity. That will be the main purpose of this trial. The main issue here is how and why he entered the US using a different name. Now if he simply used a fake name and that fake name was accepted by the US Government, the prosecution task of establishing that fake name would be made very easy. However, if, and I must insist here if, the US Government assisted him to enter the US using the fake name, then there will big complications to attack the fake name. Charlotte, attacking the fake name will amount attacking the US Government. This is where the meeting got very tense. But the defense team was very quiet about this. The defense team did not say one way or another how and why the man got the name to enter the US. I believe that the defense team probably wants to see all that the witness evidence we have before making a pronouncement about this topic. Charlotte, this case will be very complicated from the get-go. There will be a lot of stop-go motions from the prosecution and the defense. You should expect this. Did I help?"

"Oh yes, Ludmilla, as expected indeed!"

"What was the second topic?"

"I believe you already answered it when you mention Government. I believe that is what the Judge was talking about National Security issues, right!"

"Exactly, woooah, I am happy you are tying things so quickly in this trail proceeding. Is there anything else?"

"No, Ludmilla, you have helped me understand the letter better now!

Thank you and will be in touch."

"Bye!"

When she hanged up, Charlotte remembered what her Uncle Stanis told her about, "the District Attorney Office, part of the government attacking the Government that made it easy for Adamas to come to the US." It was now clear what Uncle Stanis predicted. She scratched her head wondering where the case would go from here.

About three days after the Judge meeting, the defense team for Jefferson Okito reached what resembled a stage of panic. The lead lawyer Miles Everett almost resigned after a riotous conversation with his client. The defense team had collected the voluminous prosecution evidence that it was entitled to review before the trial. It turned out to be a nightmarish discovery process. It finally dawned on the big shoes lawyer, Miles Everett, the Yale-Georgetown Universities product, that he had underestimated what he called, the lowly backward District Attorney Office staff in Raleigh. The voluminous documentation revealed the mocking obnoxious behavior that the old man Mr. O'Grady, the District Attorney has shown at the Judge meeting. Miles can tell and read how thorough the voluminous witness presentation was. Miles knew that the issue of his client identity was done with, his pretense in advancing Jefferson Okito identity demolished and shot.

"Mr. Okito, I must tell you right now that, the prosecution is producing your life identity at complete variance from what we have, which it not much from your immigration entry papers. We have got a problem. I am sorry we have got a major problem, Mr. Okito. How can you explain that?"

"What a stupid question is this? Your government extracted me overnight from Masisi to bring me here. I never requested this transfer. They told me that was necessary, otherwise I was going to be a dead man. So, I obliged, I packed myself and my family. Now you are asking who the hell I am, well goddam, I was told that I am Jefferson Okito. That is who I am. Your role is to make sure that I remain Jefferson Okito, you got that!"

"What do you think you are? I couldn't care less about what the government did or did not do. I am sure you were not supposed to expose the government which took care to save your miserable life to come here. Now you are getting annoyed because you, the ungrateful of all people, are dragging the government, your savior, into the court system you were never supposed to go through. It is very regrettable that our government goes through so many pains to deal with the rascals like you."

At that instant, Mr. Okito lunged a violent uppercut over Miles' head and missed. The junior lawyers rushed to push Mr. Okito to the other side of the room to calm him down. Miles went to his main office and poured a good size of bourbon. He stayed there for a while only to hear his client leaving the premises abruptly. He composed himself for about ten more minutes then came out. His staff looked very defeated as well and he talked to them.

"Sorry, I got out of line, guys. But it does not look any better for us in this case. In all honesty, we will be better off to get him to renounce his fake identity, resumed that Adamas whatever identity, plead guilty to the sleuth of crimes he had committed and be deported from Us to whatever country the government would take him to. That would be the proper course of judicial venue for him. This is what I am going to propose to the government when I would leave to go to the D.C. tonight. I don't know what the government will say. Maybe he had a very compelling reason to be hidden behind the classified papers on ground of National Security, I don't know. But you read the prosecution discovery voluminous documentation, we cannot match it from birth to now. Worse, I don't believe this man is capable to assume his fake identity anyway. Imagine the prosecution guiding him through his own fake life and he cannot answer simple vital questions like: Where were you born? Who was your preferred teacher in maternal school, primary and secondary school? What did you study in college, where and for how long? Did you do jail time in college and for what reasons? And on and on and on… They have all the answers in their documentation, but all associated to that Adamas guy! And what do we have? Nothing absolutely nothing about this Jefferson Okito. We will be the laughingstock at the trial. I don't want to go through that. Guys, I am not throwing the sink yet. I just want to know what the government got to help us now. I would take my chances with the unavailability of classified papers on National Security ground. We will fight it over with the usual delay or appeal. I can play there. But we got nothing today to stand on. So, stay put, I will get back in one or two days or just give up. But stay put! I will get back to you."

The aggravation that Jefferson Okito – Adamas Kagita had suffered in the hands of his defense counsel left him disjointed and paralyzed. He drove at such a high speed without realizing it on the two-ways still narrow main street of the outer banks. He was lucky that he was not stopped by the cops. He missed making a left turn to get him out the outer banks on the US-158 Road to get him to his home at Barco Corolla. He kept driving for the next 4 miles until he realized he did not know where he was going. He was very mad. He managed to make a U-turn, went back to the bridge he missed. This time instead of going north to his house, he kept going west on another road he could not remember until he decided to stop in an outdoor sea food restaurant giving on the Albermale Sound. He sat quietly alone as far as possible to the next customers. He ordered a full sea food plate with everything with a good pint of dark beer. He reflected over what the silly lawyer told me. He concluded that he was being dropped by those who have decided to extract him to the US. But why now! He finished the meal and ordered another huge glass of dark beer. When he felt that he was fully composed he called Colonel Laurens.

"All right I am ready to go back home. I believe that I am no longer serving the purpose you brought me here."

"I don't understand what you are talking about. The trial is just about to start, and you want to go home. Do you know what is waiting for you back home?"

"It does not really matter. I don't know what I am doing here in the US. And the racist lawyer you got for me is working hard to get back home. He said that I cannot be defended. So, I am telling you that I am making things easy for everybody. Let me go home to die in peace."

"Even if I agree with what you want now, do you know where you want to go back to, is it RDC, Rwanda or Uganda?"

'I don't care which country I go back to, I just want to go back home in Africa, anywhere in Africa will be better for me."

"All right, tell me exactly what the lawyer said to you."

"I cannot repeat what he said. It was just a chain of racist comments about me. He treated me lower than a dog. He said that I was not worth defending in any court in the US. I don't know anything about my own life, at least the one you folk made for me when I entered the

US. The man called me stupid, rascal and some awful names I just cannot repeat. I don't want to see that lawyer jerk again. I don't think he is skilled enough to defend me. How did you manage to hire such a racist lawyer for me. I was so mad I rushed him with an upper cut, we started fist fighting. We had to be separated and I left."

"Woooah that bad, I am terribly sorry. Mr. Okito, I must strongly advise you to take it easy, to go home and to relax. Let me get to the bottom of this. I must assure you that you are not going anywhere. Go home. Will call you very soon."

The accused left the restaurant after about twenty-five minutes when he finished the dark beer and went home.

CHAPTER 12

THE FIRST DELAY

Two weeks after her meeting with the prosecution and the defense teams, Judge Leighton-Garver surprised everybody with a terse communication which reads:

"The trial proceedings for the Case No. 56397, "US vs Jefferson Okito" are being postponed for three months."

No reason for the delay was provided. The following day, Mr. O'Grady, the District Attorney called a 2:30pm meeting at his office for all concerned, including Charlotte.

"I was advised by Judge Leighton-Garver that the defense team has requested a delay in the trial proceedings because the entire team was being changed including two new lead counsels, three new junior associates and two support staff members. The defense team has elected to conduct their business in new premises in Chapel Hill. This was very unexpected. I am trying to understand this new venue, why the team has changed. I can only speculate that the change came about after the first meeting which did not go well for the defense. My further speculation must go to the following fact: when the defense team went through the discovery process over our voluminous witness evidence, they realized that they could not proceed without changing the defense strategy. The defense team was blown over by our presentation. Now imagine what they are bringing back: two lead lawyers, three junior associates and two support staff. And they got rid of the former lead lawyer and his team. You have noticed that the Judged did not include any reason for the delay. She did not write that "Discovery in this case is voluminous and will require substantial time to review and digest in accordance with the accused right to a fair trial. "That was implied obviously. Besides I have already made her angry at the first meeting. She did not want to give me any credit about the so inept way the old defense acted. She was not going to tell me "Dear District Attorney, this old defense team has been fired, we are getting a new more skilled team to match your office skills." No sir, she would not do that nor get there. That would be unprofessional, unethical, and unfair to the defense team and the accused. I understand that. But what happened on the other hand is still very unusual. I must tell you that the new lead lawyers are veteran lawyers very skilled in Classified Information Protection and National Security issues. As far as I am concerned, we already won the first PR battle. I can also tell you that the Judge is angry. She was expecting to lighten her Court load during the upcoming election and that is not going to happen. Well, it is worse on the defense but on us from the prosecution. That is all I have for you. Thank you."

On their way out, Charlotte and Ludmilla remained quiet until they were in Ludmilla's office.

"What all this means?" Charlotte asked,

"Just like the Boss said, it is a delay in the trial proceedings. It is better for us as we are better prepared while the defense has to learn everything in three months while developing a new defense strategy. That is not easy. When you are in such rush, no matter what, you are bound to make mistakes during the trial proceedings. If you ask me, I will say that I am not surprised. I have already told you your witness evidence cut so well against Adamas, it would take a long time to match it against whatever the defense team would come up with in identifying that Jefferson Okito. Believe me the defense's main issue or problem is whether to put Adamas on the stand denying day after day what he is. Just think about it, can you take the stand and deny the prosecution telling you about your entire life in most specific details as developed in the witness evidence, day after day. That will be horrific. Soon or later, anybody will give up screaming "OK, OK it is me Adamas!" So, I believe the only recourse left for the defense is to hide Jefferson Okito behind a pile of Classified Information protected by law under some National Security scheme. This is what the Boss was talking about. And guess what if this happens, we in the prosecution will have no choice but to ask the Judge to break that protection or appeal that protection to a higher court. That will make the trial proceedings even longer. Charlotte, all right, we are not there ye. I am just warning you about what could happen."

"Don't you worry, Ludmilla, I have waited this long to get to this stage,

I am not going to give up now."

"Thank you!"

As soon as Mr. O'Grady dismissed his staff, he called his niece, Gwendolyn, at the National Security Office attached to the US Attorney General in D.C...

"What are you going to do now, waste the taxpayer's money on more big shoes lawyers?"

"I told you that you should have dismissed that accusation a long time ago. Stubborn, you want to fight the big boys. Well, they got deep pockets to drag this thing forever.?

"But for God's sake, who are protecting?"

"National Security!"

"Please don't ever mention these two words in our call. Just say Apple, Intel, Samsung, IBM, Texas Instruments, or their high paid D.C. lobbyists, but National Security, that is so hollow."

"Dear Uncle, when would you understand the companies you named drive our National Security in the Digital domain. The same goes for Lockheed Martin, Northrop Grumman, Boeing which drive our National Security in the Air Force domain. I can also mention the Too-Big-to-Fail banks: JP Morgan Chase, Citibank, Wells Fargo and Bank of America which drive our National Security in the Finance Domain. When it comes to the National Security concern, anybody in the government, Democrat or Republican, must listen to them. That is the way it goes. I did not create that rule. I only execute it. Is it fair, not at all, but that is our current governing rule. And their D.C. lobbyists and their big shoes and big law firms are there to protect them. Why should I fight them."

"Now then, why the change of venue if you will win anyway."

"They will win within the prescriptions of our Constitution as established in the Court system. They will win within the Court system parameters."

"Bull shit!"

"That is the rule."

"Bull shit."

"I am sorry, Uncle, that is the rule."

"Dear niece, the people make the rule in the US through a major tool called the election. Before, all these companies you mentioned were more powerful. Do I need to take you on the long historical review? You heard of the Robber Barons at the dawn of Industrial Revolution, JP Morgan, Cornelius Vanderbilt, John D. Rockefeller, and Andrew Carnegie. They also claimed to be the guardians of National Security concerns of the US when they made fortunes by monopolizing huge industries through the formation of trusts, engaging in unethical business practices, exploiting workers, and paying little heed to their customers or competition. They mastered what was called unregulated business. Yet the Sherman Anti-trust Act of 1890 came as the result of the negative view of the trusts and monopolies from the public. From unregulated business, the US went to regulated corporate business governance with her own series of major fiascos, which received again a disapproval view from the public leading again to a new set of political or judicial intervention. I don't need to tell you, these conditions always started small, became very big and went on to commit major governance failures and I can name: lack of transparency, lax board, lax audit process, etc.... These business units have also claimed at time to represent the National Security of the US. We have seen throughout history how these claims were quickly buried in the medias as soon as these companies went under. Nobody ever went back to find out whatever happened to these spurious claims. Pages were quickly turned to make place to the new ITT, AT&T, IBM, and so on. Do you remember them. Of course, you are proud right there in D.C. to list the corporate carriers of National Security concerns. Don't you see how weak is that fallacy?"

"Absolutely not! Corporate governance abuses are going to happen now and then. The public is there to call the failures and sanction the offending corporate units for these failures. I also know that we need to keep things in perspective. Thousands of corporate business units were extremely valuable in supporting the country's war efforts in the first World War of 1917 and remarkable in the second World War in 1940. They were all very critical as far as National Security was concerned. The country came out victorious in the second World War in the back of all these business units producing everything the country needed to wage that war from the tiny needle to the food cans to the mammoth aircraft carriers. The business units have provided so much to sustain the war. I cannot how many of them have survived the transition to post-war economy. But their war contribution remained a major mark of National Security we have enjoyed."

"I wholeheartedly agreed with that statement. My point is for you, as a public evaluator and marker of National Security, to be vigilant and to ensure that you do not distribute that mark so easily to business concerns which do not deserve it. You must always and sincerely vet these business units so much so no to get the government embarrassed to have blindly accorded the National Security umbrella to the least deserving business units."

"Don't worry, we, in this office, take that vetting the most seriously and at all the time."

"So, where are you going with your Jefferson Okito?"

"The old defense team was not expert enough to tell you the truth. We are bringing very pointed big shoes lawyers. Beware!"

"I will be waiting, Bye!"

Mr. O'Grady knew what the niece wanted to say and where the defense team's strategy was going. He cut the conference call. There was no need for him to listen to the same story. But what Gwendolyn did not say or spell out was more important. She did not divulge that the powers that be was taking steps to erase Jefferson Okito's fingerprints in the state of North Carolina. Colonel Laurens convinced Jefferson Okito to lower his profile to an almost invisibility. They moved his wife and kids to Alabama in a ranch house along US-193 Road in a completely isolated wide field. The house was outside Mobile along the sea going south. The entire North Caroline household furniture was also moved leaving only a bed set in one room and a living room set. For the purposes of the trial, Jefferson Okito was moved into a furnished town house in Chapel Hill. He was instructed to never manifest his presence in the town house. He was to be moved in and out only at night. He was not to be seen outside the compound. If he ever gets tired of the seclusion, he would then be taken to his Barco Corolla near an empty house to have a change of air and environment. Colonel Laurens assured him that these precautions were necessary to prepare him for a quick evacuation from the US to another country in case the trial proceedings became thoroughly negative, and he would be reported as a "fugitive". Colonel Laurens was relieved when Jefferson Okito agreed to the precautions. He explained that he was not concerned about the precautions and that he had lived under similar circumstances twice in DRC and once in Uganda.

After about two weeks at work, the new bigger shoes defense team had a very difficult discovery process. They came to the same conclusions as the old defense team. The voluminous witness evidence documentation was thorough and well effectively prepared. It was decidedly overwhelming against the less than thirty pages that provided Jefferson Okito's identity. They have found the accused unreliable to take the stand denying his Adamas Kagita identity. They were also not ready to start invoking the Classified Information protection that they assumed buried under the guise of National Security the true nature of Adamas Kagita and why he was extracted from the Eastern Region of DRC.

After countless debates, the two lead lawyers came up with a definite defense strategy. The Jefferson Okito identity would be fiercely fought to be preserved against the Adamas Kagita identity designation. The three junior associates will manage this defense phase. They would do this with a lot of objections questioning the witness voluminous documentation. This process was going to drag the process for a long time. If it is successful, the dismissal of the claim would close the trial. Otherwise, the two lead lawyers would move the trial to the CIAP fertile grounds of protected information disclosure. With its own streams of objections and delays. The only reservation remained the preparation of the accused demeanor. With more than two months of requested delay remaining, the two lead lawyers decided that it was worthwhile to engage the accused in the process.

The latest legal strategy was surprisingly fortified by an impromptu visit from DRC. It was no other but Reverend Drago who came to Washington D.C. carrying another message from his mentors from Rwanda. It should be stated and repeated that no other person has represented, in Kinshasa, the interests of Rwanda to the new political leadership of the DRC neighboring country as well as Reverend Drago from 1997 through the time of the trial. Reverend Drago was the virtual eye and ear of Rwanda in the capital. The entire political leadership of DRC knew that when he opened his mouth, he was always conveying what Kigali wanted. The fact of coming to D.C. so unexpectedly raised a few brows for the folks who were dealing with the trial. His arrival was not welcome. It got even more worrisome when he requested to come to Raleigh area to visit with the accused. He was requested to wait for him in the Washington D.C. metropolitan area where he was going to be retained in a closely guarded home in the Virginia suburban section across the capital. As the defense team prepared for the case, the last thing it wanted was any press coverage of the Reverend visit anywhere in the US, and certainly not in Raleigh nor Washington D.C. The defense team convinced Reverend Drago to hold the unplanned meeting with Adamas in the capital area, for no longer than two days.

One of the defense lead attorneys met with Judge Leighton-Garver and made the request to get Adamas to come to the capital for an important family visit. Adamas was under strict Court orders not to leave North Carolina without permission. The Judge agreed to the request and allowed Adamas to travel to D.C. under the Court monitoring supervision. Adamas was surprised about the request. He was not told who in the world came all the way from DRC and wanted to see him. He resisted taking the trip. The defense team convinced him that it was very important for him to go. He was told that he needed a bit of fresh air from the tense legal environment in Raleigh. He was also assured that the trip would bring a lot of salvation and clarification.

When Adamas saw Reverend Drago seating in the living house in the Virginia suburb town of Oakton, his heart started racing. He sweated profusely. He rushed to his reserved bedroom to calm down. He wiped his damped face from a cold splash from the bathroom at the end of the huge bedroom. He took him a while to compose himself. He asked why and what the Reverend was doing in the house. He told one of his handlers that there was no worse murderer he needs to face at that time but the man seating in the living room. The handler was shocked to hear this. He knew that the Reverend was not checked by the other trip handlers for carrying guns or anything dangerous to cause bodily harm. The handler pulled a small device from his jacket back pocket and pressed something to alert his colleagues about a dire present emergency in the house. At that very instant, the other handlers rushed the seating Reverend on the floor and started to body search him. The surprised and shocked Reverend screamed to be left alone to no avail. When they were done frisking him, they raised him back to his chair apologizing extensively for the body search.

The Reverend got up and started going to his reserved room. He screamed to the handlers saying that he has never been so disrespected in his whole life. He protested that he was a major political dignitary in DRC. He was not going to stay one more second in the house and wanted to leave right away. He asked to get a taxicab to go to the international Dulles airport to go back home. The handlers, realizing the grave mistake they made, started calling their supervisor or whoever to come to calm the man while Adamas listened to the entire incident smiling in the bedroom. He would not come out. The aggravated Reverend packed his suitcase and stood next to the house big entrance door. In about thirty minutes, an associated lawyer who had traveled with Adamas from Raleigh showed up. He tried to calm the Reverend who was still very aggravated. After about an hour or so, the Reverend went back to his bedroom. It was only then that Adamas was authorized to see him after getting his cell phone ready to tape everything the Reverend would say.

"What happened, Reverend Drago, you look very irritated?"

"I have never been so insulted in my life. I don't know about your stupid American guests. They have no manners at all. I was sitting there waiting for you. I heard a car coming and I thought that you came.in the house. I was still watching the TV and all of sudden, I was thrown on the floor by four guys and they started frisking me for what I didn't know. I was terribly shocked. My good man, I am accused of many things, but I must tell you, I have never carried a gun all my life. Yes, I have given orders, but I have never carried a gun in my life. Tell me why I should carry a gun all the way from Kinshasa, go through security checks, board two planes and come right here under a tight escort. These folks must be so stupid. I must be superman to evade detection from Kinshasa through Casablanca to Dulles International Airport and to get in this house with a gun. Do they have any logic? And why should I carry a gun, to kill you? What a silly and stupid plan I must have made? Was it not for my utmost respect for the Enterprise and the Leadership, I would have taken the first flight straight back home, I can tell you that. I am sorry, give me a few minutes to compose myself."

Reverend Drago sat quietly on the long sofa adjoining the bed. For the first time I saw him get up toward the bedroom small bar and poured at a good size of bourbon he could find. He offered to give Adamas a glass, but he declined. He drank the bourbon till the third glass bottom. Then he opened his attached case and pulled a French Bible. Deliberately and calmly, he found the famous quote in Revelation 12:11:

"And they overcame him by the blood of the Lamb, and by the word of their testimony; and they loved not their lives unto the death."

He read slowly read the verse three times. Adamas could not tell whether Reverend Drago read the quote to forgive the handlers or to admonish them. But the Reverend read it so slowly, Adamas decided that the Reverend was not used to calm himself with a glass of the liquor, and that the bourbon took over many of his senses, physically and mentally. He slumped on the sofa as if begging him to give him space to sleep. He started to snore. Adamas understood that Reverend Drago needed to rest for a while. He got up and closed the door behind him and went back to his reserved bedroom.

A few minutes later, the lawyer who traveled with him knocked at the door. He wanted to know if he had any conversation with the Reverend.

"He was so upset, took a glass of bourbon and went to sleep." Adamas answered.

CHAPTER 13

A WARNING FROM HOME

Adamas had a good afternoon rest when he went back to his room. At about five thirty, there was a knock at his door. This time there was a lady with a kitchen apron around her neck telling him that the dinner was served, and he was expected to join his colleague at the dinner table. Adma was surprised to see this lady for the first time. There were no upkeep personnel when he arrived at the house. He went to the dining room, and on his way, he noticed that there were no handlers around. The Reverend was already seated at the dining table. The lawyer was standing close to the dining table, he greeted him and apologized for not being able to join them for dinner. He mumbled that he had some family visits to make in the area and he would come back later. He advised him not to wait for him. He did not add that the whole house was bugged to the till to pick every sound of exchange the African guests were going to make. Before leaving his room, Adamas verified whether his cell phone taping system was on. It was.

Adamas finally sat down joining the Reverend already enjoying the sumptuous dinner that the middle-aged lady wearing a kitchen apron has apparently cooked. The table was well stocked. There were big trays of cut-up angus beef and chicken in the middle of the table surrounded by medium trays of rice, potatoes, and salad. The food was made for twenty people. There were also big red and white bottles at the table next to tall wine glasses. The Reverend was at his first full plate serving.

"Your American hosts have greatly improved the welcome in this house. It looks like they kicked out the stupid guards who assaulted me. Before you came down, I took a visitor tour of the house. It is a big mansion indeed and well protected with high walls that we find in big cities of DRC, mainly in Kinshasa where the big shots live. You cannot see the roads from this house which looks like hidden from the neighbors. A very strange house. Oh my God, I am so confused after that incident, I did not pray to bless the food. I did not quote my famous verse from Revelations 12:11. Please eat Adamas. Don't wait on me. I believe the American have gone to so much trouble to get us together. Of course, leaving aside the stupid incident."

"Again Reverend, I am terribly sorry for it."

"Please, do not apologize for these scoundrels. I came here simply as a messenger. What they did was uncalled for. Forget it, they are already making amend. Let's enjoy the meal. As I was saying, I came as a messenger from the Enterprise Leadership. Now I hope there is no listening bug here. Even if there is, it does not matter. I would be using our contact language anyway. You did not forget that the Enterprise Leadership is spread in three parts, one in Malebo, another on Lake Victoria and another far from the road leading to Gisenyi. The combined leadership asked me to come here and talk to you. The leadership is not happy about what is going on in your quarter. The Leadership is in fact nervous and wants to get assurances that no beans will be spilled in that trial you are going to have in Raleigh. They strongly believe that the mountain is setting up the three parts. They want you to answer three questions before the start of that trial."

"But it has been postponed for three more months."

"Oh, they did not know this and why the delay?

"Some legal technicality that I did not quite understand. You know their legal system is very complicated and sometimes childish. I am just learning it as it goes. I just want to get over it."

"The three parts don't believe it is going to be so easily done with as you say. They are convinced that there would be some traps against them in the way."

"Frankly, I don't know what they are thinking out there. They seem to know more than I do, that is me, the one being accused knows."

"Well, they want assurances from you not to spell any bean. You understand!"

"Reverend, I am sorry, you keep talking about beans to be spilled by me, so they said. What beans, you are not being precise. As far as I am concerned, I have no beans to spill. I never worked for or close to any of them. So how in the world would I spill their beans. You need to help me here. If you came all the way from Kinshasa to warn me about spilling some beans, I don't know anything about, then your trip was well useless."

"Adamas, I don't think so. My trip was urgent and necessary. This trip took a lot of conversations and meetings among them at the highest level. I am their main messenger. It is not a game. It is not a service they want you to execute and that you can dismiss. No Sir! Absolutely not! Let me tell you, the minute you start working in that mine you joined the Enterprise, you have been working for the three parts. Is that clear! You owe them that much! So be careful about what you are saying and what you will say from then on."

"Reverend, believe me, I am not disrespecting the Leadership. They made me what I am today. I am extremely grateful for that. Still, I also believe when I don't understand what they send you to get from me, I need to get some clarifications from you. I am getting the feeling that you are going in a very infernal vicious circle, if I may say so."

"All right, as I said before I have about three questions for you to answer. Are you ready?"

"Yes!"

"The first is this; how many times did you go to Mauritius Island or Seychelles Island in the past ten years?"

"I have never been to Mauritius Island. I went to Seychelles Island for a long holiday stay at the Four Seasons Resort. I went there with a beautiful beauty from Somali I met in Mombassa. As a matter of fact, I loved it so much, I went back there maybe two or three times. The lady was always available when I wanted to go there."

"So, it was some kind of honeymoon you enjoyed there."

"Yes, that is the only thing you go there for. Sex and party, party, and sex. I enjoyed it very much."

"Did you meet anybody there for business?"

"No, I told you it was for sex and play. I don't like any other activities in that resort like fishing, snorkeling or deep-sea swimming. That is not for me. I spent most if not all of my time between bed sheets, cavorting with that lady."

"I got the picture and not business, right!"

"No other business."

"Have you ever met a gentleman by the name of Denish Rajeev?"

"No!"

"Now think and remember hard, in your management of logistics for Coltan from the mines to the Rwanda border."

"No, never! I met a lot of Indian businessmen, but that name does not mean anything to me!"

"Rajeev used to hang around a lot around Butembo-Beni junction road. No idea who he is?"

'Never heard of him, never met him!"

"The last question: "Have you ever met a gentleman by the name of Ferenc Zolty?"

"No, who the hell is this one?"

"He is a Coltan trader of German-Hungary descent with a lot of traffic right there in Goma. Sometimes he claimed to be an American expatriate by the name of Freddy Zoltan. Never crossed this one?"

"Never met nor crossed this one?"

"Now I need to go over some very difficult questions for you coming to the US. These questions would be asked to you at the trial. The Leadership wants to get them answer now so they have a good background if ever your name starts flying in the medias."

"Why were you selected to come to the US as a political refugee?"

"I ran into a serious business trouble with a close family member of the President of Uganda. I was threatened to be killed. I went to the American embassy and requested the asylum. I was extracted from Kampala under a new name and flown out in an American military jet cargo from Kampala to Nairobi where I took a commercial flight to New York and Raleigh. This is how I came to the US. "

"Do you have another motivation in mind?"

"What do you mean, that is the only reason that was used for me to get here/!"

"That was, I am afraid to say this like the American love to say, the bull shit story that was used. But for yourself, you know that there was more to that. Did you discuss anything else with the American hosts?"

"Reverend Drago, I did not discuss anything less with anybody. Personally, I know I started having issues with the Congolese General who was protecting the entire logistic operations in DRC. The General was getting very greedy. It came down to either keeping his cover or keeping my management supervision. The Leadership thanked me for the good job and flew me here. That is all I know and nothing else. But I have never discussed this with anybody when I was coming here. I was only happy that the Leadership was able to find a new life for me here in the US. I was not complaining, and I know I screwed up with this trial. We talked about this already, so I don't have anything to add to this. '

"Very good, that will satisfy the Leadership, everything you have said. Who is your main contact here in the US?"

"Colonel Laurens."

"Have you ever met him?"

"No!"

"Do you want to meet him?"

"No really, I never want to meet with the Leadership in my previous job. I understand how our job is designed. I always need everything and every response I need from Colonel Laurens and always remotely from afar. He has treated me very good from day one. I don't need any more than he has been willing to give. It is really a win-win equation."

"Did any other person from the Leadership has ever contacted you besides me?"

"No Sir, never!"

"Very good, that would be all for today. You did not touch your food, it is getting cold. Let me try to get it warmed up for you."

125

"That would be nice."

The Reverend called upon the kitchen Lady who showed up at the third call. She took Adamas's plate back to the kitchen to get it warmed over. At the same time, Reverend Drago was completing furtively his conversation notes on a scattered piece of paper. Adamas was observing the Reverend still taking notes of their lengthy conversation. Adamas was still not clear of the urgent trip that Reverend Drago took to see him. He was still convinced that the trip was useless despite all that the Reverend said. He decided that he could answer the same questions from the confines of his new bedroom in Raleigh. He has also noticed the deep and serious aggravation that Reverend Drago showed every time he pushed back about the trip motivations, he had already determined to be bogus. He went mentally to his previous conclusion: the Leadership was getting ready to drop him ungraciously as it has done before to countless expendable free lancers like himself. But he reflected that he was not going to go down that easy. The lady brought back his hot plate interrupting his wandering thought. The two guests continued the dinner reminiscing about so many pleasant and not so pleasant episodes when they crossed paths in the Eastern DRC. About an hour later, they both quietly retired to their respective reserved rooms. They never heard the lawyer who came back from the back area of the strange house. He never left the house, listening to the entire conversation of the African guests while sitting in the house back corner station full of best spy listening devices.

The African guests spent the night without any more contacts, each staying in the respective reserved bedroom. It became very transparent to both guests that their meeting was inopportune and guided by distant powerful people. It was evident that they did not want to exchange anything further if they did not have to. They were eager to get over the meeting imposed on them. It was so much so that in the morning, Reverend Drago packed his suitcase to leave and brought it closer to the house big exit door. He let the hosting lawyer that, after the breakfast, he was going to pay visit to few family acquaintances in Washington D.C. area during the day in preparation for his departure back to DRC with the 9:45pm flight leaving for Addis Abeba, Ethiopia. The lawyer assured him that a limousine transportation would be made available to him. The lawyer did not bother to ask him whether the planned conversation with Adamas was completed. The lawyer already realized that the planned conversation did not go as expected. Reverend Drago took a seat in the house main living room while the breakfast was being prepared. Adamas came down about twenty minutes later. He did not bring his suitcase to leave. He just joined Reverend Drago for another conversation.

"Good morning, Adamas, don't worry, I am not blowing your covert. The lawyer left again for his errands. It is just you and I in the house with the cook getting our breakfast ready. I told the man that I must leave after the breakfast. I got a busy schedule of family appointments in the D.C. area before leaving for back home tonight. I will miss you. Now before breakfast is served, I hope to close our conversation with a few questions, if you don't mind. The questions came from the Leadership last night. They want to know what your estimates are, your projections of how this trial would end. They figured that you have a definitive idea or hope of how this thing would end. Now this does not mean that what you believe is what would happen. They want you to share your best shot."

"This is very funny, I never thought about the end of this trial. I got assurances from the lawyers that everything would be all right. They never explained what "all right" meant. You know when you go through what I am going, you go from the most positive outcome to the worst in a split second. You could be dreaming the pie in the sky in one instant, two minutes later you see yourself enchained in a dungeon twenty feet underground, surrounded by bars, you are lying on the floor smelling your vomit. It is a mental zigzag that is very depressing. You want an objective projection, well, at worse I believe that I will be expelled from the US on the ground of entering the US under a misappropriated and mistaken identity. The issue would then be where the US would expel me to. I don't know, it could be back to Uganda or Rwanda or DRC. Or it could be in another country here in North, Central of South America. I don't know. That is the worst case. The other case would be that the US government could decide to give another different identity and move me and my family to a very distant state in the North, East, Midwest, or Western state. I don't know. Whatever the outcome would be, I know that I would no longer live in the state of North Carolina."

"Either way, that sounds positive, don't you think so? The leadership was afraid that you would be sentenced for the crimes that lady had accused you of?"

"Well, that is not going to happen. The lawyers have been clear about that. There is no court in the US to litigate what happened in Africa. They also said that the end of the trial would mean more restrictions of movement for me. It would be an open jail anywhere I would be from then on. In addition, I would be under constant watch and supervision. However, the lawyers repeated that afterwards, if I committed the slightest offense, I would then suffer the full burden of the American Justice leading to a ten to twenty years of jail time with no parole. Tell the leadership that, from then on, I am looking forward to an awful life between precarious freedom and certain jail. A living hell anyway you look at it."

"Still better than being shredded by bullets you cannot tell where they are coming from. Adamas, let's face it, you and I have made a lot of enemies in our enterprise life in Africa. We have chosen it and in consequence we are living that secluded life. The Leadership parts have condemned themselves to the same life. Don't expect from them any sympathy about that life. They have assumed it. That is why the leadership would prefer a quicker trial where the outcome is fixed right away. You see your presentation of the end is clear and ominous, right, so why go through the charade of a trial."

"I am not making those decisions about the length of the trial. My American guests are taking the lead on this for their own reasons. I have no means to contest or challenge their decisions. In all truth, I am a dead man walking here."

"The Leadership is not comfortable about what your hosts are doing. They believe that there must be some ulterior motive that is making them anxious. Do you know that motive? Have they shared it/"

"I am sorry I don't know it, that so called motive. When I hear you talking, it seems to me that the leadership knows precisely that motive and they are not sharing it, you are not sharing it. For you to cross that big Atlantic Ocean through two long international flights to ask me that question, that tells me where they are standing. And I am afraid it is not comforting for me. Well, as I said it, I am a dead man walking, entirely resigned to my fate."

"Adamas, you can tell, feel, say anything you want, the Leadership has thoroughly analyzed your hosts legal defense strategy and it came to the precious conclusion, a quick trial. That is the opposite of where the hosts want to drag you. Their question is that simple: are you going to survive the cross examination about your borrowed identity? If you can answer that question, then my trip was useless as you said yesterday. Otherwise, the leadership has a strong point."

"I cannot answer that question until I am on that court stand. By the way, Reverend Drago, it is my life after all we are talking about here. I will continue fighting for my life in that court. I am no different from the Leadership parts who have lived so many different lives to get to where they are today. I am no different from you when you have also lived so many lives through the present. All of us have somehow survived those many different lives and continued to fight for our lives. Let be assured that I will also continue fighting for my life."

At that instant, Reverand Drago rose suddenly from the sofa deep seat as if bitten by a stinging bee and exclaimed loudly:

"I knew that you would not be unable to answer that question, and, on that note, I must close my line of questions. The house cook has brought the breakfast, let's eat."

Reverend Drago ate his breakfast without saying a word. He pretended to concentrate on listening to news that was blared from the big TV. He had raised the volume from the beginning to prevent any more exchange with Adamas while eating. When he finished his breakfast as quickly as he had started, he went back to seat looking at the BBC world news on TV, ignoring Adamas who remained at the dinner table. In less than ten minutes later, the lawyer walked back in the house to announce that the limousine ride for Reverend Drago was pulling in the driveway. Reverend Drago got up and walked to the entrance door, collected his suitcase, and walked out of the house. He never turned back to bid farewell to Adamas, the man he came all the way from Africa to see urgently. The sound of the limousine leaving the house driveway was heard ten minutes later while a flustered angry Adamas continued slowly eating his breakfast.

CHAPTER 14
TRIAL PRELIMINARIES

Adamas's return flight to Raleigh with the associate lawyer was just aggravating as when he was summoned to come to Washington D.C. This time, the urgent request to take the trip still escaped him. He remained flustered during the flight. He mentally searched the reason why the enterprise leadership sent Reverend Drago to meet with him. He believed that he had answered all the questions that the Reverend raised. He did not care at present whether he answered satisfactorily these questions. As far as he was concerned on this flight back, the meeting strengthened his belief that the leadership had already abandoned him. Adamas smiled when thinking about his repeated rebuttal to the Reverand Drago when he said that he was basically a dead man walking. That was his strong message to his former keepers that he has been abandoned to his sorry fate.

Adamas knew that he had aggravated Reverend Drago when he suggested that all of them and including the Reverend have led multiple different lives and remained determined to fight for their lives. He knew that was a very touching subject for the leadership parts, a sad truth, still a taboo never raised in their conversations. For him to dare the Reverend Drago by raising it was the last straw. He was not surprised that the Reverend did not bid him any farewell. He left visibly upset and Adamas could not care a bit. As the jet pilot announced the preparation for landing the plane after about an hour flight, Adamas resolved that he was ready to continue to fight for his life.

Adamas was very perturbed when he reviewed the line of questions that Reverend Drago raised, specifically the list of people he may or may have not seen when he was vacationing in the Seychelles Island at least the two times he was there. He did not mention that there was an American who literally followed him throughout the island spots. His name was Colonel Carl Thorthon. The American said that he came from the backwaters of Thailand, Cambodia, Laos, and Myanmar. He added that he never returned to the US after his Vietnam army services, he claimed to have been honorably discharged at the rank of Colonel. He let him know that he was making a lot of money involved in drugs trade from Asia-Pacific to Europe and the US. He was getting tired of drugs trade and wanted to join what he called the coltan and gold big game in Eastern DRC. It was obvious that he knew his background. Adamas listened to him trying to find oud what he knew about him. He knew a lot. He said that he had already set up contacts in Kampala, Kigali, and Kinshasa with high-ranking military officers willing to set up a parallel logistic route to evacuate the minerals through a third country he would not specify. He said that I should join this new set up. Adamas told him that he would think about it. Adamas surmised that in the line of business he was involved in, you run into these kinds of mysterious free lancers, and he was not surprised. Most of the time he just listen and forget about them. But this man, Colonel Carl Thorthon showed up in Goma and Beni at the end of two later caravans' trips. They continued the Seychelles conversation. They talked for a long time. And after a long analysis and prospection, Adamas mentioned to him that he was not interested, and his proposal was too dangerous for him at the time. His proposal reminded him a similar undertaking laid by one of the leadership members, precisely the DRC President, and without the consent of the other leadership members. Adamas also struggled to find out if this was not a trap laid by the enterprise, a bait he resolved not to fall for. No less than four months later, the American folks came up with the evacuation trip to the US and warned him that services were no longer appreciated by the enterprise. He left Eastern DRC.

He rejoined his defense team in Raleigh, gearing up for the trial that was fast approaching. He dedicated himself to a strenuous effort of remembering his made-up biography:

"Jefferson Ohio was born on August 14, 1968. He spent his youth in Mbarara area around Kamukuzi Hill neighborhood and took secondary school classes in a Mbarara High School where a notable prominent alumnus was no other but the Uganda President Yoweri Museveni. When he graduated from high school in 1986, Museveni's rebel army chased out the dictator Idi Amin and Yoweri Museveni was sworn in as President. The protracted war between Idi Amin regime and the Museveni guerilla disrupted the country's economy from

1972 through 1986. Okito's family already had meager survival and bleak conditions worsen. Jefferson Okito could not pursue University education. He became a supervisor of a cattle farm belonging to a big land-owning family north of Mbarara. He quickly became aware and learned the business trade of many agricultural products and cattle trading along the big high traffic roads which came from DRC border going to Kampala and further west toward Dar-Es-Salam in Tanzania, or Mombassa in Kenya. Slowly and surely, Jefferson left Mbarara and became a trader for every product that transited along these East-West roads. With time he discovered that he could make more money trading in all sorts of ores composites or minerals that were being trafficked along these roads from DRC to the ports of Mombassa in Kenya or Dar-Es- Salam in Tanzania. He became a powerful trader in gold and coltan ores. However, with no military background or reliable contacts, he chose to restrict himself to waiting for minerals shipment at the DRC and Uganda border. He knew very well that the minerals shipments originated from war ravaged areas in Eastern DRC and without a strong military background and backing he would not stand a chance to engage in any business activity or to simply survive. He decided to be involved in logistics operations that consisted of buying the minerals at two or three safe border towns in Uganda, lodging them in the huge warehouses he has built and controlled, and carrying the minerals to Mombassa or Dar-es-Salam. This shrewd business strategy paid off handsomely. However, Jefferson Okito made a lot of money and enemies in this lucrative trade. Before he knew it, Army Generals, some very close to the members of the President family, started harassing him. The strongest warning, he received came about when two of his younger brothers, assisting him in the extensive logistics of the trade were assassinated by armed bandits at Busia, the border town of Masui, on the Western Road that goes through Kenya and then takes the southern turn toward Dar-Es-Salam port of Tanzania. He tried to raise his profile and contacts with the central government members in Kampala for protection, but this did not work, the generals have already managed to block all access. He even tried to access powerful interests in Kigali sharing the same evacuation of minerals from DRC to Tanzania, he did not get any help. He tried to hang around a bit longer but when one of his big warehouses was burned down at one of the DRC border towns and another assassination attempt took place when he came to surveil the incident leaving two bodyguards and his driver killed, Jefferson knew that he was no longer safe in Uganda and started making plan to leave the country. He tried to move his operations to Rwanda only to meet the same military obstacles. His political contacts advised him to get out of Uganda, the sooner, the better. His quiet request for exile to the US was granted about eight months later while he maintained a very low profile, hiding in the country in very remote residences. He finally boarded a night flight to Nairobi from where he rested a while and came to the US with his family."

This biography had a lot of plausible venues if delivered appropriately to the jury. The defense was determined to work on it. The defense team prepared Adamas-Jefferson very hard. They made him repeat every facet of his "biography" to make him wear it like a custom-made suit, both mentally and physically. Adamas practiced so much to the point he started believing that he was Jefferson Okito. When he woke up in the morning, he hailed himself as Jefferson. He repeated the name over and over throughout the day. He went as far as introducing himself as Jefferson when he called his very surprised and frightened wife to inquire about his kids in that remote compound outside Mobile, Alabama. He reassured his wife that he was just practicing his role in a very secret business operation. And for the first time, his always submissive and docile wife asked him a lot of questions about his mental and physical health. She revealed that she was having a lot of nightmares about their family future after the sudden departure to Alabama, the fact he was not home was becoming very difficult compared to the time with them when he was home all the time before when they came to the US. At the end she asked whether he was abandoning his family. This was from a wife who never asked any question about their whereabouts, did everything Adamas asked her to do, never stepped out to the house nor its compound, did not know anything about their neighborhood, did not drive and worse did not speak English. Everything was provided to her on the silver plate. Except for breastfeeding their last one year old child, Adamas took care of everything. While away in Raleigh Adamas did the same remotely. The whole situation was becoming a bit frightening for the poor lady. So much so, when Adamas introduced himself as Jefferson in Swahili, the lady literally lost it. It dawned on Adamas then the terrible impact on his family, the major upside-down conditions his reckless adventure had created that fateful Saturday, outside the safe cocoon that had sheltered the family in the US from the beginning. Looking at himself in the bathroom mirror, Adamas shed a few tears, wondering if he would be able to recover that shelter, that safe cocoon by the end of the trying episode in the court system.

As quickly as he felt sorry for himself and his family, Adamas wiped out his tears on his face and resolved to apply himself as Jefferson Okito for his sake and family.

The defense team was elated and convinced of the tremendous progress that Adamas made metamorphosing into Jefferson Okito. The team became slowly and profoundly assured of the risks of the change. However, to protect their strategy, the lead lawyers requested another trial preliminary meeting with Judge Leighton-Garver. They wanted to introduce a mountain of legal safeguards about the lines of questioning to establish the identity of the accused. The defense team claimed that since the accused's identity was provided by the government, the lines of probing that identity must respect government confidentialities. Judge Leighton-Garver, very curious to know the intent and the purpose of the request, obliged the request and called the meeting inviting the District Attorney team. Mr. O'Grady had already warned his team that he expected such defense team's request. As soon as Judged made the request, he gathered his team to instruct them of his strategy. He stated the DA would not accept any legal boundary in its line of questioning unless the defense team invokes CIPA (Classified Information Procedures Act) legal boundaries. He knew that the defense team was on a fishing expedition to see how long the trial would progress before invoking CIPA. As usual he had concluded, the longer the trial would take, the longer the delay, the better for the defense.

"Welcome, ladies and gentlemen, I called this preliminary trial meeting requested by the defense team." Judge Leighton-Garver started the meeting, I want to invite the defense team to explain the purpose of their request."

"Thank you, Your Honor, in the interest of a timely review, the defense wants to introduce a set of legal safeguards or legal boundaries around the lines of questioning that should be brought up during the trial. We want to introduce these boundaries at this time to facilitate the smooth progress of the trial because in our opinion, since we must start determining the identity of the accused and knowing that the accused has entered the US under strict government procedures and declarations, we strongly believe that we must abide by the government procedures and declarations. That is what the defense team preliminary request."

"Thank you, Counsel, what does the Prosecutor team say about this request?"

"May it please the court, we strongly believe that there should not be any boundary during the trial unless the defense wants to invoke CIPA legal boundaries. We know perfectly well that before anything, we need to clear out the identity of the accused. We know that the accused had entered the US under what the defense team has stated to be government procedures and declarations. Those procedures and declarations are also public documents that can be reviewed at request. We stand ready to dispute that these government procedures and declarations are confidential. They are not. For all I know, any person coming to the US brings a passport with a valid visa provided by the US embassy or consular services abroad. The key word in that statement is a valid visa that the government provides to the foreign person who has requested to come to the US. The defense team is pretending that the process by which the government determines the delivery of that valid visa is confidential. But we beg the question of what that confidentiality involves. We accept the validity of the delivery of the visa. The presumption here is that the government has determined that the delivery of the visa has followed the lawful instructions of the process and the foreign person requesting the visa has provided truthful declarations that are found in the visa document. That is the heart of this trial. We are not contesting the validity of the accused's visa of entry. We are disputing the declarations contained in the request for visa. That is the reason why we cannot agree to the so-called boundaries the defense wants to circumscribe our discovery."

"Your Honor, may it please the court, the Prosecutor team is already pleading the case in this trial. That is most unfortunate. We are talking of boundaries in terms of confidentiality surrounding the visa that the government has provided our client. That is all. Every person entering the US is entitled to a certain amount of confidentiality regarding declarations made to get the visa of entry. Let us be clear about that. We live in a democratic country where four fundamental inalienable rights are exercised and for a reminder, they are, freedom of speech and expression, freedom of religion and conscience, freedom of assembly, and the right to equal protection before the law. These rights are never parked when a foreign person enters the US with a visa. On the contrary, these rights are proudly exhibited to remind especially the foreign persons that we are going to live by these rights. I submit that my esteemed colleagues would agree with me."

135

"My esteemed colleague, I agree with you wholeheartedly about our four fundamental rights indeed. For the sake of time and moving the schedule, and to make a point of what we have said from the start, I am willing to review your list of boundaries with my team and to reply within two days or so whether we will consider and abide by these boundaries. Of course, if it so please the court."

"Counsels, my role is to move the trial proceedings within a legal consensual platform agreed by both the defense and the prosecution. It makes my life much easier to move the proceedings when both teams agreed to go along according to the same procedures. Believe me, I never enjoy dictating procedures. For the highest interest of justice for all, my inclination is always to let the two parties reach agreement around procedures. I would be expecting a review of the boundaries by the prosecution team and its decision. Thank you, ladies, and gentlemen, for a good session. This meeting is adjourned."

As soon as the DA team went back to the office, Mr. O'Grady asked Ludmila and a younger associate to review the list of boundaries to the lines of questioning that the defense team shared. It was with revolting horror that Ludmila surmised the list of boundaries which revealed the first intent of the defense team to prevent and to reject the full presentation of the voluminous biography of Adamas Kagita in court. The boundaries were developed to accomplish the following: debate only the biographic narrative found in the 18 pages visa application request signed by Jefferson Okito, limit the lines of questioning only around the life of Jefferson Okito in Uganda, never address Mr. Jefferson Okito by any other name but his Ugandan name with no mention of an Adamas Kagita of Congolese descent, never mention political, economic, business and military activities happening in other countries but Uganda, and more other boundary in similar vain. Ludmilla completed her summary by nine o'clock the same day. She called her boss who was already home and expected her call.

"Thank you, Ludmilla, I expected the same stupid boundaries. Our answer will be a big no. But hold the summary. Do not share until the time and date of the meeting. Just for your ears only, we got to be diplomatic here. Our strategy is this: We reject the boundaries, but we play along the boundaries! Do you understand? First, we give the defense team the noble opportunity to do the grandiose spill of Jefferson Okito life. We give them all the time in the world to provide whatever that visa request declaration gyrated. We leave them embellish it on the till. They will. We do not, I repeat, we do not raise any objection as if we agree to the beautiful life of Jefferson Then we come back disassembly it slowly and surely. Believe me, we are going to get the accused to reject the fallacy of his own declarations in the visa request application. Trust me on this one. The voluminous biography of the accused that we have accumulated will expose him somewhere along the charade he wants to pull. If you want to know why, well It is hard to live a double life. Soon or latter things would catch up with him. I have seen this before."

Ludmilla did not understand what the Boss was talking about. She was simply enraged by the list of boundaries which were designed to throw away the extraordinary work she had done assembling the voluminous biography of Adamas Kagita from birth through to present. How would this despicable defense team dare reject her work. She was blindsided by her own involvement. She went as far as to think that the Boss had a bit of bourbon to put him to sleep. Well, it was ten pm.

Ludmilla was surprised that the Boss did not invite the big DA team to a follow up meeting. She was the only one senior lawyer with her junior associate to accompany the Boss to the meeting. The DA gave a brief statement that she was going to read in response to the request from the defense team. After Judge Leighton-Gaver welcomed the two teams, Ludmilla read the following:

"Your Honor, dear esteemed colleagues from the defense, after substantial review and consideration of the list of suggested legal boundaries you shared, the prosecution team decided unfortunately to decline to abide by the purported list of legal boundaries. While respecting the intent of the said boundaries, the prosecution team fully reserves the right to follow closely the presentation of the visa request declarations and procedures within these boundaries and challenge where appropriate its content. Sincerely, the prosecution team. Thank you."

There was about a minute of silence in the conference room while the Judge and the defense team struggled to understand what the prosecution team was saying. Judge Leighton-Garver cut to the chase and addressed the defense team:

"Counsels from the defense team, do you understand and agreed what the prosecution just said and proposed?"

"Your Honor, we do understand and agree!"

"That is fantastic, Counsel Mr. Grady, you surprise me again by this proposition. As I said, I second your agreement and I would like to see you in court as we have already predetermined. Thank you."

Throughout the meeting, Mr. O'Grady looked absent and sullen as if he had lost an important venue for the legal procedures. It was just an act of fooling the defense team. He did not want to drag the meeting conversation into another debate. A fine poker player, Mr. O'Grady was not about to divulge the trump card of his legal strategy the same way the defense lead lawyers had done with theirs. He quickly left the court. Ludmilla, still clear about what the Boss was trying to accomplish, drove back to the office with her junior associate equally sullen and absent.

CHAPTER 15

JEFFERSON OKITO

The first trial delay brought the beginning of the actual trial proceedings to the first week of December after the festive Thanksgiving weekend. The trial will start on Monday December 5, 2016. It was partly cloudy in Raleigh, North Carolina, but the summer weather was still lingering on with the temperature still projected in mid-90-degree Fahrenheit. But this did not prevent Judge Leighton-Garver's Court from being fully packed. Her court was in the imposing tall building of the US District Court for the Eastern District of North Carolina on 310 New Bern Avenue. Reverend Patrick Chibere, "Papa Chi", Elder Pastor of the Raleigh Metropolitan Church of Our Savior, had harangued, during the Thanksgiving sermons, his congregation of Congolese immigrants to come to show their support for Charlotte Keregi in the lawsuit filed against Adamas Kagita, a presumed warlord in the Eastern DRC. Most of the church congregants fled from that region of DRC to come to Raleigh. Charlotte was not keen on the noisy presence of her church people. She failed to discourage "Papa Chi" from inviting so many people to the trial proceedings. She was aware of the strict court appearance that Judge Leighton-Garver imposed in her court. Reverend "Papa Chi' ignored Charlotte's advice.

Judge Leighton-Garver was surprised to see so many people in her court. She had underestimated the importance of the trial proceedings for these immigrants she never met before in most of legal undertakings. She did not expect to see a packed court for a trial she was inclined to expedite to a quick resolution. She did not indulge Mr. O'Grady, nor the lead defense lawyers over the ramifications of the case in front of her. She assumed that all she needed to do was to adhere to strict Judge conduct as in any court business. The packed court attendance disturbed her. She quickly invited the DA, and the lead defense lawyers to understand why her court was packed. Mr. O'Grady informed her of the deep and great interest that these immigrants have in this trial.

Judge Leighton-Garver decided then to secure her court with a presence of about ten court police agents stationed in every crucial corner of the court. She was finally ready to start the trial proceeding after sitting the jury which has been selected as neutral as possible, ensuring that no African immigrants were to be members.

The trial, presided by Judge Leighton-Garver, included about ten members of the defense team including Jefferson Okito and eight members of the District Attorney Office including Charlotte Keregi seated next to Ludmilla Garrov. An associate lawyer from the defense team gave the opening statement.

"Members of the Jury, we intend to show that this case is a case of mistaken identity that has grown into a case of violation of the basic inalienable rights of freedom of speech and expression, freedom of religion and conscience, freedom of assembly, and the right to equal protection before the law, rights that the prosecution wants to deny the accused, a case of unlawful persecution of the accused on basis of mountain of hearsay, a case which should be quickly dismissed on grounds of resting on a grumbling slope of sands. Members of the Jury, we implore you to stop this masquerade of justice as quickly as possible by dismissing this terrible waste of judicial energy and time. We should be better than this. Thank you!"

Ludmilla rose to give the Prosecution Opening Statement:

"Members of the Jury, we intend to awaken your conscience about something very important about this case. How would you like to live next to a person such as the accused with a despicable past of thousand murders, rapes, thefts, plundering on a scale rivaling those committed during the last second world war? Would you live next to that person? I don't think so! The only remedy for such an accused is either reminded to jail for the rest of his life or deported from your neighborhood, from North Carolina, from the US so not to risk suffering the same brutal crimes the many people who came to witness this trial have suffered back home …"

At that instant Judge Leighton-Garver screamed at Ludmilla from the bench:

"Counsel, I would not tolerate such inflammatory language in my court. And I would join the members of the Jury to disregard the counsel's opening statement. I am inviting both bench teams to my chamber. Bailiff, please get the members of the jury evacuated to a secure conference room."

The Judge got up and walked quickly to her office followed by Mr. O'Grady, Ludmilla, the lead defense attorney, and the associate lawyer who delivered the defense opening statement. After they were seated and the Judge distributed cold water in plastic bottles, she took a long sip and stared at the window for a minute reflecting on what she was going to say. Then she faced the lawyers.

"This would be the last time I would make this statement. I have been very flexible and kind, letting both teams run the proceedings in a consensual manner. To tell you the truth I underestimate the impacts of this case on the community at hand. I did not expect so many people to attend the trial proceedings. But here we are, and we must manage these proceedings. I would not tolerate any disturbance of any kind in my court. I must remind you that the accused is presumed innocent until proven guilty beyond the shadow of any doubt. That is our norm. So, I would not tolerate any inflammatory language during the proceedings, and you know very well where such language will lead us, to court disturbances we will regret. I would not tolerate any inflammatory language and the next time I heard this I would clear the court. Your sole recipients of court statements are the members of the Jury and the court staff, me including, not the assembly out there. Am I clear and understood now?"

Ludmilla raised her hand," Your Honor, I am very sorry to have caused such a uproar. I wanted to match the defense opening statement. I must have gone overboard. My sincere apologies, Your Honor!"

"Counsel, my statement is for everybody here. I can tell the dynamics of the court. I am sending a message to all of you. Let's be civil about the trial proceedings. Let's go back there now in an orderly way. Thank you!"

The Judge led the way out of her chamber followed by the defense team and last the DA. As they were about to get out Judge chamber, Mr. O'Grady slowed down, turned to his protegee, and whispered, "You did great, keep it up!"

As soon as the members regained their seats, the Judge restarted the proceedings by inviting Jefferson Okito to the stand. The bailiff asked him to restate his legal name and address and to swear on the Bible that all that he was about to say true and nothing but the truth. He did it. The same associate lawyer who read the defense opening statement rose to start his line of questioning.

"Good morning, Sir, for my benefit can yo state again your name?"

"My name is Jefferson. Okito."

"When were you born and where?"

"I was born on August 4, 1968, in the town of Mbarara. This is a city in the Western Region of Uganda. I was born in the Kamukizi Division of the town which counts five more other divisions; Kakoba, Nyamitanga, Biharwe, Nyakayojo and Kakiika."

"Can you talk about your family?"

"I was the second boy in a family of five including three boys and two sisters. My father's name was Cyrill Okito, and my mother was born as Brenda Bagari."

"Can you talk about life in Mbarara, what you like to do there, any particular hobby of interest?"

"Life in Mbarara was very simple. My father was essentially a handy man working in large cattle farms surrounding the town. My father and my mother came from the Banyankole tribe which is mainly cattle raising. Though from cattle raising family, my best hobby was fishing. I loved going to see a family uncle living along the river Ruizi, every chance I got to escape the city life of Mbarara to go fishing. When I grew older, I got a few friends to go fishing on lake Kachera in Lake Mburo National Park."

"Oh, I see, who were your friends you grew up with then!"

"Well, I fondly remember Xavier Bhatia and Andre Muinga. Those two were my best friends. We grew together through high school years. We started parting our ways later when I went to work as a supervisor for one of the largest cattle farms in the Nord area of Mbarara. I never saw Muinga again. I heard he died during the civil war that toppled Idi Amin. I stayed in touch with my good friend Bhatia until about two or three years before leaving Uganda. Xavier Bhatia had entered politics and was doing well for himself in Kampala.'

"Any girlfriend or girlfriends!"

"I rather say girlfriends after high school. The one I adored was Geraldine Birogo. Gerro, I loved to call her. She was the best girlfriend I could have married if I did not get into the trading business. She did not appreciate the constant traveling of trading business. But I could not stay still in that business always on the road from DRC border to the ports of Dar-Es-Salam in Tanzania or Mombassa in Kenya. Always on the road to make money trading, always trading. Another girl I remembered fondly was Manlisa Kasiva. She was much younger but a bit precocious. I am not afraid to say that she initiated me into sexual relationships. She lived in the same area where my uncle was along the river Ruizi. I must say that I went there as often as I did to be with her. I enjoyed our long many walks along the river, our carefree swimming at the edge of the river and our nightly escapades. I stopped going back to the area when I learned that she became pregnant indulging so many other young men.'

"Still, you got married right!"

"Yes, but my current wife was from my third marriage. When you are on the road all the time, no woman would trust you to stay in the marriage. Soon or later, they leave or split. I married twice before this last marriage. I had three kids from the first, two from the second. They are back home in Uganda. A bit too painful to talk about."

"Why was it difficult to maintain a home life when you were making so much money. Can you delegate the supervision and stay home?"

"That is easy to say if we had the same road system you have in the US. You know what when I came to the US, I tried to see if I could resume my road running business. I rode with a truck driver from Jacksonville, Florida to Green Bay, Wisconsin in the spring. It was beautiful but no encounters like what I faced back in Uganda. It was very easy on the clock. Back home, you can never know when you will be back in days, weeks, or months. It was always a one-way adventure. No woman would wait for you. You know that and you indulge whoever you meet on the road. When you come home, you find nobody waiting for you. And you move on. It was not easy. But when you are so engaged to the till, you make so much money, you don't want to leave. You start practicing what they sing back home, 'a woman at every port', or 'a woman at every major gas station'."

"Let me ask you a very important question to clear the air for everybody in this court: in your trading business, have you ever cross the DRC border to go in the war torn regions of North Kivu, South Kivu or Ituri?"

"Never, never, never.! In the trading business, in what you call war torn regions, you cannot operate if you don't know how to use guns, machetes, of these killer tools. In other words, you must someone who knows how to kill or get killed. You must be a man of military background. That was the reality of it. You cannot learn it. You must be trained in it. You must practice all the time. At the end you become a killer, a murderer with no respect for human being, with no respect for life. I never joined any military group even during the time of the worst dictatorship of Idi Amin. I stayed clear of that. I am being persecuted because I developed a strategy to profit from those who lived with guns, machetes, and tools to kill. My strategy was simple, you of military background go in the field and bring back for me something of value, gold, coltan, coffee, tea, I will wait for you at the border town, I will buy what you will bring back at a premium and will sell it abroad. That is, I will put them first in the warehouses at the border and search for buyers abroad, then I will bring them in huge trucking caravans to the ports, mount them in boats for delivery as requested. That was my business. Of course, the military people understood the strategy and started to muscle me out. Finally, they kicked me out to take over the business. Was it dangerous, yes, was it risky, yes, but every business is risky? A business without risk is no business, in my opinion again!"

"Well thank you, many folks in this free enterprise society of ours, will understand and appreciate what you just say. But tell me for clarification, did you need the cover of powerful military people to move your huge trucking caravans from DRC border to the ports and through two or three countries? Please explain how you manage it."

"Well, the situation in war torn areas of DRC required military people protection, generals or colonels of various armies investing in the areas. They could be Congolese, Rwandan, Ugandan and many war lords from countless well-armed militias. When the merchandises leave DRC, you did not need the military cover at the same level as before the border. The cover amounts to bribes you provide the police force in Uganda, Rwanda, Kenya, or Tanzania. To ensure that your trucking caravans are not stopped for a long time on the road, or inspection sites, or border towns. This police supervision can be done sometime by military people or police force. That is the reason I have mentioned that at least in Uganda military officers are most of time leading police supervision. They know and understand better the logistics that people like me are engaged in. If they become less satisfied with the way you share the bribe money along the way, they would start causing problems with your logistics operation. That is what happened with me."

At that instant, the associate lawyer requested a lunch recess. He informed the court that he wanted to come back to show a video demonstrating the logistics operations that Jefferson Okito had mounted from DRC border to the ports of Mombassa and Dar-Es-Salam. Judge Leighton-Garver granted the recess. However, it was remarkably noted that the morning attendance was cut in half by the time the Judged granted the recess. It was past two pm. Most church congregants, that Reverend "Papa Chi" has invited, have left the court. The court far back benches were empty. These congregants were not happy with two things. They were increasingly irritated by the favorable line of questioning of Jefferson Okito alias Adamas Kagita. They could not stand to see the accused having fun, enjoying the line of questioning and at time smiling while conversing with the defense lawyer. They also noticed that there was no visible or loud objection from the prosecution to the strange line of questioning. The prosecution bench was awfully quiet. The congregants assumed that the fierce admonition from the Judge against the prosecution opening statement has tempered and intimidated the prosecution. They readily concluded that this was an instance of bias that did not look good for Charlotte Keregi's case. Few congregants left messages with "Papa Chi" expressing that feeling. The Reverend shared the same feeling with Charlotte when they broke for lunch at a nearby restaurant. Charlotte did not agree with that assessment but had no way, no tools to push back. In fact, she had noticed the resignation from Ludmilla when she came back from the early meeting that the Judge after she had interrupted her opening statement which she thought was very powerful. Charlotte has noticed the same lack of dynamism, the same resignation from the entire prosecution bench listening to the happy conversation that the defense lawyer was having with Adamas. Still during the long entire morning proceedings, she was encouraged by the furtive notes taking that Ludmilla was exchanging with her subordinate junior associate and Mr. O'Grady, who at times sent them back for more editing or simply kept them as satisfactory. Charlotte had no idea what they were exchanging but assumed they were pieces they would use for objections later. But there was no objection follow-up, none, so much so that she finally concurred with and confided to the Reverend:

"You are right, I did not hear any objection! That is very strange! I don't understand the prosecution strategy. I guess we must wait and see. I can assure you they worked so hard. I have seen it."

The afternoon became even more alarming for the prosecution, Charlotte, and the Reverend. They were shocked to see the whole afternoon proceedings dedicated to a video presentation by the defense team of the logistics operations of Jefferson Okito company. The video lasted two hours and half from three pm. It was a clever presentation of what Jefferson Okito tried to explain about the ways his company received the products from war torn DRC at the border towns, packed them in his warehouses, mounted them into the double or triple deck trucking caravans and left the warehouses and take the different roads that left DRC border through Mbarara, Kampala along the great lake Victoria going Est to Kenya or through Mbarara going South to Tanzania all the way to Dar-Es-Salam through Tarangire National Park. The proceedings became a lovely video distraction for the members of Jury enjoying an afternoon viewing of various African parks with sights of lions and various wild animals. Some members of Jury took time to get an afternoon nap. Judge Leighton-Garver struggled herself not to fall asleep until she excused herself to her chamber for thirty minutes. Everybody struggled to follow the narrator of the video when he navigated from Swahili to English and some time to local dialects. The longer the presentation lasted, it became obvious to the Judge and the prosecution that the defense team was eating proceedings time with the video for lack of any other presentation. After about an hour and thirty minutes, the exasperated judge halted the video presentation, she called both teams to her bench to find out if there were any more scenes of major interest to the case, the defense insisted that the whole video was of incremental interest for the accused defense. The Judge relented and the video continued until the end. It was five thirty pm. The Judge adjourned the proceedings to the entire court relief.

The prosecution was equally relieved to note that nowhere in the video there was any indication of Jefferson Okito company name inscription.

The name could not be found anywhere, on the trucking caravans, on the warehouses, on the office buildings where the trucks were maintained, nowhere. The junior associate added another significant remark. During the entire video presentation there was no picture of Jefferson Okito anywhere in the company premises, in the offices, in the warehouses, around or inside the trucks. It was quite unusual that the owner or the presumed managing director of the company could not post a single picture in the video presentation of the company.

When Charlotte got to her car to go home, she was surprised to see Mr. O'Grady approaching her and he said:

"Don't be fooled by the theatrics the defense team put out today. We were monitoring all the charades they presented today. We gave them the latitude and the impression of being civil. Wait and see when we will start challenging all the nonsenses, and ridiculous lies they gave in the court today. They will beg us to stop pushing them hard. Go home and rest. We will see you tomorrow. Good night, Charlotte."

Charlotte thanked the DA and regained her smiling face on the way home.

CHAPTER 16

ADAMAS KAGITA

The following day, the court attendance decreased further than it was at the end of the previous day's session. Judge Leighton-Garver cut the number of the court police agents to half. She expedited the routine calls of the court. She requested Jefferson Okito back on the stand and asked the prosecution to start its rebuttal, its line of questioning. Ludmilla rose and approached the Members of the Jury.

"May it please the court, Members of the Jury. We were presented yesterday a fantastic biography of a Mister Jefferson Okito who, I am afraid to tell you, never existed in Uganda nor anywhere in this world until he materialized on May 19, 2009, in the Immigration box of the International Airport of Raleigh in North Carolina. I would help you to understand this if you follow me diligently as I approach the bench to talk to … Sir can you for my benefit, the benefit of this court restates your legal name?"

"My name if Jefferson Okito?"

"Are you sure that is your name?"

"Yes, Maam, that is my name?"

"For the second time, are you sure that is your name?"

"Your Honor, Counsel is badgering the witness" the defense lawyer said loudly,

"Please, Counsel, ask one question and do not repeat the question." The Judge intervened.

"I am sorry, Your Honor, I would ask the question again for the last time, are you sure that is your name?"

"Yes, that is my name."

'All right, so you said. I will take you back to what you said when your Counsel asked you and I quote "Can you talk about life in Mbarara, what you like to do there, any particular hobby of interest?" Do you remember what you said. Let me remind what you said: "When I grew older, I got a few friends to go fishing on lake Kachera in Lake Mburo National Park." Do you remember that answer?"

'Yes, I do!'

"And your counsel enchained with this question: "Oh, I see, who were your friends you grew up with then!" And you came back with the following answer:

"Well, I fondly remember Xavier Bhatia and Andre Muinga. Those two were my best friends. We grew together through high school years. We started parting our ways later when I went to work as a supervisor for one of the largest cattle farms in the Nord area of Mbarara. I never saw Muinga again. I heard he died during the civil war that toppled Idi Amin. I stayed in touch with my good friend Bhatia until about two or three years before leaving Uganda. Xavier Bhatia had entered politics and was doing well for himself in Kampala.'

"Did I quote your answer correctly?"

"Yes, Maam?"

"But that was funny, I don't know if your brain was playing tricks with you, or you did not quite remember what you have spent so many days cramming in your brain, and it started coming out a bit jumbled when your Counsel asked you that question. Did your counsel get your brain mixed up with your actual identity? Are you following me?"

"No at all, what are you talking about?"

"I will be glad to do this. When I said it was funny, I meant it. Do you know why, well it is that simple: the two friends that you fondly remembered, Xavier Bhatia and Andre Muinga, were your friends. I wholeheartedly agree with you there. But unfortunately, they were your friends you went fishing with you, not in Uganda but in DRC in a town called Butembo where you were born and named Damien Kagita, the same man we have accused in this case named Adamas Kagita. Tell me how you can remember the same friends with the same

149

names in a different town, in a different country. I know why, when you became comfortable yesterday, you went back to your primary identity of Adamas Kagita and spilling your identity references. Am I correct?"

"I don't think so, these are my friends I have known in Uganda, I have never been in DRC, never!"

"By the way, in your follow-up answer you were also correct to have Xavier Bhatia who went into politics, but, not in Kampala in Uganda, but we have found a Xavier Bhatia as a "Depute National" from Butembo in the Parliament in, are you ready, Kinshasa in DRC. Furthermore, Andre Muinga was also killed, not during the civil war that toppled Idi Amin in Uganda, but in the civil war that toppled Mobutu Sesse Seko in DRC. Did I not say that your brain was playing tricks with you on the stand. "

"I am sorry, Maam, you have a case of mistaken identity for me and my friends as well."

"Don't you worry, I got more of the same from your own statements yesterday. Let us talk about your girlfriends. Members of the Jury, here I must call your attention about a behavior that the accused I address as Adamas Kagita has shown throughout his life in relationship with women. Again, he bungled the presentation of his biography, transporting events that happened in DRC to Uganda. Yes, he mentioned Manlisa Kasiva. He called her his girlfriend. He designated her as a precocious girl, in common language, he meant that Manlisa Kasiva was a nymphomaniac girl, she liked to have multiple sexual partners. He added that he stopped seeing her when he learned that she became pregnant sleeping around with many boys in that area of river Ruizi. In a twist of tongue, he confessed that he enjoyed taking long walks with her, swimming care-free with her, meaning that they swim naked together most of time, and he added they had a lot of nightly escapades. I don't need to tell you or explain to you what two young people of opposite do in nightly escapades. In summary, he gave a portrait of Manlisa Kasiva as a very bad girl, a sexually active girl he enjoyed going out with until she got pregnant. But ladies and gentlemen of the jury, the accused started that description of Manlisa Kasiva by introducing her as a much younger girl. By how much we don't know. Our research has also identified a Manlisa not in Uganda but in DRC, not somewhere along the river Ruizi, but outside the town of Butembo, in a village where he loved to spend vacation by his uncle small farm. There was a Manlisa in the household, a niece of his uncle's wife. Here his memory got her name twisted. Manlisa last name was not Kasiva, but Kavisa. Close enough. When our Romeo started indulging Manlisa, she was indeed much younger by six years. The accused was sixteen and Manlisa was nine years old. The accused ran off from his uncle's farm and never went back there because he was caught by his uncle's wife raping the poor nine-year-old Manlisa. He was chased after by his uncle who searched him armed with a machete. He disappeared in the bush, and it took him two days to reach his parents' home in Butembo. He disappeared again for a week in town when his uncle showed up at his parents' home searching for him. He never crossed that uncle until he passed away. Now do you know who shared that despicable episode of Adamas Kagita, well no other his best friend Xavier Bhatia. Do you remember this story?"

"Absolutely not, this is also another made up story of grave mistaken identity about me and Manlisa Kasiva!"

"All right, I must still submit that you are not good at getting your stories straight, at remembering what the defense team has tried unsuccessfully to cram in your head to make you Jefferson Okito that you are not. You will see that I am not done yet. Ladies and gentlemen of the jury, I need to also debunk the drama about what the accused had fondly called Gerro, Geraldine Birogo. This one entered faithfully into the strict criminal journey the accused has traced after he graduated from high school. By the way we have all your genuine academic references when you completed what they call in DRC secondary school, or high school here in the US. Back there all students must take the secondary school State Exam to go to university. Members of the jury, Adamas took that exam along with his friend Xavier Bhatia. Both decided to go to the big regional university that was in the big urban center of Kisangani. Adamas wanted to take law studies while Xavier wanted to major in Construction engineering by concentrating in mathematics, physics, and chemistry. Their different academic paths eventually separated them, each following different social interests. Adamas's path took a different nonacademic path. He started spending more time in social evening gatherings chasing after female students. These social evening gatherings also attracted the big town well-off older folks and big shots ready to splurge on younger female students. Adamas quickly discovered that he could make a lot of money by acting as intermediary between the beautiful young female students and their older pretenders who prefer to indulge them secretly away in the confines of rented rooms or apartments, leaving the preliminary contacts to intermediaries. Adamas excelled in this pimp game but had no personal residence where to prepare the female students to change from regular academic girls to sexy attractive high class call girls. Soon enough he found a young army Major, named Bernard Molekeni, with a decent apartment in a secluded corner downtown to accommodate his business. The army major was a nephew to the town army garrison commander a General named Ogpado, in other words in the army culture of the times, another spoiled brat. Adamas and Major B, as he liked to be called, agreed to share the bounty of the intermediary pimp business. The young major spent most of his time in the military camp and left Adamas conduct the business literally unsupervised. The young major will show up on Thursday or Friday evening to spend the whole weekend at home. This arrangement got Adamas to gradually skip both campus residency and attending law study classes. By the end of his first academic year, Adamas was no longer a college student. In addition, he would no longer entertain his friend Xavier warnings and they simply stopped seeing each other. It was at that time that Geraldine Birogo joined the stable. It was very difficult to understand why a girl from a prominent family in town would join a call girl joint. Compared to most other girls, she was not desperate or in need of money or goods. She had all she needed at home and even more. Her family had owned large tracks of real estate in town for years. The family also owned two major cars and trucks dealerships. The family name Birogo was synonym with health. When Gerro joined the stable, she was careful to entertain any older client. She made sure that her clients were out of town folks. After a while, she convinced Adamas that she would no longer indulge the rich old folks, she would become his permanent staid-at-home lover while she would supply the stable with better and sexier girls, she knew from the university campus. But she recruited younger girls from the town. Their age ranged from thirteen to seventeen years old. These immature girls became pregnant before long. A big scandal broke out when three of them died during abortion attempts by an unlicensed medical assistant."

"Mr. Kagita, do you remember this scandal?"

"Not at all, I never lived nor studied in that town, … Kisangani."

"Members of the jury, I must refresh your memory while I am navigating the increasingly perilous criminal journey of Mr. Kagita, allow me to give you a good perspective of the DRC country at that time. DRC, then called Zaire, was entering the last ten years of the administration of the president dictator, Marechal Mobutu Sesse Seko. That is the time the central government started to disappear, its authority collapsed, the economy confronted a galloping inflation like for the time of Germany Wagner Republic before Hitler came to power, when to buy a loaf of bread you need to produce a bag of hundred thousand of Deutch marks. It was the same with its "Zaire" paper money. It was also the time when the dictator Mobutu unable and incapable to address a conflagration of national issues, retired to his sumptuous compound in his village named Gbadolite near the Sudan border. The compound was very near an airport built to receive international jet flights. It was the time the DRC-Zaire population languished in bottomless misery, an infernal economic catastrophe. With the complete collapse of central government authority, the provincial authority was literally confiscated by military garrison commander. It was no different for the town of Kisangani. General Ogpado, uncle to major Molekeni, effectively took over running the town. He decided to stifle the prostitution scandal very quickly. He called a meeting with Gerro parents and the elders of Birogo family. The meeting closed with astute agreement. Major Molekeni and Gerro will be removed and extracted from any legal pursuit. Both will disappear. Major Molekeni will be immediately transferred to a very remote military garrison at the town of Djugu at the extreme northeast border with Uganda, while Gerro will leave DRC to study abroad under an assumed new name at the University of Strasburg in France. Poor unconnected Adamas will bear the full brunt of the legal prosecution. For the first time in his life, Adamas learned about the power of social connection, the iniquity of legally applied injustice, the abusive political power. He was brought in front of a panel of three corrupt magistrates who deliberated for less than two days to declare him guilty and give him a six years sentence. "

"And there is more to this episode. The next morning after he was sentenced, Adamas was awaken at about five thirty in the morning by a group of heavily armed military men. They handcuffed him and threw him in the back of a jeep. Adamas took the ride lying on the floor of the jeep trunk surrounded by armed military people who rested their feet all over his body. Adamas was certain that he was going to be killed to pay the price of the three dead young girls. The jeep took the direction of the town military large base. And it stopped next to the shooting range where military recruits practice shooting all kinds of military guns. Adamas said his last prayers. He was then dragged to the office of the commander Ogpado, who he had never met. They made him seat to wait for him from about six am until he showed up at around ten thirty.am. By that time, Adamas has exhausted all the last prayers he could think of waiting for his death in the shooting range next door."

When obviously tired of waiting, Adamas started to doze off, he was then awakened by a stern salute by the armed people guarding him and welcoming the General who dismissed all of them after they had removed his handcuffs.

"Young man, you made a mess of a lot of things in town. Did you see what is happening outside? You belong to the shredded trees that the recruits are pulverizing out there. Yet, my stupid nephew said that you are good in business. Is that true?"

"Yes, Sir!"

"Now, I have a deal for you, and you cannot refuse. You know why, I am the boss of this town, and everybody does what I want. All right, here is my proposal, my nephew who is gone now because of your stupidity, used to run a racket of military provisions for me. I need somebody I can trust to run it now. I believe you are the right person to do this job. Now I see you wondering how, why! Well, he said that, and I agreed, the racket was becoming a bit too apparent for a lot of people to see and to report it. He suggested that the racket must be run from an invisible place like well the jail. That is where you come. I will protect you to run the racket from the jail. I will provide you with a team to come and go with the goods as instructed. You can even resume your prostitution ring with trusted mature girls if you want. That also will be protected. And you can run whatever other rackets that don't compromise me. That will be all right. There are conditions and terms for this job. If you do it well, I can assure you, you will be out of jail in about two years with probation. That is my offer. What do you think?"

"It sounds very good, but do you trust me on this?"

"Bernard trusts you on this, I don't know you. His words, my word. Fair enough?"

"It is a deal!"

"Members of the jury, this is how Mr. Kagita made the jump in his criminal career. He was duly recompensed two years as promised when the military conditions deteriorated in Eastern DRC and many military garrisons were moved there including the people under General Ogpado who was moved to the military garrison of Beni-Butembo, Adamas's hometown. General Ogpado already knew that his next assignment would put him in the center of the logistics for trafficked minerals leaving the area to Uganda. He was bound to make a lot of bribe money more than the racket of military provisions in Kisangani. He jumped on the opportunity. This time he reunited Major Molekeni, his nephew, with his old buddy Adamas in the area."

"Mr. Kagita, if you are wondering where this detailed episode came from, well it came from your old friend Xavier Bhatia. Remember when he was on his way, to complete his academic degree in Civil Engineering at the prestigious university of Makerere in Kampala, Uganda. You spent a whole week sharing this episode. When he graduated with a Master in Civil Engineering, Xavier could not come back home with the civil wars raging then. He went to work in South Africa."

"What else do you want me to do to refresh your memory, Mr. Kagita."

"You don't have to in your story of mistaken identity."

"All right, there was another story you told Xavier, do you remember? I must refresh your memory also."

"I am getting tired of stories you are bringing now on Xavier's account, well he is not here to confirm these stories, isn't he?

"Don't worry we will get to that confirmation very soon. Yes, I am on the roll, Members of the jury, during the same week Mr. Kagita confided to Xavier about what he would do to his uncle who threatened him with a machete after he raped that young girl, the niece to his uncle wife. Do you remember what you told him?"

"Another story, another speculation!"

"Absolutely not, but you said; By the time you will come back from Uganda, you will learn that I have taken care of that uncle. Now that I am about to become Adamas, the town Danger, I would be without mercy, I would pump as many bullets as possible in that uncle's stupid brain to remind him to never mess with me, never. Do you remember that? This is important when we travel the murderous journey of Adamas Kagita and we will learn what would happen to the uncle, we will learn the sadistic revenge that Adamas had promised Xavier. Still cannot remember this!"

"No!"

"Very well, Your Honor, I want to request a lunch recess at this time." It was almost two pm.

"So granted!"

When Ludmilla rejoined the prosecution bench, Charlotte was smiling at her. A sign of great approval and admiration for a job well done. Mr. O'Grady shared the same adulation:

"Now you see what I meant when I said that we are going to use his own words to challenge his status. I told you that nobody can deny his or her past forever. Yo have worn him verbally. Wait to see how he will react with the video presentation this afternoon."

"I wish I trusted that strategy from the start. I had my doubts but the more I talked, it makes more sense. Thank you so much, Mr. O'Grady."

"You are welcome!"

When the trial proceedings resumed, Jefferson Okito alias Adamas Kagita was called back to the stand. Ludmilla took over the line of questioning where she left off.

"Mr. Kagita, I am sorry, Mr. Okito, what was the name of the company you owned in Uganda?"

"Who wants to know?"

"I do, Your Honor!"

"Please, answer the question!"

"My company went by many different names depending on where my trucking caravans were on the road, in Uganda, it was Okito Unlimited, in Kenya it was Jeffo Lanes, in Tanzania it became Bagati Express."

"Were these names legally registered in each specific country?"

"Of course?"

"Ladies and Gentlemen of the Jury, yesterday the defense team entertained us with a beautiful two hour and half safari show video. The defense told us that we must suffer watching what they called the logistics operations of Mr. Jefferson Okito's company. We just heard the accused telling us the different names of his business company. But I don't remember seeing any of these company names anywhere in the safari video. I did not see these names at what were supposed to be the warehouses at the border, I did not see any name inscription on the truck, the double or triple deck caravans. There were no names on the trucks in Kenya nor in Tanzania. Now you can allow me. Mr. Adamas just had another double take in his brain. He just gave his Congolese mother's name Bagati to the company name while in operating in Tanzania. What a big slip! Furthermore, if we can go back to the safari video, Members of Jury, I must remind you about another very telling point. There was no picture of the owner in the famous safari video. Would you not think that the proud owner of the enterprise would show a picture of himself and his staff, and his drivers when he was celebrating the logistics operations of his company. That escaped Adamas Kagita who never owned any logistics operations in Uganda, Never?"

"Now, after yesterday's safari video, we worked almost all night to provide you, Ladies and Gentlemen, a video of Adamas Kagita in DRC from infancy until he came from the two years jail in Kisangani. We want to show the progressive descent to hell, to the life of war lord before he crossed paths with our distinguished witness Charlotte Keregi. If anything, this video must refresh a lot of memory for the accused Adamas Kagita who must remain on the stand."

The video started with a family picture of Kagita family with his father Cyrill Kagita, his mother Brenda Bagati, his two younger sisters Helen and Magida Kagita. Adamas closed his eyes when Magida photo was zoomed on the screen on purpose. The narrator said that Magida was born and grew up with a lot of challenges for his parents. She was finally diagnosed as retarded. Magida was probably the only woman figure that Adamas had shown or extended a lot of affection growing up. He could not look at her. The next batch of photos showed his friends: Andre Muinga and Xavier Bhatia when they were about sixteen. There were pictures of them playing soccer and going fishing. This set was followed with a newspaper clip of his uncle's picture, how he was found dead along the same river he used to go fishing. The photo showed his uncle's body riddled with machine gun bullets. The high school graduation scenes came afterwards showing the three friends enjoying the graduation party with other friends. The narrator then started to explain the University of Kisangani episode. It started with Xavier's company then Major Molekeni came in with a group of call girls in extravagant sexy dresses. Before long Geraldine "Gerro" Birogo was seen lying on the big sofa playing seductively with three other very young girls. Next there was Adamas on the court stand facing a panel of three judges. The following set of pictures showed the trio of General Ogpado, Major Molekeni and Adamas having a great time in a bar in either town of Beni or Butembo. The video stopped with a beautiful picture of Adamas's parents with his two sisters at a wedding. The scene was remarkable in that his sister Helene is holding Magida very tight. With the zoomed family still picture flooding the court, Ludmilla stood up and went to the stand where Adamas was covering his eyes and could no longer look at this family photo. His hands still covering his eyes were trembling. He looked very exhausted and remote as if he was seeing spirits, as if he was going in trance. He could no longer face Ludmilla who knew then that she got him in his worst mental stage and went for the jugular.

"How old was Magida then?"

"I don't remember."

"I cannot hear you!"

"I don't remember>"

"I cannot hear you."

"She passed away after that wedding."

"Who passed away?"

"Magida!"

"Who is Magida?"

"My sister Magida."

"What was her last name?"

"Kagita."

"I cannot hear you."

"Objection, Your Honor, Counsel is badgering the witness!"

"Objection overruled!"

"I cannot hear you."

"Magida Kagita, my sister!"

"Where was that wedding taking place?"

"In Butembo."

"Is Butembo in Uganda?"

"Objection, Your Honor, Counsel is badgering the witness!"

"Objection overruled!"

"No Maam, in DRC, please leave me alone, I am not feeling well, leave … me alone!"

"I cannot hear you!"

"Objection, Your Honor, Counsel is badgering the witness!"

"Objection Sustained! Does the accused need a recess?"

"Leave me alone, I am not feeling well, leave me alone, leave me alone, leave me alone, leave me… leave …."

"Witness is collapsing on the stand, please get the medics right away!"

Judge Leighton-Garver pressed some kind of alarm signal on her desk. In less than two minutes, medics barged into her court with respirator masks and the air flow box on top of a rolling bed. In no time, Adamas was wearing the respirator mask and was wheeled out of the court room. Judge Leighton-Garver yelled orders in her court.

"The court is adjourned and will be in indefinite recess now. Bailiff, please escort the Members of the Jury to the adjoining conference room right away. I will join after I hold a brief conference with the prosecution and defense teams in my chamber. Please join me in my chamber." Judge Leighton was walking ahead and removing her black robe. She took her seat while wiping her face.'

"Woooah, I have never witnessed what happened in court a while ago. I heard the witness was breathing heavily. I knew something was going wrong. I am sorry counsels, I should have stopped the line of questioning sooner. I hope he will come out all right. I tell you what, I don't think we will reconvene tomorrow nor the day after until I get a doctor certified statement that the witness would be able to bear the brunt of another line of questioning. Now let me find out from the defense team, which way you believe we need to go after the witness has literally and virtually abandoned his Jefferson Okito legal name. He has reassumed his old Adamas Kagita identity. Where do we go from here, that is my question?"

"Your Honor, after the tragic scene we have all witnessed, I would tend to agree with your assumption. But the witness is the only one in need to reconcile his identity. He is on his way to the hospital, and we will interview him later when he would feel better. I want to request a week or more of recess. We will reconvene then to share our next legal step."

"And what does the DA say about the defense proposal?"

"We certainly will wait and see what the defense would come up with after the recess>"

"All right, I am proposing that we reconvene in a week and half. I will keep you posted about the witness health evolution. Thank you and good evening. Sorry, the Members of the Jury are waiting for my statement about the next legal step. I really thank you all for indulging me in this tragic scene."

Members of prosecution and defense teams left the Judge's chamber under alarming shock. None of these lawyers could have predicted this turn of events. The defense team was in a worse position. The lead lawyers expected that the identity trial phase was going to involve slowly. They expected Jefferson Okito to prevail under the assaults of prosecution. They were not prepared to see their client crumbled like a two-bit mangoes' thief in an open farm market They did not expect the imposing Jefferson Okito, a purported war lord of frightening posture to collapse in the witness stand after a mondain review of his family portrait. They were now realizing the biggest mistake they had made. Unlike Ludmilla from the prosecution team, the defense team did not dwell on, nor ever asked him much about his life from infancy and all these steps marking his progression into the criminal journey to war lord status. In front the members of the Jury, they missed the marks that Ludmilla managed to establish so eloquently and persuasively. The lead attorneys knew that they had to cut their losses fast. The health debacle was now a great opportunity to change the defense strategy.

The prosecution team left the court very quickly, avoiding showing any sign of remarkable triumph from its successful presentation. The prosecution team looked sad and was sympathizing with the defense team over the fate of the accused. On the District Attorney discrete signal, the prosecution team left the court to get back together at the office.

As soon as they were gathered in the DA conference room along with their Charlotte Keregi, the main witness, the DA Boss closed the conference room door.

"This was a very much excellent teamwork. I am very proud of all your contributions. As I predicted, there was no way that Jefferson Okito would have survived the preparation that we have accumulated to bring about the identity of Adamas Kagita that he wanted to deny. However, I did not expect the end to come so quickly and this fast before bringing up the core of the accusation from our main witness Charlotte. My theory is this, there always would come a moment when people living double or triple identities would fall into the trap of reconciling the multiple identity lies against their true identity. It is no different from the work we do here when we push the accused to reconcile with the act he or she has committed, when we push the accused to enter a guilty plea. I have told each one of you here present that this is the core of our work in the District Attorney Office. Everything we do here must get us to that station. If we don't, then we have failed in our mission. It is as simple as that. That is why I must thank Ludmilla for having so cleverly led Jefferson Okito to get rid of his fake identity to wear Adamas Kagita's identity in a tragic moment. Now we must remember we would not have gotten to that end without the incredible voluminous testimony that our very dear witness Charlotte Keregi has assembled here, and that Ludmilla had arranged and filtered with utmost legal professional care. I congratulate both of you."

"I don't have to tell you that our work in this case is far from over. Yes, we have taken an important step in litigating this case. But we have not won the case yet. We did not get Adamas Kagita held accountable for his despicable war lor acts in DRCi It is only then that we would be able to get him to pay for these deeds, either getting him expelled from the US or getting him imprisoned in a jail in the US. That is our legal judicial goal, remember it. Believe me or not, it is not going to be easy. First, we must get Adamas Kagita in good health to be able to come back to the stand. God only know what the defense team would try to push that next step. After we have crossed that step, I know that the defense team would not let us get Adamas to confess his crimes. The defense will raise all kinds of legal procedural venues including invoking CIPA or Classified Information Protect Act to hide and cover Adamas's background and the reasons why the government allowed him to enter the US. Ladies and Gentlemen, we still got a lot to do."

.

CHAPTER 17

D.C. AGENDA

The next morning, Mr. O'Grady refused to pick up multiple calls that her niece made from Washington D.C. starting from eight am. The DA's instructions were clear; he would not pick her niece's calls until after ten am, after he had his morning breakfast with two cups of coffee, and after receiving his morning progress report about various pending cases he managed. He was done with both tasks by nine fifteen am. He then started reviewing CIPA instructions until ten am. Id did not have to call, Gwendolyn called.

"Good morning, Uncle O'Grady. I hope I am not disturbing your breakfast this morning. I heard that your Russian protegee blew away our man all the way to a coma at the hospital."

"I am sorry to hear that. I did not get any update from Judge Leighton-Garver, the only reliable authority I expect to get reliable medical updates about Mr. Adamas Kagita. What a waste, your high-priced lawyers. When I think you are paying them twelve hundred dollars an hour from our people hard earned tax money, I must cry "what a waste". And they could not get Jefferson Okito to artfully cram his own fake identity in his own dull head. What a pity! Did your big shoes lawyers tell you what a lousy work they did? Did they tell how Jefferson Okito got his own fake life jumbled up, mixed up from one end to another? Did they tell you that they could not prevent the accused war lord to start crying in front of my young protégé you called Russian? She would be seriously offended to be called Russian. She is from the former People Republic of Yugoslavia. She was born in the old capital of Belgrade. A brilliant lawyer from the UNC prestigious law school, thank you!"

"So, we heard she did very well. We heard that she took poor Okito on a steady clever path of removing bit by bit Okito masks. We will be honored to have the Lady in our side."

"You will have to wait in line, I am sorry. She could have joined your big law firms in Manhattan or D.C. straight form law school. She declined because she is going for a higher principled legal career. After the human right abuses, she witnessed when Yugoslavia was being broken apart, she then raised her profile goals. What she is doing now is a tremendous professional building step. She is at the right place and at the right time to grow. I sincerely wished you had benefited from such a training. Unfortunately, you preferred to burn those building blocks and you are now advocating empty mondain goals and pursuits."

"No matter what you think of my career, I had excellent law training at Yale, and my career growth was excellent. Thank you!"

"Indeed, no price paid, no pursuit earned, and I rest my case!"

"Why do you keep insulting your own family professional pedigree, I will never understand it? Are you ashamed of your family name? We are what we are, we have ancestors who prepared our lineage very well. I am proud of it. I would not make any excuse about it. No sir. I was not born poor. I got it. I got more opportunities, more chances than the next bloke. I know that. My family helped me with mountain of references to get me here. I know that. I will never apologize for that. At the same time I never abused these opportunities. Is the next guy more deserving than me to exercise such or such job opportunity, possibly. But I was interviewed for this job, and I was hired on merit. Case closed!"

"Did you hear me, I repeat, no price paid, no pursuit earned?"

"Is it me or our entire family?"

"Our entire family, me included!"

"Oh, I see! Last time I heard that you were elected to be District Attorney of that district of Raleigh County? Did you cheat your way to get elected, Uncle O'Grady?"

"No, I was duly elected! I see that you don't understand my chain of thought. My election to become District Attorney was traced from the time I was born. I did not earn it. It was given to me as an O'Grady. All I have to do was to scratch some steps in the right schools from maternal, elementary, high school, university, and legal assignments and bam I was elected DA! If you don't understand this, you will continue in the same path of no price paid, no pursuit earned until one day you will be seriously tested in an environment where you must earn your pursuit and you will falter. Now do you understand what I am trying to convey to you my dear niece?"

"I hope so, I am still not certain! But uncle O'Grady, if I may ask, what drove you to share that observation today when you said, no price paid, no pursuit earned?"

"Well, I am so glad you got to ask that question. It is relevant to my frame of mind today. You see I sat through two days of trial proceedings this week. I saw a man with an awful past dressed by our government in a straight identity he could not assume. This man struggled for two full days to go along the identity that was not his. He has been rehearsing to be somebody he was not for the past three months. In other words, the government, our government insisted that he wears a mask that the government has chosen for him for whatever reason. Remember what I said, this man had an awful life of war lord, he has done things in life in that part of the world, things you and I would never vouch for near or far from our own family. So, the awful man struggled with the borrowed identity for two days. At the end. after confused and confusing identity missteps, he revealed his true identity and collapsed in overwhelming shame when he dared to deny the most precious memory he had of his retarded sister he loved so much, and so dearly. And guess who were on the opposite sides of that despicable legal scenario, two members of the famous legal family in the state of North Carolina, my own niece on the side of the very government dressing the poor slob into a borrowed identity, and me on the side of the prosecution that legally and cleverly undressed the same slob back into his lifetime war lord criminal identity. Do you recognize your side in this tragedy, in this mockery of the poor slob. I do and I beg you to do the same. Think of what our family has done to prepare us to get to this poor slob. What price did we pay and what pursuit have we earned to get to the poor slob, one pulling him this side while the other pulling him the other side. One dressing him up and the other undressing him down. And you know what at the end of the day. I congratulated my team for the job well done, while you curse your high-priced lawyers for missing the beat, for failing in their task to protect … the government. Now tell me again what price did we pay and what pursuit have we earned? I answer you; none, absolutely none."

"Oh, I see, you made an excellent point there. Here I was taking it so personally. I thought that you were insulting me, my legal competence and expertise. So, what do you and I, us, to do, resign our job, our duties, Uncle O'Grady? We are already fully engaged to abandon all now to undertake other pursuits."

"You are right, we are already fully engaged not to abandon our duties. We cannot go back and start all over. I am too old for that. I am just telling you, advising you to reflect on our duties sometime. That is all."

"Thank you! I will keep this analogy going forward."

"Now you call me so many times today. I took time to reflect over what I just shared with you privately and confidentially. What do you have in mind now?"

"Well, I want to sound you about our next steps."

"I am listening."

"The man is in a coma. He won't be able to testify any more, why don't you abandon the criminal pursuit and let him be. He won't hurt anybody right?"

"Absolutely not! My goal is to get him back where he came from, at least out of the US. I owe this to the lady who brought up the accusation. What if he comes out of the coma in a full healthy stage? Would he stay in the US in his original identity of Adamas Kagita, the war lord? Furthermore, what if this collapsing scenario was all contrived to lead to a legal exculpation? What would that make me look, a fool for sure? My dear niece, I can see where you want to go with this. I am not going to allow it. We are prepared to litigate this to get the appropriate outcome according to one person, the offended Charlotte Keregi who has suffered the loss of an entire family killed by this scoundrel."

"That would become problematic, and you know it?"

"Please indulge me."

"Adamas Kagita entered the US under some government specifications?"

"I knew it, it is leading to CIPA cover? We will go there too, we must exhaust this CIPA bull shit?"

"Uncle O'Grady!"

"I am sorry, we will go there?"

"You will lose!"

"I will take my chances."

"Will talk!"

"Bye!"

CHAPTER 18

JUDGE LEIGHTON-GARVER'S AGENDA

The prosecution and defense teams reconvened in Judge Leighton-Garver's chamber the day scheduled for the update over Adamas Kagita's health condition. Mr. O'Grady, the DA and his protégé Counsel, Ms. Ludmilla Garrov, represented the prosecution team. The lead lawyers and the associate lawyer represented the defense team. They were all comfortably seated in the spacious chamber of the Judge.

"Good morning, counsels! I received good news from the clinic where Mr. Adamas Kagita, otherwise called Jefferson Okito, was admitted about a week and half ago. He has fully recovered from what was determined to be a mild heart attack. He needs more rest in the clinic setting. I was not told how long he would need to stay there. Let us just say that he won't be released tomorrow or next week. He is recovering, thanks God. So much so, I have dismissed the Jury for the time being and I want to communicate to you some preliminary legal decisions I am about to take."

"After reviewing the trial proceedings about the case No. 56397 in this District Court, I have determined that the accused, Mr. Jefferson Okito alias Adamas Kagita, was caught using fraud or willful misrepresentation of identity to gain an immigration visa to the US. Mr. Jefferson Okito provided false and misleading information about his identity, nationality, and background to obtain immigration entry benefits to the US. Now that the court has established that Mr. Okito never existed and has substituted in lieu and place of a Mr. Adamas Kagita, a war lord in DRC, Mr. Okito is currently deemed inadmissible to the United States and subject to deportation proceedings from the US as stipulated in 18 US Code & 1546 around Fraud and misuse of visas, permits, and other documents."

"What does the defense team think of these legal decisions I am about to issue.?"

"Your Honor, we understand the level of deception you expressed in these decisions, but the defense must respectfully submit that these decisions would be a bit premature as the accused is entitled to various legal waivers in filing waiver Form 212(I) or I-601 Waiver for Prior Fraud or Misrepresentation."

"I understand that the accused is entitled to these legal waivers. But in the meantime, I am turning the case 56397 to the Immigration Cour oft Raleigh-Durham field office and I am also turning the accused, Mr. Jefferson Okito, into the custody of the immigration police force."

"Your Honor, Mr. Okito is in failing health. Such a custody transfer would aggravate his health condition. We were hoping that the case would remain in your court jurisdiction while we are filing the waivers with the Immigration services. Besides, Mr. Okito is very weak and still in the hospital. He is not going anywhere."

"Counsel, as you know very well, the transfer of case 56397 to the Immigration Court includes the physical custody of the accused. The Immigration Court is well prepared and aware about how to handle such a case. I am not throwing the case in the vacuum on the other side. Adequate preparations have been made to adjudicate the case appropriately. I would no longer handle this case. Let me find out from the prosecution how they would like to proceed."

"Thank you Honor! The prosecutor is relieved to hear that the medical case of the accused has improved remarkably. The prosecution seconds your legal decisions that we find highly appropriate. We understand that the Immigration Court will take over the case. Our goals have not changed. We want to see Mr. Jefferson Okito stripped of the immigration entry visa benefits he has gained fraudulently by misrepresenting his identity as Adamas Kagita. We stand ready to litigate the case in every court in the US until Mr. Kagita is either deported from the US or is jailed in the US to pay for the endless series of crime he has perpetrated as a war lord. We will pursue this case till the end, to that end, Your Honor, this District Attorney Office is ready to be constituted as Special Counsel at any Federal Court to prosecute this case."

"I want to thank both teams for the indulgence you have shown me during the last difficult two weeks. I wish you good luck in your respective endeavors."

The defense team departed as quickly as they could to the clinic where Mr. Okito was being taken care of. They were rushing to announce the decisions that the Judge had taken. The prosecution team stayed behind chatting with Judge Leighton-Garver about the rapid turn of the case disposition.

"Mr. O'Grady, have you ever pleaded a case in the Immigration Court?"

"No, this will be the first."

"Most of them are very political except for acts of terrorism and cases involving drug traffic. Most take human rights abuse coloration. Less than two per cent are CIPA related. I tell you, the way the defense is getting agitated about Mr. Okito-Kagita, it would wind up with a huge CIPA coloration. I don't understand why this man seems to be so well protected. Sounds Langley if you want my speculative opinion. That is the reason I wanted out of that case. Are you sure you want a Special Counsel assignment on that one. It could go on for a long time, an eternity."

"Maybe my last assignment. I am sixty-eight."

"Well good luck and thank you for your voluminous testimony. It helped and cleared the case very quickly for me."

The lead lawyers were obviously alarmed by the Judge decisions. They were not surprised by the chain of events from the time Jefferson Okito alias Adamas Kagita collapsed and was quickly transferred to the hospital. They were upset by the quick defeat their strategy suffered under the clever legal pummeling the Counsel Ludmilla Garrow delivered. They gasped for legal relief after the court plain admission by Jefferson Okito that he was the war lord Adamas Kagita after all. There was no possible legal relief coming their way. They spent the next week and half sounding all legal contacts and tools to execute some kind of last-ditch rescue. Nothing materialized. They would not dare approach Judge Leighton-Garver knowing the legal inclination she had expressed from the beginning of the trial proceedings. She did not want to get involved in a case with national security ramifications. They suspected that she would quickly turn the case to a different court if she could. And she just did that in a heart bit. The lead lawyers must now earn their big shoes lawyer fees in a difficult Immigration legal terrain.

When the defense team reached the hospital, Mr. Jefferson Okito had already been moved to a section for incarcerated patients with armed guards posted on both sides of the hall. The violent patients had cuff chain on their ankle. Jefferson was spared the ankle chain. He was found sleeping and almost relaxed. In this section, the patients were restricted to having only one visitor at a time. The lead lawyers stayed behind. The associate lawyer walked in. When he got to Jefferson, he was still deep in sleep, and he did not want to wake him up. He signaled to the lead lawyers to leave while he would stay to keep him company. In about two hours later Jefferson wake up.

"Hello, counsel, that lady judge could not wait to throw me in jail already!"

"Oh, really, when I arrived here at the hospital, I went to the cardiology department and was told that you were already here. I was shocked."

"Well, don't worry, I resigned myself already to this fate after the debacle at the court. How did it go at the court, did you reconvene today?"

"Yes, that was then we learned that the Judge already decided to turn you to the immigration court. When did they move you?"

"Yesterday around five o'clock. I was tired and sleeping, reacting to the medicines I had been taking and when I woke up, I was already here. The folks who brought me here were dressed as armed jail guards, they did not say anything. They just rolled my bed in. When I noticed the ankle chain on a few patients I knew it. Tell you what, for me it does not matter anymore. I just want my wife and kids to be all right. They can do whatever they want as long as they don't send me back to those three countries, DRC, Rwanda, or Uganda. I would be killed as soon as I leave the plane in any one of these three countries."

"Why are you talking like that. We will get you out of here soon enough. We have already filed waivers against the immigration penalties. Money is no object. We will raise your bail as soon as you are to walk out of the hospital. Did you call your contacts since you came to the hospital?"

"No man, what is the use. I am abandoned to my fate. That is all right. But I am sorry for letting you down after the long training and preparation we did for the trial. I am very sorry. But my sister Magida did it to me. I could not hold it. She died when I was in jail in Kisangani. I know you all in the court thought that that lady lawyer

171

got me. No way! I fucked a dozen of her kind anywhere I used to go. I met a lot of Russian girls like her in Seychelles Islands. They came there on prostitution binge. Bang a lot of them all day and all night anyway I wanted. What is her name again?"

"Counsel Ludmilla Garrov!"

"She looked like them virgins I used to bang in Seychelles. They screamed all night, cannot take it, too tight. I can tell. And she probably went on celebrating that she got me. Hell no! But when she put Magida's picture, I could not hold it more. I must confess that there was no woman in the world I care far more than my sister Magida, she was so helpless and retarded. The only thing I wanted to do was to help her any way I could. Then I did not because she passed away when I was in jail, the only place I could not help her from. That really upset me then. And again, right there when I was fighting for my life on that stand, they had the nerve to put her picture. That brought back the same feeling of upset, I could not face it. Anyway, that was going to happen soon or later. I am sorry. So, where we go from here?"

"As I was saying, the first thing is to get you a waiver."

"But under which identity?"

"Adamas Kagita now. No more hiding, all right. Then fight as hell any deportation proceeding on ground of being killed if you go back as you said, in any of three countries. Now if that does not work, we would get to another safe country in Central or Latin America. The first I can think of is Belize. Nice place."

"That is fine, a beach place raising my kids quietly. I like that! You know what, maybe I should call the Colonel. I miss talking with him. But they took all my cell phones. Oh no!"

"Take it easy, you will get them back. Think of it this way, you are recovering, you need rest. Let us do the work. We will get you out. Talking about your wife and kids. Again, don't worry. The day after you came to the hospital, we realized that there was no more priority but to reassure your wife with the kids about your whereabouts, to give them a very comfortable setting there around Mobile, Alabama. We did not tell her anything about what happened in court. We knew that she could call you anytime just to check on you. We anticipated that by bringing in a very nice lady from Tanzania speaking fluent Swahili.

This lady had parents from Kenya and Tanzania. She has worked for us in many difficult cases like yours. At this moment she is staying with your family in Alabama claiming to be from South Kivu. She knows the Eastern DRC area very well, claiming to be from the city of Uvira. She also speaks French very well. She told your wife that you sent her there to keep her company until you show up. Remember her name is Issana Baruti. The first time you get your cell phones back you must give her a call. The most important thing is that she drives a rented big family SUV and is getting around to help your wife with household stuffs. Your wife really appreciates the help. And she is slowly opening slowly with Issana. She said that she misses you dearly."

"Mr. Okito, all we are asking you is to stay calm. We are working as hard as hell to get you out of this mess. It will take time and hopefully not too much time. As far as I am concerned, I will come back here every day until you get out all right. Have a lovely day. Take your medicines to get back in shape and strong."

CHAPTER 19

UNCLE STANIS' RESERVATION

Charlotte Keregi spent the same two weeks and half of trial proceedings in permanent euphoria from the chain of events that followed at an incredible speed. The first day was disappointing, of course, but the next day was a total change, almost from a confusing dark night to a shining day, when Ludmilla proudly took over the prosecution of Jefferson Okito alias Adamas Kagita. She cried inside when the smirking smile that Jefferson Okito wore the first day slowly evaporated under the legal punches that Ludmilla was raining on his face. The whole scenario reminded her of the famous boxing match between Georges Foreman vs Mohammad Ali on October 30, 1974, billed as "The Rumble in the Jungle" in Kinshasa. When she was growing up, that boxing match was shown many times on TV in place of any sport event that was scheduled but was not broadcast. This became a fixture of sport event on TV for a long time. Most kids then learned Mohammad Ali's rope and dope strategy. Charlotte observed how Ludmilla legally built her case by encircling poor Jefferson in a rope and dope style to give a final blow that sent him to the hospital with a mild heart attack.

Saying that Charlotte enjoyed Ludmilla's knock out was an understatement. While the Judge screamed for help from medics for the collapsed Adamas, Charlotte felt extasy of the nth kind. She did not move but her whole body responded as in a trance, as in a cup of orgasm. She remained still when Adamas was wheeled away with respirator mask over his face She remained calm not believing what she was witnessing in front of her, absorbing the front row fall of the war lord who had terrorized thousands of people in her native Greater Kivu. Charlotte kept still when Judged Leighton-Garver invited the prosecution and defense teams to her chamber while ordering the Members of the Jury to leave her Court to go to a different conference room. She kept still for a long time waiting for the prosecution to come back. In fact, Charlotte felt her body shaking for no reason, she felt a cold sweat from her neck down to her spine, she felt paralyzed, and her hands were damp. Charlotte became afraid to move from her prime seat. She thought that she had an unfortunate and uncontrolled discharge down below from the overwhelming emotions that invaded her body during the collapse of the accused. Only after surveying the court that was emptying fast, Charlotte rose to check herself, her dress, and the seat. There was no discharge. She was relieved and smiled. But she was still shaking from the emotions that were still invading overwhelmingly her whole body. She decided that she would wait for the prosecution team outside in the parking lot. She got up and ran outside to her car. When she was seated inside her car, she lowered her front windows and checked her mirror. She was heavily perspiring. She wiped her face. Then she saw a glow on her face she did not recognize, a triumphant glow that frightened her. She started her car and left the parking around the court imposing building and kept driving to nowhere. After about ten minutes of unscheduled driving Charlotte pulled into an undistinguished mall parking. She drove to the far opposite empty side in front of tall trees. She stopped the car and rolled down the front windows. The autumn breeze calmed her down. She started praying. She opened her small pocket bible and landed on Psalm 37. She read loudly from verse 7:

"Be still before the LORD and wait patiently for Him;

Do not fret when people succeed in their ways,

When they carry out their wicked schemes.

Refrain from anger and turn from wrath:

Do not fret – it leads only to evil.

For those who are evil will be destroyed,

But those who hope in the LORD will inherit the land."

Charlotte read these verses about three times to regain her composure. She kept praying a little bit more to the point of dozing for a while until the loud cell phone ring awakened her. That was Ludmilla from the court building.

"Hello, Charlotte, are you all right. We looked for you around the court building, but you were not to be found. Are you ok?"

"Yes, I am all right! We were asked to leave the court while I was waiting for you. I waited outside in the car for a while. You were still not coming out. I decided to leave, and I was parked not far from the building in this mall parking lot. I will come back if you need me."

"No, you don't need to, everybody is still under shock The Judge suspended the trial proceedings at this time. Please go home and take some rest. I will give you a call later tonight to share what would happen next. We are going back to the office and will be released for the rest of the day. Take good care of yourself."

When Ludmilla reached Charlotte that evening, she was awakening from a long afternoon nap that started after she reached home from that mall parking lot stop. She reached home extremely tired as if from strenuous exercise. The shock from the trial proceeding was still acting on her body. She was still tense. She took a long hot shower and on a rare occasion she had a good size of bourbon she never touched. She went to sleep at about five in the afternoon. When Ludmilla called back, she has been up for about twenty minutes revisiting the trial episode.

"What do you think of the trial session today?"

"You did wonder today, Ludmilla! Beyond excellent! I suspected that you were going to nail him from the way the trial was evolving in the morning. His denials were strong and firm in the beginning, but he started to come down and even doubt himself. It was becoming obvious that he was going to get caught. I did not expect it to happen so soon and over a picture . That was a surprise to me."

"Not to me, your Uncle Reverend Stanis laid that surprise for me. I carefully read the notes he had on the back of that famous picture. He said that Adamas was very attached to that sister Magida who happened to be retarded. Apparently Adamas confided to his close friend Xavier Bhatia that there was nothing more outrageous to me but being in jail in Kisangani and learning after about three weeks that Magida passed away and he was not informed of this to request a temporary release to come back home to attend her funerals. Adamas knew that he could have gained that release from his close relationship with General Ogpado. Besides, he had less than three months to get released by the

General anyway. He guessed his parents did not want him to come home to bury his siter. His parents did not appreciate his wayward ways in Kisangani, abandoning his academic studies to become a big-time pimp so they learned. Adamas was no longer valued by his parents. He never forgave them for that affront. He never talked nor visited them after that affront. In the same vein, killing his own blood uncle was no big deal. From that affront he stepped up erasing his blood family memories with one major exception, Magida. The picture brought back personal drama now under new dire circumstances of losing his protection from being deported back to the Eastern DRC hell he came from. You must thank your Uncle Reverend Stanis for the outstanding contribution he provided to nail Adamas."

"I will do just that at our usual weekend call. But what would happen now?

"Well, the Judge stated that she would monitor Adamas's health progress and will reconvene a meeting within a week and half to share the progress of the trial."

"But for all practical purposes Adamas confessed that he was no more that Jefferson Okito. Did I miss something?"

"No, you are correct. Everybody heard his confession. The issue is what the Judge will do with that clear confession. The fact is there is no longer Jefferson Okito who entered the US under false identity. Adamas Kagita, the war lord was resurrected at the place of Jefferson Okito. But Adamas Kagita is not registered in the US. He does not exist in the US. Do you see the legal confusion? The Judge can simply arrest Adamas Kagita who should not be in the US because there are no immigration documents validating his entry. The Judge should simply transfer him to the US Immigration services to dispose of his case. I am leaning towards the latter disposition. But time will tell, we don't know how Adamas Kagita became Jefferson Okito. We don't know which powerful people pulled the strings to make it happen. As far as we are concerned, the persecution wants to ensure that Adamas is punished for the crimes he committed against you and your family. Remember that is why we are in court after you accused Adamas Kagita of masquerading as Jefferson Okito. Now that we have removed Okito masks, we must find the court to prosecute Adamas Kagita, a non-entity in US. Are you following me?"

"I am and it does not sound easy."

"Now keep the faith, we won the first step, the identity step, we must go for the prosecution now. Keep the faith!"

"Ludmilla, when I was waiting to hear from you and parked my car in that mall parking lot, I did not know where I was. But I pray and read Psalm 37:7-9 and it said something about keeping the faith: "Be still before the LORD and wait patiently for him ... For those who are evil will be destroyed, but those who hope in the LORD, those who keep the faith with the LORD, will inherit the Land!""

"Amen!"

"Ludmilla, I have always kept the faith of the LORD. This has brought us to the winning episode that we witnessed today. I will not give up."

"And I am all the way with you. I will keep you posted about what the Judge will tell us when we reconvene. Stay calm and keep the faith!"

Charlotte was confused when she did not receive an invitation to attend the meeting that Judge Leighton-Garver called to reconvene the prosecution and defense team. Ludmilla reassured her that she would share everything that the Judge would tell them. As soon as Ludmilla got out of the meeting, she asked Charlotte to meet her at their favorite restaurant. When Charlotte arrived, she noticed that Ludmilla had ordered two glasses of Champagne.

"Charlotte, this is to celebrate a great victory as I have expected and as I tried to explain to you. Adamas Kagita has been arrested and turned over to the Immigration Court for entering the US under false pretense and misrepresenting his identity as Jefferson Okito. Adamas Kagita is in a terrible judicial condition as we speak. He is not registered under any Immigration document in the US, but he is in the US. He is still in the hospital recovering from what they said was a mild heart attack. Since he came to the US and thanks to your accusation when you identified him as Adamas Kagita, he has finally been arrested. I heard that he is lying in bed chained to his ankle in the prisoner's ward section of the hospital. When he is fully recovered, he will be brought to the Immigration jail, I believe, in Charlotte or somewhere in one of the federal court jails. The judge communicated that decision today when we reconvened. Of course, his defense team wanted the Judge to maintain him as Jefferson Okito and turned him over to the Immigration Court when he would leave the hospital. The Judge declined that procedure. She made her decision effective immediately. The defense said that they will pursue some kind of immigration waivers. That will take a lot of time while Adamas is spending time in jail where he belongs. My Boss advised the Judge and the defense that he will continue his prosecution of Adamas Kagita until he is deported, or he is jailed in the US!"

"I agree! I have been waiting for this for a long time. I must raise this glass for celebration not just for me, but your team, for you, and especially for many more in the thousands who have been mowed, killed by Adamas for no other reason but running across his murderous path. One evil is being destroyed by the will of our Lord. We have been patiently waiting for the will of the Lord and it is being fulfilled. Amen!"

As soon as their celebration dinner was over, Charlotte rushed to share the extraordinary news with her friend Suzanne and her husband Reverend "Papa Chi". Another bottle of Champagne was chilled and shared by the longtime friends. The rest of the evening was shared in a lot of laughter and prayers. Charlotte needed about three cups of strong coffee to continue her trip home. She could not wait to be home to wake up the next day on Saturday morning to share the news with her Uncle Reverend Stanislas Keregi. The champagne glasses Charlotte still prevented her from waking up as scheduled at 6:30am on Saturday morning. It was 7:00am when Charlotte opened her eyes. She rushed to heat up water for two cups of coffee she desperately needed.

"Hello, Uncle Stanis, how are you on this beautiful late November morning. Are you already getting buried in the arctic snow?".

"Not yet, my dear niece. We have had a series of freezing rains all this week. It did not help folks of my age. We got to be more than careful navigating every street. Saturday morning is not welcome. With less people on the street, every walking path freezes, and short walking distance becomes a nightmare. I decided to stay home today. You sound very happy, what is the good news you are about to share?"

"More than good news, Uncle Stanis, and we owe all to you indeed!"

"And what have I done?"

"A lot, Uncle Stanis, a mountain of a lot. The voluminous testimony that you sent finally bore its fruit. The news is that our nemesis, Adamas

Kagita, the war lord is now arrested, chained to his ankle, resting in bed in a prisoner's section of a local hospital."

"Hospital, whatever happened to the scoundrel?"

"Well, he collapsed, had a heart attack when he was being questioned about his sister Magida. Apparently, he could not bear looking at the picture of his sister Magida, who turned out to be retarded and passed away when he was pulling time in jail in Kisangani."

"So, Adamas had emotions after all. Collapsing just after seeing the picture of his retarded sister. Are you sure that he was not faking it. This does not sound like the war lord Adamas "Danger de Mort!" Are you certain that Adamas collapsed because of this. I don't believe it. Tell me more!"

"I am not kidding. I was right there in the front row where the main witness seats. I saw him convulsing when he was being ravaged by relentless questioning from this young lady prosecutor. I heard him saying "leave me alone, leave me alone leave …" and he fainted while his body was coming down and the Judge yelled for medics help. It was a very tragic scene, Uncle Stanis. It was surrealistic. Even for me, who had wished him a thousand deaths, I felt sorry for him seeing the medics rushing in the court, reanimating him, putting the respiratory masks next to this breathing machine and rushing out of there to the hospital. What a pandemonium, I staid frozen for a long time witnessing all that!"

"And then what happened?"

"Well, he was rushed to the hospital where he was diagnosed having had a mild heart attack. He stayed there recuperating for a week and half. If I may back out to the incident, what happened then was very revealing. Under intense questioning, Adamas Kagita came out saying for everybody to hear, he was actually brother to Magida Kagita, that he was, in fact Adamas Kagita, not the masquerading Jefferson Okito he has been trying to be since he came here in the US. That was an ultimate confession that the Members of the Jury, the Judge, the prosecuting team, and the defense team, I mean everybody, heard and he could not take back/"

"So!"

"Well yesterday, the Judge had reconvened the prosecution and defense team to share Adam's medical status. After she gave it, she also shared her decision after reviewing the incident. The Judge decided that the court has witnessed Adamas Kagita revealing that he was not Jefferson Okito who has entered the US under false pretense misrepresenting Adamas Kagita, the war lord. She ordered the arrest of Adamas Kagita and turned him over to the Immigrations Court. As soon as Adamas gets better, he will be transferred to an Immigration jail where he would wait for his Immigration Court disposition."

"Wonderful, wonderful, wonderful! Amen, Amen, Amen! I thank Our Lord for bringing the Shining Light over the Evil Night our family had endured for so long! I did not believe that you would reach this point of reckoning. I thank you for your persistence in carrying the Keregi's torch to the end. You did very well, my niece, more than very well. The family owes you a great debt of gratitude."

"Amen, Amen, Amen! Again, all that thanks to the meticulous testimony you provided us. Would you believe it, the young prosecutor saw what you wrote on the back of that picture of Magida's picture. She said that she used it to pummel Adamas about that testimony. Apparently, you collected it talking to Adamas's close former friend, Xavier Bhatia!"

"Oh, Lord, I remembered that picture now and the notes I scribbled on the back. Hallelujah!"

"You see, my dearest niece, Charlotte, many times people try to bring down the mighty evil one with big guns, bazookas and so on. And here, a tiny simple picture did the job. Would you believe it? So, where we go from here?"

"As I said, the case is now an Immigration case. The prosecution team has sworn that Adamas must pay for his acts as a war lord. They mentioned two dispositions: he must be deported from the US, or he must do time in jail in the US, based on the voluminous testimony you provided. So, it is not over yet."

"My very dearest niece Charlotte, you know I always stand on the side of truth. Truth confused Adamas to confess his identity, truth will always set us free. Unfortunately, your American hosts have problems sitting on the side of the truth. I appreciate that you raised the misrepresentation Adamas was carrying all this time in the eyes of the American Justice in its court. But my question remains: who has managed to provide Adamas, a notorious war lord, with that extraordinary cover to leave Eastern DRC to get here in the US and stay for this long undetected until you got his veil and masks removed in a court, in a trial proceeding. I must still submit that powerful people and forces have banded together to bring Adamas here for whatever reason. These powerful people and forces would not allow you to disturb what motivated them to bring Adamas to the US. I would not burst the bubble we are enjoying today. But we have a long way to go before declaring victory. Time will tell."

"Uncle Stanis, I know where you are going, and I struggled to avoid that path. But I never thought that I would witness the collapse of Adamas. I saw it. I trust in Our Lord managing His time for the Good of all of us. I would not give up."

"And I would be right next to you all the way. I am telling you this for a very good reason. I had a long discussion with an eminent professor of History at the prestigious University of Uppsala. We talked about all what we have done lately about the confusing identity of Adamas, this old man shared a lot of reservations about the case. I share his reservations when he gave me the following lecture.:"

"From 1790 through present, there have been about 32 Immigration Acts in the US including a variety of amendments. The laws were established principally to determine who should or should not allow to enter the US, and who should reside or should not reside in the US. In addition, in specific cases, these laws established how these laws should be managed and by which federal agency or institution. As far as immigration laws that would or would not apply over Adamas case, you must realize that starting 1948, after the second world war, Immigration laws were focused on people designated sometimes Displaced or Refugees. Their cases happened because of wars, violence or persecution. Such as in Europe after the war of 1940, Indochina-Vietnam after the war period of 1940, Iraq, and Afghanistan after the war period of 2001-2003, "

"The professor also added by saying that this:"

"These laws took a political coloration at the end of the second world war when the Us came out as a major superpower opposed to the Communist Block of the Soviet Union. That was the case when the US opened its borders to Displaced people who were leaving the war torn and devastated Europa, and as Refugees running from political persecution from the Communist Soviet Union."

"The professor emphasized a very important point:"

"In this wave, the US received not only the persecuted Jews, but also their oppressors, the Nazi and Nazi collaborators and sympathizers who arrived at the US misrepresenting their identity by lying in their application for visa entry into the US. Just like Adamas Kagita had done, they came in with different identity the immigration services could not possibly verify given the unbelievable churn of people that was taking place in the Europe after the second world war, and for Adamas the incredible population churn still taking place in Eastern DRC."

"The professor concluded:"

"It took about forty year later for the US immigration services to correct the grave prejudice when one after another the hidden Nazi and their collaborators started being denounced and identified. It took that much time to debunk their misrepresentation as in cases of John Damjanjuk originally as Ivan Grosny or Ivan the Terrible of Treblinka, Alois Anich originally Anrija Artubovuc, the enforcer of the Croatian racial purity, Klaus Altmann originally Klaus Barbie, the butcher of Lyons and thousands more evil and scoundrel people who lived as "quiet neighbors" throughout the US and Latin America."

"My very dearest niece, this above lecture tells me that the issue is not the Court system where justice must be adjudicated. The real issue is the way the Immigration laws are codified in a such way, big loopholes are designed and integrated in law to accommodate political coloration of the moment and always on short term basis. Yesterday it was the drive against Communism, then it changed into against anything Islamic as after September 11, 2001, then against anything Mexican or Japanese or Chinese. And worse, to favor coltan in a major industrial drive for the next technological digital revolution etc... When a law, any law, is colored by the political wind of the moment, it usually takes time to bring it back to its preliminary intent of fairness, justice, and compassion. In the meantime, we must deal with its unfairness, its injustice, its illegality, its inequality, and various attempts to make it …just. And I can tell you now these imperfections of law are being cooked up and manipulated in court by the same powerful people and forces which have created Adamas Kagita as a war lord and brought him there in the US to suit their purpose. They are not going to give up that easily, You and I will be waiting for them at each turn of the law or whatever the Court system allows us. And I will guard myself to see the evolution of the case against Adamas Kagita evolve and be exhausted to that end."

"Uncle Stanis, I must stand with you in the same pursuit. I don't know where I would be without your wisdom. Will talk!"

CHAPTER 20

IMMIGRA AGGRAVATING VENUE

Mr. O'Grady was not amused by the prospect of the legal proceedings that were being forecasted during the trial preliminaries at the Immigration Court in Charlotte, North Caroline. He found himself with Counsel Ludmilla Garrov trying to relearn basic differences between the Immigration court system and the traditional court system. Ludmilla proposed a lengthy and thorough preparation in the hands of her former UNC Law Professor, Mr. Steve McIntosh, an eminent expert in the US Immigration Court system. Professor obliged with two late afternoon seminar reviews in the DA conference rooms. The DA entire staff was invited but only two members showed up: Mr. O'Grady and Ludmilla. The Professor proposed to advance the seminar deliver through a series of questions and answers. This narrows the review on specifics of major interest of and in respect of the DA office.

Mr. O'Grady started with the obvious: "What were the basic differences between the traditional court system and the Immigration court system?"

Professor McIntosh provided a long story of the evolution of the immigration court after the civil war through and the purpose of the Immigration Court system and added:

"Immigration court was a specialized court that handles cases related to immigration and deportation, while federal court handled cases related to federal law and constitutional issues. Immigration courts were part of the Executive Office for Immigration Review (EOIR) Immigration courts were a part of the United States Department of Justice (DOJ) while criminal and civil courts were part of the United States constitutional judicial branch. The Immigration court system was the emanation of the Executive Branch trusted to manage the entry of foreign people and their evolution to become citizens pf the US."

This was becoming an important distinction and consideration that the District Attorney team was reacquainting itself with.

Professor McIntosh also added that "The Traditional Court System they were most familiar with, as opposed to the Immigration Court system, was comprised of Criminal and Civil courts Criminal courts which were based on local state laws while immigration courts must abide by federal immigration laws."

"Criminal cases focused on actions taken against the state. Criminal charges could impact a person's immigration status. However, a criminal court did not have the legal authority to make decisions related to immigration law. Criminal court judges could only make rulings related to criminal charges, and immigration judges may base their decisions on these rulings."

He inferred that:

"The DA team knew from experience that Civil courts processed cases related to personal damages that result from torts, which are civil actions that cause another party to experience some loss or harm. Common examples include assault, vandalism, or defamation. Civil cases typically determine the liability of one party as well as the financial compensation that must be paid to the plaintiff for injuries and other damages. Criminal penalties include fines, jail time, and community service. In Immigration Courts, Immigration cases must abide by federal laws. Immigration judges can consider criminal convictions when ruling on an immigration status. But their primary objective is to rule on cases that pertain to deportation, asylum, and other immigration issues. "

For an obvious reason, the professor focused on a major tenet difference of the two courts system:

"Unlike criminal and civil cases, immigration cases cannot be ruled on by a jury. The right to be tried by a jury of peers, enshrined in the Sixth and Seventh Amendments of the Constitution was extended only to the US Citizens and not to people seeking entry to the US through immigration venue. Therefore, only an immigration judge can decide on the arguments made for and against a case. Immigration judges were appointed by the Department of Justice, and opposing attorneys represent the U.S. government. After the case is presented by the client attorney and the opposing legal government counsel, the immigration judge will decide. The Decisions taken by an Immigration Judge can be appealed through the Board of Immigration Appeals (BIA). This process involves the review of an immigration case by one or more judges to overturn or uphold the decision made by the original immigration judge. Immigration cases must abide by federal laws. Immigration judges can consider criminal convictions when ruling on our immigration status. But their primary objective is to rule on cases that pertain to deportation, asylum, and other immigration issues."

The professor started then to explain the functions of Immigration judges:

"They are charged to execute following functions: advising noncitizens of their legal rights, hearing testimony, making credibility findings and rulings on the admissibility of evidence, entertaining legal arguments, adjudicating waivers and applications for relief, making factual findings and legal rulings, and issuing final orders of removal. Immigration judges are therefore administrative law judges.

"Immigration Judges administer their courts according to an elaborate set of rules of procedure according to types of hearing: master calendar hearing in case of removal proceedings or individual calendar hearing for other hearings or merits hearings. The Immigration Judge is usually assisted by the clerk of the court who is useful in answering questions regarding filing requirements, deadlines, and other miscellaneous questions that arise."

Along the way, Mr. O'Grady and Ludmilla learned about the types of cases that are heard in immigration court including:

"-Removal proceedings: These are cases where the U.S. government is seeking to remove an individual from the country due to a violation of immigration law.

-Asylum cases: These are cases where an individual is seeking protection in the United States due to persecution or a well-founded fear of persecution in their home country.

-Bond hearings: These are hearings where an individual who is in custody can request to be released on bond while their case is pending.

-Cancellation of removal: This is a form of relief that allows an individual who has been in the United States for a certain period of time and meets other requirements to avoid removal from the country.

-Adjustment of status: This is a process that allows certain individuals who are already in the United States to apply for lawful permanent resident status (also known as a green card)."

Another procedure of major interest to Mr. O'Grady and Ludmilla was reviewed by the Professor:

"How motions, evidence, and objections are going to be dealt with in the immigration court. During direct testimony and cross-examination, oral objections to questioning by either side are permitted as stipulated by the general guidelines on motions and courtroom procedure from the EOIR Immigration Court Practice Manual the team resolved to familiarize with very quickly."

They learned that:

"Neither the Federal Rules of Civil Procedure nor the Federal Rules of Evidence formally apply in immigration proceedings.

Overall, the admission of evidence in immigration court is extremely broad. The immigration judge "may receive as evidence any oral or written statement made by the respondent or any other person" if the statement is "material and relevant to any issue in the case. Further, hearsay is generally admissible in immigration court unless it is "fundamentally unfair".

As far as the voluminous testimony that the DA team was planning to offer in the case against Adamas Kagita, Professor McIntosh provided a different set of procedures when it comes to testimony processing:

"Most judges will deal with evidentiary issues prior to any testimony. Documents can be offered into evidence (without having to lay a foundation through testimony. The trial attorney, or government counsel, may make objections to the evidence, most often based on authentication, relevance, undue repetitiveness, or hearsay. Based on the relaxed evidentiary standards applicable in immigration court, any objection by the trial attorney should go to the weight of the evidence, not its admissibility. In response to an objection that a document is unduly repetitive (most often arising with respect to country conditions of information), it is helpful to be able to pick out one issue from each report that is not necessarily covered by others. In addition, while the information contained within several reports is similar, they each come from distinct sources, which proves that it is more likely that the information is accurate and/or widely accepted.

Another important point that the DA team became increasingly aware was that:

"Since the trial attorney, the government counsel will be the prime driver of their case against the accused Adamas Kagita, they needed to ensure that the counsel's access, availability, and concurrence were assured at all the time. In addition, his or her amenability to work out issues before the hearing must occur as often as regularly possibles. A trial attorney's enormous workload makes her or him likely to consider requests for continuances (within reason) and the stipulation of various issues. If there is a question or a need to know the trial attorney's view on an aspect of the case, the trial attorney's accessibility to discuss the case will become primordial."

Mr. O'Grady and Ludmilla were not pleased of the role that will be assigned to them from then on in the immigration court system, when they will be reduced to the function of "AMICUS CURIAE" of "FRIEND OF THE COURT" offering the court information (the voluminous testimony information that they have gathered) or perspective about the case.

Professor closed the first seminar on that note to completely weary DA team.

The next day evening, Mr. O'Grady and Ludmilla made inquiries about the possibility to appeal the Immigration Judge decision. Professor McIntosh obliged them with a difficult and long process that will take place at different stages of the appeal from the Immigration Court system back to the appeal process within the traditional court system as stated below:

"Immigration judge's decisions are usually rendered orally in the courtroom at the conclusion of the hearing. If it is not favorable, a decision about whether to pursue an appeal will have to be made without the advantage of a written decision or transcript. Because the Notice of Appeal must state the errors of law and/or fact to be

189

reviewed, it is a good idea to have a colleague in the courtroom to take contemporaneous notes of the judge's decision."

"Prior to filing an appeal with the Board of Immigration Appeals, the losing party can file a motion with the immigration judge to reconsider the decision. This must be done within 30 days of the decision and before filing a motion with the BIA because once a Notice of Appeal has been filed with the BIA, the immigration judge loses jurisdiction over the case. These motions are usually filed when there is a request that the judge reexamine or reconsider his or her own decision based on either new evidence or new case law. Again, any motion to reopen or reconsider must be filed with the correct fee within 30 days of the decision and before filing a Notice of Appeal."

"The Board of Immigration Appeals, which is part of the U.S Department of Justice's Executive Office for Immigration Review (EOIR), is the appellate administrative body for interpreting and applying immigration laws. The BIA is comprised of 15 Board Members, who are aided by staff lawyers. A Chairman and Vice Chairman share responsibility for BIA management. Decisions rendered by immigration courts nationwide may be directly appealed to the Board of Immigration Appeals (BIA), headquartered in Falls Church, VA.".

"The BIA has jurisdiction to hear appeals from removal orders and other decisions rendered by any immigration judge. BIA decisions are binding unless modified or overruled by the Attorney General or a federal court. Most BIA decisions are reviewable by federal courts. Most appeals reaching the BIA involve orders of removal and applications for relief from removal."

"The BIA designates some decisions as precedential. These decisions are binding on all Department of Homeland Security officers and immigration judges unless modified or overruled by the Attorney General or a federal court. "

"The BIA reviews findings of fact by the immigration judge under a "clearly erroneous" standard and applies a de novo standard to issues of law. Most appeals are decided after the submission of written briefs and are issued as written decisions. Oral arguments are allowed only on rare occasions. To file an appeal with the BIA, the appealing party must reserve the right to appeal at the time the immigration judge renders a decision in the case. If the losing party waives her right to appeal, the immigration judge's decision will become final."

"In the Notice of Appeal and brief, you may request that a three-judge panel review the decision of the immigration judge. Otherwise, a single judge will decide the appeal. Requests for a three-judge panel are evaluated based on certain factors.

The filing of a direct appeal of a decision by the immigration judge in a timely manner, within the 30-day period, results in an automatic stay of execution of that order. Once the BIA decision is issued, the losing party (now referred to as the "petitioner") may be entitled to judicial review of the decision in the federal circuit courts of appeal. However, not all issues are entitled to judicial review by the federal circuit courts."

Again, the prohibition does not apply to cases that raise a constitutional claim or a question of law. Not all courts agree on what constitutes a "question of law." The ninth and second circuits have held that questions of law include the application of statutes or

regulations to undisputed facts, or mixed questions of facts and law. Therefore, in the ninth and second circuits, a decision on "changed circumstances" or "extraordinary circumstances" is a mixed question of law and fact over which the court has jurisdiction.

A petitioner has 30 days to file a petition for review with the federal circuit court from the date the BIA renders its decision.

There is no automatic stay of removal when filing for a Petition for Review. A separate request for a stay of removal must be filed with the federal circuit court. If the petitioner is detained or is in danger of being imminently removed, the request must be entitled as "emergency request for stay of removal." The federal courts give considerable deference to agency decisions, but they do not hesitate to reverse the BIA when error is clear, such as when the BIA fails to follow the legal reasoning of its own precedential decisions."

Mr. Ogrady and Ludmilla were thankful for the substantial review and appreciation of the immigration court system where the case against Adamas Kagita was going to be litigated from then on. They were not thrilled by the prospect of amicus curiae against actual prosecuting the case in the immigration court. But they also knew that the voluminous testimony they have developed would come in handy and crucial every step of the next immigration court system way.

CHAPTER 21

NATIONAL TERRITORY

A couple of days after the review of the immigration court system, given by the UNC professor McIntosh, Mr. O'Grady was not spared by new jabs from his niece from the office of the US Attorney General in Washington, D.C.

"Hello, Uncle O'Grady, I heard that you were having problems learning how our court system, I mean, the immigration court system operates. I have told you from the gate go that in this case, you would eventually come back to us on the Executive side of the Attorney General of the US. I am very happy that you need two days to learn that we run the Immigration procedures in the country. The President of the US is the sole arbiter of all issues related to the Immigration. Of course, he delegates that function to the Attorney General office where I am …"

"Gwendolyn, you are still back to the political nonsense of territorial domain of the Immigration domain. I need to remind you that if your Boss managed the Immigration procedures within the constraints of the Constitution, there would be no problems. Any time there is any derogation from the law of the land, then there will be problems. Tell me where your scoundrel of Jefferson Okito alias Adamas Kagita is currently. Let me answer it, he is in the Immigration jail section of maximum-security federal jail somewhere in western North Carolina area. I have been telling you, your political deal to bring him here to the US would never hold. We have already managed to strip him of his fake identity. We are not done yet. He would pay for all the crimes he committed in Eastern DRC. Mark my words on that."

"No, he won't. Our political deal, as you call it, will prevail, and would stand at the end for national security purposes. I don't know why you won't let it go. I also work every day for the vigorous implementation of the rule of law in this country. But I also recognize that we cannot have a rule of law in this country while the world outside is burning with people willing to bring that very edifice of rule of law down. That is why we have national security purposes that abide by the same rudeness we live in the world outside the US. Why is it so difficult for you to understand this. I am very proud to operate in both worlds."

"More power to you, my dear lovely niece. I cannot live in that cocoon where there is rule of law in the morning and that disappeared around four thirty pm for the sake of national security purposes. I cannot. Absolutely not. For me, the clarity of the rule of law is primordial in the morning, in the evening and at night. That is why I won't be able to operate, and I quote, as a politician. I cannot, I won't!"

"What I am trying to tell you today is this. That judiciary ball is now in the hand of the Attorney General, in the Immigration Court System that he controls. You have made your marks by stripping that man of the old identity. A great victory indeed! Can you just enjoy that victory and let it go. I must tell that you would aggravate a lot of people by pushing the agenda to upset what has been put in place for paramount national security purposes."

"And what has been put in place, let us know of the scheme that has been put in place. And it better be lawful. Otherwise, no deal. Put it in your thick skull that we have to answer not to the President, not to the Attorney General, not to my lovely niece, but to a very respectful lovely lady who raised the initial concerns about that scoundrel murderer Adamas Kagita when you hided him as Jefferson Okito who never existed. She recognized Adamas Kagita and screamed in horror. She screamed in horror, in the same manners as those, who survived the extermination camps of Auschwitz-Birkenau, Treblinka, Sobibor, Chelmno, Belzec, Majdanek, only to see the Nazi and the Nazi-collaborators, their very torturers, calmly living among them after so many years, in New York, Chicago, Cleveland, Pittsburg or whatever city in the good old US. Did you hear that scream of horror. I guess not. I heard it and did not like it. That is why I will continue to ignore your petty politics and will push the agenda until all the Adamas Kagita of this world answer for their crimes. And if this country will celebrate and honor the rule of law, I will continue to do that."

"Now you are going to the deep end as we are standing here to defend the Nazi or every violator of human rights in the world. You know very well that this is far from the truth. What you just said is also an extreme political speech. Going back to the case in point, and you know this very well, his defense team will introduce a series of legal waivers against his misrepresentation at the port of entry to the US. For God's sake, the man did not speak or understand English when he came to the US. He signed any papers under any identity to enter the US. Fine, he was found guilty of misrepresentation. The fine Judge Leighton-Garver said so. The immigration court recognized it and the procedure for removal has been put in motion. As I said, the procedures for waivers are also being filed and will be adjudicated in the immigration court system. That is the rule of law process that we are following. What is wrong with that?"

"Then why bring about national security purposes here if that is all that is there? In addition, what are we supposed to do about his loaded criminal background, should it be tossed aside because Adamas Kagita has become, all of the sudden, a Pentecostal Church or Baptist Church choir boy in North Carolina! Come on, Gwendolyn, come back to us down on earth for a second. Don't you see that you are becoming a conduit for amazing grave contradictions. This D.C. assignment has turned your head into a scary deposit of nonsense. Too many D.C. bull shit conversations have gone to your brain. I know that you want to tow the official line, nothing wrong with that, but spare us the same nonsense official line."

"There you go again. I am tracing for you the evolution of the case and you are coming back with load of disparagements. All I am saying is that, as you move along the immigration court system, the defense would be right beyond or beside you with appeal over appeal to wear you down with endless of motions until you will be exhausted and at the end we will confront national security purposes you won't be able to overcome. That is all I am warning you about. Don't come back and tell me that I did not warn you."

"Well let me say that I am prepared to get there. Thank you!"

"You are warned anyway!"

"Thank you again. That review of the immigration court system came in handy. Professor MacIntosh prepared me for the pitfalls you are talking about. You see, it was not a waste of time after all. I learned a lot. I know now that you control the process in that but of national territory. I also came to appreciate something else, that delegation comes after a big question mark, that is you must execute that delegation within the premises of the rule of law as prescribed by the Constitution. You must act in such way that there should not be, as it was well advanced and emphasized by the highly esteemed Law Professor McIntosh, "a question of law' in other words a derogation of law.'"

"Very dear Uncle, we do not derogate from the implementation of law, not that I have seen it nor anticipated it. Thank you for your attention."

"Gwendolyne, my very dear niece, as we march now in what you call your immigration court system territory, I must beg your mercy in making an urgent request. Professor McIntosh said that we need to set up a very good and working relationship with, what you call in the immigration court system, a trial attorney, the government counsel as opposed to the accused counsel. He insisted that to move this case efficiently within this new court process, the working relationship in term of access, availability, confidence with the trial attorney must be very high. I don't know anybody in that territory. Do you have any strong reference in the Charlotte area? Think about it and provide me with a good name, a good contact as soon as you can. Thank you!"

"I know few immigration court judges in the area. They should be able to identify a good contact who will be selected for the case. I will let you know. Bye!"

CHAPTER 22

IMMIGRA PRELIMINARIES

The DA Mr. O'Grady advised his staff counsel, Ms. Ludmilla Garrov to take an overnight trip to Charlotte for the first meeting he has scheduled with the Immigration Court folks in Charlotte, NC for the trial preliminaries around the first waiver that the defense team has filed for the incarcerated Adamas Kagita. The DA was dead set to contest that waiver and any other waiver for the accused. Mr. O'Grady warned that the three-hour car ride from Raleigh to Charlotte in the morning could reserve a lot of surprised delays. As far as he was concerned the eight thirty am appointment could be jeopardized. Mr. O'Grady planned to spend the night in Charlotte and not to fight the morning traffic from Raleigh to Charlotte. He did not trust himself to negotiate first the West bound 64 from Raleigh then the South bound 85 to Charlotte any time in the morning before ten. Ludmilla agreed and made the advised overnight hotel reservation.

The DA team arrived well before the appointment at the Charlotte Immigration Court at 5701 Executive Center Drive in Charlotte. The DA team was promptly received by a member of the Assistant Chief Immigration Judge. That was a surprise for the DA Team. They were led directly to the conference room of the judge where another lady was waiting for them. She introduced herself as Ms. Faye Manley, Trial Attorney. She said that she was going to be the government counsel during the hearings concerning the immigration case of the accused Adamas Kagita alias Jefferson Okito. Ms. Manley surprised Ludmilla by telling her that she was also a Law graduate from UNC, two years after Ludmilla's promotion. She added that she heard about Ludmilla's high level legal scholarship and proficiency in UNC academic circles. This note was very endearing for Mr. O'Grady to have recruited her to the top of her class.

Faye announced that she was lucky to have been selected to lead the hearing of the case. She said that she knew that the legal support that Ludmilla was going to provide would be above the top after reading the summary of the voluminous testimony that the Raleigh DA Staff Office was bringing against the accused Adamas Kagita. She confessed that in the execution and delivery of her functions as Trial Attorney, she had not seen such a thorough extensive level of legal testimony against an accused in the immigration court. She assured the DA team that she was honored to prosecute the case at hand to the highest possible level.

Faye advised the DA team to be reserved during the preliminary hearing of the first waiver that the defense team will bring for the accused. It is always better to see what strategy the defense team will adopt, under what constraints the defense team would want to box the government counsel in prosecuting the case, therefore eliminating the extensive legal venues that the voluminous testimony can bring to squash the waiver. Faye said that the best venue would be to listen attentively to what the defense team would be up to.

Faye proved to be correct on the defense team's strategy when the hearing started under the Immigration Court Judge. The defense team went straight to file I-601 Waiver for Prior Fraud or Misrepresentation. The purpose of the Form I-601 is usually used in a case for Adamas Kagita who is ineligible to be admitted to the US as an immigrant or to adjust status in the US. He must file the application to seek a waiver of certain grounds of inadmissibility. For Adamas Kagita, there were three grounds of inadmissibility that the defense team wanted to waive:

-Immigration fraud and Misrepresentation when he entered the US under the identity of Jefferson Okito who never existed,

-The 3-year or 10-year bar due to previous unlawful presence in the US as Jefferson Okito

-Criminal grounds of inadmissibility which Jefferson Okito alias Adamas Kagita hid when he entered the US.

Faye and the DA team listened motionless when the defense team completed its plea. The immigration court judge then asked the trial lawyer what she intended to do regarding the waiver filing. Faye calmly responded:

"Your Honor, the three grounds appear rather of high order in the grounds of inadmissibility backed by the voluminous testimony against the accused Adamas Kagita. The voluminous testimony that our esteemed Raleigh District Attorney Staff Office team had accumulated and is ready to share to contest this application for waiver. Your Honor and for your information, this very voluminous testimony was the basis of discovery when the accused was forced to confess to the misrepresentation of identity from Jefferson Okito to the war lord Adamas Kagita. The government counsel intends to use the same testimony to prosecute to the full instance of the law for all crimes the accused Adamas Kagita had committed as a war lord."

The immigration judge invited the defense team for a rebuttal.

"Your Honor, the defense counsel intends to pursue the waiver application against the three grounds of inadmissibility as stated. Accumulating a voluminous testimony without verifying the hearsay displayed herein would amount to a grave prejudice to the applicant of the waiver. The defense counsel intends to dispute the voluminous testimony as hearsay with no basis for factual verification."

The immigration judge delivered his conclusion:

"I hereby request that the government counsel provides factual verification for the testimony that she intends to introduce as evidence to contest and to dismiss the waiver application submitted by the accused."

At that instant, the defense lead counsel made an urgent request:

"Your Honor, the defense counsel is requesting that the court provides conditions for probation release of the defendant Adamas Kagita currently in administrative custody of ICE."

The immigration judge replied tersely:

"Counsel knows very well that the three grounds of inadmissibility you are requesting to be waived require that the defendant remains in the ICE administrative custody until the waive is granted, not before. Your request is therefore denied. This hearing meeting is adjourned."

The hearing meeting was swift and took less than fifteen minutes.

Faye was delighted by the judge's stand. The last thing she did not want to argue about was the continued incarceration of Adamas Kagita, in the administrative custody of ICE. And she did not want to do this while she had the DA team visiting from Raleigh. Faye was in an even more relaxed mood. She invited the DA team to have an important legal strategizing meeting if they want to listen to new venues that she wanted to explore and share while they were still in Charlotte Immigration Court premises. Mr. O'Grady agreed to the meeting along with Ludmilla. The meeting was going to take place in about an hour after Faye had cleaned her morning schedule. The DA team went back to the same conference room to wait for Faye. As soon as Faye came, she eagerly started sharing information about an agency that the DA team was not quite familiar with operating within the Department of Homeland Security Investigations (HIS) in direct support of the Immigration and Customs Enforcement (ICE) agency. Faye went on to define a center fully dedicated to assisting in the prosecution of the Adamas Kagita's case.

"In 2008, HSI created the Human Rights Violators and War Crimes Center (HRVWCC). The purpose of this center was to leverage the knowledge and expertise of a select group of special agents, attorneys, intelligence analysts, criminal research specialists and historians across multiple national security apparatus of the US government to work collaboratively to prevent the United States from becoming a safe haven for individuals who engage in the commission of war crimes, genocide, torture and other forms of serious human rights violations from conflicts around the globe. This center is the only U.S. government entity focused entirely on investigating these global atrocities."

"The HRVWCC focuses on its mission in two ways: by identifying, investigating, prosecuting, and removing human rights violators and war criminals found within the jurisdiction of the United States; and by preventing entry into the United States of known or suspected human rights violators and war criminals. The center works with foreign law enforcement and international partners and tribunals to further global accountability covering the geographic areas of the Americas, Europe, Africa, the Middle East, and Asia."

"Specifically, and as far as the Adamas Kagita case goes, the HRVWCC is also home to HSI's Human Rights Target Tracking Team which is comprised of criminal research specialists and intelligence analysts. These specialists are dedicated to identifying suspected human rights violators and war criminals abroad and to preventing their entry into the United States. I strongly believe that we can use these specialists to assist us in verifying factually the bulk of the voluminous testimony that you have collected about Adamas Kagita. Before you raise any doubt about the effectiveness of these specialists, let me tell you that these specialists have successfully assisted in the prosecution of a war lord criminal from Liberia who fit perfectly Adamas Kagita war lord profile from DRC This Liberian war lord was found guilty in a Federal District Court in Philadelphia and was condemned for thirty years of jail time."

"According to multiple reporting, you will find the story of Mohammed Jabbateh very similar if not close to Adamas Kagita's. **He was** born September 1966 also known by his war namesake "Jungle Jabbah" just as Adamas was known as "Danger de Mort". He served as a general in the United Liberation Movement for Democracy in Liberia (ULIMO), a rebel group that battled for control of Liberia in the 1990s during the first Liberian civil war from 1989 through 1997. This is not different from what I read in your voluminous testimony submission about Adamas Kagita, about his long criminal journey, about his joining all kinds of armed militias in Eastern DRC to rise to the top of endless criminal enterprises to assert power, to kill people, to rape women, and always to make a lot of money. This is how and why he joined armed militias to control minerals murderous traffic from Eastern DRC to neighboring countries of Uganda, Rwanda, and Burundi. This is how and why he rose to the rank of Colonel or General of armed militias who controlled the mines and the logistics in the hands of armed militias controlled by rebellious groups which invested the area such as RCD, CNDP and M23.'

"In the same path as Adamas Kagita, but before him in December 1998, Jabbateh submitted his application for US asylum and later for US permanent residency. While Adamas Kagita entered the US as a Uganda citizen, a businessman named Jefferson Okito fleeing whatever we must find out his criminal enterprise, Jabbateh disclosed that he was a member of ULIMO, but he did not reveal his alleged "General" capacity. In January 1999, an immigration asylum officer interviewed Jabbateh to determine whether his asylum application should be granted. Jabbateh responded "no" to these two questions: 1. "Have you ever committed a crime?" and 2. Have you ever harmed anyone else?" In January 1999, Jabbateh received US asylum based on his answers to questions posed on his Form I-589 asylum application form."

"Jabbateh also applied for permanent residency (also known as a green card) using Form I-485. He responded "No" to these two questions: 1. "Have you ever engaged in genocide, or otherwise ordered, incited, assisted or otherwise participated in the killing of any person because of race, religion, nationality, ethnic origin or political opinion?" 2. "Are you under a final order of civil penalty for violating section 274C of the Immigration and Nationality Act for use of fraudulent documents of have you, by fraud or willful misrepresentation of a material fact, ever sought to procure or procured a visa, other documentation, or entry into the US or any immigration benefit?"

"Jabbateh settled in Lansdowne, Pa, where he remained until his conviction in October 2017. Jabbateh had a wife and five children who live in Philadelphia. He also had an ex-wife and at least seven children who live in Liberia or elsewhere on the African continent, who he attempted to sponsor to immigrate to the US. Jabbateh started a shipping company in 2008, Jabbateh Brothers Loading Services, which packages, and ships containers to Liberia. It remains in operation. Friends and family in his community around Philadelphia regarded him favorably. He did not hold a US passport and had not left the country since his arrival in 1998."

"On March 10, 2016, Jabbateh was indicted and charged by the US Attorney's Office for the Eastern District of Pennsylvania with two counts of fraud in immigration documents and two counts of perjury. The indictment was unsealed on April 13, 2016, and Jabbateh was arrested in his Delaware County home in Lansdowne, Pa "

"On October 18, 2017, Jabbateh was convicted of two counts of fraud in immigration documents and two counts of perjury stemming from statements he made in connection with his applications for asylum and permanent residence.] Jabbateh was sentenced to 30 years in prison on April 19, 2018. Although federal guidelines generally only call for 15 to 21 months in prison for the charges he was convicted, U.S. District Judge Paul S. Diamond instead sentenced him to the statutory maximum, saying it would be "not only unreasonable but outrageously offensive" considering his past."

"I want to be clear, I am departing not based on the horror of the atrocities the defendant committed abroad," Diamond said. "Rather, I am departing based on the egregiousness of his lies…and their effect on our asylum laws and immigration system." He said Jabbateh had made a "mockery" of the U.S. asylum system that had been established to protect people fleeing from human rights abusers like himself.[

"HSI agents from Philadelphia, the HRVWCC's Africa intel analyst and members of the United States Attorney's Office for the Eastern District of Pennsylvania traveled to Liberia to interview over 30 eyewitnesses. These eyewitnesses provided firsthand accounts of torture, rape, cannibalism, and murder committed by Jabbateh and his band of soldiers. Judge Diamond relied heavily of these factual accounts of Jabbateh past to render that lengthy sentence."

"These factual accounts established that Jabbateh was a commander or higher-ranking officer in ULIMO and ULIMO-K, and during that time he either personally committed, or ordered ULIMO troops under his command to commit the following list of acts:

1. The murder of civilian non-combatants

2. The sexual enslavement of women

3. The public raping of women

4. The maiming of civilian non-combatants

5. The torturing of civilian non-combatants

6. The enslavement of civilian non-combatants

7. The conscription of child soldiers

8. The execution of prisoners of war

9. The desecration and mutilation of corpses

The killing of persons because of race, religion, nationality, ethnic origin or political opinion"

"I don't think we will have any problem prosecuting the above listing of ten charges against Adamas Kagita according to the testimony you got, and which can be easily verified by the HRVWCC.'

After a brief pause, Mr. O'Grady, the Eastern District of North Carolina DA, thanked Ms. Faye Maley, the trial lawyer.

"Counsel Ms. Ludmilla Garrov here and I are very grateful that you did not wait for us to get thoroughly informed and acquainted about the case against Adamas Kagita. Your appraisal will help us tremendously. We realized that we have been lucky to land on your dedicated service in the immigration court system we were not fully informed of. To tell the truth that was a matter of grave concern for us. As you have already found out, we have dedicated a serious amount of energy and resources to advance the prosecution of this scoundrel. We were seriously concerned above all that the accused could be released on technicality by the immigration court judge. I must tell you that the accused has strong financial and political backing in support of his case. You saw the kind of legal representation he is affording for himself. His legal representation is top notch indeed. We were afraid that he could be freed after posting any sizable caution thanks to his powerful backers. We were relieved to hear the judge tersely rejecting the defense team request for any probation venue. We are extremely happy with the amount of preparation you have dedicated to the case. We are very much interested in the new reference you have mentioned. I am talking about the HRVWCC. We did know about this center. But we are ready and willing to work with it. We know that you will guide us superbly. Thank you again. Ludmilla what do you think?"

"Mr. O'Grady, this trip has exceeded all my expectations. Counsel Faye, you have no idea how helpful you have been to us. Our District Staff Office is concerned mainly with domestic legal issues. This is the first time we are venturing in international areas. I must confess, even for me from a region which has experienced the terrible background of grave human right violations, this has been a difficult re-education. I share my Boss's utmost gratitude. I forgot to mention that we just had a two review of the immigration court system by one of your eminent Professor McIntosh. Now my question to you is this simple: did he convince you to immerse in this legal career?"

"Yes, he did! I am glad to ask. He also guided me in my legal graduation paper project which focused on the Yugoslavia sectarian break up wars. I never stopped consulting with Professor McIntosh, a tremendous resource!"

"He is indeed!"

"Ladies, I second that appraisal! Now, back to our business matters. Faye, you have mentioned the involvement with the HRVWCC. What is the procedure, how can we avail of this support?"

"Mr. O'Grady, the sooner you align that support the better. I am sure that Professor McIntosh has shared with you the immigration court system and how it evolved from the judge decision to appeal with Board of Immigration Appeals (BIA) to Federal Court of Appeals to the US Supreme Court back to the Federal Court of Appeals down to the Immigration Court. Of course, if the Judge's decision is generally accepted, then the case will be closed. Otherwise, it will navigate the lengthy appeal process. In this case, the immigration court judge has already indicated to me the trial lawyer to get the voluminous testimony verified. That is a decision that amounts to an appeal already. In other words, the defense team is saying it is rejecting the voluminous testimony as hearsay, irrelevant to the case of Adamas Kagita. I am anticipating that the defense team will plead some kind of death threats waiting on Adamas Kagita if he is deported back to DRC. The defense team will state that Adamas Kagita was forced to lie, to assume this Uganda identity of Jefferson Okito, because he knew that if he has entered his name as Adamas Kagita, he was never going to get a chance to enter the US. All right, the debate becomes now under what immigration statutes his background would prevent him to enter the US. The immigration court judge must weigh all these immigration admissibility and inadmissibility statutes. The defense team could appeal his decision for whatever reasons, preferably for what we call "question of law". That means is the decision rendered by the immigration court judge abridges the constitutional rights of Adamas Kagita in term of all the basic human rights affordable to all residents of the US. These Rights are freedom of speech, freedom of movement, freedom of assembly, right to a fair trial, freedom of association, freedom of belief and religion, right to privacy, and for Adamas Kagita the Supreme Right to Life if he can plead that being deported back to DRC, that right to life will certainly be abridged. The immigration court judge has basically instructed me to show that Adamas Kagita will not be deserving of these rights in the US by living here unless he answers the series of crimes he has committed while in DRC. Otherwise, he would be deported or would spend time in jail in the US."

"Are you saying that we can go right now start the process of verifying the facts reported in the voluminous testimony using the HRVWCC services. But that could be very expensive."

"Yes, it is costly. But it is lawfully funded by the Department of Justice if it is requested by the immigration court judge and the Attorney General office. I will initiate the request. Don't you worry at this stage it should be routine. You have already done tremendous research work. Validating it would not be difficult. Remember in the Liberian case, there was no documentation to start with. The verification process was done from the interviews that did not exist before. You have already dated materials to bring to court. I know the bulk of them is in French. We can select the most important ones and verify them to satisfy the judge inquiry. We have people who have done this, and they will be willing to help."

"Any particular reference or references?"

"Of course, we have references in the HRVWCC to make direct use after we determine the most important key events and themes, I have noticed that you have already done an excellent classification and filter of the voluminous testimony."

"Well, that is wonderful. Ludmilla has done all that work already. She also has an excellent local reference to work with you. Just indicate for us the references in that agency to work with."

"Certainly, I have in mind a very dynamic specialist in HRVWCC who worked in the Liberian case. His name is Pascal Bodavi. He is full French-English bilingual, originally from Cameroon. He has a J.D. Law degree from University of Georgia in Athens, Ga. A very resourceful gentleman. I would rather let you meet with him when you are ready or better yet inviting him to come to meet with you in Raleigh. I can assure you would not be disappointed.'

"We would invite him as soon as he will be available."

"I have talked with him, he is available now before another big assignment. Grab him as soon as possible."

"Please, please share his reference. We want to talk with him today."

"My pleasure!"

CHAPTER 23

BODAVI FROM MAMIE

On the way back to Raleigh, Ludmilla was instructed by her Boss, the DA Mr. O'Grady to get urgently in touch with Charlote Keregi.

After the wonderful feedback help, they got in Charlotte from the immigration court trial lawyer Faye Manley, it was more than obvious to share the next steps that the DA office needed to undertake. Charlotte was the main contact to accomplish what Faye suggested to do in contact with the HRVWCC staff. Ludmilla arranged to meet with Charlotte the next day evening at their regular restaurant drop.

"Hello Charlotte, I must let you know right away that we had a very productive meeting at the Immigration Court building in Charlotte. Woooah, I did not realize that they named that town after you. Yo must be an important Southern belle to be celebrated this way. Ah, Ah, Ah… On a serious note, the visit went very well for the DA Staff office. For your concern, Adamas Kagita will remain in the jail if the case is not resolved or concluded, according to the immigrant judge who is handling the case. We were very concerned that he could be released on probation. It is not going to happen, so we happily learned. We were concerned because Adamas appeared to have very powerful financial and political support. And whether we like it or not, money talks in the US. Now rest assured that he won't be released. The simple reason being that he had no document today to attest that he is in the US since he entered the US through fraudulent misrepresentation as Jefferson Okito who has been found as a person that does not exist. Now he cannot set foot outside the immigration jail until he has lawfully regularized his status as a resident. And he won't be able to do that because, and this is very important, Charlotte Keregi along with the Raleigh Eastern District Attorney Office have determined that he is a war lord with a long murderous baggage in Eastern DRC. Charlotte and the same DA office would see to that either he is deported, or he is jailed to pay for his crimes. The immigration judge repeated the same decision that Judge Leighton-Garver made. We were delighted with that decision."

"Furthermore Charlotte, the same immigration court judge decided that he would make a final disposition of Adamas Kagita after he is convinced that the voluminous testimony that you have helped us gather is, and this is very important, verified. That is the reason I came back, and I set up this meeting so urgently. Now you must be wondering how we need to verify all that you have helped us gather. Now rest assured that the voluminous testimony has already been verified to the range of sixty percent or more. It is up to us to raise that range to close to ninety-nine, nine, nine, nine … percent. It is up to us to convince the judge that what was reported was verified. We were very pleased to meet what they call in immigration court terms, a trial lawyer who is the government lawyer who represents the US government in ensuring that people enter the US territory lawfully. I need to pull back here for your information, well, in the immigration court system, this trial lawyer pleads the government case for or against the entry into the US of any foreign person who may be represented by an immigration private lawyer. Currently, Adamas Kagita is represented by a powerful law firm from D.C. with very expert private immigration lawyers. Now the trial lawyer we met provided us with very good information, very good steps around the process to get the voluminous testimony verified.'

"That is very interesting, Ludmilla, and what is the process?"

"This is where we came back very relieved to get this case to more than a satisfactory conclusion. The trial lawyer named is Faye Manley. She said that there is an office with a long name: HRVWCC for Human Rights Violators and War Crimes Center, funded by the Department of Justice that would assist us to verify the voluminous testimony. Faye explained that we would need to select key events in the voluminous testimony and get them verify through interviews and factual verification at the local level in Eastern DRC."

"Do you mean right there in Eastern DRC area?"

"Yes indeed, Charlotte!"

"Ludmilla, you are not asking me to go back in that area and interview people about various events where Adamas was implicated. That would be impossible. I would be killed, assassinated!"

"You would not be asked to do none of this, Charlotte! A professional team of experts would do that verification process. I am not saying that it would be easy, but it can be done. Just to reassure you it was done in Liberia and successfully to get this war lord put in jail here in the US for thirty years."

"I hate to tell you this, Liberia is not DRC! You are talking about two different countries, two different areas."

"Charlotte, before you close your mind about this venue, I beg you to calm down. I beg you to wait to hear the conversation from one of the people who had conducted such verification process in the Liberia case. We have invited this gentleman from D.C. He should be here in a day or two. Charlotte, remember what you told me when we started this process. You said that you would leave it all in the Lord's hands to carry his final judgement over Adamas Kagita. I would not let you close your mind now that we are getting to the final judgment. I know that you don't want Adamas Kagita to go free. I don't!"

"Ludmilla don't get me wrong. Of course, I want this man to suffer my Lord's final judgement. But that should not happen by paying another course of killing and assassinations. You know very well that the powerful forces that are backing Adamas are still in place back in Eastern DRC, just as omnipotent as ever. I follow very carefully all that is going on there. The killings have never stopped, Ludmilla. I left and run away because of the same. Would I expose anybody to the same killings, I wouldn't! The price of retribution is getting a bit steep, my God, help me!"

"I am, we are! Charlotte, I repeat, keep you mind open until you hear this specialist, OK!"

"OK, I would!"

After a day, Charlotte was invited to come to the DA Office at about ten thirty in the morning. Ludmilla took her straight to the DA Staff conference room where a young black man of about thirty-five years was waiting for them. Pascal Bodavi introduced himself as a lawyer attached to HRVWCC. He said this jokingly with an exaggerated thick

French accent. That broke the tense outlook that Charlotte wore with her walking into the room. He added in French:

"Bonjour, Mademoiselle Charlotte Keregi", in a professional French accent now.

"Bonjour, Monsieur …."

"Monsieur Pascal Bodavi from Mamie, British Cameroon, SVP, Mademoiselle Charlotte et Enchate!"

The last reference brought a big laughter from the two African expatriates.

"Where are these British references coming from a young man of Cameroon descent?" Charlotte shot back.

"I knew that a beautiful Congolese lady would never greet a young buck from Cameroon as British, pardon me, English speaking, only French. Well, I am sorry to disappoint you. I was born in a town called Mamie in the British section of Cameroon on the big highway going to the neighboring brotherly state of Nigeria which abandoned us in the throes of French colonialists, a terrible fate we have been suffering forever …"

"Very sorry, young buck from Mamie, British Cameroon! I knew that there were two colonial sections in Cameroon, the French and the British. I thought that the same tribes are shared in two sections, one French another British. The colonial burden we all shared in Africa. Believe me a Bamilike in the British section can always communicate with a Bamilike in the French section in Bamilike. So, what is your problem. From a Pan African stand, it should really matter. Well, I am very happy to meet you as a special counsel from that agency I cannot spell. Greetings!"

"I am so relieved you know each other. I was a bit lost a while ago thinking that I came to a family reunion."

"Ludmilla, I am grateful that you got me a bilingual African to exchange in such serious legal matter. That is refreshing. You got me all nervous yesterday talking about sending God knows who to Eastern DRC to interview people there. Today I am relieved that a bilingual not speaking Swahili from Cameroon would go there. 'Habari kani'"

"Habari muzuri!"

"Oh my, he also speaks Swahili! I am in good hands. Ludmilla, sign him up!"

"All right, guys, enough of joking around!"

"Mr. Pascal Bodavi, it is my pleasure to introduce you to Ms. Charlotte Keregi from Eastern DRC. I am happy that you have lowered Charlotte's anxiety about going into troubled areas as you did in Liberia."

"Point of correction, Ludmilla, he did not lessen my anxiety yet. He has not gone there yet. The fact he speaks three languages spoken in the area is a plus for startup. That is the point I was making. I know that the ladies would appreciate his presence there, but the armed and wild militia may not take it kindly that this polished lawyer comes in the area interviewing people about the murderous traffic of gold and coltan. And you got tons of militias in the area. This is no joke. Enough of me scaring the British buck from Cameroon."

"I see that Ms. Charlotte Keregi has zero confidence over the illustrious team from HRVWCC. You know what, Charlotte is right. It is no joke. It was not joke in Liberia. It was no joke to go to Liberia conduct those interviews to provide verification to hearsay that was more and less documented about that war lord. Let me just say, the verification process followed a logical procedure. To ascertain the verification, we decided to proceed to drive the most significant events of the war lord involvement in the country civil war story and that were found in the documented hearsay reports. We assumed that significant events were events that impacted a larger or wider section of the country. We reviewed the Liberia territorial administration. The country map comprised of territorial divisions or counties with major capitals, the counties were subdivided into districts which in turn were subdivided into clans. To track the military engagement of the war lord required to follow how he emerged from whatever status in the militia from the lowest territorial subdivision of clan or district to higher division of county or the county capital. The beautiful thing about this tracking is that along the way, people remember, and people talk."

"However, the problem here is that we were not tracking a picknick, we were tracking the evolution of the war lord in the context of civil war. The event or events of interest were no joke. These events occurred in areas invested by drugged up armed militias. You did not know what these war combatants were going to do from one minute to another, whether they were going to share willingly their war memories, whether they were fantasizing or sharing realities. The most unpredictable and dangerous were the younger ones who needed to be called by their superiors to attention all the time. You never knew whether they were following orders or were simply improvising them. You won't believe when I said my biggest surprise was seeing how the female combatants behaved. They combined all the worse war attributes in trying to prove themselves in front of male combatants. They were the most stoned, the most violent, the loudest and always the most dangerous. I personally avoided them. Most combatants, male or female would not engage in any conversation. They were always standing apart. The most difficult thing was to gain their confidence to share stories they would never want to talk about when the civil war would be over. Anybody who goes around telling you that he or she had the best approaches to reach these combatants is lying. After a person has gone beyond basic humanity, that person is well marked, that person is lost. You must be lucky to retrieve a slice of their deep memories around the events they have witnessed."

"So how did you manage to verify the atrocities they were engaged in or have witnessed, if these combatants did not want to talk?"

"We got to the victims if they were not killed. The way we got to the victims was probing the combatants about events and locations. The combatants will share the event, the approximate date of the event and the location. That was the start of the conversation. They would not go further about what they did. They were not fools to share the crimes that would implicate them. Then we will go to the general population and make general inquiries. If the whole village population was exterminated well that was the end of the interview. Now you must also remember that these combatants did not conduct themselves under predetermined rules of engagement of organized armed forces. They were wild guerilla forces and very disorganized. The chain of command was fluid. That chain of command started and ended with self-appointed Commandant or "Generals" who mainly inspired fear and imposed brutal, harsh discipline among combatants. They never hesitated to kill on the spot combatants who did not obey their orders, small or big. So, during these war campaigns there were always some people, old folks, women, and infants who were spared or were hiding during the murderous event at a particular location on a particular date. These folks were interviewed at length. It did take a long time to compare the same story being told more than two or three times from the lowest territory level. That was the extent of the first verification step. When the same story gets repeated more than three times and is confirmed by combatants and other high-ranking commandants, that was the second level of verification gaining more meat. And when the event gained military significance that was a third level of verification, and the event was tabled. Using that iteration, we came up with a list of more than thirty significant event cases implicating that war lord. Now is that methodology valid in Eastern DRC, I don't know. But we can only try to find out if it would and could be validated."

"If you put it that way, I would strongly agree that your verification process would work in Eastern DRC. But I still have a major reservation. Of course, Liberia is not DRC, and you already said it. My reservation comes from the political environment that allowed you to conduct those interviews. I am assuming that your team arrived to conduct these interviews after the civil war."

"True, we got there about more than ten years after the events, after the first civil war from 1989 through 1996, the second civil war from 1997 through 2003, the transitional government from 2003 through 2005, the first elected presidency of Ellen Johnson Sirleaf from 2005. I must say that we conduct the interviews in a peaceful environment. But finding combatants and people to talk was still very difficult."

"Unfortunately, the interviews you are planning to take would not happen in a peaceful environment, I am afraid. And that will be a very major obstacle you would face in Eastern DRC. What you would find in Kinshasa, the capital of DRC, is totally different from what is still happening in Eastern DRC. The state of war has never stopped. The killing has continued until now. The combatant's environment is still prevalent. How in God goodness Grace are you going to accomplish that verification? And I must tell you a political reality about DRC today, people you will see in Kinshasa, in political power position, are the same people who are pulling the strings to maintain that state of war in Eastern DRC. If the civil war in Liberia was political around power sharing and that has been negotiated to a form of peaceful transition to elected government, DRC has not known that peaceful transition, at least not in the Eastern DRC. The civil war is continuing with more killing, all the way to the staggering tune of eight million dead people now. And I am not exaggerating.!. The fighting is now over the control of mineral resources, gold, coltan and diamond. Everybody, I mean everybody wants to share in plundering those mineral resources including the central government in Kinshasa, the Armed Forces, the local militias, the militias governments from neighboring countries of Uganda, Rwanda and Burundi, the UN forces. They fight over both the extraction of minerals and the logistic to get the minerals from DRC to border towns of Uganda and Rwanda from where they are shipped overseas. I am telling you, we have thoroughly documented this murderous plundering, everybody is involved in this war waged by the surrogates war lords like Adamas Kagita. My question, again, is how you are going to conduct your interviews under these murderous circumstances."

"Ms. Charlotte Keregi, if we must conduct these interviews in that area, we certainly will find a way. We will be covered by some lethal forces to accomplish this if we must. That process will be designed by the powers that be. Let them design it. I will certainly be involved."

"Mr. Bodavi, I can assure you that I must alert the same folks who provided us with the voluminous testimony to assist you in the area. They know the terrain better than anybody else."

"You read my mind. I was going to ask you the same thing. I want to do better. I would review the entire voluminous testimony with you and Ludmilla. Together we would select thirty or so most significant events in the criminal journey of this war lord. I would take over then and there. Thanks to your references, I would work with our worldwide team to set up these interviews. I beg you to leave to the team the execution of these interviews in DRC and the delivery of documented interviews back to you, the DA Staff Office, and Counsel Faye Manley in Charlotte. Will that work for you?"

"Definitely and certainly if nobody is exposed and harmed in the process, and as long as you are not exposed or harmed in the process. "

"Don't worry about me, I am not about to get unnecessarily exposed or harmed. And thank you for your concern."

Ludmilla, who has followed attentively the difficult exchange, jumped in:

213

"Hello guys, I am so relieved to notice that you have reached a common understanding over how to move ahead in this verification process. Mr. Bodavi, thank you so very much for clarifying what we need to do to help ourselves. To tell you the truth, I was also concerned about the verification process given the political instability in Eastern DRC. I trust that Mr. Bodavi knows exactly what it would take to accomplish the verification process. I am ready to assist his team anyway I can. Charlotte, I hope that our guest has answered your concerns and questions."

"He did, indeed! as I said, so many people have already lost their life in this case. I pray that our involvement does not add more exposure nor harm to anybody."

"I understand and appreciate your overall concern."

"Still, Mr. Bodavi, can you help me understand why and how you chose such a difficult career path? You could have been helping a lot of immigrants representing them as immigration lawyer with your unique background?"

"I was born in a town called Mamie in the Anglophone or British section of Cameroon. The town is located on the major road that led to the Eastern border to Nigeria. That section has always been considered as a stepchild and minority in the Cameroon evolution to an independent state since 19661 when the region people elected through a referendum to remain in a Union with the majority French Cameroon as opposed to the union with Nigeria. Things never improved for these English-speaking people from that time through to date to a point that since 1985, the region people have contested the political union and integration with Cameroon pushing for an independent Republic of Ambazonia. A lot of my family members joined political movements to achieve that political goal. My father, a former lawyer, got my family to leave the area and migrated to the city of Calabar in the Southwest "Cross River State in Nigeria. The family gained political refugee status in the city of Calabar where I grew up. The family-maintained still attaches in both Cameroon and Nigeria. I came to the US right after high school graduation and lived with an uncle family outside Atlanta while going to Georgia State University. I finally followed my father's path when I went to the University of Georgia Law School in Athens. After Graduation, I wanted to practice International Business Law in both Cameroon and Nigeria. But I was advised by my father to return to the US as the political situation in the English section of Cameroon has deteriorated to a full-blown rebellion against the central government of Yaoundé. He warned me that life was not going to be easy as a lawyer from the Ambazonia region, in both Cameroon and Nigeria. That was then I came back to Atlanta and started a legal career first as an immigration lawyer and when I became a US citizen, I joined the HRVWCC for obvious reasons. The biggest case I was involved in was the Mohammed Jabbateh case which awakened me to incredible atrocities that we watched from afar on TV documentaries without full appreciation of the impacts and consequences of these follies on the impacted people in Africa. I intend to personally prosecute the drivers of these atrocities wherever they hid in the world. And this is where I am now."

"That is a tremendous goal I have not heard of among many young professionals of African descent. I certainly commend you at such a young age. How old are you?"

"About thirty-four about to be thirty-five in a month or two."

"Still very young, again congratulations. It sounds like you and I have similar goals. Mine, as you can see is very specific: I want that son of bitch jailed for the crimes against me, my family and many, many, many people. I have dedicated my life to that goal. I thought that it was a faraway mirage, but God has preserved me to get there slowly and surely thanks to Ludmilla of this world, of the DA here, my church members, and now thanks to you, Mr. Bodavi. I thank you so much for giving me hope!"

"I would not make any promise, but you would get a relief, so Gold help us!"

"Amen!"

Ludmilla observed and listened with attuned emotion and wonder at the two victims of human rights violations in Africa and the resolutions they have fixed themselves and did not easily share them.

"Mr. Bodavi, we have held Charlotte much longer than I expected. She had to go to work to attend to patients in one of our hospitals. As you can see, we are lucky to get people in all kinds of life to assist us in our prosecution of criminals. Charlotte has been our shining star to that effect. Thank you, Charlotte, thank you again for coming. We will be in touch."

"Thank you, Ludmilla, you are getting a hell of support in the hands of Mr. Bodavi, will see you again, young buck!"

Ludmilla led Charlotte to the DA Staff Office exit door.

CHAPTER 24

BODAVI'S INITIATIVE

As soon as Charlotte departed, Ludmilla brought Mr. Bodavi to a brief meeting with Boss DA. The man from HRVCC raised another surprise:

"I must share with you another verification process that I was not at liberty to talk about when Charlotte was around. This process was devised by the concerted team put together to handle verification process. I must share it officially with you. Charlotte and her contacts back did a hell of job providing all that background that accumulate to the voluminous testimony. The documentation was impressive, and we are not disputing the veracity of it. Yes, the judge requested further verification. It sounded simple. But as Charlotte explained it, the government in place is just as much part of the problem. The government in Kinshasa is fully engaging in the same plundering that the accused was master of. It is difficult to tell who is doing the stealing, the killing, the savage plundering from the team that is really protecting the national resources in DRC. I don't want to talk about the neighboring country governments which are equally involved in the plundering. The judge was briefed about this by our concerted team. If the judge requested further verification, it is simply a political step to ensure that the Immigration department is not blamed for messing up the government engagement in this very bizarre external dossier. The immigration department is disposed to move the case as legally as far it can. The immigration department is also ready to drop it on the higher judicial circle if it needs be. Are you following me so far?"

"I am, and I hope Ludmilla is too, are you?"

"I am following you and I want to hold my reservation until the end, until I am convinced, I understood. Please, proceed!"

"Thank you, lady, and gentleman! As I was saying, this bizarre dossier has a lot of foreign strategic implications, at the intersection of four concerned countries: DRC, Rwanda, Uganda, and the US. We have got to be careful about how we handle this case and especially this so-called verification. I have shared what I believe will be a two-pronged initiative to get a positive progressive outcome for the immigration department. I have proposed a two steps process. The first step is the step that will openly engage the DRC government from Kinshasa whereby the US Justice Department will make all the regular request to interview a set of contacts who could assist us but they will not be as significative as we have decided, The second step will be the step whereby undercover operatives from Kenya, South Africa and Tanzania will go to the area under various masks and covers. These undercover operatives will be well protected and will conduct the most significative interviews as indicated by the filter of the voluminous testimony. Hopefully the undercover operatives will be successful in their tasks and collect the interviews without any problem.

The bottom line is that the interviews are done, collected, and reviewed either in Kenya or South Africa and finally forwarded to Faye who will present them to the judge. Case closed! What I want from your office and a good selection of significant and less significant events to carry to Kinshasa and the fields in Eastern DRC. What do you think?"

"It is a wonderful plan, Mr. Bodavi! Ludmilla and I had the same concerns after we talked with Counsel Faye Manley and with our very brave Lady Charlotte. I hope you are aware that the bulk of the testimony came from Charlotte's Uncle who resides in Sweden. I would strongly suggest that you get in touch with him for a better selection of events. He had a tremendous selection reach back home. He should be the principal guide for the most significant events."

"Thank you, I expect Charlotte to share his references. Thank you."

"Mr. Bodavi, from the beginning when we got involved in this case, I had this gut feeling that the case had many myriad trails. Today, you have removed a lot of misgivings about our government's external engagements. I guess in this world, you cannot expect other people to share our values and to march in the same tunes. Can you imagine the central government so crooked spoiling its own country's mineral resources for the benefit of a few people at the top of government chain. I always wonder what our political leaders should do faced with such tragedy, should they go along, look the other way, or seriously engage them to correct their way with the risk of being kicked out of the country or the external engagement. That cannot be easy for our leaders."

"And imagine when that political leader must face this disconnect every day and come back to face the American people and decline to say anything about. No wonder they age so fast running the country! Ah, ah, ah!"

"On the serious note, I believe from what you say that there is a bit of disconnect in the administration around the US standing in Eastern DRC!"

"A major one if you ask me! A major one, indeed! On one hand you have folks from Clinton political camp and on the other hand folks who came with Obama. They were supposed to work together. But it was obvious they showed different allegiances here and there. The Clintonistas who lived and suffered what they called the calamity of the Genocide of Tutsi in Rwanda and had stood and continue to stand by the new Rwanda political leadership no matter what and the Obama folks who came later and put in place the legislation against blood minerals. Guess what, this legislation went entirely against the blind support that the Clintonistas gave the new Rwanda leadership which now pushed and aggravated the plundering of mineral resources in Eastern DRC. I wonder sometime whether this support was a guilty "quid pro quo" trip for missing to prevent and to stop the genocide on its track. It was very hard for them to ignore the fact that the Rwanda leadership has chased the genocidaire troops from the DRC eastern mountains through the dense equatorial forest of the Congo River basin all the way to the country capital of Kinshasa over the South West corner of the country, to have overthrown the dictatorial regime of Marechal Mobutu, to have established a new political regime in DRC, only to be chased from Kinshasa by Mze Kabila, the same very puppet they have put in place. It is again difficult for them to ignore that the Rwanda leadership was upstaged and kicked out Kinshasa for the simple reason that Congolese, with four hundred fifty tribes, would never have gone to accept to be governed for a long time by a new tribal group from a different country. It was more than incredible that the sectarian factor of tribalism escaped the Clintonistas and the Rwandan Leadership plan to take over militarily DRC when the terrible genocide was triggered by the same. So much so when the new Rwanda leadership was sent back home, it set up armed militia to extract mineral resources in the Eastern DRC. The Clintonistas looked the other way. However, the new Senator of Illinois, Barack Obama came up with a new legislative against what he designated "blood minerals". The Clintonistas still continue to support the established Rwanda leadership and looked the other way This happened before Obama run and was elected President. The Clintonistas joined the Obama Administration with coveted assignment in Foreign Affairs where they maintained their support of the Rwandan leadership despite "blood minerals" extraction in Eastern DRC. And here we are, the two-pronged allegiances have survived, and the contradiction maintained."

"I see, so how this Adamas Kagita issue would be resolved given the contradiction of these two allegiances?"

"Hard to tell! The contradiction does not need to be resolved until the next time we have another democratic administration and when all is put under another national strategic interest rug. Unless you can tell me, who wants to take responsibility of supporting a Rwanda leadership which has been aiding and abetting another genocide now to the tune of more than eight million people and counting because of the plundering of mineral resources in the Eastern DRC. That is the big question. Sooner or later responsibility would be assigned to some party. Now look how that assignment was done when the Rwandan leadership was kicked out from Kinshasa. Would you believe it, Lauren Desire Mze Kabila, the puppet president put in power by the invading Rwanda leadership, was held responsible for mass graves holding more than thousands of fleeing Hutu people across the Congo River basin. These people were massacred by invading Tutsi Rwanda forces throughout DRC. The American Administration held Mze Kabila responsible for these massacres until he was assassinated. There was no mention of the invading forces who carried out the massacres and dug the mass graves. This is a good illustration of how the Adamas Kagita case would be resolved. A political way would be found, I am sure!"

"Are you saying that we are wasting our precious time, and the fix is in, the outcome is already fixed?"

"Absolutely not, I am not! The contradiction of these allegiances would go on, that is the D.C. game we don't need to play. That is not new. Every administration comes with its own set of contradictions. Some are maximized causing major scandals, some are internally managed with maximum restraints for all especially when the risks of scandal are quietly assessed to bury everybody. Remember self-political interest always triumphs in most cases, because political instinct, whether you like it or not, is one of survival. And most always manage to move the post and undesirable political baggage to the next administration. If you don't know this, politicians would say "well get out of the hot kitchen". Mr. O'Grady, to that remarkable vain, how long ago this Eastern DRC tragedy has been reported?"

"Well let me answer this question since 1997. That means we have gone through five American administrations, two Republican and three Democrat. And the Eastern DRC issue is still being debated. I have no intention to play the D.C. game, my objective is to provide the verification of what has been determined to be voluminous testimony to cover the criminal journey of Adamas Kagita. My role is to assist the immigration judge with that verification. The judge will decide regarding the immigration status of Adamas Kagita based on verified testimony. I know that if I satisfy the judge requested verification, Adamas Kagita would be prevented from staying in the US or would be jailed for the crimes he has committed. That is the end of my assignment. Now if the judge is prevented from enacting his decision for whatever reason, the appeal process would take over. The case would go up the judicial ladder until it is sent back in whatever form and the upper ladder would decide."

"All right what if the appeal is brought up in relation to National Strategic Concerns, what will you do?"

"Any time I hear National Strategic Concerns, I know we are talking about the contradictions I touched upon above. That is CIPA. That is strictly D.C. domain, political game. That comes when I have exhausted my legal perimeters and constraints. I cannot play there. Here the litigation evolves into what I enjoy hearing "A Question or A Matter of Law". It is way above my low salary grade and function. It is also a domain where the public is seldom invited in, it is excluded. It is where the political game is played to the till, covered by a myriad of exceptions, most of the time plain ridiculous and far from the tenets of law. To tell the truth, I am most uncomfortable in this circle. I just don't like it because this is where the criminals evade justice. This is where the breakdown of the foundation of justice takes place and the beginning of delusion over the justice framework begins."

"I should not surprise you that I feel entirely exactly the same."

"Mr. O'Grady and Counsel Garrov, I hope you understand now why I was not at liberty to exchange all that I shared above in the presence of Charlotte. I wanted to spare her the trials of our legal professional undertaking, especially on the prosecution side. Don't get me wrong, I love my job, I deeply love what I do. But I also feel to be duty bound to share my background and my objectives when we will be working together and assessing the good, the bad and the in between contours of my engagement."

"I don't know about Ludmilla, but you have enlightened me about a lot of questions I get from D.C. related to this case. I assumed the contradiction of allegiances in this administration over the case. But not to the extent you have exposed it today. That will help me to lower a lot of reservations I had carried before. We really appreciated your input greatly. We will be in touch. Thank you."

CHAPTER 25

UPPSALA BONZES

Lawyer Analyst Pascal Bodavi was not eager to come to Sweden in the middle of the winter. The forecast minus twenty degrees Fahrenheit during the week stay in Stockholm area was far from an incentive to take the trip. However, the more he reviewed the voluminous testimony over Adamas Kagita, one name, Reverend Stanislas Keregi, Charlotte's uncle in Uppsala, Sweden, kept coming back as the main contact and provider of more than seventy five percent of the documentation. Pascal wished to push the trip to the beginning of Spring, but the tight schedule that the immigration judge had imposed on the government counsel left him not much time when combined with the scheduled trip to DRC for the key interviews in mid-February. Charlotte provided Pascal excellent references to meet with his uncle in Sweden.

When the plane landed in Stockholm, Pascal was relieved that the actual weather forecast was below minus ten. In addition, he did not have to step outside from the moment he left the airport to reach the hotel room he reserved in Uppsala. Pascal was also surprised to learn that Reverend Stanis was disposed to see him that day in the afternoon if he was available. He was and they agreed to get together at the hotel restaurant late in the afternoon.

"It is a great pleasure to come to see you Reverend in this beautiful town of Uppsala", Pascal greeted, in impeccable French, Reverend Stanis, an imposing tall man in mid-sixty of age.

"That is refreshing. My niece Charlotte did not tell me that you speak French. That is very refreshing for me. I don't have much luck to practice here in Uppsala. It is always either English or Swedish. As a matter of fact, I cherished those Saturday calls with Charlotte, my weekly chance to speak French or Swahili."

"What about at home with your wife!"

"Oh, Charlotte missed telling you this. I am a widower. Leonie was called back to the Lord around 2003 back home. I was in Butembo-Beni area at one theological seminar when some armed militia people invaded this village not far from the Kwazimu coltan mines and killed more than three hundred people including my wife and two young children. I managed to come back and to retrieve my two older children, two boys, who were on the church school premises. With the help of the Lutheran church, I came here to Uppsala. I then managed to raise my kids here who are now gone. They are now taking graduate classes in the university. They are all grown and happily living their life, thank God. When I came here, I decided to go back to school taking advanced Theological seminary classes. I work as a researcher at the seminary African Studies. The Johannelund School of Theology has built a tremendous African Studies center of which I am a board member. This center has been extremely resourceful in driving the voluminous testimony you have seen."

"It is top notch, Reverend, I wish we had similar research center when we were collecting Liberia civil war data for the war lord case I worked on recently."

"We do, we could have helped you if we were approached. But our Great Lakes documentation is very expensive. It started before I came here about the Rwanda genocide of 1990. I expanded it over the genocide evolving in Eastern DRC. We get so much material daily, it is unbelievable. You will notice this tomorrow when you will visit the center."

"But who is sending these documents!"

"Everybody, it is from the Congolese, Rwandan, Ugandan, and Burundian diasporas first. All these immigrants have decided that they must document every event taking place back home. Some people have issues to settle with those in power back home. They probably considered themselves political refugees from each one of these countries. Other people just pass on whatever falls on their laps. I have a tremendous respect for social networks. Many times, I am reading a mondain report from God knows whoever. Before you know it, that very mondain reporting becomes a significant basis in a chain of reporting a very significant event such as an assassination, a big political change, a demotion in the government, a military retirement and so on. We also get all kinds of precise reporting from back home, from disgruntled government employees. For instance, as far as DRC is concerned, I am very surprised how we are getting the news from the government inner circle, very close to the head of state. I am talking about very secret stuff from the President and his family entourage. We get these reports right away on the same day the events occurred, sometime less than two or three hours later. I believe that a lot of secret services people, still attached to the previous regime, do not hesitate to broadcast these documents, videos, and news. There is absolutely no allegiance to the current regime. It is the same for Rwanda and Uganda. In addition, every time we try to verify these videos, documents, and news, they are verified as fully authentic. I guess these regimes are all resting on very precarious shaking stand!"

"It could also be the level of endemic corruption that is so rotten eating away the fabric of the inner circle in those regimes!"

"Possible, but we have never paid anybody for all that we get. I simply think that the level of government delusion is so high among many people at home and abroad, nobody trusts anybody. And let's face it, in a country like DRC, people cannot live with their monthly salary which comes very short in the face of endless obligations, family and other obligations. At the highest public administration level, people will break even with the equivalent of two thousand dollars of monthly salary. When you add all these obligations, some tangible, other just ridiculous and self-destructive like supporting many mistresses, everybody seems to rely on additional income from made-up function bonus and primes, bribes, overbilling, ghost payroll, dead employees' payroll, all kinds of schemes to increase the monthly salary. Furthermore, you must add external income derived from a variety of hidden business such as real estate or retailing. Now this is possible for people in higher public administration salary grade. However, it becomes a real nightmare when you go down the salary ladder, the inclination to bend the rules to increase one's salary increases. You can only guess and imagine the nightmare in a particular domain or function like Intelligence Services. Here, the level of abuses expands exponentially. Employees are dearly compensated based on their ability to bring charges against other people, in other words they get inflated bonus salary when they have raised accusations against other people, whether made-up or verifiable accusations. If these accusations are significative enough for the country's political leadership, the employee can land twenty to fifty thousand dollars that month. But this employee may not see such a onetime bonanza for a long time unless he or she comes up with major charges against other people every month. But in that case, the utility of this employee's accusations will decrease under the suspicion that the accusations were becoming bogus and made-up. This employee will risk being reprimanded or worse arrested. Knowing very well how the Intelligence Services operate, this employee would reduce the number of monthly reported charges. With reduced monthly income, the employee would become very disgruntled and disillusioned. This employee would not hesitate to send us all kinds of information."

"There you got it. It is very sad. But it is good for us in business to verify whether what we must use is authentic. If it is relevant and authentic, it would make it easy for us to bring it in the court of law."

"Exactly, but we cannot build the country when nobody trusts anybody. That will bring sheer chaos and absolutely nothing can be developed or created from such generalized delusional paranoid. I pray it is not raised at a family level!"

"Maybe not, but who knows! It is possible at the level of tribe, I presume."

The new partners continued the discussion of the quality and size of the reports received at the African Studies Center during the late afternoon dinner. The next day they met around mid-morning at the center. Reverend Stanis introduced Pascal to his young staff. He was provided with an impressive management of gathering past and current coverage of each of African states. The objective was to provide a digital catalogue of each state with extensive references regarding the country's etymology, history, geography. demographics, government, economy, infrastructure, culture, and references. Additional extended articles of key political leaders of the country were also provided. Each country also had a feature of political evolution for the past thirty years where were dumped the various social media references. This feature could be digitally filtered and organized to drive a sequence of references for a pertinent subject. This is the feature that was used to trace Adamas Kagita criminal journey and every other topic of biographical interest. Pascal used the feature to trace the biography of a prominent Anglophone opposition leader in his native Cameroon. He was surprised about the details that the feature provided. The references included authentic documents, videos, and news attached to the political leader. Pascal was impressed. The feature led Pascal to reorganize the initiative he had presented to Mr. O'Grady and Ludmilla about dividing interviews between open and hidden interviews. The initiative was now divided between interviews in Kinshasa and Goma, and interviews in the logistical fields of the mineral resources murderous traffic. Pascal realized that the initiative was risking arbitrarily to drive and separate significant from insignificant interviews by location. The digital feature will be used to determine the significance of interviews whether they happen in Kinshasa, Goma or in the logistical traffic fields. Pascal also insisted that the selected events included the following charges that have already been retained against Adamas Kagita: in his long criminal journey:

-Led armed attacks and confiscation of dangerous caravans of coltan and gold minerals on their way to Uganda and Rwanda,

-Led kidnapping and holding in slavery bondage of minors to work in artisanal coltan and gold mines he supervised,

-Led kidnapping and holding of young girls as sex workers in remote jungle camps,

-Brutalized, tortured, and killed recalcitrant minors and sex workers

-Intimidated, brutalized, tortured, and killed workers and family members at odd with operating practices in coltan and gold mines he supervised

-Intimidated, brutalized, tortured, and killed workers and family members at odd with logistical practices he supervised to carry coltan and gold minerals to Uganda and Rwanda,

-Led armed campaigns to raze entire villages suspected of hiding and providing shelter to self-defense militias opposed to unauthorized artisanal mining of coltan and gold in their areas.

Pascal provided Reverend Stanis the description of his original versus revised initiative objectives. Reverend Stanis agreed to the new changes of direction. But he also shared his reservation:

"I was relieved to hear that a young man from Cameroon was leading this process of interviews around major human rights violations. I knew then I did not have to educate you about reporting ambiguity in our respective countries. Coming from an area of Cameroon with major political disturbances, I knew that you carry a political awareness your other American colleagues would not have nor understand. In fact, Charlotte, my niece, you have met, and I come from similar background and areas. Whether we like or not, we are attuned to that ambiguity of reporting, in our case, that not all Congolese can connect to. I don't know if Charlotte shared this, but you would find in Kinshasa and Goma a lot of political leaders who are involved in the same crimes that you are prosecuting against Adamas Kagita. I can go as far as to tell you that the current political leader of DRC is a major accomplice of the same crimes. That is a terrible fact you will confront when you arrive in DRC. So, beware of what you will collect in those interviews. I am happy that to find out you are struggling to come up with a good strategy to lead you to a much powerful probable cause."

"Reverend Stanis, please rest assured that what you have eminently qualified as reporting ambiguity has been my major concern in this selection process of interviews. This was a major reason I decided to come here to visit with you in the middle of winter in Sweden. When I noticed that you were the source of the bulk of the voluminous testimony, I decided that you were the man. I am now gratified that I came only to discover a power tool to guide our selection process. "

"My staff and I would assist you as much as we can. I would provide further filter if needs to be when it comes to significance of interviews. I should also be able to direct you to credible people to interview to avoid wasting time and the run around my people are famous for. My big advice in this selection process of interviews is this: the least obvious people would be the ones with the most significant input in this process. Of course, you will touch base with the obvious and the showy references and that will only be for the sake of covering the most relevant ones. Remember that when you get to Kinshasa and dealing with what the native call the "kinoiseries", or endless talks to say and to mean absolutely nothing."

For the next two more days, Pascal worked with the staff in selecting events related to Adamas Kagita criminal journey. Altogether they accumulated about fifty-five events. Reverand Stanis and Pascal spent another whole day spreading them by significance level, location, contact names and two levels of interview where applied. Pascal was very pleased with the final products and the redesigned initiative. He left the following day to go back to Raleigh, Nc.

CHAPTER 26

KINSHASA KINOISERIES

As soon as Pascal Bodavi returned to Raleigh, Nc, he shared with Charlotte and Ludmilla the very productive meeting he had with Reverend Stanis, the African Studies Center he supervised at the Johannelund School of Theology in Uppsala, the digital data base the staff used there and the extraordinary analytical feature that filtered the basic questionnaires of the interviews that would be conducted in DRC. He surprised the ladies by announcing why the feature directed him to change the directions of the interviews process. The ladies were effectively impressed by the documents he brought back and readily agreed with the change in the interviews process that will now rely exclusively on people being interviewed rather than predetermined significance of the event being reviewed through the interview. They agreed with the suggestion from Reverend Stanis to drag the significance of events from the outcome and the outlook of the interviews. They went on to assist Pascal in planning the interviews process in terms of team's composition, interview documentation, travel itineraries, travel support and protection in Kinshasa, Goma, and logistical field key points. In the new design, Pascal will lead the Kinshasa team with about four people. An attached FBI Super-Agent will lead the Goma and logistical field stops. The travel cover and protection were going to be assumed by UN forces and undercover South African soldiers and Marine soldiers attached to the American Consulate in Goma for the Eastern DRC area, while the Kinshasa team protection was going to be assumed essentially by undercover Marine soldiers attached to the American Embassy. Ludmilla volunteered to be part of the Kinshasa team, but the DA Mr. O'Grady declined the request. Pascal was upbeat about the Kinshasa coverage. His bilingual status was going to help to overcome a lot of communication shortcomings. He was not convinced of the same around Eastern DRC coverage, despite the Kenyan and Tanzanian members of the team who were fluent in Swahili and who also were reported to be very familiar with the area. The process was on schedule about a week and half later.

Arriving in Kinshasa reminded Pascal of many trips he made going back to Cameroon and landing in Yaoundé, the capital or Douala, the economic center, and taking a long trip to the Anglophone section to his native section. This time, Pascal was relieved that while the plane would land in the capital airport of Ndjili, the international disembarkation formalities would take place in the newly built international terminal which opened a while ago in 2015. He had heard about the terrible nightmare confronting international travelers when the domestic and international disembarkation operations were handled in the same terminal facilities. There was a substantial improvement in services as some computerized upgrades to the arrival's terminal have been implemented. Still the lack of clear signals, instructions, and a shortage of bilingual communications made for a disturbing welcome. Constant requests for money and bribery from airport and security staff were a bit annoying. As anywhere on the continent, corruption remains a problem. Our team's arrival was still a manageable experience.

As the Kinshasa team left the Ndjili international airport, they noticed on the way to town a crowded big street called Boulevard Lumumba. Along the way are the vibrant and noisy districts of Masina, Kingasani and Ndjili. It will take about two more hours, depending on the intractable traffic to arrive at the hotel Memling in town, one of the major hotels in Kinshasa that had been renovated consistently to maintain its five stars standing. The US embassy had already assured the team that its confidential documentation of the interviews will be secured within the embassy premises, avoiding unnecessary leaks of the team legal works throughout their itineraries and movements about the complex town of Kinshasa.

The day before the team started the interviews, a long-time staff member of the embassy appraised the team members about what they should guard themselves while moving around and about the very crowded city. He mentioned that the visitors will encounter what is locally called "Kinoiseries."

"From the beginning "Kinoiseries" were identified as objects of art or craftsmanship from the city of Kinshasa. The types of objects that are considered kinoiseries may include wooden sculptures, masks, textiles, jewelry, and decorative objects made of various materials such as metal, ceramic, and glass. These objects are often characterized by their originality and creativity, reflecting the history and culture of the city of Kinshasa. However, when Kinshasa grew from a town of less than two million in 1960 to an agglomeration of more than 10 million people around 2014, the term "Kinoiseries" became a character trait specific to Kinshasa inhabitants who are never short of ideas to ensure survival in an inclement and tough environment, a population that is certainly deprived but overflowing with fertile survival imagination. "

"The fertile survival imagination comes from the fact that Kinshasa is home to about thirteen percent of the DRC's population, but accounts for eighty five percent of the Congolese economy. It was also found that seventy percent of Kinshasa people are employed informally, seventeen percent in the public sector, nine percent in the formal private sector, and three percent. Most new jobs are classified as informal. Finally, the mean household spending amounted to one dollar per day per person in Kinshasa, and that spending goes for food."

""Kinoiseries" is reflected in good and bad behavior, from people bossing endlessly to make ends meet to those investing in petty and violent crimes. It should be noted that after the last civil war of late 1990, the city has been striving to recover from disorder, with many youth gangs hailing from Kinshasa's slums. Kinshasa is generally safe for daytime travel, but to beware of robbers, especially in traffic jams and in areas near hotels and stores. By some accounts, crime in Kinshasa is not so rampant, due to relatively good relations among residents and perhaps to the severity with which even petty crime is punished."

"Unfortunately, in the 2010s, a peculiar crime phenomenon to seriously guard against as a visitor, has grown in alarming proportion in Kinshasa. It is about street children or "Shegués", who are generally orphaned or abandoned by parents, and are subject to abuse by the police and military. Of the estimated 20,000 children living on Kinshasa's streets, almost a quarter are beggars, some are street vendors and about a third have some kind of informal employment. Some have fled from physically abusive families, notably stepparents, others were expelled from their families as they were believed to be witches, and have become outcasts. Previously a significant number were civil war orphans. Street children are mainly boys, but the percentage of girls is increasing."

Armed with warnings from the Embassy staff, the Kinshasa team was scattered all over town to attend the interview process the first day. Pascal reached out to the main target witness who happened to be Adamas Kagita long-time close friend, Xavier Bhatia, now a very influential Representative of Butembo-Beni territory in the Congolese Parliament in Kinshasa. The man was beyond sadness to report on his childhood friend.

"I never thought that we would diverge so remarkably in our maturity, in our outlook of life and professionally. We were always attuned academically. I did not know why Adamas decided to follow such a violent path in his life. I absolutely don't take pride to talk about Adamas I still consider a close friend. I wished to meet him and ask him why? Why did he have to cause such much calamity and tears around him? I am at loss to understand and to witness all that he did from the time we reach Kisangani, the University of Kisangani. I did not understand the vein attraction to the life of crime from that time. He told me that it was power, power over women, power over people, power over money. He said something to that effect:

'Xavier, you don't know what is like ordering a beautiful sexy girl to go have sex with such man and bring back the money the man pays for her services! Xavier such a power over girls who would never look at you if you were not her pimp! That is power you would never get with your mathematics degree!"

That is what attracted him, and no matter how I plead with him, he rejected all my counsels. I warned him that all that would lead to one place, jail, sooner or later. He did not listen, he did not mind until he was jailed. Then I saw him and asked him what he had gained out of the pimp life after the three young were dead. I realized that he was gone, lost to the other side when he confided to me and said:

"Xavier, you don't understand, I got only part of the equation. I got power without connection, that is why I have been jailed. Watch out for me when I would get out of here, I will get the entire equation: power and connection."

Indeed, he got both power and connection when he got back to Butembo and joined the General Commandant Ogpado and his nephew. He went full blown in life of crime kidnapping caravans of precious minerals. He was completely lost then. I did not know then that the three of them were partners in Kisangani. It was too late. I knew I lost him when he confessed killing his own uncle who had punished him for rapping his wife's niece. That was the no return descent into the bottomless crime pit."

Xavier went on repeated what Pascal had already read in the voluminous testimony. Then he asked him about Charlotte. The response was a big surprise.

"Did Adamas ever mention a lady by the name of Charlotte Keregi?"

"No, but he used to mention a Justina Keregi he claimed to have kidnapped her near the Kwazimu mines area, when she was about fourteen and took her to what he called was his sex workers compound in the mountain surrounding Walikale. I could not believe what he was saying. I thought that he was just blowing winds to show me how much power he had in the area. Anyway, he said that Justina became his main lady in charge of managing the sex workers compound which catered to military people who came from Rwanda to collect the minerals and did not want to mix up with local women. He said that Justina was the daughter of a pastor named Stanislas Keregi. He said that if there was somebody, he worried about most it was that Reverend Stanislas. Because he searched for him all over, killed his wife and never had a chance to find him. Later he learned that Reverend Stanis had fled to Sweden with his two sons. He also confided that he managed to kill all the Keregi he run across in the area. Just to erase the Keregi memory, Adamas strangled Justina before leaving for the US. This Charlotte Keregi must be Justina's cousin. She must have run away from the massacre of the Keregi family."

"That is very interesting!"

"And why?"

"Well, that is a name that came up in the voluminous testimony I received about Adamas."

"Well, any Keregi would have to settle major family counts with Adamas, I can tell you that. I personally have not run into that name again. But I know someone in Goma who can provide you with the whereabouts of this Charlotte if you are still looking for her. Oh, before I forget, a colleague representative from Goma should have even more stories about Adamas criminal background. Adamas always stopped by his office in Goma at the end of his own caravan from the mines to Rwanda's frontier. He is here in Kinshasa during the parliament session, here is his contact."

"Thank you, I will call upon him very soon. Let him that my team will call upon him."

Pascal next two interviews were with military officers, colonels to be exact. They turned out to be attached to the President own Brigade. They were not forthcoming talking about Adamas Kagita. They gave the impression of having been warned not to share much about the accused. The last contact was a three star General about to be transferred from Kinshasa to a remote assignment at the Central African Republic border. He was not happy about the transfer. He provided all needed verification of Adamas Kagita's murderous supervision of artisanal mining operations with sixty percent of minor recruits. Adamas confided to him that he killed the minors at the rate of twenty a week for punishment. He added another key verification of the erasing two villages when parents of dead minors protested the wanton killing of their children. The General provided pictures documentations of the massacre. All in all, the first day of his interview process was satisfactorily productive with rather goulash stories. He rushed to the embassy to translate the interview documentations. When he reached the embassy, his team associates reported achieving the same rate of productive interviews. They had about fifteen completed interviews out of twenty-three assigned.

The Goma team was just as productive the first day of interviews as the Kinshasa team, they completed about twelve out of eighteen, while they were waiting to hear the team members covering the logistic key points, who were expected to report their rate the next day as expected. Pascal was more relieved that there has been no report of violent pushback from most respondents. In all sincere honesty, the area was still tense with numerous armed uncontrollable militia groups, he did not know how he would have tempered or eliminated them. If anything, he was seriously counting on Mother Luck.

Pascal had not read all the reported interviews, he would review them quietly perhaps on his way back to the US. Yet, the biggest surprise he got the first day was the revelation from Xavier that Reverend Stanis involvement was more personal that he imagined. Losing both his wife and his daughter in the hands of Adamas Kagita was enough motivation to pursue and incriminate him to the end of the world in any court he could expose him. He was also surprised that Charlotte has not mentioned this in addition to her own well-documented terrible odyssey. Was this a deep family secret? Do the niece and the uncle know what has been revealed to him. If the Keregi family wished Adamas dead, he knew that there were many other families wishing him a similar fate. That should be a strong reason not to go back to the area. The Kinshasa team left the embassy compound around nine thirty p.m. to rush to the hotel for a late group dinner.

The next day, Pascal managed to get an early appointment with Xavier's representative colleague. He was an affable gentleman, very quick to smile at the mention of Adamas Kagita. He recounted the horror stories Adamas Kagita shared about his logistic caravan trips. The Goma representative listened to his stories more for laughter than anything. He could not believe the extent of cruelty he added to the stories. He never took him seriously. He said that Adamas talked most of time as he was narrating a fiction script of the movie. He simply listened to him share laughter. He never engaged him to verify the stories which, in his own estimate, were too far-fetched. He was surprised and a bit shaken to hear that Adamas was being legally prosecuted on account of the same stories he shared with him so casually.

"Seriously, when Adamas came here in my office, he loved to sit on that chair and he looks at the window and started spilling his stories, he never looked at me. I spent my time laughing and patting him on his back. He kept repeating "For real, really, for real". He would go on for hours while we are drinking beer. All that time, he never looked at me. Then he will get up and go about whatever business he had. Sir, now thinking back, he was confessing to me some horrible and grave crimes. For instance, he mentioned that when two caravan minors started disputing over some silly games, who was better than who, he said he got annoyed to hear them, and from his seat next to the truck driver, he struck both dead and balanced them off the truck without stopping. I laughed stupidly for five minutes, and he kept repeating, "For real, really, for real!" Then he left as cold as he shared the story. My God, he was probably trying to get me to stop, I did not."

"But did he mention a lady by the name of Charlotte Keregi?"

"Oh yes, he did! He said that if there was a woman he was going to marry. He said that he met her on the bus trip to Butembo. Then he added that she was a knock-out virgin girl. I was surprised and I asked him how in the world he knew that. That was the only time I wanted to verify his story. He looked at me and said quietly that her hands looked so soft as if she had never held anything that was impure. He went on saying a girl like that must have as never seen a man member. That was so unreal, I did not challenge his fantasy. Then I asked him if he tried to take her as a spouse. He responded that he tried but the family did not want to give her away to me. The family got her to run to Goma. I never saw her again. I punished the whole family. I did not want to find out what he meant by saying that he punished the whole family. He cut the conversation abruptly and left. To tell you the truth, I never asked him about Charlotte again. I classified that story as one of his many fantasies. Now the funny thing was that when he was about to leave the country and I learned later that he was going to the US, he came to the office and for the first time he showed up with a lady. She looked like Charlotte he had described, I asked him if he had found Charlotte. He lowered his voice and said in French probably to confuse the Lady that she was a close substitute."

"I see, please Sir, in your estimate, was he making a lot of money?"

"I would think so. The company he kept in town would tell me that he was making a lot of money. Adamas controlled the whole coltan traffic from Walikale to the Rwanda border. So, his cut was in the half million to a million dollars every month. His problem, I presume now, was that he had no time to enjoy a lot of money he made. Now I realized that he killed so many people, he could not sit in the park with a bunch of people to drink or eat at leisure. He was always on the run. He was more comfortable in the jungle areas where he reigns as king. Now and then he also mentioned that he went to Seychelles Island or Maurice Island for long weekends He said that he went there to make love to a lot of young Russian girls. He claimed that they were too tight for his big member. He spent long weekend to get them opened up he said. I did not know whether to believe these so-called love escapades. But at the same time, I knew he could afford them."

"Do yo know why he left the area to go to the US?"

"I heard many stories. You know he got so big for his own good I believe. I strongly believe he started annoying the big boys at the top of echelon of some countries. I mean some chiefs of state."

"Oh really!"

"Oh yes, he started mentioning to me stories about dealing with members of presidential families, brothers, sons, daughters, uncles! He said he was traveling with some of them to Seychelles and Maurice Island. Here again, I drew my deep reservation. You never know with the man. It was always difficult to tell whether he was fantasizing or not. Adamas was the type of guy who would walk and starts telling me that the wife of this president had a tattoo on her left inner thigh or upper left of her right breast. Now would you take somebody like that seriously, of course not. Maybe he got himself so compromised that he had to be shipped out where he would not be touched. Or worse, maybe powerful people in the US are playing him against the powerful people here in Africa for whatever reason. I don't know, only Adamas knows. I believe you need to interview the so-called Reverend Drago who deal with these powerful here in Africa?"

"I never heard of him, of this Reverend Drago. Who is he, and what rapport he has with Adamas Kagita?"

"But he comes often to the US pretending to be a Reverend representing DRC in your National Day of Prayer! He is the man who manages Adamas Kagita worldwide. Your Embassy entertains Reverend Drago all the time. Maybe I am pushing the envelope here. Check with your ambassador."

"I will, I certainly will! Thank you for the tips, I really appreciate your input. Are there any more horror stories you want to share about Adamas?"

"Well, no more than what you have heard. But I must say that you just gave me a cold sweat to realize that the man was literally confessing his horror stories, his many crimes and the only thing I could do is just laugh about them. I am very sorry about this."

"Well, let us do this, since you are learning more about the man than his stories, I want you to remember as much as you can recollect and send these stories to me. If you can put them in writing in term of event, date, location, people affected that would be great. Adamas Kagita was and is a monster, a very dangerous man with trail of crimes so long he should be locked up in jail. Your colleague Xavier knows quite a bit about him. Ask him, he would share a lot of horror stories. Here are my references. It will great if you can help us."

237

The Goma Representative looked very sad by the end of the exchange. Pascal felt very sorry for him. Pascal started learning more about the psycho side of Adamas Kagita. When he was requested to get involved in his prosecution, Pascal leaned on his strong inclination to become rich. But the two interviews with the two Parliament Representatives convinced him that Adamas was a psycho. The way Adamas exchanged with these two colleagues told him something he needed to research further. And this so-called Reverend Drago was also a puzzle. He was very eager to engage the Ambassador. But he also needed to be careful. He could be shaking a very complex imbroglio. He wrapped his assigned interviews with two ore security officers from the country intelligence agency called ANR for "Agence National des Renseignements" in French. The officers repeated what was already recorded in the voluminous testimony about Adamas Kagita. They were not willing to add or to go any further than that. Pascal rushed back to the Embassy and requested an urgent appointment with the ambassador.

"Your excellency, I did not have the chance to thank you for extending wonderful hospitality to our team in this very delicate mission. I wanted to take this time to thank you and your staff in case we must rush from here without saying bye. I want also to let you know that the interviews process is going very well, and we should be able to close our Kinshasa mission by tomorrow and leave right away. We have a very tight schedule. I made this urgent request to also get your feedback about a prominent person here in Kinshasa. His name kept being raised in all our interviews. I was taken a back because his name was not mentioned anywhere in the testimony we were asked to verify. I was wondering if you had any dealing with this person, I am talking about Reverend Drago. We heard that he is a frequent contact visitor with the embassy."

"Oh yes, Reverend Drago is a very good source for intelligence services here in the capital outside the entire intelligence apparatus we rely upon. Mr. Bodavi, I must tell you that we have a good expansive intelligence structure in the country. We don't have to search for it. It comes to us daily in a diverse variety I may add. Every politician here believes that we control everything of strategic importance in the government, the army, the security domain, the economy. They tend to give us more strategic weight that we are sometimes surprised to possess. Of course, we concur with the Congolese political elite's assessment of our ability. We don't have a choice but to claim it. It is the same about Reverend

Drago who in all fairness represents Tutsi tribe interests in the Congolese political plethora of four hundred fifty tribes. He has been involved in every political event in the Eastern DRC since 1997. He was also a Minister in the Central Government for about two or three years. He seems to have a strong affinity with the government of Rwanda. So, he comes here most of the time in public relation pretention to impress on other politicians that he has our strong support. I am afraid it is all PR exercise. I was asked just recently if he was in the US about a month ago. I did not ask him what he went to do there. I know that he has three years repeat visa allowing him to go to the US any time he wants. I believe he has his immediate family living as residents in Delaware State. So, on that basis every other politician believes he has some very powerful support from the US government. Do you know how the Reverend plays that PR to the till, he invites other politicians to come with him to the National Prayer Day organized by the Congress every year. A lot of Christian politicians around the world are invited by Congressmen and Senators to that event. Of course, we give a short stay visa to Congolese politicians who go there as co-invited by some Senators. Is that so strategic to make him the American supported politician? Remember we are talking about National Prayer Day! This is, I am afraid, ridiculous from the Congolese political elite to give him a powerful American connection on that basis. Please, talk to me about a Wall Street venue or a Pentagon venue, then we can evaluate, but National Prayer Day! I must tell you, here we start falling for what our staff employee reviewed with your team. I am talking about Kinshasa "Kinoiseries"! I would ask you to ignore the Reverend."

"Thank you, Sir, for your clarifications. And thank you again for the warm hospitality."

"It was our Embassy pleasure!"

The Kinshasa team managed to wrap the interviews process and forwarded electronically the interviews to the US Immigration agency database. The team left the next day for Nairobi, Kenya, to wait for the Goma Team. The wait was extended for two more days to an increasing worry for the whole Kinshasa team and Pascal. An urgent message finally came from Goma advising that one of the logistical groups was ambushed while getting closer to the famous coltan mine enclave where Adamas Kagita used to reign supreme. The management of mines operations simply refused to accord the interviews scheduled and predetermined a month ago. The group informed Pascal that the management was guided by a Reverend Drago. That reporting shocked Pascal remembering what the ambassador told him about the Reverend Drago. Was he supposed to abide by the ambassador's suggestion to ignore the Reverend Drago. He did not think so. He really wished that the group had a chance to take the picture of the famous reverend. The group did! The group also stated that the UN protection convoy had to take a longer western retreat trip to avoid another ambush. That trip took them to the western province of Maniema where a UN helicopter collected the group safely back to Goma. There was no serious harm to the group members who survived the episode. The Goma team arrived in Nairobi on the third day to everybody's relief. The entire interview process team rested another day and returned to respective countries the following day.

In the direct Nairobi to JFK Lufthansa flight of about fifteen hours, Lawyer Analyst Pascal Bodavi was still intrigued by the subtle yet pervasive presence of Reverend Drago in Kinshasa and in the coltan mining operations in Walikale territory in North Kivu. It became puzzling for Pascal to notice that a person pretending to be a reverend, a man of God, should be associated with brutal mining operations where Adamas Kagita had reigned as an unchallenged killer war lord. In addition, Pascal raised for himself more unanswered questions; It was noted through Immigration documentation that Reverend Drago has visited D.C. area about a month before the Raleigh District Court trial, he landed in Dulles International Airport, he stayed in a residence in a town in Virginia across from D.C. This had happened when Adamas Kagita took a sudden authorized trip to see family members in the same area at the same time. Was reverend Drago visiting with Adamas Kagita? And why? What relationships if any were there between the Reverend Drago and Adamas Kagita? Why does Reverend Drago seem to have so many entrees with the US Embassy in Kinshasa?

Pascal checked the entire interviews set for any Reverend Drago references, they were plenty about fifteen. The other report, just as interesting as the Ambassador's, was the one that another member of the Kinshasa team had from the Embassy Political Counselor who was cautioning the team about what they would collect in those interviews:

"You should realize that after the overthrow of Mobutu in 1997, the Congolese natives grew restive about the central government being controlled and led by the Rwandan invaders. The worst case was the situation that was cleverly kept from the public from May 1997 through July 1998. It was then revealed that a Rwandan General, James Kabarebe was Chief of Staff of the Congolese Army. The Rwandan imposed puppet President, Laurent Mze Kabila, grew himself nervous about his hold on power. He managed to impose his own Congolese natives slowly and gradually in strategic positions, preferably from the Katanga province tribes. The Rwandan invaders did not appreciate that change and tried to unseat President Kabila through a military coup. That failed because the Angolan government intervened quickly squashing the Rwandan troops who left to go back to the Eastern region of DRC where they have remained, to date, fomenting a whole series of rebellions against the central government while engaging in plundering the coltan and gold minerals in the area for Rwanda benefits. However, a successful infiltration of Congolese government at all levels by Rwandan elements took place after the assassination of President Laurent Mze Kabila in 2001. Successive governments, put in place to appease Rwandan grievances, have implemented multiple high level army officer appointments taken by Rwandan citizens. The purported son of Laurent Kabila, who was appointed to succeed his assassinated father, increased these appointments throughout the entire security infrastructure of the country and in other key strategic positions. That is the main reason why you should be very reserved about the responses you would get in those interviews. The responses you would get would come from the very enablers of the mineral resources plundering in the Eastern DRC, the very enablers of the killing going on in the Eastern DRC, the very enablers of the war lords of Adamas Kagita temperament. In other words, you would get fake responses as you would be talking to a bunch of Reverend Drago's! It is clear to me that all these Reverend Drago's speak only one language, take only one directive, from Kigali, the capital of Rwanda."

CHAPTER 27

INTERVIEWS SUMMARY

The process to summarize the interviews took two steps: first in Raleigh attended by Charlotte Keregi in permanent touch with Uncle Reverend Stanis Keregi in Uppsala, Sweden, Ludmilla Garrov, Pascal Bodavi; then in Charlotte attended by DA O'Grady, Ludmilla Garrov, Pascal Bodavi in permanent touch with Uncle Reverend Stanis Keregi in Uppsala, Sweden, Faye Manley and two DRC interviews members. Pascal Bodavi insisted on the crucial apport from Uncle Reverend Stanis. Charlotte Keregi was not comfortable about including two family members in this legal representation until both DA O'Grady and Trail Lawyer Faye Manley convinced her that Adamas brutalization and killing of so many Keregi family members would give a powerful legal weight and causes in prosecuting Adamas Kagita. At the end Faye Manley selected the top sixteen out of sixty that were generated. By order of significance the two groups agreed to align the sixteen interviews according to charges leveled against Adamas Kagita:

A. 3 interviews for cases where Adamas intimidated, brutalized, tortured, and killed workers and family members at odd with operating practices in coltan and gold mines he supervised,

B. 3 interviews for case where Adamas intimidated, brutalized, tortured, and killed workers and family members at odd with logistical practices he supervised to carry coltan and gold minerals to Uganda and Rwanda,

C. 3 interviews for cases where Adamas led armed campaigns to raze entire villages suspected of hiding and providing shelter to self-defense militias opposed to unauthorized artisanal mining of coltan and gold in their areas.

D. 2 interviews for cases where Adamas led kidnapping and holding in slavery bondage of minors to work in artisanal coltan and gold mines he supervised,

E. 2 interviews for cases where Adamas led kidnapping and holding of young girls as sex workers in remote jungle camps,

F. 1 interview for cases where Adamas brutalized, tortured, and killed recalcitrant minors and sex workers,

G. 1 interview for cases where Adamas led armed attacks and confiscation of dangerous caravans of coltan and gold minerals on their way to Uganda and Rwanda,

While still in Charlotte, Nc, the prosecution team including DA O'Grady, Ludmilla Garrov, Faye Manley and Pascal Bodavi had a strategic review meeting to determine what legal strategic steps to take depending on what the Immigration Court Judge will decide after hearing the key interviews he has requested. Faye Manley led this meeting.

"The immigration court Judge can follow two paths in his decision in this case. He can reject Adamas Kagita culpability we have demonstrated in the interviews and starts legal proceedings to deport him out of the USA for violating Immigration laws concerning Fraud and Misuse of Visas, Permits, and Related Documents, and Perjury related to False Personation. Or the judge accepts Adamas Kagita's culpability demonstrated in the interviews, find him guilty of violating Immigration laws concerning Fraud and Misuse of Visas, Permits, and Related Documents, and Perjury related to False Personation, transfer him back to the US District Court in Raleigh, NC to be tried for violation of human rights perpetrated in Eastern DRC. The latter was the course that was followed in Mohamed Jabbateh case in Philadelphia, Pa. Our esteemed colleague Pascal Bodavi was thoroughly involved in that case and that is why he has been expanding his expertise in this matter. I am personally favoring the second course. I don't see how Adamas can be released out there and allow him to continue the same maihem he had already done against countless people."

At that instant DA O'Grady intervened:

"Dear esteemed counsels, I want us to get to the second decision and to get this scoundrel nailed as you said, amply demonstrated through the voluminous testimony we have collected and the sixty interviews that were gathered recently and about to presented to the Judge. Unfortunately, I must share the reservation that Reverend Stanislas Keregi continued to share with us. I want to go back to what I heard among the interviews that Pascal's group came back with from DRC. Two interviews have bothered me a lot. The one Pascal had with the ambassador and the other one from the Embassy Political Counselor. These two interviews talk about the enablers of Adamas Kagita found not just in the murderous logistical fields of the plundered mineral resources, these enablers are found in highest levels of government in Kinshasa, DRC, in Kigali, Rwanda, and in Kampala, Uganda. These enablers are here also in the highest level of government in Washington D.C., and in some boardrooms in the top high technology corporations, major beneficiaries of the plundering of mineral resources in DRC. Adamas Kagita is only the smallest link in the chain that is brutalizing the Eastern DRC people for the past twenty years or so. These enablers are powerful and have corrupted both parties in DC. They are going to do everything to save that link, Adamas Kagita, from being exposed in a public trial. I can tell you at this time that they are mobilizing every legal resource to see we don't get to the second favorable decision. I could be wrong about this, but time would tell."

Pascal Bodavi jumped in:

"I agree with DA O'Grady. I must also submit that I felt the same way in Philadelphia. Powerful political forces were pulling in different ways the trial venues of Mohamed Jabbateh. I certainly realize that there is a big difference between what happened in Liberia versus what is happening in DRC, the stakes are totally different if not bigger. I know and observe that. I came back from DRC dejected by the probable intervention of powerful forces in this case as DA O'Grady observed and mentioned. The embassy folks are witnessing the DRC unfolding drama on the front row. Maybe their reporting interviews are cries in the desert. Our role, ladies and gentlemen should be to use these cries at the right time to expose the enablers.to a public trial. That is what we should do. That is the only way to prevent the hidden and negative intervention of the powerful forces."

"I have no hesitation to confront these powerful forces, whichever they are or come from, in the matters concerning the legal immigration resolution. I am getting used to these battles. If you feel strongly that they should be named let me know." The trial lawyer, Faye Manley, interjected.

"But we should not allow them to undercut our legal strategy. We should invite them to fall into the legal trap we would build slowly and efficiently the same way we did it in Judge Lehighton-Garver Court. Ludmilla got the bastard to reveal his identity when he was emotionally exhausted. I submit that we must do the same in the next step when we subtly name these obscure forces. This will only be possible if the case is sent back to Raleigh District court. That is why it will be very important that we overwhelmed the immigration court judge with a definite presentation of Adamas Kagita guilty disposition to allow the judge to follow the second legal venue of this case. That is not only deciding his future deportation and at the same time conduct a thorough review of his major violation of human rights under the international legal framework." DA O'Grady cautioned the team.

Faye concurred:

"I agree with the DA. But let us not fool ourselves, this legal strategy will be feasible if we are not constrained by the defense raising the specter of CIPA. That can block he second venue depending on the judge venue."

"I doubt that the defense will raise that card so soon. That is their trump card. The minute the defense will raise the CIPA card, all bets will be off. The defense would not risk betting the whole house so soon. That is my opinion." Pascal finally spoke.

"I feel the same way, counsel, that is an important card for them. Using it at this juncture will show that the defense is ready to throw the towel. That is not the way they operate. I could be wrong but let us strengthen our interviews presentation in front of the judge and see where it will lead." The DA closed his legal suggestion.

The trial lawyer, Faye Manley, closed the meeting on that final legal resolution.

CHAPTER 28

DOOMED ADAMAS

After less than an hour and half of reviewing interviews from DRC, his Honorable Amos Vance-Parrington, Senior Immigration Court Judge agreed to the entire line of criminal prosecution presented by the trial lawyer, Faye Manley. He agreed that Adamas Kagita should not step foot in the USA territory. Furthermore, he rejected with strong revulsion the defense objection that Adamas be tried for the widespread violation of human rights in Eastern DRC. Judge Vance-Parrington addressed the defense counsels' team in following harsh terms:

"Counsels, I have occupied this chair for far too long, reviewing immigration cases from many people, some from unfortunate dispositions I could do nothing for them because the immigration laws of our nation would still not allow them to enter the US territory, other from clear and present dangers for the citizens of this great country of ours. Your client, in my opinion, has apparently crossed the boundary of unfortunate disposition, he appears to belong to the extreme opposite extremity of that chain of immigration considerations. From what I have seen and read, your client has been accused of having lived the life of an unbound and unrepentant criminal for more than the time I spent on this chair. If his criminal pursuit was purely for financial gain, there could be room for some exceptional considerations, but his pursuit was simply criminal for the sake of being criminal. His wanton demoniac crimes tell me that he should bear the full extent of responsibility according to criminal laws as prescribed by many human rights conventions especially the 1948 Universal Declaration of Human Rights in its articles 1,2, 3, 4, 5, 9, 13, 14… I have decided that he should respond to the crimes he has been accused of having committed in that Eastern region of DRC. The Universal Declaration of Human Rights, which I have mentioned, allows that any nation court jurisdiction prosecutes violations of human rights your client has been accused of. I have decided to remind him to the Eastern District Court of North Carolina in Raleigh to be tried over the long chain of accusations leveled against him. I would not be exercising plainly my function of Senior Immigration Court Judge if I neglect the opportunity of getting your client to answer for these accusations.in that court in Raleigh, NC. This court is adjourned.'"

Judge Vance-Parrington's decision fell on soft hears for the new prosecuting team including Trial lawyer Faye Manley, Analyst Lawyer Pascal Bodavi, Counsel Ludmilla Garrov and her boss DA O'Grady. Adamas Kagita's defense team was beyond being crushed. The defense counsels were so beaten by the judge's lecture, they missed the chance of even raising the specter of CIPA's as an objection. They collect themselves to confront the same Judge Leighton-Garver who has quickly sent them packing from the unraveling defense in Raleigh to the Immigration court in Charlotte. They were not looking forward to this prospect unless they could request a new cumbersome jury trial.

If Adamas' legal defense team was beaten, Ms. Gwendolyn O'Grady, the Associate Attorney General, National Security Division in Washington D.C. was mortified by the Judge Amos Vance-Parrington's decision. Her job was basically to contain the political ramifications of Adams' case from the beginning. Gwendolyn was the political mantle of the so-called hidden below the radar powerful forces pulling the strings of the case internally in the US and externally in many embassies and political governments in the region of Great Lakes including DRC, Rwanda, and Uganda. Gwendolyn was shocked that the case was about to blow out into the open public, into the realm of unregulated and undisciplined worldwide social media. She knew that the minute that the Judge, in charge of carrying the case in court in Raleigh, bangs the gavel to start the case court proceedings, she would be in the worst prick of her function and her life. She would be lucky to keep her job because she has failed to keep the lead over this case. She might as well resign and dump the whole mess over anybody stupid enough to take it over. She called her uncle two hours after the judge's decision.

"What should I do now after you have blown our cover wide open in this Adamas' case?"

"Good morning, Gwendolyn, you start a conversation with elders, with uncles and aunts, with a good morning, young lady. If you want my opinion, you should resign your position as quickly as possible and don't tell your successor how bad it will get for that position."

"Good morning, Uncle O'Grady, good morning! I hate to tell you this as unethically as vulgar it is, I am fucked!"

"Spare me the vulgar pronouncements, it is not like you! And that very good-looking gentleman, I heard, a high level Ph. D economist at Brookings Institution would not appreciate that language. How long have you been dating, six years? Please, get marry and give yourself a good excuse to quit now. Your boss, the Attorney General, would understand it! "

"Funny, that crossed my mind yesterday. But the O'Grady are not quitters, I remember you telling me this a while back when I graduate from Yale Law School. I would not quit now. I must finish my job?"

"How are you going to finish what is looking like a train wreck. By the time the DRC interviews would come out, your office would be bombarded from all sides. You know that."

"Do I, I don't! What social media outfit knows about the Associate Attorney General, National Security Division, nobody! Our office runs below two or five radars. Nobody knows this office that pulls so many strings that sometimes cross each other. We have an elaborate command center answering to only one person, the Attorney General, who lives to never expose this office. That is why I selected this office for a job. I knew it from the best, my very uncle DA O'Grady! Now what do you got for me in these DRC interviews!'

"What a joke, you think that you can fool me. Why do you want to know about the interviews if they are not bound to bury your office and your boss'! Enough of the power play game. Resign and marry yourself away, Gwendolyn, a pride counsel from Uncle O'Grady!"

"My dear niece, we intend to cut off your intervention in our new legal strategy. To date we have not yet gone after the financial resources of Adamas Kagita. Remember that he has been stripped of his old identity of Jefferson Okito. He used that identity to live a very expensive life in the US affording himself the most expense legal defense. We intend to deprive him of these financial resources now that he is a prisoner of the Immigration Court system until he gets sentenced to a long stay in jail for his flagrant human rights violations. This is where and when he will be forced to cough up his protection in the US, all these hidden powerful forces covering him!"

"But dear uncle, you are forgetting that articles 6,7,8,9,10 and 11 of the 1948 Universal Declaration of Human Rights state the fundamental legality of right to be defended in the court of law. These articles are for all accused irrespective of where they live or are, whether they are citizens of the US or not. Adamas is entitled to any legal defense he can afford. You know the law, Uncle O'Grady!"

"Not using the financial resources from killing so many people! We will pursuit that line of prosecution as well?"

"Please, if you cannot use that line against mafia members in the US, how can you use it against Adamas?"

"We will try it?"

"Good luck!"

DA O'Grady knew very well that the prosecution wouldn't go there. He just wanted to get his niece to get off her the phone when she started inquiring about the DRC interviews. He did not want to give any inclination of what these interviews contained. Uncle O'Grady knew that his niece was in constant communication with Adamas' defense team which has been very ineffective so far in protecting Adamas and the government commitment in the case. DA O'Grady wondered at times whether his niece was sharing her disappointment over Adamas' legal representation.

The inquiry about Adamas' financial resources has been in DA O'Grady's mind from the time Judge Leighton-Garver sent the case to the Immigration Court and got locked up in jail. He wondered aloud how Adamas managed to hold on for this long with no visible means of support. He wondered about his family out in the Outer Banks. How was the family managing? He was convinced that his niece Gwendolyn was hiding something around Adamas cover and support from whatever obscure forces which have ensured his immigration entry into the US. For further clarity he took steps to find out. He made a request to the North Carolina State police Superintendent to run a check about Adamas' family in that house in the Outer Banks. To his surprise, the house was empty and for sale by a real estate company located in Washington D.C. Further inquiries revealed that this company was executing the sale on behalf of Adamas's big shoes law firm. The

Outer Banks house was listed for sale at $785,000. Adamas' family was apparently relocated to an area outside Mobile in the state of Alabama, according to the same real estate contacts. That probably explained why Adamas has not been visited by anybody since he has been incarcerated in the immigration jail near Raleigh. But there was still no explanation about Adamas and his family's financial support. DA O'Grady decided that he must blow up this cover during the upcoming trial of Adamas. He was convinced that the elements and sources of the financial support would go a long way to establish the reasons and motivations of why Adamas came and gains an immigration into the US along his family.

Charlotte Keregi did not share the DA's ambivalence when she learned the decision taken by the Immigration Court Senior Judge. She raised her hands to thank God for the positive evolution of the legal case she had initiated. For a major exception she did not want to wait for the Saturday morning call to share the news with Uncle Reverend Stanis. She also added how crucial his overall input in the process has been according to the entire defense team.

"Uncle Stanis, I had many doubts about the way the case has evolved lately from the Raleigh court to the Charlotte Immigration court. I was convinced that Adamas was going to be kicked out of the US and probably return him to Rwanda, Uganda, or DRC to enjoy the rest of his life in undeserving opulence until the time would come his political masters were going to get rid of him through assassination or whatever. He was going to be killed by these unforgiving people, that is for sure. But that was not what I wanted. I wanted Adamas to be tried to answer for so many crimes he committed not just against our family but many, many, many other families. The decision that came back was exactly what I had dreamed of since I came to the US, the decision confirms to me that in addition to the word of our testimony, the blood of the lamb that was shed in Eastern DRC will triumph over Adamas. I never stop dreaming about these two events and the Lord has carried me to witness this day. Amen! Amen! Amen! Furthermore, and this is for you, Uncle Stanis, it has also been confirmed by DA O'Grady that you, yes you will be the first witness to testify against Adamas in that court in Raleigh. The DA is ready to get you to come here to Raleigh, all expenses paid. Do you see how far we are going, Uncle Stanis?"

"Dear niece Charlotte, I must sing like you Amen! Amen! Amen! Indeed, you have done an outstanding miracle! I had my reservation and doubts. I did not believe that we would get this far. I am ready to testify, I will come without hesitation. That is very good news you are sharing today! I would not say anymore but thank you, Charlotte! Bye and we will talk again!"

Charlotte was not done sharing the good news. She called her dear friend Suzanne Chibere, Pastor Chi's wife:

"My dear Suzanne, the Lord has given thanks, the Lord has honored his beloved daughter, your dear friend Charlotte!"

"Hold on, hold on, my dear friend Charlotte! You are going a bit too fast for me! I am to give thanks to the Lord who has honored you! Please, hold on, hold on! Speak slowly for me to understand, what has happened to you? Are you pregnant, are you about to get married? Charlotte, help me!"

"I am not going to let you spoil my joyous moment, Suzanne, not today, not when the Lord has honored me in every way possible!"

"OK, tell your lowly friend, your friend full of sins! What has happened?"

"In what language do I need to tell you, to explain to you that the decision has been taken in Charlotte to send Adamas case back to Raleigh to be tried so that Adamas must finally answer for all the crimes he has committed against my family."

"Oh, I see! But, Charlotte, you have a very strange way to communicate such a grave news. You did not have to invoke the Lord's name for that. You got me worried and overjoyed at the same trying to figure out what you were celebrating. My very dear, I am happy for you. But why do you think that the Lord has honored you around this matter? Was it not evolving in immigration and district courts as you explained to me last time we talked. I remembered that you were a bit saddened about the back-and-forth legal engagement. To tell you the truth, I did not understand what the fuss was you were sad about as long as the scoundrel Adamas was in jail where he belongs all along. Help me now, what has changed?"

"OK, Suzanne, a very big deal has changed! Let me tell you and I must simply repeat myself for the nth time for your thick scull. Since I came to the US, I dreamed of dragging Adamas Kagita to court to answer for the crimes he subjected my family back in DRC. You got that right!"

"Yes, I did, and I do!"

"And the great opportunity came at your daughter's wedding when I saw him, right, are you following me?"

"Yes, I am!"

"And we took him to court when it was revealed that he was using a fake identity as Jefferson Okito, and he was arrested as fugitive as Adamas Kagita. He was put in the immigration jail right."

"His case was moved to Charlotte where his immigration status was to be determined. At the same time, the Immigration Court Judge wanted to determine what kind of fugitive he was. Was he a criminal as our extensive testimony said he was? The Immigration Judge sent a team to DRC to collect additional facts about Adamas background by conduct interviews in Kinshasa, Goma, and the dangerous trails where coltan and gold are mined and shipped to Rwanda and Uganda. That was Adamas main occupation, and he made a lot of people pay for their lives in that business. Well, the team that went to DRC came back with worse damaging interviews about Adamas. So, the Immigrant Court Judge decided two things I am celebrating today: first he decided to get Adamas deported, second he also decided that before being deported, Adamas will be tried for all the crimes he has committed according to both the voluminous testimony we have developed and the last interviews that were conducted. Now, Suzanne, do you understand my joy, do you understand that my dream has finally become a reality?"

"I do, Charlotte, and I am very happy for you! I am sorry that I got carried away with pregnancy and marriage. You know my screwed mind!"

"Don't be sorry, I felt the equivalent of what you can relate to, I felt a rapid sexual extasy running on my loin, on my bottom, when I got home rejoicing about the news. If a man was around, I believe I would have indulged him without question! I never felt it so hard, it frightened me. I rushed to take a cold shower. Suzanne, for the first time in a very long time, I felt woman. This is the second time I had this strange feeling, Suzanne. Am I recovering my primal libidinal sensations? Is that what you feel when you must indulge your husband. What am I going to do?"

"Hallelujah! Amen! All these years, I thought that I was an oversexed slut! I am relieved that you are coming back to our world. I just need to find you a suitable gentleman. Now I am afraid you would kill the poor man. But that is OK! Just be careful not to give in so quickly and naively. You must enjoy it with the right one! I strongly suggest that you practice on yourself to temperate your ardor when the time would come. You see, men can detect woman desperation and would abuse of it. Don't go out there being desperate. So, practice on yourself, I mean masturbate now and then when the urge becomes intense. Most of us do it alone, in the bathroom."

"Oh my God, now I am going to hear from you all kinds of horror stories! God help us! Of course, I want you to share the good news with your husband. In addition, I want you to tell him that I am requesting that we organize a thanksgiving service to honor the Lord for his thanks sometime before the start of the next court proceedings. I must tell you also that my Uncle Reverend Stanislas Keregi has been invited from Sweden to be the first to testify against Adamas. It would be awesome if my uncle could join us in that thanksgiving service. I don't know the protocols of such a thanksgiving service at the church, but I leave it to Pastor Chi to determine how my uncle, a Revered, would love to participate."

"Charlotte, it would be an honor for my husband and I to organize such a thanksgiving service and to welcome your beloved uncle from Sweden. Remember also that you have always been part of our family. Your uncle will be welcome as part not only our church family but our restrained family. Now I understand why you have been keeping such a low profile lately. You were keeping grave events to yourself. Charlotte, and I seriously mean what I am about to say. We are family. It does not help you to keep all these concerns bottled up when you can share them and get friendly perspectives. We don't want you to fight this battle alone. All of us have suffered the same Eastern DRC events. You are not alone. We all want to help anyway we can."

"I know this, please bear with me when it looks as if I am taking distance. I am not really! We will talk!"

As has been the case many times in the prosecution of Adamas Kagita, the progress made in transferring the case from the Charlotte Immigration Court to the North Carolina Eastern District Court hits a bump. The hope of having Judge Leighton-Garver presiding over the case was dashed. It was obvious from the beginning that Judge Leighton-Garver was not enthusiastic in retrying the case. She was concerned about the political implications of the case. She was warned many times about it. She was happy when the case was moved to the immigration services for early disposition. But every time she ran into DA O'Grady, she expressed her disbelief to get the case return to Raleigh District Court. One afternoon, she shared a political confidence with the DA. She said that the case was torn between two sides of Democrat party: the holdovers of Cliton era and the new folks from Obama's campaign. The latter being entirely unsupportive of the political compromise the Clinton holdovers have made around the Eastern DRC endless civil war. Judge Leighton-Garver did not cherish the prospect of getting caught in that political stalemate, a political nightmare with no clear winning side. It was obvious that Judge Leighton-Garver had a long political agenda after the Raleigh Federal District Court Judgeship. It was not a surprise for the veteran DA to learn that the young bright Judge Leighton-Garver. was appointed to a diplomatic judgeship assignment representing the US in an International Criminal Court under the United Nations organization in La Haye, Netherlands. Judge Leighton-Garver had a strong preference for the collegial judgeship function in that assignment, keeping her long-term political prospect clean. Unfortunately, this judge vacancy disturbed the assignment of Adamas' case for about two months until Judge Alvaro Lopez from Texas Federal Western District Court was reassigned to Raleigh District Court. The Judge was reassigned on the account of his wife, Pr. Amelia Franscisco Lopez, an eminent Biomedical Engineering Professor, who has accepted a tenured Deanship at UNC Biomedical Engineering Department.

Replacing a sitting judge during a transfer of a case was a difficult process as should it be expected. It was more so when the case has already been reviewed and vetted by the sitting judge. The very voluminous testimony afforded in Adamas case did not help. The prosecutor team was entirely taken back. But the leading DA O'Grady was not. He welcomed the new Judge, he was better appraised of Judge Leighton-Graver's disposition to the case than the rest of the team. He was determined to instruct Judge Alvaro Lopez as long and as deeply as the opportunity offered him. In addition, he collected confidential background about the judge. He learned that Judge Alvaro Lopez showed zero merci to people accused of trafficking narcotics from Mexico and people enabling and abetting drug traffic for the Mexican cartels. All he needed was to equate the same murderous coltan and gold traffic in Eastern DRC to gain supportive ears from Judge Alvaro Lopez. Adamas defense team had none of this inclination when Judge Alvaro Lopez banged his gavel to start the trial proceedings.

255

CHAPTER 29
FROM SWEDEN WITH SYMPATHIES

The Sunday before the start of the new trial proceedings against Adamas Kagita turned out to be a big celebration service at Pastor Chi's church, the Raleigh Metropolitan Church of Our Savior. At Charlotte Keregi's request, Pastor Chi asked the congregation to come in large numbers to welcome Reverend Stanislas Keregi invited to testify at the trial that was to resume the next day. This was going to be a huge thanksgiving celebration service to thank the Almighty Lord for having listened to his children to make those who were responsible for shedding the blood of the lamb, his Son's blood accountable. The church was packed with no spare seats, the late comers were held outside the Church to follow the service looking at the large TV Screen mounted inside the Church Recreation center. When Reverend Stanislas was asked to address the packed congregation, he did not disappoint, he addressed them in Swahili:

"Sisters and Brothers in Christ, when my beloved niece Charlotte asked me to come to testify in this trial, I was interrupted in conversation with colleagues discussing some issues at the office. My niece did not know this, and she is learning this now. I interrupted her call. I went down on knees in front of my colleagues who were stunned to see me display a thankful honor to Our Awesome God! They joined me kneeling when I screamed in Swahili the same way I am talking to you now and they did not understand yet they raised their hands as you are raising yours now as I said: Thank you Lord, Thank you Lord, Thank you Almighty Lord, the blood of the lamb has been shed far too long back home, let that blood triumph over the evils who have never stopped to crucify the innocent ones. Lord Almighty stop the shedding of the blood of the lamb! Amen! Amen, Amen! Please be seated."

"Sisters and Brothers in Christ, I must share this with you. After that ominous invitation, I went home to start preparing for this trip. If you saw me during the week before coming here, you would think that I was going well berserk. Wherever I was, I implore our Lord to guide me, and I recite the Lord Prayer every chance I got. Sisters and Brothers, I would ask you to recite that prayer at the end of my note. But I wanted to let you know that while reciting the prayer, I keep repeating two sentences that I want the Lord to stamp in my heard and my mind and they are:

'And forgive us our trespasses,

As we forgive those who trespass against us'

Those two sentences have not left me on my way from Sweden to Raleigh. Sisters and Brothers in Christ, I am not saying this not to lo look any better or to appear superior to anybody. But my sisters and brothers in Christ, remember these sentences, the first, we ask the Lord daily 'To forgive us our trespasses', followed by a promise we make daily to our Lord 'As we forgive those who trespass against us'. I am asking you to pray for me as I go there tomorrow in court in the Lord's grace of these two sentences. With your prayers I would be able to leave the witness stand worthy of our Lord's grace in these two sentences. Now again I must ask you to recite together the Lord's prayer: Our Father Who art in Heaven …"

The Reverend Stanislas rendition vibrated in every congregation member's heart as a thunder jolt. Very few members understood what he was talking about. His niece Charlotte knew exactly what his uncle was talking about, having lost his entire family in the hands of the accused Adamas. Charlotte could not stop crying next to his uncle, being reconfronted vigorously by her friend Suzanne who sat next to her. Charlotte was wondering whether they would be able to overcome the pain that would be relived at the trial the next day.

After Judge Alvaro Lopez has concluded the trial preliminaries by seating a new jury panel and sharing the witness's appearance schedule for the first day, he asked the prosecution and defense teams whether they were ready to start the trial proceedings. He was surprised by an objection by the defense team.

"May it please the court, the defense rises to object to the current trial proceedings as the defense has not completed the discovery process in reviewing all the prosecution findings and documentations as expected."

"Counsels, that is elementary, I know I am a new kid on the block. I assumed that the discovery process has taken place around this case already. Am I missing something, what is the prosecution saying about this? Counsels, please, all of you in my chamber, now!"

"Counsels, please I am not available to play any trial delay game now. We have already waisted two months on this, what is going on?"

"Your honor, the prosecution is at loss around this defense objection. Counsels, would you be kind enough to tell the court what is missing?"

"The reports from DRC interviews!"

"We provided all these documentations the day of the decision made by Honorable Senior Judge Vance-Parrington of Charlotte Immigration Court! We used the same reference for both the Immigration and District Court references. This took place about two and half months ago. I am sorry if your associates have not updated your platform. That is not our job. Your honor, you can verify the same,"

"Counsel, I am verifying the same. All is there, we are going back there to start the proceedings. Are you on board, counsels from the defense team?"

"May it please the court, we have all the documentations including the DRC interviews. Our sincere apologies. We have them indeed! Our sincere apologies!"

As soon all counsels returned to their stands, Judge Alvaro Lopez admonished all the counsels:

"Counsels, let it be the first and last time, I need to suspect any trial delay on any counsel part. Has the prosecution call the first witness?"

"Yes, your Honor!"

"Please, proceed!"

Reverend Stanislas Keregi rose from the witness bench and took his witness seat next to the Judge highchair. For the first time since he left DRC about twelve years, he saw Adamas Kigali, seated at the end of the defense team stand, but in a separate desk with two uniformed immigration court guards standing behind him. He wore an expensive suit with a dark tie and polished shoes. He looked as restrained to the chair, but his hands were not handcuffed. Adamas had a clean shaved face. Adamas looked like an ordinary bank officer. He did not look like the abominable scoundrel he has been described in the voluminous testimony splashed all over the prosecution stand. There was also a mike in front of him that will be operated remotely by the judge if he needs to talk to the court.

Counsel Ludmilla Garrov approached the witness stand:

"Good morning, Reverend Stanislas Keregi, how are you this morning?"

"I am Ok by the Good Lord's Grace!"

"Can I ask you something this early this morning, if you are, OK?"

"Certainly!"

"Have you ever seen the accused Adamas Kagita?"

"Never, this is the first time I saw him in person. The pictures of the accused Adamas Kagita showed most of time a different person I am looking at today. He was always well armed, not polished as he is seating there!"

"Most serial murderers always looked polished in court!"

"Objection, your Honor!"

"Sustained, counsel there is no need to inflame the conversation so early in the morning!"

"So noted, your Honor, my apologies! Reverend Stanislas, I believe you have a description of what you believe the accused Adamas Kagita has done against you and your family. I think you have prepared it, and you want to read it in court if your Honor would allow it."

"Please, proceed!"

Reverend Stanislas turned toward the jury panel and started reading from a stash of paper he pulled from his suit:

"Ladies and gentlemen of the Jury, I am about to read what has been transcribed from the interview that was conducted with the former close friend of the accused Adamas Kagita named Xavier Bhatia, a

Representative of People in the DRC Parliament. The interview took place about three months ago in Kinshasa, DRC.

'I met Adamas sometime around Mars in 2007, when I came to Goma. I just came back from Johannesburg where I completed my Master degree in Construction Engineering at the University of Johannesburg. Adamas looked very prosperous then. He said that he was now second in command at the big coltan mines of Kwazimu in Walikale territory. I did ask him what kinds of functions he was fulfilling as second in command of mining operations. It was the third time he went about the same conversation. Every time he had a completely different version of his functions. This time he was a little bit precise. He said that he was master of life and death in the territory. He was at time sarcastic and dead serious. He would not let me interrupt. He said that my academic degree was worthless in his world. He was amassing the equivalent of three to four hundred thousand dollars a month. When I asked again doing what, he exploded. Coltan my man, Coltan! This is what the world wants, and we are providing it daily. And he was on top of the coltan food chain from Walikale to Rwanda border warehouses. Unfortunately, he added, bringing it to Rwanda is not picnic, everybody wants to get our stuffs. It is to kill or to get killed if you see what I mean. That is my life man, it is no picnic! When I asked him whether it was worthwhile compared to working as a construction engineer as I intended to do, he laughed at me. Then he said he got all the ladies he wanted to get. He gravely added my only concern is about this man of God called Reverend Keregi, Reverent Stanislas Keregi. I think it will be either he kills me, or I kill him He said that there will be no middle escape between us. I asked him then why? Adamas stayed quiet for a few seconds, checking that nobody else was listening to our conversation. But we were alone in my hotel room. Then he said, he had kidnapped his daughter and made her his sex slave somewhere in his jungle compound about ten miles from the mines. The Reverend left me no choice. I loved his daughter, she was about fifteen or sixteen years old. A goddess of a girl. The moment I saw her in the road leading to her father's compound, I was smitten. I sent delegates to marry her. I was turned flatly down by her parents and the whole Keregi family. Well, I took matters in my own hands, kidnapped her when her father was away in a conference in Beni-Butembo area. When the family started looking for her, I killed his wife and a baby she was carrying. I killed everyone who was in the compound. Later I was told that the girl had two younger brothers who were away in school. When they came back, they were hidden in the area. This Reverend used his Church network to retrieve the kids and left the country for good. I never heard from him again. I held the girl for about five more years but never gave her a chance to know whatever happened. Well, when I was ordered to close my sex slaves' compound, I simply cut her throat and buried her in that compound. I could not deal to think of her whoring with anybody else. She belonged eternally to me. Man, that is my life now, kill or get killed. I told him that to each person, his cross. I could not join him in that life. He left me in the hotel room, and I never saw him again.'

Ladies and gentlemen of the jury, that is the witness testimony I wanted to share with you today about this man accused of many other crimes. The testimony comes from the conversation he had with his close friend who has reported it in form of an interview Altogether, Adamas has killed more than twenty members of my family because of one reason to keep my daughter as his sex slave. But yesterday I had a wonderful thanksgiving celebration service at the Raleigh Metropolitan Church of Our Savior when I shared with the congregation what I was feeling coming from Sweden to Raleigh. I told them that I kept reciting the Lord's Prayer every day and every hour when I received the invitation to come testify in this court. I told them that in that prayer there were two sentences that will motivate me while seating on the witness chair and they are 'And forgive us our trespasses, as we forgive those who trespass against us'! Ladies and gentlemen, I feel relieved that I am being guided by these two sentences. I must tell you that all the feeling of revenge built up for so many years against this man has been washed away by the mercy and the grace that the Lord's prayer anointed my soul at this moment. I feel this enormous pity for him surrounded by guards, shackled as he is on that chair. It is a pitiful sight when the blood of the lamb is triumphing over the evil he represents, over the evil he is. I thank the Lord Almighty, Amen! Ladies and gentlemen of the jury, thank you for listening to me!"

At that instant, Counsel Ludmilla Garrov came to collect Reverent Stanislas from the witness bench and addressing the court, she said:

"May it please the court, our first witness has completed his testimony. I am requesting a recess, your Honor!"

"So granted!"

261

Ludmilla guided the terribly and mentally exhausted Reverend to his seat behind her niece who was tearing up a flood. That was the reason why Ludmilla requested a recess. Charlotte Keregi was scheduled to follow her uncle Reverend Stanislas who displayed a remarkable God-fearing restraint at the witness stand, a restraint that spooked the packed court of attendees, most from Pastor Chi's church. Charlotte Keregi was still trembling at the prosecution bench side, mumbling a prayer in a soft voice, wondering whether she would be able to hold her own once on the witness stand. To allow Charlotte to recover, Ludmilla stood up to ask a few worldly questions to Adamas Kagita.

"May it please the court, Counsel wants to direct few refreshing questions to the accused, Adamas Kagita."

"Please, proceed!"

"Thank you, your Honor, Mr. Adamas Kagita or former Mr. Jefferson Okito, have you ever seen Reverend Stanislas Keregi?"

"No!"

"Then why have you sworn to your close friend Xavier Bhatia that it will be kill or get kill if ever you face the Reverend?"

"I never said anything of the sort, never!"

"In other words, your close friend Xavier Bhatia was lying when he reminisced the last conversation you two had in that hotel room?"

"I don't remember such a conversation."

"Fair enough, but I presume you remember Nyagatero Pass along the elevation leading to Mount Benya."

"I do."

"Wonderful, we are getting something and somewhere here. Now tell the jury what was remarkable about Nyagatero Pass?"

"This is where my Boss has built his expansive farm compound. It was in a beautiful, lush valley with a small running river. My Boss farm was built on the left side of the elevation?"

"How far was it from the Kwazimu mining area?"

"About seven miles?"

"Now listen very carefully before answering the next question. What was the next big compound as you rose along the elevation to Mount Benya?"

"Mmmm …"

"I did not hear you!"

"The next big compound was my compound?"

"Please, repeat what you just say."

"The next big compound was my compound?"

"And how far was it from your Boss compound?"

"About three miles."

"So, we can count about ten miles from the Kwazimu mines area, am I correct!"

"Yes, my compound was about ten miles from the Kwazimu mines area."

"Now let me refresh your memory, to get to your big compound from the mines area, you had to take the Nyagatero Pass going up the elevation to Mount Benya, is that correct?"

"Yes!"

"How can your close friend, Xavier Bhatia, possibly know in the reported interview that a compound you just said belonging to you was about ten miles from the Kwazimu mines area the same way as you told him? "

"I never had that conversation with whoever you are talking about?"

"How can your close friend, Xavier Bhatia remember that you said you were ordered to close the compound and for what reason?"

"I never had that conversation with whoever you are talking about?"

"Let me help you, your Boss was not amused, your Boss was not happy to learn that your compound, next to his family farm compound, your compound was in fact a sex slaves compound attending to vile debauchery for a lot of people who supported the murderous traffic of coltan and gold minerals from the Kwazimu to the lawless warehouses at Rwanda and Uganda borders. That was the main reason you were ordered to close the sex slave's compound. That is also the reason you killed the Reverend's Daughter that you wantonly kidnapped at the minor age of fifteen. What was her name, do you remember?"

"I don't know her name!"

"Justina Keregi, does this name ring any bell in your evil range?"

"I did not kill Justina Keregi!"

"You did worse, you cut her throat!"

"No, she run into the jungle when the compound was ordered closed. She did not return to her parents. She disappeared into the jungle, I never heard or seen her again. She just disappeared for ever. I did not kill her, I loved her so much, Justina!"

"So, why did you confess to have cut her throat, why, Adamas?"

"That was the tough talk of the jungle, kill or get killed?"

"How many people did you kill according to your law of the jungle, to kill or to get killed?"

"I did not kill anybody, it was all tough talk!"

"That is a new revelation, it was all tough talk, to kill or to get killed! Do you reasonably think that anybody would believe that?"

"You don't have to but that was the reality of the law of jungle, kill or get killed?"

"Accused Adamas Kagita, tell that to Reverend Stanislas who already has forgiven your trespasses against his daughter Justina, his wife Penelope and his baby born Stanis Junior! Tell him that you did not kill them!"

"I did not!"

"Tell him!"

"Badgering the witness!"

"Sustained, Counsel you should know the time of the day when the witness closes answering your questions!"

"I am sorry, your Honor! But if I may, members of jury, accused Adamas Kagita has finally acknowledged knowing, kidnapping Justina Keregi, the teenage minor daughter of Reverend Stanislas, he also claimed to quote loving her end quote and witnessing her disappear in the jungle. He was the last person to have seen her. What the accused Adamas Kagita would not confess to is the fact that a burial site was found in his abandoned sex slave compound where the corpse of Justina Keregi was unearthed with marks of her throat cut in the same manner he has shared with and revealed to his close friend, Xavier Bhatia. Members of the jury, thank you for your sustained attention. "

"Counsels from the prosecution, I believe it is about time for lunch recess before you call your next witness. This court is adjourned!"

Ludmilla returned to the prosecution bench. She found Charlotte fully recovered from her uncle Reverend Stanislas' testimony. Ludmilla asked her if she would be ready for the next witness testimony. She raised her hands saying she would be.

Soon after Judge Alvaro Lopez bands his gavel to start the second session of the court proceedings in US vs Adamas Kagita case.

"May it please the court, Counsel is calling witness Charlotte Keregi to share what she had endured in the hands of the accused Adamas Kagita."

After swearing on the same Bible that her Uncle Reverend Stanislas has used in the morning testimony, Charlotte was finally ready to provide her testimony.

"Members of the jury, it has been close to fourteen years, I have been ready to provide this testimony against the accused Adamas Kagita. I may not be as eloquent as my uncle who preceded me on this witness chair this morning, but I must marshal all the strengths in my body and bones to do this. I must beg you to bear with me if I stumble here and there during my presentation. My story started with a trip I took right after graduation from high school. I aspired to become a nurse after my graduation. I talked with my parents and my husband about my academic ambitions. You must understand that was a very difficult time back then. The country went through a violent regime change, from a dictatorship that went on for thirty-two years to a new uncertain violent political transition. My region saw multiple waves of military campaigns. There was first a rebellion that took place in the neighboring country that toppled the regime in place, followed by a terrible genocide of about million dead people. This tragedy sent genocidaire military troops and refugees packing in our area. These troops and refugees were in turn chased by the new military contingents who took over the neighboring country. The invasion of our area changed into a full-fledged rebellion that toppled the dictator in the capital of the DRC in Kinshasa. No sooner after we learned that the new President installed by that rebellion was assassinated and the military troops who put this man in power retreated to our area to start a new rebellion and started to plunder mineral resources in the area. In the process they started fighting with local militias. The area or province called North Kivu became extremely militarized with pockets of military groups all over the place. The local population managed as best it could to hang in, being displaced or killed or protected or chased from its territory. This was the prevailing anarchic time we lived in and pursued our education. As far as I was concerned, I wanted to leave the area after graduation and go to another neighboring country called Uganda to pursue my nursing education. My parents and my husband reluctantly agreed to let me go. I took a trip with an aunt to go a big urban center called Beni-Butembo much closer to the Uganda border. I was supposed to meet a paternal uncle in that town to assist me to go to Uganda. It was on that precarious trip that I ran into Adamas Kagita on a trip bus. Adamas was there next to the driver. He was heavily armed wearing a military uniform. It was difficult to tell whether he was protecting the bus trip or was on some perilous business. However, Adamas never stopped harassing me and other younger women at every bus stop. My protective aunt had few harsh exchanges with Adamas. When we arrived at Beni-Butembo final stop, we were welcome by my paternal uncle who rushed us to his house somewhere in town. That is when I learned about Adamas. My uncle informed us that the man was from Beni-Butembo, and he has been identified as a murderous leader in the dangerous traffic of minerals from many artisanal mines throughout the North Kivu province to Uganda and Rwanda. My uncle said that he was very dangerous, and he had earned a very sad nickname for his murderous rampage. He was called in French: 'Danger de Mort' or "Danger of Death". My uncle sounded very fearful of Adamas and warned us that after having unsuccessfully harassed us, he was probably trying to find out through his many contacts where we were hiding in town. He added that under the difficult circumstances he could no longer guarantee a safe passage through the borders of Uganda which are also heavily militarized. At the end the uncle strongly advised us to take another southern trip straight to the town of Goma to wait for a better quieter opportunity. I was very surprised by my uncle's apprehension. I could not believe that an innocent chance encounter with this man could turn to a calamity. I was wrong. Sometime later that evening, my uncle had a scary visitor who warned him of what he was the most afraid of. Adamas had found out that he was hiding his next conquest. At about four in the morning, the uncle took me and my protective aunt to a town south of Beni-Butembo where we boarded a bus trip to Goma. We were lucky to arrive safely in Goma the next day at around noon after multiple stops. I was stunned. By the unexpected turn of events. All these years I was growing up, I was well protected in our area, surrounded by members of a very large well-known family in the area. I never really paid attention to all the political turmoil's which visited our area. I always assumed that our family was big enough to provide all of us with great protection. When I was married, my family insisted that my husband na d I resided in our family compound to enjoy the same protection. The many military campaign waves did not touch our family per se. And all the sudden, I became a mark to run for my life in places I did not know."

"My stay in Goma became even more revealing. I was staying in the beautiful compound of another distant maternal uncle. He was a judge in the territorial court in town. After about four days of stay, the uncle asked to talk to me in private. He had terrifying news. He announced that a highly revered grandfather was killed by the guards at the Kwazimu mining operations. Apparently, the grandfather had intervened in the adjudication of a mining operation. There was a landslide which had buried ten miners. The grandfather complained about the increasing risk that miners were facing because of the multiple landslides which have occurred lately. Four family members were among the last victims. As an old veteran of mining operations, the grandfather raised his voice at the management meeting, and he was kicked out. It was reported that he then called for a strike against the mining operations. The guards followed him on his way home then shot him. The next day the Kwazimu mines were completely paralyzed. Everybody reported to the family compound to show their sympathy. The Kwazimu mines management did not appreciate the strike and sent military guards to the family compound which was burned down. A lot of unaccounted family members were shots or disappeared. I lost my husband, two other brothers and parents in the burn down family compound. The man who led that campaign was no other Adamas Kagita. Every person named Keregi in the area was running for life. Adamas embellished the whole story saying that two of your uncles and two brothers stole a company truck or van when they were running from the massacre. He killed all of them on the road to Goma. I was later told that this was the second time that Adamas went after the Keregi family. The uncle judge also told me the story about what happened to Justina Keregi, her father, the Reverend Stanislas, her mother, and her baby born brother. I guess Adamas wanted to eliminate any trace of the Keregi family. I had no idea about Justina Keregi. No family member ever mentioned it. I must assume now that Adamas knew exactly who I was when he saw me on the bus. I was also told that I looked very much like Justina. I also learned that the Keregi family refused Adamas' proposal to marry Justinia at first when she was only fourteen. He took matters into his own hands by kidnapping her until he killed her later. When Adamas saw me in the bus, he confused me with Justinia. He went as far as to contact my family to propose to marry me also when I was already married. People in the area said that he decided to kill everybody in the burn down family compound to teach my family lesson, to avenge the affront of denying him marriage proposals to two Keregi cousins. From that time, I started making plans to leave the country. I came back to the burn down family compound under a heavily armed escort from area residents to retrieve some important documents and managed to take the difficult escape route to Uganda and to Raleigh. Members of jury, as soon as I reached Raleigh, I swore to testify in court to give this presentation against this accused Adamas Kagita. God helping, I fulfilled my academic ambitions to become a nurse and above all to testify today, to report the killing of more than twenty members of my family by the same Adamas Kagita. Thank you."

At that instant, Ludmilla came to the witness bench holding a box of paper towels and said:

"Hallelujah, Charlotte, you did it and you did not need any paper towel! I am very proud of you to have delivered this testimony as you said fourteen years later. And this accused never imagined that this day in court wouldn't happen, but it did.".

"Now let me ask the accused a few questions while he is in that witness chair."

"Accused Adamas Kagita, do you remember this beautiful lady on the witness chair?"

"I am afraid I don't! Never met her in my entire life!"

"Well, you said the same about Justina Keregi this morning, but we learned also that you never stopped loving her."

"Did you not deny knowing her when you claim to be Jefferson Okito!

My question is not about Charlotte Keregi, it is about the whole Keregi family, why such an obsession with this family, why did you kill about twenty members of that family, that is what the court wants to know."

"I don't know what you are talking about!"

"Oh, you certainly do, you went berserk about Justina, kill the whole Reverend family, then you see Charlotte in the trip bus, you harassed her, you cannot get her, you go on burning her family compound, killing a lot of people! Two ladies in the raw, twenty and more victims, that is unbelievable, there must be a deep motivation you need to share with the members of the jury and this court."

"I don't know what you are talking about?"

"Accused Adama Kagita, do you want me to help you refresh your deep memory, well I would do it! Now look at the projection I have prepared for you on the left projection screen! What do you see?"

"My God, why bring up my wife?"

"And next to your wife on the right-hand side is, well Charlotte and further on the right-hand side we have, exactly Justina! Now anybody looking at these zoomed pictures would believe that these three ladies are related. In fact, for your information, you went as far as looking for another Keregi to marry to bring to the US as your wife. Adamas, you have been obsessed with these Keregi ladies, you could not resist falling for another Keregi lady. We checked your wife's background in Beni-Butembo area. Her biological father is a Keregi. You were again smitten by another Justina and went on marrying her precipitously when you were doing your immigration papers to the US. The man who gave

269

her away was her adoptive father, Benjamin Buseri. Thank God, she is married to a monster who never engages his wife over anything, except impregnating her with the two children while maintaining separate living spaces. Do you know why you maintained separate living spaces in that big house in the Outer Banks? Well, you did not want to get closer as married couple, you did not want to reveal that you were still pursuing Justina you killed by cutting her throat. I strongly believe that your wife would have had her throat cut up if Charlotte has not pressed this case to this court. You look surprised about these revelations. Don't worry! We know that the Outer Banks house has been emptied and now on sale and your family is outside of Mobile, Alabama and your wife is in good care of Issana Baruti who is taking good care of your entire family.'

"By the way how are you still managing your family financial support when you have been incarcerated for this long. "

"I believe that is none of your business."

"Badgering witness!"

"Sustained, Counsel, where are you going with that line of questioning, is Adamas not entitled to secure his family financially!"

"Just asking, your Honor, just asking! Well, members of the jury, I strongly believe that we have established the enigmatic motivation for the accused Adamas Kagita to kill twenty members of the Keregi family. We have established his obsession with the Keregi ladies to the present wife. It was so obsessive that he had now the Keregi blood running his own children."

"May it please the court, when reviewing this line of questioning, I had a few question marks about the accused interactions with a major element or contact he had when he was involved in whatever functions he was assuming with the Kwazimu mining operations. This line of questioning, I am certain will also explain the obsession with the Keregi family."

"Please, proceed!"

"Thank you, can you tell us what relationship you had with a Reverend Drago when you were assuming whatever functions in the Kwazimu mining operations?"

"I don't understand the question?"

"Did you work with a Reverend Drago when you were working for Kwazimu Mines? In other words, what were the functions that a Reverend Drago had with Kwazimu mining operations?"

"I don't know, you should ask him?"

"Your Honor, the accused is refusing to answer the question!"

"Please, answer the question?"

"Your Honor, I don't understand the question?"

"Let me ask you, do you know this Reverend Drago, does the defense team is aware of this Reverend Drago, was he mentioned in the discovery, if the answer is yes, then answer this question, do you know this Reverend Drago?"

"Yes, your honor!"

"You see, that was very easy. Now you know this Reverend Drago, the prosecution can answer any question relative to him, and I did not hear your counsel, I mean the defense team raising any objection, please proceed!"

"Thank you, your Honor, let me again ask the question, can you tell us what relationship you had with a Reverend Drago when you were assuming whatever functions in the Kwazimu mining operations?"

"I believe he was a member of the Board of Administration of the Kwazimu Mines company."

"Do you believe that your response is correct, are you not certain."

"I am certain!"

"If he was a member of Board of Administration, what if any relationship you had with this Reverend Drago? Did he initiated any task or function you need to perform?"

"No that I know of, he gave general directives!"

"Such as!"

"Security directives about the mining operations."

"Which security directives, for instance breaking strikes, preventing employees stealing equipment's or minerals shipments, advising best secure logistics, do you see where I am going here?"

"Yes, he gave many different directives."

"Did he give directives about how to handle complaints relative to mining landslides?"

"Well, not really, we took care of those complaints?"

"How did you handle these complaints?"

"We penalized those who complain up to firing repeated offenders?"

"And sometime killing right?"

"Never!"

"Who decided never!"

"I never decided to kill anybody!"

"With the Reverend input?"

"But those were operations issues, the Reverend was dealing with the Board administration issues?"

"So, not killings right?"

"Yes, Maam!"

"Then who decided to kill the Elderly Keregi when he complained about the ten people who were buried because of mining landslides?"

"I don't know, I came in a day later."

"Then who decided to burn down the Keregi family compound when you came back, killing more than twenty people from the same family?"

"Who made the decision to engage in that wanton murderous operation?"

"You cannot answer this question, Adamas, was it you or Reverend Drago?"

"I did!"

"I did not hear you!"

"I did!"

"You seem to answer this question out of fear of Reverend Drago?"

"No, he was not there to make that decision, I did it!"

"Members of jury, again, you heard the accused confessing to have made the decision to burn down the Keregi family compound and killing more than twenty members of the Keregi family!"

"May it please the court, it is late in the day, I will continue this line of questioning tomorrow!"

"Thank you, Counsel, this court is adjourned!"

Ludmilla closed convincingly and remarkably two major testimonies with elegant lines of questioning which forced Adamas to plead guilty twice in the row. DA O'Grady was extremely proud of his protégé.

CHAPTER 30
REVEREND DRAGO'S LINE OF QUESTIONING

The triumphant closing, that Ludmilla Garrov celebrated in lines of questioning on the first day of the trial, raised a lot of concerns at multiple levels and in many quarters. The first question mark hit the accused Adamas Kagita who became very alarmed when Ludmilla started talking about Reverend Drago. That was the last person he wanted to talk about in any way or fashion during the trial. Precisely speaking, he became fearful during the questioning. He suspected that Reverend Drago had sent people to monitor this trial evolution. And to sit there and being questioned about his working relationship with Reverend Drago was entirely unexpected. He answered the line of questioning as quickly as he could do. As Ludmilla insisted on probing their working relationship, he became prepared to implicate himself if that would spare him further questioning. He reasoned that he would be better off to hang himself rather than talk about Reverend Drago. He remembered what the man strongly advised him the last time they met. He intimated to him to speed up the trial by taking the guilty plea in such a way to spare as he put it the "Enterprise" further embarrassment. He suggested that the "Enterprise" would take good care of him if he toes the "Enterprise" line and plead guilty and remain in jail for five to ten years. The "Enterprise" would stand by him during and after jail time. He also remembered that he responded arrogantly that he would take his own chances by "fighting for his life'. That was how they parted company and he had not heard from the "Enterprise" from that day. Well, things have not gone any better. He lost his borrowed identity and was about to be sent to jail for a long time without the "Enterprise" support. Adamas was clearly convinced as he was being driven back to the Immigration jail cell, Reverend Drago had already received the full transcript of the trial first day proceedings. Furthermore, Reverend Drago had also already provided the "Enterprise" gang with the summary of the same and what need to be done about it. He knew that he was being abandoned to his own fate of long time in jail or death if he was to be released now. Jail time looked a better prospect.

While Adamas reconciled to a long-time jail prospect, he was shocked to hear that his wife Lisa was a Keregi. He could not believe that the "Enterprise" had manipulated him to a point where he was to be trapped in the US wearing his obsession with Keregi girls. He could not believe that he was forced to leave his Eastern DRC domain, by marrying a Keregi girl who looked like Justina. Did the "Enterprise" place this Keregi girl on his path when he needed to get married to assume that Ugandan Jefferson Okito identity. Adamas remembered that the entire ordeal to leave DRC took less than a month. Adamas shook his head. He was very confused. He could not decide which of the groups managed to place this Keregi girl on his path. Was it the "Enterprise" or the American Intelligence service or both? Was he being played all along from the start by these two groups, under the steady mentoring and guidance of Reverend Drago. And now that he is done, the two groups must be having a good long laugh at his expense. Did the Keregi girl know what game she has been thrown into? He dismissed that thought. Lisa has been so absent minded from the start, he could not suspect she even knew or cared to know who she was forced to marry if she was leaving DRC to go far away in the milk land of the US. The most shocking thing for Adamas was around the details that the prosecution provided during the court proceedings. The details must have been provided by somebody who was thoroughly knowledgeable about the motivations which were used to get him from the terrain of plundering minerals to carry them to Uganda and Rwanda before shipping them overseas. As far as he knew, Reverend Drago set and executed the entire migration to US plan. He remembered that the first requirement to go was to marry that girl. Reverend Drago indicated that Lisa was a rather docile marriageable woman. Reverend Drago told him that he did not trust him to pick one of his multiple wayward girlfriends.

"Adamas, you must appear respectable in this project. Your prostitute girlfriends should not apply. A very good friend of mine named Benjamin Busire has exactly what you need, a beautiful and willing girl to marry you. We can close everything by this weekend if you agree', so he said.

He was right, Lisa fit the bill perfectly. And she was a complete copy of

275

Justina. Adamas was beyond smitten. He controlled his emotion and did not say anything to Reverend Drago who was reading his mind. Adamas was happy. In addition, at seventeen Lisa looked so pure and obviously virgin from far. The prospect of her carrying his kids was enchanting. He did not count the money he gave for the dowry that weekend. He gave more than five hundred thousand American dollars. Lisa never said a word but yes or no. She obeyed at the drop of every of his requests. She was the type of wife he always wanted, excessively obedient. He even told her that he would not touch her until they have settled down in that big house in the Outer Banks. She agreed, having no idea what he was talking about, with no inclination about that he was postponing, their first lovemaking. When that happened, she submitted as naturally as she could despite his roughness and violent sexual perversion. She held the bargain dictated by her parents and did not complain. She was a revelation for Adamas. She then pumped two beautiful children in less than three years. Still not complained, never raising her voice, never speaking to her husband unless asked or spoken to, attending to her children, entirely obedient and docile to a fault.

And now, back to his jail cell, Adamas was stricken to hear that Lisa was just a well-executed part of a package plan. He could not believe that the prosecution had mapped his life down pat from the time he left DRC to the present. As he struggled to make sense of the prosecution's statement that afternoon, Adamas was only left to assume that the two groups, the "Enterprise" and the American intelligence service have collided to play him, and he was played all along. In addition, the thought of being subjected to another round of questions involving Reverend Drago the next day did not sit well with Adamas. He sat on his tiny cell bed for a moment but felt like he was falling. He stood up and had the same feeling of collapsing on his own weight. He looked around and in a dream that he saw as if the ceiling and the walls of his cell were also collapsing. The whole scene started driving Adamas crazy. How could he, the merciless war lord, not see this huge betrayal coming? How could he have been played so disdainfully? A pounding migraine was now ravaging his head. He felt like his head was spinning around and leaving his body. From his cell he screamed for help. By the time the medics arrived, he was found lying on the floor, convulsing his body like a maniac, vomiting everything he had eaten that day. The medics said that Adamas looked like someone in an exorcist trance. He was quickly evacuated to the jail infirmary where he was restrained in bed by three guards to be calmed down, and where he spent the night under heavy doses of anxiety disorder medicines to keep me sedated and to allow him to sleep.

The same triumphant closing that Ludmilla delivered was in fact noted with a considerable alarm by two "Enterprise" spies who were sent to attend and monitor the court proceedings by Reverend Drago, as Adamas has suspected. The spies were shocked when they heard the line of questions involving Reverend Drago with his name loudly mentioned by Counsel Ludmilla Garrov from the prosecution team. They did not believe their ears and eyes about the sudden turn of prosecution questioning and the responses that Adamas was giving. They did not need to wait for the Judge adjournment gavel to rush back to their hotel room to share the news with Reverend Drago back in Kinshasa.

"Reverend, you won't believe what we have witnessed in the court today. You were namely cited by the prosecution lady trying to get Adamas to talk about the working relationships between you and Adamas. Thank God, Adamas reduced it to an ordinary working arrangement. The prosecution tried to implicate you as the responsible giving orders to kill people. Adamas stood his ground and assumed that responsibility. Sadly, the defense team did not raise any objection to the sudden turn to that line of questioning. It was so unexpected out of nowhere."

Reverend Drago listened attentively to the reporting and became livid and very quickly restrained himself. He reassured the spies by saying that the court exchange was in the natural flow of any trial in the US. He then changed the conversation call into a different coded language to signify the spies not to call his number and to wait for a message from a different source in about an hour. When the new call came from a restricted source, the reverend told the spies that he has warned Adamas already when they met to speed up his guilty plea to close the case and to move on to other things. Adamas did not listen and now everything must be done not to expose the "Enterprise" top leadership. He advised the spies to continue following very closely the trial proceedings while the reverend was getting new directives from the "Enterprise" top leadership which rested on the political leaders in DRC, Rwanda and Uganda.

While DA O'Grady congratulated Ludmilla Garrov in her very productive first day of trial proceedings, Charlotte Keregi was stunned and very surprised by the revelation she threw about Lisa, Adamas' wife, being a Keregi. She was disappointed that she was not informed of that major revelation story. She asked her uncle Reverend Stanislas if he was aware of this. The wise man tried to calm his niece:

"The fact I was not aware of this does not mean that it was purposely kept from us. Believe me Charlotte, I don't know who has read the entire voluminous testimony we have produced. I have not read everything. I know you did not. The lawyers were duty bound to read everything during the discovery. And on top of that you got sixty to eighty interviews that came from DRC. I heard that they rose to more than three thousand pages. You and I have not read a tenth of these interviews. We don't know what the legal prosecution team found in these interviews. I am not defending the team. But I am assuming, as it is routine in the American judicial process and what I have also seen in the Swedish judicial system, you convict the accused if you can develop a solid motive for the crime. You convict a bank robber because the robber needs to get money that is stored and protected in a bank. There cannot be a bank robbery case but in a bank location, right, and case close. That is the way it is in the American and most European legal trial. If you cannot come up with a good motivation for a crime, the conviction and sentencing may become very moot. Now if there is a murder for instance, the prosecution would spend a great deal of time searching for a motive. A cheated husband or wife who kills his or her partner would amount to a crime of passion. This crime is punished at a much lower sentence than a crime committed by a lawless bandit or robber who randomly kills a person in a dark alley. And you know why, in both cases the crime may or may not be premeditated, a strong motive must be established. While the first crime can be determined as a crime of passion, the second will be established as a deliberate wanton crime. Believe me, in the crime of passion, the accused can easily get suspended sentence or minimal sentence while the robber would get no excuse and will be sentenced starting to twenty to life jail sentence. That is the way crime is punished in the US. And the strategy for the prosecution is always to search for the motive. Going back to Adamas case and how it was being prosecuted, it was established today that he killed more than twenty people in our Keregi family. Back home in DRC, the punishment would be death not for the motive but for the large number of dead people. In the US judicial system, the motive for killing twenty people must be established. The prosecution must work hard to remove the insanity plea motive, that is the accused was insane and got busy killing people for no reasons. Insanity conviction does not lead to harsh punishment, so the prosecution works very hard to stay far away from it. Believe me, in the Adamas case, he seemed to direct his incentive to kill toward our family. Twenty and more people were killed. The prosecution needed to find out why Adamas targeted our family with so much hatred. The prosecution here must have gone through voluminous testimony and interviews looking for that hard factual evidence of the motive. Whether you and I do not like it or do not believe it, Adamas had shown many instances of obsession over the Keregi girls. First there was his obsession over my daughter Justina he kidnapped and killed, then his awakened obsession over you when he saw you briefly in a bus trip and went about searching for you that night in Beni-Butembo, and now his obsession over a Justina looked alike by precipitously marrying this Lisa Keregi we did not know, all that established a clear obsessive motive pattern. The prosecution will pursue that line of motivation to get a maximum sentencing of Adamas at the end of this trial. That is the way of the US judicial process whether we like it or not. Charlotte, I want you to know, and rest assured, that I will get to the bottom of that Lisa family relationship. I will keep you posted."

Charlotte Keregi was appeased somewhat but still raised the issue when she crossed Pascal Bodavi who had a quick answer:

"I am sorry that we did not share this prosecution strategy with you and your uncle. I told the DA and Ludmilla that you may not have established or known about that shocking family relationship with Lisa Keregi. We learned from a chance interview we had yes with Lisa's adoptive father, Benjamin Busire. We had a few untranslated interviews still in Swahili when we came back. As we evolved in finding the crucial killing motives, I circled back to my team members from Kenya who mentioned this man Busire. When we translated this interview, we were very stunned and surprised. It was one of Ah-AH-AH judicial moment. I was observing Adamas when Ludmilla raised it, I saw him becoming very uncomfortable. He laid his head low as if blown away. I don't know how he is feeling now but I can see the revelation must have hit Adamas as a major betrayal by his higher up in Eastern DRC. That marriage strongly reinforced his motive to kill as many members as possible of your family. It was obvious that his obsession grew by the fact he was rejected as unsuitable to marry the first two Keregi girls, Justina Keregi and another Keregi girl that is you, Charlotte. He took upon himself to burn down your family compound to eliminate all

279

Keregi who stood against his obsession. The precipitous marriage to Lisa Keregi was a victory sign of revenge in his lifetime quest and obsession. Charlotte, to tell the truth we developed and tied this motivation chain of all these events this last weekend before Monday. We did not have the time nor the courage to share this with you. We were afraid that letting you know would have led you and your uncle to pushback and to logically insist on verifying the family relationship with Lisa. That would have taken few days of delay we could not afford. We took a big chance to lay the revelation out there at the end after Adamas had already pled guilty to the massacre in your family. And guess what, the defense team was so overwhelmed, it did not cross-examine you to ascertain that this Lisa Keregi was your relative. That was a very bold strategic step and it worked. If there is blame to direct to anybody, please blame me for this lapse. I would explain this to your uncle, just the same.'

"Don't you worry, I will talk to my uncle. I was very silly again not trusting your very impressive legal strategy. I am very sorry. Please don't mention this to Ludmilla."

"You are not a lawyer. Like in any trade or work domain, the experts take risks to move the process. I understand!"

CHAPTER 31

ADAMAS' DELAY

As Charlotte got ready to go back to the Raleigh District Court building the next day morning, she noticed an urgent call from Counsel Ludmilla Garrov:

"Good morning, Charlotte, I am calling to advise you to come straight to the DA office. We are facing another court proceedings delay. This time, Adamas had serious health setback after yesterday's difficult trial proceedings. We have called your uncle who is also coming straight here. See you later."

Charlotte alerted her friend Suzanne to share the same news with her husband, Pastor Chi. Both were scheduled to attend the Tuesday court proceeding. She drove to the DA office where Ludmilla guided to the DA conference room. Her uncle was already in the conference room including Pascal Bodavi and the DA who addressed the team as soon they sat down.

"I am afraid that we are going to experience another delay in the trial of Adamas. He did not take it too well the line of questioning our esteemed counsel Ludmilla started yesterday. I was called by the manager of the immigration court jail at around nine pm last night. They told me that Adamas was having a serious bout of anxiety disorder when he came back from the trial. He collapsed on the jail cell floor, screaming, vomiting like a deranged maniac. It took about three guards to restrain him in bed with chains and give antidepressant very heavy doses to calm him down and to keep him sedated and at sleep. The defense lead lawyer also called and advised me that Adamas won't be able to attend his trial today. Judge Alvaro Lopez agreed, and he has adjourned the trial proceedings for the time being. The Judge would call the meeting sometime today about what would happen. He did say whether the proceedings would resume tomorrow. This is the second time that Adamas has reacted violently during the trial proceedings. We must be prepared to advise the Judge and the defense about the legal consequences of this interruption. I don't like what I am seeing. I don't want this scoundrel to escape the full legal retribution that will be called against him at the end of this trial. Well, we must let the process take its course and the professional medical experts will guide us anyway."

"The Lord has already set the course for Adamas, I don't think he would escape it." Reverend Stanislas told the team.

"Thank you Reverend, I am starting to suspect that this Reverend Drago must be seriously vetted in these proceedings. The way Adamas had reacted at the mere mention of this Drago is telling. He reacted as if he is seriously afraid of this man. What do you know about him, Revered Stanislas?"

"Dear DA O'Grady, there is nothing that hurt me more than to listen to people mentioning this Drago and associating the title Reverend next to his name. As far as I am concerned it is pure abomination to call him Reverend. He had no right to call himself Reverend. I know, I know, it has become standard for so many people to call and to use our Lord name in vain. What is even more tragic is that it does not shock anybody anymore. It used to be sacrilegious to enter the Lord house. I certainly remember the Smiling Pope, the two hundred sixty third Pope in Vatican, whatever his name was. I believe he was named John Paul I. I am not catholic, but this one was a saint. He lasted only thirty-three days, he was so afraid of, trembled every instance for being Pope. I am mentioning him for the humility, the reverence and the respect he had shown for the divinity of God. Do you know what he said? Well, we are talking about a Pope. He said something to that effect and pardon me if I am not translating what he said properly, but it went like this;

"I felt less deserving to enter the church where the cross of our Lord is prominently displayed. I rather stand outside the church and admire Our Lord awesomeness from the church door."

Now how many Popes have you heard saying something like that. And according to the extensive documentation I managed in the African Institute in Uppsala, Sweden, here we got this so-called Reverend Drago, a so-called-man of God, when in fact he was and remains the main political intermediary between the political leaders of DRC, Rwanda and Uganda. In fact, he is the main messenger for Rwanda political leader at this time, telling the current DRC president what, when, why, and how to exercise his political power, how to carry the water for the Rwanda regime which installed him in Kinshasa in the first place. This is a Reverend who led the Rwandan faction to the DRC political peace conference that took place in Sun City in South Africa. He came out of this conference as a Vice-President in Charge of Security. Now remember that in Sun City, he was the leader of Rwandan faction that invaded DRC in 1997 from the Eastern mountains to Kinshasa, only to be kicked out by the first President it installed and to get him assassinated. This Reverend Drago is feared in Kinshasa more than anybody because everybody knows that he represents the power behind the puppet in place. Now how many DRC dead people this Reverend had to answer to when he is in fact managing the systematic plundering of mineral resources in Eastern DRC for the benefit of Rwanda and Uganda. That is the same Reverend Drago who has supervised Adamas Kagita as a war lord. Now Adamas was in for one thing only, to make a lot of money. He did not care about the political orientation of those who are plundering the Eastern DRC where he was born in a local tribe called Tande. Adams answers only to Reverend Drago. And he had killed so many of his own tribe people to earn his strange war lord title. Adamas knows that he owes his life to Reverend Drago's protection and to those Reverend Drago answers to. I don't need to tell you that line of questioning involving Reverend Drago is the death certification for Adamas. I am not surprised by his reaction."

"Are you saying that Adamas could be killed anytime even in immigration jail?"

"Mr. O'Grady, Adamas is a dead man walking anywhere including here in the US. By the way, your Reverend Drago has been welcomed for the past ten years or so at the highest level of the US government and Congress. Does he not come here every year to the Congress National Day of Prayer with a long and extensive contingent of DRC elite politicians? My Good Lord, the Congress National Day of Prayer!! And he comes here parading the crème of the crème of the American Government and Congress! Imagine how that extraordinary spectacle of Reverend Drago being attended, wined, and dined by the crème of the creme in Washington D.C. play on TV in Kinshasa! Reverend Drago had become an untouchable back home in Kinshasa. Reverend

Drago is extremely feared in DRC If Adamas is a marked dead man by Reverend Drago, there is nothing you can do about that., I am afraid!"

"This is not gonna happen! We are still in the US! Let me make a few calls. Excuse me!"

DA O'Grady left the conference room, leaving behind a deafening silence among the team members!

DA O'Grady rushed to call the manager of the immigration court jail. He strongly advised him to keep the accused Adamas Kagita in a secured separated twenty-four hours guard room. He should communicate with any visitor only through a cage like divider. He lets the manager know that the accused meals must be essentially protected from poisoning as well. The manager informed the DA that two people came to pay Adamas visit. They claimed to be family members, but they were never seen on the premise before. They were refused visitation rights on the account that Adamas was still under heavy sedation. They waited for about three hours then they left. DA O'Grady was alarmed to hear this and requested to get some surveillance tapes identifying these visitors. He called the defense lead lawyer to share his alarm.

As soon as DA O'Grady clarified Adamas status, he called his niece Gwendolyn in D.C.

"Can you tell me, Gwen, why this administration has to bend backward dealing with these petty dictators in the Great Lakes in Africa? This is becoming way behind ridiculous!"

"What are you talking about, I heard that you are winning all winds blasting, what happened now?"

"I am talking about your Reverend Drago trying to kill my prisoner here in the US! Better warn them, what they can get away in the jungle, would not work here in the US. We still abide by the Constitution, last time I checked!"

"Are you serious? Adamas is zero quantity for everybody now. He has been abandoned. From all sides. He did not want to follow the line. He has been dropped from all sides. Believe me! You can hang him as high as you want, nobody, absolutely nobody cares!"

"What about Reverend Drago?"

"What about him?"

"I just verified that he has sent some hired killers to do away with Adamas? How ridiculous is this?

"I don't know who is feeding you this garbage. It cannot be true."

"We got surveillance tapes of these goons daring to show up at the immigration court jail. The nerve of them! This is not Kigali, Kinshasa, or Kampala, please tell your low life gangsters. We got twenty to life sentence here for these kinds of goons."

"I am at loss and cannot follow what you are saying. Who the hell is Reverend Drago?"

"I must be damned for you to ask this question. This Drago man has been your intermediary for ten years now and you don't know him, what kind of intelligence service you are running when this man visits your Embassy in Kinshasa every day, and you don't know him!! Oh, I see, Langley does not tell what or how they run the shop in Kinshasa, very, very sad!"

"I see, my dear uncle, you are becoming victim of the game of influence that African politicians play so well there. It is called in French "jeux d'approximate". That is when people can mirror for you a whole scheme or sequence of events, people that have nothing to do with reality. And they do it for a long time. If you are not vigilant, if you don't ask the right questions, you can lose very big, you can lose a lot of money, your reputation, your family in those games. At the end when you realize that it was simply a stagging, a set up to get you to do something, to give up something, in other words to be fooled, then it is too late. Now you heard about Yahoo Boys in Nigeria, that is exactly what it is but at a political level. Sometimes it can get as high as at a government level, yes, I say the government level. Only when the whole thing starts collapsing, then you hear the president, the premier minister or the general denies that there was the authorization to do this or that came from them. Now if that Reverend Drago visits the Embassy every day, you should ask who he is visiting like that every day and for what purpose. There is a lot of influence peddling that goes on in place like Kinshasa where people are not always working eight hours a day if ever. There are a lot of Reverend Drago pretending, all the time, to do things on behalf of this one or that one. When in fact they are simply doing influence peddling. Forget this Reverend Drago."

"Well, well, well, Gwen, bravo! My God, you are talking the same way as our ambassador spoke not long ago in Kinshasa. I heard it in one of those interviews. It is all so confusionist. All right, I must assure you that I will get to the bottom of this Reverend Drago scheme."

"Well, be my guest."

DA O'Grady dropped the call, seriously aggravated by his niece talking nonsense. He reached out to the State Police Superintendent. He had asked him to review the surveillance tapes at the immigration court jail. Two gentlemen were identified in the tapes. They were quickly located and still staying in a local five-star hotel very close to the District Court building. They were also identified in the court surveillance tapes. They were attending the Monday court proceedings and showed up in the morning at the court. They asked a lot of questions about the cancelled Tuesday session. Later that afternoon, they were found at the hotel and interrogated by the state police detectives. They were very polite and identified themselves as two Congolese pastors from a small church outside Chicago. They claimed to be family relatives to Adamas. They quickly provided a few background checks as Adamas relatives, but could not explain why Adamas never tried to contact them after coming to the US. They insisted that they were requested by family members back home to come support Adamas during the difficult ordeal he was confronting. They did not hesitate to provide their contacts in Illinois including addresses and telephone numbers. They claimed to have a residence status in the state of Illinois. They appeared to be shaken up a little bit for being subjected to so many police checks. They were alarmed when told that more follow up checks of their backgrounds would be made by the Illinois state police and the FBI, and that they must make themselves available for these follow up checks. They also claimed to have no idea who Reverend Drago was even when the North Carolina established calls made from their cell phones and hotel room phones to Kinshasa into well monitored and indexed Reverend Drago. They left Raleigh the next day while DA O'Grady promptly received the complete reports of their whereabouts during their Raleigh visits..

At the end of the same week, on Friday morning, Judge Alvaro Lopez convened a meeting gathering the immigration court jail director, the prosecution, and defense teams. He also invited the doctors who had conducted a thorough physical and psychiatric reviews of Adamas

Kagita. They concluded that Adamas has suffered an anxiety attack after the first day of the court proceedings. They believed that he was stable now and should be able to attend the court proceedings if he takes the prescribed anxiety medicines. As soon as the doctors departed, Judge Alvaro Lopez turned to the defense team to find out whether they were ready and willing to resume the trial proceedings given the status of their client. The defense team stated that their client was ready to plead guilty but to a limited range of infractions, preferably about the twenty indictments which were reviewed on Monday. The defense team did not want to expose Adamas to the full extent of prosecution that was scheduled and that would amount for him to answer to all the indictments covering a full range of criminal infractions Adamas faced including:

-brutalizing, torturing, and killing workers and family members

-intimidating, brutalizing, torturing, and killing workers and family members at odd with logistical practices

-conducting armed campaigns to raze entire villages suspected of hiding and providing shelter to self-defense militias opposed to unauthorized artisanal mining of coltan and gold in their areas.

-brutalizing, torturing, and killing minors to work in artisanal coltan and gold mines he supervised,

-kidnapping and holding young girls as sex workers in remote jungle camps,

-brutalizing, torturing, and killing recalcitrant minors and sex workers,

-conducting armed attacks and confiscation of dangerous caravans of coltan and gold minerals on their way to Uganda or Rwanda,

DA O'Grady was surprised by the defense team's proposal that he found a bit premature. In addition, he knew from the side conversation he had with the immigration court jail director a bit about the defense team's strange behavior on behalf of the accused. The defense team had not visited, seen nor spoken to Adamas after he left the Monday court proceedings and after the anxiety attack set back, he had suffered that evening. The defense team behavior was, in fact, confirming what his niece Gwen has said; "Adamas has been abandoned to his own fate." The proposal fitted the pattern of what Gwendolyn was trying to share.

DA O'Grady sternly rejected the defense team's proposal offer.

"Very esteemed Counsels from the defense, I am very surprised that you dare proposing that the prosecution accepts a plea deal on only twenty indictments out of more than twelve hundred indictments we intend to vigorously prosecute, or in other words, 1.6 percent of the criminal package the accused has to answer. I must tell you right now and there that is ridiculous. We must reject your proposal."

"Esteemed counsel, that was our first proposal, a simple talking point. What would be your counter proposal?"

"I don't think you would like it. First Adamas must plead guilty to the entire set of indictments, and second Adamas must assist the prosecution to prosecute the entire chain of command that has enabled his execution of his small share in the entire civil war that has raged for more than fifteen years in Eastern DRC to the current holocaust of more than eight million dead, and third Adamas must assist the prosecution to prosecute the entire chain of command that ensured that Adamas escaped the war zone and quietly immigrate to the US."

"Mr. O'Grady, that would be impossible! May it please the court, the prosecution is no longer prosecute the accused at hand. The prosecution is blowing the prosecution to a range beyond its call, beyond this court. This is becoming a political trial and the defense team had not signed up for this."

"Counsels, this is becoming very interesting. I would not allow this case to become a political football in my court. I tell you what I would do. Since you appear to be so far apart, I want to hold separate meetings today with each party. And we will reconvene on Monday to determine what we would do. I would start with the defense team then close with the prosecution. This court is adjourned!"

The first meeting Judge Alvaro Lopez held with the defense team was rather short. The defense team complained about the intransigence of the prosecution trying to widen the scope of the trial beyond the only accused at hand, Adamas Kagita. Judge Alvaro Lopez advised the defense team to be a bit patient while he probes the DA and his team to determine what the prosecution was up to.

"I don't know what DA O'Grady is up to. I don't know him very well. We are building our working relationship starting from this first case

I was assigned to. After talking with the man, I would know what he wants. Of course, I would not allow any political grand standing in my court as I have warned him. I am just suspecting a hidden motive here, just give me a chance to find out. Will talk on Monday."

DA O'Grady joined the Judge right after the defense team left. The DA was alone after wishing his staff a good weekend.

"Your Honor Judge Lopez!"

"Please, spare me the formalities. Give me a chance to remove this black robe? Now let us relax, it is Friday's afternoon before the long weekend! I don't know what you prefer, a good bourdon or a good whiskey?"

"Sir, I am a Southern bourbon man!"

"All right, I am Texan pure breed, no Tequila applied despite my Lopez last name! I am a Texan torn between a good bourbon from Kentucky or a good whiskey from Tennessee! So, what is gonna be for the Southern honorable gentleman?"

"Kentucky bourbon, Sir!"

"Sorry, you did not specify a brand. What will it be between Maker's Mark or Jack Daniels?"

"I know where you are going, Sir, I would not be tricked or confused by the difficult choice. I would stick to Maker's Mark, a true Kentucky bourbon."

"OK, you win!"

"Now, DA O'Grady, what is eating you to blow up the defense team proposal so categorically? I heard that you had some political ambition to be elected Senator from the state of North Carolina. But the virulent attack you have expressed against the higher powers that be, powers anybody can assume and see must be the high technology American corporations. And I don't need to tell you that they would not appreciate that line of questioning."

"Judge Alvaro Lopez, I am relieved that you have that keen sense of appreciation of what I was leading too. I am also glad that you are giving me a relaxed opportunity to explain. Honorable Alvaro Lopez,

I am far gone in age and ambition at this time to be concerned about political ambition. I am more concerned about what is sadly becoming more and more irrelevant lately, and that is the pursuit of justice and precisely in our courts of Justice. Remember what you told me about your thinking, or if I may, philosophy around our judicial system. You say that you were most upset to see how in the prosecution of drug traffic, the country is so versed on one side of the tragedy, the offer while neglecting the concentration on the demand. You said that the politicians hardly talk about the demand for drug because the demand includes people who vote. While the offer is driven by people in faraway place like Columbia and Mexico, by people who, well, do not vote, people who will never elect them. You say that you were sitting there in that Judge chair in San Antonio, sadly watching a long parade of mainly small time drug traffickers from Mexico trying to cross the US border with less than thirty kilos of heroin or cocaine, while big containers of the same drug in thousand tones were quietly being offloaded in thousand ports on both coast ports of the US from Miami to Portland on the East Coast, from San Diego to Seattle on the West Coast. This is where the demand needs to be attacked. But you hardly hear that from the politicians. The pushback is always that it is too complicated. And you said that you sit in San Antonio handing out twenty to life sentencing to these small-time dealers. Honorable Alvaro Lopez, it is the same thing analogy in this Adamas case. The Eastern DRC has been plundered for mineral resources for the past fifteen years by neighboring countries. These mineral resources are crucial for the manufacturing of what we use every day, I am talking about cell phones, laptops and all kind of small household equipment's made by high technology corporations around the world. The large-scale plundering has caused millions of victims we have shared in this trial. And who are we prosecuting, Adama Kagita? You will never hear about those who are profiting in that chain of murderous production from the mine field to the display stand of these high devices. It is the same logical you have witnessed."

"My good honorable DA, believe me, I have extensively read your voluminous testimony. I have reached the same conclusion you are portraying, my question to you is simple, what do you want to do within the context of your prosecution? You know very well throwing the wide net you raise a while ago would not work. Adamas is already assured to get a sentence, maybe a long sentence, but how do you want to expand concretely your prosecution? This is what I want to know.

Please be specific!"

"I was getting there. The best way to expand the prosecution will be to remove Adamas from his current defense team who has already, for all practical purposes, abandoned defending him. That defense wants now to cut a deal to a lesser sentence. If I rose to reject the defense proposal by widening the prosecution domain, it was on purpose to upset the defense scheme. Honorable Alvaro Lopez, I know very well that you would not grant me that sudden change of prosecution venue. But if Adamas drops this current defense team on grounds of not getting the expected defense then I would start gaining his cooperation in prosecuting the chain of command above him, the chain of command that had direct him to execute his share in the large scheme of plundering the Eastern DRC for accessing the mineral resources."

"I see, I see, but DA O'Grady what are the instances of neglect the defense team that Adamas has literally suffered?"

"Yes, I do have many instances when the defense team did not raise objections nor try to cross-examine the statements from witnesses. It was obvious that the defense team had abandoned the accused. Worse, twice when the accused was stricken, the defense team did not visit him at the hospital, as if hoping that he would not recover. The last straw was when I found out that the defense team never shared with the accused the fact that a higher up in the chain of command had sent goons to monitor the court proceedings and attempted to visit Adamas in jail and probably to harm him. To date, the defense team has never alerted the accused. As a matter of fact, I decided to secure Adamas safety in jail. The truth is that Adamas has been abandoned and his chain of command is betting on his early demise."

"That is serious. I would not allow that. I need to check with the immigration court jail director. If he concurred, I would interrogate Adamas and advises him about proper course of action including a definitive change of defense team that he will need to pursue. You know this is very delicate. He needs to state that the defense team provided by his current chain of command has abandoned him. I will determine his current state of mind to reach that decision. This is grave and serious. Thank you, honorable DA O'Grady."

CHAPTER 32

ADAMAS' REVENGE

Judge Alvaro Lopez was so revolted and incensed by the conversation he had with DA O'Grady, he decided to come back on Saturday to have the immigration court jail director bring the accused Adams Kagita to his court for a lengthy conversation. First in absence of Adamas, the Judge verified what the DA O'Grady had revealed the day before. He was not disappointed. There was much more calamity than DA O'Grady had shared. The jail director admitted that the defense team did not visit Adamas after two of his medical setbacks while in custody at the immigration jail. He also admitted that he called by phone and shared with the defense team the unexpected visit from the two pastors from Chicago. The director went even further, he claimed to become very alarmed by the visit when he noticed that the pastors looked so unfamiliar with Raleigh environment, he asked Adamas if he knew the two pastors. Adamas looked shocked and very frightened. The director was inclined to dismiss his behavior because of his acute anxiety but Adamas told the director that, not only he did not know them, but Adamas started to incessantly beg the director not to allow the visitors to see or talk to him. He claimed that the visitors were sent to kill him by spreading poison or by transferring demoniac spirits by physical contact. The director said that he was amused by the suggestion but could not help noticing how very distraught and increasingly frightened Adamas became. That was the time he called DA O'Grady to share his concerns. He was deeply surprised that the defense team was still not communicating with the accused to learn more about the unexpected visitors.

In the privacy of his chambers, with two prison guards standing at a safe but inaudible distance, Adamas revealed even more than both DA O'Grady and the jail director touched upon. Judge Alvaro Lopez was confused when Adamas stated that Reverend Drago, the "Enterprise" and the American intelligence service have all conspired to abandon him in his miserable fate at this time. Judge Alvaro Lopez requested more information, more examples of abandonment. Adamas went straight to the revelation by the prosecutor about his wife being a Keregi. Adamas stated that that revelation must have come from only one-person, Reverend Drago who manipulated him to marry that lady to apply for his immigration visa to come to the US. Now he said that he was certain that Reverend Drago has been paying for his legal defense team in this trial. He proclaimed that he was screwed from the start. That was a monumental accusation, a definitive ground to change his defense team if Adamas wanted so. Judge Alvaro Lopez probed him further.

"Mr. Adamas Kagita, do you feel that you are being poorly represented and defended in this trial?"

"Judge Lopez, I am, there is no doubt about it. I am screwed. This has been a complete betrayal from the start. They wanted to get me out of the operations in DRC. They could have just killed me. I don't know why they had to get me here to the US!"

"Mr. Adama Kagita, those are grave accusations, I am prepared to get you some help under the law if you can get me evidence of what you are talking about. I would not look like a fool to proceed based on your words. I need solid proofs that your legal defense has been shortcoming from the start answering not your interests but the interests of those you claim have abandoned you. Do you have such evidence/"

"Judge Lopez, I can assure you that I do and from the start of this betrayal. Guess what, my contact from the Intelligence Service here in the US advised me to tape all important conversations I would have with my lawyers and save them in my cell phone. The immigration court services took that cell phone from the time I was arrested. I hope the cell phone is still working OK. I have saved all conversations I had with my lawyers. If you listen to these conversations, you will find out how I have been treated and lied to all along. And guess what you would also find out that the same lawyers arranged to get Reverend Drago to come from back home to a big house somewhere in Virginia across Washington D.C. I also tape the conversations I had with Reverend Drago. He came expressly to warn me that the whole cabal, the "Enterprise' wanted me to speed up the trial by pleading guilty very quickly to lesser charges and be sentenced to a few years. He said

293

that all that has been taken care of. Reverend Drago assured me that I would be taken care before, during and after I would do time in jail. To his big surprise, I turned him down. He left the US very upset. From that time, I knew that I have been abandoned by everybody. After that I have been going with the flow knowing that I have been screwed and only death is waiting for me. I know that these lawyers have also taped the same last conversation I had with Reverend Drago. Yes, Judge Lopez, I have the evidence in that cell phone. Listen to these conversations you would know the truth."

"Mr. Adams Kagita, what you say is more serious than I thought. Let me get the immigration court jail director to retrieve the cell phone and I will take some urgent decisions. Now after I have verified the evidence, I would propose that you change your defense team that you do not trust anymore. Is that what you want to do?"

"Yes, I do! But I don't know how I would be able to afford a good legal representation."

"One thing at the time, we will get to that later, one thing at the time. Give me the chance to retrieve the cell phone."

"But, Judge Lopez, I know that this defense team is not there to defend me. It is there for Reverend Drago, the "Enterprise" and the American intelligence service. How many times do I need to repeat this. But what good would it be there for me to get another defense team here in the US when I have to go against the Intelligence Service, I am, as you love to say it, a Dead Man Walking. I am screwed!"

"Mr. Adamas Kagita, you will be surprised what can be done. Again, one thing at a time. You would wait in my chamber for the time being."

Judge Lopez talked with the immigration court jail director to go very urgently to retrieve the cell phone and bring it back to him. He called DA O'Grady to share the conversation with Adamas Kagita. DA O'Grady told the Judge that he was dropping everything he was going to do the weekend to come and to be at his disposable.

"Your Honor, I had no idea that Adamas was leaning in this direction. But this will help us to start prosecuting the chain of command behind his crimes. I don't know how high we will get but it would be a starting point. I am coming, Sir!"

In no time, the cell phone was retrieved. It took about three hours to get it recharged. A court clerk was called upon to transcribe the many conversations that Adamas taped by date, place, and participants. Adamas helped the court clerk all along. The transcription took the rest of Saturday and all day on Sunday. Judge Alvaro Lopez cancelled all his Monday appointments. He spent time listening to the tapes and reading the transcribed tape documents amounting to around seventy-five pages. At about four in the afternoon, he completed writing his decision. He then ordered the defense and prosecution teams to reconvene on Tuesday at about ten-thirty am in his chambers.

"Counsels, I have called this meeting to inform you of an important development that has occurred this weekend. Defendant Adamas Kagita has filed a motion with the court requesting to substitute their current attorney team. The court will then hold a hearing to determine if the substitution is appropriate and in the best interest of the defendant. The defendant has introduced this motion for the following reasons:

-Lack of trust. The accused stated that he has lost trust in his current defense team due to a complete breakdown in communication.

-Incompetence. The defendant felt that the current defense team has demonstrated time and again not to be competent enough to handle the case by limiting objections against the prosecution positions and or not cross-examining prosecution statements,

-Demonstrating a conflict of interests between the defendant's interests and the interests of various groups providing legal fee payments for the defendant

To that effect, the defendant has provided a lengthy list of conversations he taped revealing the above conditions that the court is examining. Counsels will be provided with copies of transcribed taped conversations by the court clerk.

Counsels, I will hold a hearing in two days to determine if the substitution is in the best interest of the defendant.

This court is adjourned."

There was an embarrassing and deafening silence in the Judge Alvaro Lopez chambers. The defense team was at a loss and shocked to hear what the Judge just said. They collected copies of the motion and copies of transcribed taped conversations. And left the court premises very quickly.

The time for hearing to substitute defense team turned to be a very short meeting. The defense team agreed to be substituted and advised the court that it has been amply compensated for the legal services it has rendered using the proceed of the sale of the defendant's house at the North Carolina Outer banks to the tune of one hundred thirty thousand four hundred forty-seven and 84 cents. ($130,447.84) out of a balance of $1,250,000. The defense team agreed to move the retainer balance escrow to whichever financial institution that would assume the legal fee payment transactions as soon as a new defense team is determined and identified.

Two local law firms were asked to take over the legal defense for Adamas Kagita. A Chapel Hill law firm named Braxton and Associates was chosen and was given about a month and half to come up to speed to take over the entire legal defense for Adamas Kagita, covering both the immigration issues as well as the human rights criminal proceedings.

As far as the prosecution team was concerned, the substitution of the defense team opened new venues for its charges. But the team was not certain how it would be able to push its drive. DA O'Grady was plainly explicit. He wanted to go as high as he could, but he knew that it was not going easy. The new defense team was assumed to have, well, no clues of what it has signed up to. The defense team seemed more eager to close the deal, but it did profess to have no idea of what the accused wanted except that Adamas was tired and very resigned waiting for whatever sentenced that was coming down the pipe. The new defense team appeared to fit that program. It was small and had no big shoes, big references law firm.

It was a totally different gut-wrenching universe for what Adamas rejected in a block. That was the case for all the obscure contacts in the Intelligence Service, the Attorney General contacts including Gwendolyn O'Grady, and their accomplices back in the Great Lakes region, the political leadership gang in DRC, Rwanda, and Uganda and principally their intermediary: Reverend Drago. This man felt the entire weight of Adamas Kagita's fiasco falling squarely over him. And for him to learn that Adamas Kagita had taped most of their conversations where he repeatedly mentioned the "Enterprise", that was a terrible lapse, a major intelligence mistake. Reverend Drago knew that for all practical intents and purposes in the "Enterprise", he was now the new Dead Man Walking and he must find ways to extract himself very soon from that predicament.

Still there was a motion of saving grace for the entire cabal which thanked the confusion that was coming in the American power superstructure. Precisely, it was the quadrennial political change that was about to take place in Washington D.C The advent of a new administration, which, this time, was replete with people so driven to blow the arcane workings of the previous administration, the cabal was predicting that it will probably be given the unexpected reprieve by being ignored and forgiven from major overseas blunders that were taking place so late in the process. The cabal knew that these blunders, in entirely misunderstood corners of Africa in the Great Lakes region, would not be subjected to any urgent review priority by the new administration know-it-all experts. China, Russia, Central European Theater, Middle East, Iran, Afghanistan, Korea peninsula to say the least, were already commanding urgent priority from the new masters of the world. Nobody welcomed the change more than Gwendolyn who could not wait to vacate her function before the end of year, neglecting and discarding the regular handover to new unidentified staff agents. She went on a long-postponed trip to Australia, Singapore and South-East. There was nobody Uncle DA O'Grady could reach and exchange views over the politics and outstanding issues occupying the staff in charge of National Strategic Affairs under the US Attorney General. Langley dedicated its time before Christmas to blur the entire picture. Colonel Laurens phone was disconnected. Adamas stopped trying to reach him. Both the Rwandan and Uganda political leadership lowered their profile in Eastern DRC. They subcontracted the plundering of mineral resources to well-connected Congolese politicians around the young puppet political leader more interested in quickly amassing an unheard fortune of more than twenty billion of dollar according to a Forbes magazine listing, by confiscating the entire mineral resources rent of the country while playing and masquerading another brutal quest of a third magistrature succession.

This confusing and confused political and judicial landscape did not escape DA O'Grady's review when he sat down with his now drinking buddy, Judge Alvaro Lopez. It was apparent that they were handed an empty slate and plate. No matter how and no matter what they try to do, they were facing a tremendous delay in advancing their

297

judicial foray. They appreciate now why the old Adamas defense team vacated the Raleigh legal premises as quickly as they could to return to the festive new opportunity grounds of Washington D.C. The good friends resolved to call the endless delay that was pervasive everywhere, the Adamas's delay.

Judge Alvaro was forced to pause Adamas Kagita's court proceeding during the delay. He suspended the prestation of the jury members. DA O'Grady had a very difficult choice. He was no going to hold the witness he brought from Sweden, Reverend Stanislas Keregi. Although, his testimony was completed and done the first day of the trial. DA O'Grady was not eager to let me go back. If he was around, he suspected he would come to some very important usefulness. But he was at a loss justifying to hold on to him. DA O'Grady suspected that Reverend was a pivotal reference to an extensive database of people, issues, events which have accumulated in Eastern DRC from 1990 through the present. He was very modest about the role he played in bringing about the African Studies Center in Uppsala. DA O'Grady thought that it was part of the prestigious University of Uppsala. It was not. As a matter of fact, Reverend has single handily build the center to become a prestigious academic center recognized worldwide. He knew that he would not have made so much drastic advances in the prosecution of the case without the Reverend and the center. The Lawyer-Analyst Pascal Bodavi confessed to the same. After much soul searching, DA O'Grady circled back to his primary goal to prosecute the chain of command that enabled Adamas Kagita. He held two long thinking sessions with Pascal Bodavi and his protegee Counsel Ludmilla Garrov. Together, they concluded again that no significant advances will be made in the direction of that goal without Reverend Stanislas's contribution. The fact that Adamas has opened the gates in sharing a lot of the so called "Enterprise" environment, Reverend Stanislas must be around to vet Adamas' references to build them to a set of solid testimonies. The Reverend stay would be prolonged.

DA O'Grady asked the prosecution team members to welcome Reverend Stanislas not as a witness but as a team member. Pascal and Ludmilla were surprised by the unexpected elevation of the Reverend, yet they could not second guess the old man with an endless set of surprising habits.

"I am inviting Reverend Stanislas into our team for a very precise reason.

I don't have to remind you that we would not have made so many advances in prosecuting this case without his awesome contribution. What I am doing is simply an obvious next step. We know very well that we are suffering another delay in our court proceedings. The main reason for his presence among us has already been fully and extraordinarily appreciated and vindicated. His eloquent witness stands literally closed the guilty plea of the accused. That, as I told the older defense team was my first goal. My next goal was always to prosecute the chain of command that enabled the accused Adamas Kagita to act the way he did, so wantonly so carelessly. That is what we need to concentrate our attention on now. We are also lucky that Pascal Bodavi has agreed to be part of pursuing the second goal. It would be completely useless and unconscionable to send Adamas away for a long time only to let the murderous field where he had caused so much distress to the very forces which are managing the plundering of Eastern DRC, the same forces which would only be ready to replace Adamas Kagita with another Adamas Kagita lookalike to continue the same murderous journey. Counsels, I did not sign up to give up in the justice quest when we have made so much progress. That is why we need Reverend Stanislas to assist us with his broad knowledge of the field."

"I believe that we have accumulated enough background to continue this prosecution. And believe me or not, thanks to the accused, we have landed on what I presume to be a description of the environment of that chain of command. Listening to the taped conversation we got from Adamas, you start to visualize how the chain of command operates. The taped conversations with Reverend Drago were in my opinion very telling. As we suffer through this delay, I want us to analyze those taped conversations, pick up the management steps of the chain of command. If you are wondering why we must do this, well I must tell right now, I want to start a process of initiating a legal extradition of Reverend Drago from DRC to Raleigh to answer for the murderous tasks he directed Adamas to execute, and all based on those taped conversations. Now I see your eyes opening wide in surprise, suspicion, and incredulity. You are already thinking that the powers would not let it happen, they would block that step. Granted, you are right, but interviews took place in DRC just recently, and we never thought that they would happen. I would submit that we may not get an extradition, but we can dispatch an FBI team to interrogate Reverend Drago. That could very well be possible. If not, we will go down on that scale of possibilities, we will conduct a forced interview of few people we will identify in our analysis of the taped conversations. I am sharing with you the scope of what we need to consider as we start going after the chain of command. Are you with me?"

"Yes, Sir!"

"This is my plan during this delay, I want you all to think through these proposals. Thank you!".

CHAPTER 33

OF BRAXTON AND ASSOCIATES

Legal references associated with Braxton and Associates, Adamas new defense team, should have raised the attention of both Judge Alvaro Lopez and the prosecution team. These references did not. The underestimation of the defense team was an understatement. Braxton and Associates appeared strangely too small for a law firm with such extensive reaches in combating violations of human rights throughout the US and worldwide. It had a very small staff but supported by a worldwide council of designated "pro bono" associates disseminated in major law schools around the world. The council function was to receive requests to represent victims of human rights violations worldwide, to identify the extent of the violations, to determine the need to represent victims locally or at any international court accepting to hear these violations, and to fund the legal representation locally or through international channels. The funding of the legal representation was mounted at two levels. The registered local 'pro bono" associates provided free legal representation at the first level. The balance of legal representation was funded through the law firm's elaborated fundraising functions. The free legal representation was shouldered most of time by law school professors and students engaged in legal clinics to assist violations victims. To date, 80 percent of the total legal representation fee had been shouldered through free representation. The remaining 20 percent was picked up by victims and the law firm fundraising proceeds. It must also be said that the law firm has managed to survive for the last fifteen years thanks to a huge financial endowment provided by law school alumni who have done exceedingly well in various law domains. It was rumored recently that three former alumni, major high technology venture capitalists, have provided the law firm with more than three billion endowment funding. Braxton and Associates was not about to suffer any financial funding of its many cases any time soon.

However, the involvement of Braxton and Associates in Adamas case begged an urgent question. Adamas was not a victim of human rights violation. He was a perpetrator of human rights violation for all his adult life. Why then volunteer to represent such a person. That was the misunderstanding and the underestimation of the challenges that Braxton and Associates confronted. The law firm was not only interested in getting the violations against human rights prosecuted, condemned, and repaired for the victims, it went further. It intended to eliminate these violations from happening by eliminating the forces which enabled these violations. After having followed Adamas' case, the firm had determined that Adamas was ready to wage some kinds of revenge against the same forces which enabled him to commit various violations of human rights and the same forces were abandoning him now. Braxton and Associates were ready to assist Adams in mounting his revenge higher up against the chain of command that had manipulated him all along. In other words, Braxton and Associates was in the same line of prosecution as … DA O'Grady. The difference being that the law firm will be offering the help while the prosecution will be making the request for help. Braxton and Associates were signing up to ensure that Adamas gets the maximum right benefits against sentencing while denouncing the forces he worked with all these years.

Two law students, Bambi Mothleni and Frank Collard, joined Lead Counsel, Criminal Law Professor Julia Fama, in the legal representation in defense of Adamas Kagita. Bambi Mothleni from South Africa and Frank Collard from Barbados Island were asked to sift through the voluminous testimony that was submitted for the purpose of the case discovery and the equally voluminous interviews that were extracted from DRC. Still their review priority was focused over the transcripts of Adamas taped conversations. This is where started the revenge that Adamas was so eager to mount against his old partners in crime. The students thoroughly analyzed the taped conversations with a lot of direction and additional inputs from Adamas. The students did the legal work as part of their legal clinic projects necessary to receive the degree of Juris Doctor. The law firm provided them with necessary rental transportation and food while in the Raleigh area. The most interesting thing about the clinic engagement was their constant reference to the database application provided by the African Affairs Center in Uppsala, Sweden. So, the two students were beyond shock to see in the witness court reports statements made by a Reverend Stanislas Keregi, Executive Director of the Center. They could not believe that

302

the Reverend came from Uppsala, Sweden to give testimony about the case. And he did this before the testimony given by his own niece, Charlotte Keregi who, for all practical purposes, initiated the criminal pursuit against Adamas right here in Raleigh area in North Carolina. It was very bizarre and frightening at the same time. The Adamas case was very strange to say the least. While the two students did two other legal clinic projects, they were in direct contact with victims of human rights violation they met most of time through remote video-conferencing sessions beamed through satellite from distant places. The Adamas case was altogether different. They had to meet with the man accused of multiple killings and who was now trying very hard to convince them that his superiors in the chain of command had directed him to commit those unspeakable crimes. It took the students a while to engage Adamas on routine basis. Many times, they will gather with Adamas in the jail designated conference rooms and will listen to his monosyllabic recounts of his crimes. And when they will complete these long sessions, they came out in horror with a distinct sense and urge to vomit. Many times, they will leave the immigration court jail premise in a cold sweat. They will then sit for a long time without talking and catching up their breath from listening to the horrors Adamas shared. It will take them a while to leave and to drive back to Chapel Hill area.

The next day, when the student resumed their clinic projects, they first handed Professor Julia Fama the summary of the previous day's legal engagement. Summary they struggled to develop. If Professor Fama noticed the distinct disturbing impact of the legal engagement on their face, she would console them to remain engaged or simply advised them to take a day off if the prospect of successive worse encounter a day after became very difficult. She also warned them that it would not get any better later in their profession. The sooner they get used to the disconcerting and troubling circumstances in the field the better it will be for them, otherwise it was probably time to consider a different line of work away from the law domain. Yet the two students stood their ground, they have invested so much in their degree, they were ready to go back and to pay Adamas another professional visit.

As the Adamas delay came to expiration, Professor Julia Fama had completed the price proposal to get Adamas to rat his precious chain of command against the lengthy sentencing time that she knew Judge Alvaro Lopez was going to recommend, on the lower side that DA O'Grady had been telegraphing for some time. The only issue the lead counsel had was to motivate the accused Adamas Kagita, completely resigned to worse outcome, to a minimum of engagement to meet the prosecution and the Judge halfway in the exchange for bargaining a lower sentence. She advised Adamas to cooperate for a lifesaving price.

While Braxton and Associates' law firm was literally joining the prosecution in ensuring that Adamas' old chain of command be prosecuted to the full extent of law, the same chain of command was shaken all over the places. That was the period when the political leadership in DRC, a strong party in that chain of command, started to crumble, unsure of maintaining its hold on power in Kinshasa, DRC. First, there was a strong push back against an obscure law that passed in the Parliament requiring that a census take place before the next presidential election projected in 2016. That law started being considered as an initial signal to postpone the programmed election, authorizing the sitting president, constitutionally prevented to run after two terms, to remain in power. The law was followed by the regime's different attempts to change term limits and to extend the president rule. At the same time, in the Eastern Region of DRC, there was an influx of many armed groups that splintered into dangerous movements killing hundreds of people. There were also major document leaks that showed in Forbes magazine and Panama papers, how the president had enriched himself and his family while ignoring the bottomless poverty pit where Congolese people were thrown into. To make matter worse, elections to determine a successor to the president were canceled and delayed for two more years until 2018. The last actions prompted massive protest demonstrations around the country. In Washington D.C., in the last months of its governance, the American departing administration implemented the mechanics of sanctions against the DRC regime in place.

The planned prosecution of Adamas' old chain of command became a bit problematic.

CHAPTER 34

ADAMAS PRICE OF REVENGE

When Judge Alvaro Lopez called the meeting, at the end of the so-called Adamas delay. to review the court proceedings in the Adama Kagita's case, there was a big surprise when in addition to defense and prosecution counsels, a government lawyer invited himself to attend the meeting. The government lawyer called the Judge the day before, advising him of the strong interest that the government, the departing administration, attached in the court proceedings around the case. In clear and grave terms, the lawyer advised the Judge that he was going to attend the court proceedings to ensure that the US highest strategic security interests were protected and preserved. Judge Alvaro Lopez was shocked to hear the request. Biting his tongue, he granted the government lawyer the request to attend the meeting, more than curious to find out what were the US highest strategic security interests the government intended to preserve in the case.

As soon as Judge Alvaro Lopez opened the meeting, he invited the government lawyer to state the government interests in the court proceedings.

"Counsels, I am resuming the court proceedings in Case No. 56397-B, "US vs Jefferson Okito/Adamas Kagita" in the additional presence of a new counsel name Vance M. Broadside, representing the government. Counsels from the defense and the prosecution, when Counsel Broadside called and announced that the government was inviting itself in these proceedings to ensure that the government security interests were protected and preserved in this matter, I told him that I was granting his request in one condition, that he clearly tell the court what if any were the government security interests he was going to protect and preserve in the case. I am now inviting the counsel to share those interests and if he feels that what he will share should be done in "huit clos", or government requested "behind closed doors", I am prepared to grant this request."

"May it please the court, I am requesting a government "behind closed doors" meeting involving primary or lead counsels only."

"So granted!" Judge Alvaro Lopez responded. He invited the lead counsels and the government lawyer to his chambers.

"Thank you, Your Honor! Thank you, Honorable Counsels, for indulging my request in these court proceedings. I realize that you have been interrupted twice in adjudicating this case. I am not here to request another delay. However I must let you know that you are engaged in a case of significant interest for the US government, and it is significant for both the incoming and departing administration. The government of the country does not stop because of a political transition. For that reason, an utmost care must be exercised during the government handoff from one administration to another in our democratic process, and it is so in case sometime of very profound different approaches from one administration to another. Let me add if these approaches are not changed through our legislative approach, what is in place will remain as a matter of law to guide the governing approach, the status quo. I hope you understand what I am saying and where your deliberations are going. Given that we are going through a transition process here in the US, our international strategic security interests will remain the same until they are changed legislatively. Our security interests in the Great Lakes region of Africa will remain the same. Your court proceedings should not be made to upset them one way or another. I will represent the government during the court proceedings to advise you whether you are upsetting these strategic interests. This is what I have been trusted to share with the court. I am here to answer your questions about any concern you might have. Thank you, Honorable counsels, thank you your Honor!"

"Counsels, you heard the government lawyer, please let me know what you think."

"May it please the court, for my part the government counsel is telling us that the government will monitor our court proceedings and if we start disturbing government interests which the counsel has vaguely alluded to and that he does not want to specify then the government will push back. That is so arrogant, the defense team will simply ignore the government suggestion. I rather see the government intervention in the Court of Appeal when and where the government will hear from the defense."

"May it please the court, I am not in the habit of agreeing with the defense most of the time, and less so the first time we are in the same room. Your Honor, the prosecution agrees entirely with the new defense team against the unfortunate premature intervention from the government counsel. I am getting the sad impression that the government had sent a counsel to replace the old defense team which had failed in representing the accused. It is terribly sad that the government counsel did not want to explicitly share what are the highest strategic security interests motivating the government to monitor the court proceedings which are public. There is no need to grant the government counsel any seat in these court proceedings. The prosecution will ignore the government counsel the same way as the defense until the government raise any matter to the Court of Appeal process."

"Counsel from the government, to tell you the truth, I share entirely what the defense and the prosecution counsels have said. But I still have much respect for the government, the incoming and the departing. The democratic process had given us the result we must abide by it. I understand the difficulties of the government transition process. We have gone through it before, and nothing had collapsed, the Court system is still there functioning. And if the government is not happy about the results of the proceedings in this court, it can avail itself of the Appeal process. Yes, I would allow the government counsel to attend our proceeding but not to monitor them as they do in some other countries. That is my decision. The Court is adjourned!"

Judge Alvaro Lopez, the defense and prosecution lead counsels returned to the court to resume the court proceedings. The government counsel left the court immediately to return to Washington D.C. for further instructions.

Judge Lopez instructed the defense and prosecution counsels to meet and discuss the tradeoff requirements they wanted to submit and agreed upon if Adamas was to plead guilty under various sentencing court guidelines. The meetings were scheduled to take place within the entire week. However, another surprise hit DA O'Grady when the defense team made an insolent request. The request was to get the prosecution prized witness, Reverend Stanislas Keregi, to answer about thirty questions that the two students aligned with Adamas legal defense clinic wanted to review. This was a bit upsetting for the DA. He was told that Judge Alvaro Lopez was aware of the request. He warned the DA that it logically amounted to a big provision in the discovery process. The prosecution could not decline it.

DA O'Grady was torn by the request. He discussed it with his staff which advised him to push back. Judge Alvaro Lopez insisted that he had no choice but lean on the Reverend to help, otherwise he could be held in contempt of the court and jeopardize the sentence of Adamas at hand and precisely the court victory he had worked on his entire adult life. He sat on the request for another day wondering how he could request this man who had suffered the brutalizing and the massacre of his entire close and distant family members in the hand of Adamas, the accused whose defense team was asking for help or support in its discovery process.

While Mr. O'Grady could swallow his pride as a DA, an office of the Court and used to crazy requests from the American Court System, he had grave doubts and reservations if he could impose the American judicial norms on the Reverend, currently living in Sweden but still of Congolese origins and who was forcefully immigrated to that distant land during an advanced age of maturity. On the third day, DA O'Grady gathered all his strength and finally approached the Reverend to make the request in very low inaudible tone.

"Reverend, you have assisted us in an incredible manner, ensuring that the prosecution against Adamas had advanced to a certain sentencing and court victory. We are thankful for your involvement. I am certain that we are entering a new phase of the prosecution. You know that Adamas is a tiny link in the murderous chain of command. Yes, we must get Adamas punished and sent away for a long time. But what about that chain of command? I am sure it has already found and replace the Adamas, the tiny link in its chain of command. It would be ridiculous for us and for you to stop now to crush that chain of command if we can blow open the prosecution of the entire chain of command. Are you following me? Now unfortunately for us, at least in the norms of the American judicial system, we must be as accommodating and cooperative with Adamas now that he has becoming willing to go after his higher up in that chain of command. We have no choice but to assist him and his defense in identifying the culprits and events in that chain of command. I must bring you in a secret at hand now. The defense is more than willing to negotiate a lot of venues to work up that chain of command in exchange for lower sentence against Adams. I am struggling with that step. I would not go there without your approval. If you tell me that we stop at Adamas lengthy sentence and we must forget the other folks in that chain of command, I will respect your wish and decline all the proposals that his new defense will be bring about. But I must tell you we will miss a chance to stop the carnage, the plundering that is still going on back in the Eastern of DRC with more dead, more displaced, more destruction and all other calamities. Please, Reverend Stanislas, what would be your answer?"

"DA O'Grady, I heard what you are trying to communicate. I appreciated it all heartly. I have painfully discussed it with my niece Charlotte. We prayed for your resolution. I would do anything, anywhere and anyhow to advance that goal to stop the death spiral we have known in that part of the country for so long approaching more than twenty years. Yes, we have been spared but what about all those who are left behind. Adamas, as you have eloquently stated it, is only a tiny drop in that ocean of nuisance and evil that had been hitting our home for so long. Anything to stop it must be done. I would cooperate anytime and anyhow."

"Reverend, I am most grateful again for your contribution. I would like to share questions from the students who are assisting the defense lead counsel. They claimed that it is only from your database that they can get answers to these questions. But they did not know the right features or combinations to use to interrogate the database appropriately. I read these questions, they were way past my old fuzzy brain. Please help them to get appropriate answers. You never know, these answers can also assist our prosecution somehow."

"Don't worry, Mr. O'Grady, I will attend to the defense request."

While DA O'Grady struggled with the request from the defense team, he was also aggravated by the sudden request by the government to "monitor" the court proceedings in the Adamas case. The dispatch by the government of this Counsel named Vance M. Broadside to Raleigh was a shocking surprise to the DA. He took it personally. He never heard of the man. Gwendolyn had never mentioned him being a member of her staff. As far as he knew, there was no one in contact with higher echelons in the office of Attorney General of US as he did with his own niece. That contact was informal contact between two family members, in fact, helping each other as the case evolved through the judiciary system. It was obvious from the start that they would not have been arguing over the case if it did not land in Raleigh District court. The exchanges between the family members were at times acerbic and contentious, but, at the end, they carried on the exchange to help each other. The help went both ways, from international security purposes that Uncle O'Grady lacked, and for US court proceedings purposes that Gwendolyn lacked. They never confessed these shortcomings between themselves. But they never stopped lifting each other in areas of need. And as the last presidential election resulted in a new administration coming in, Gwendolyn informally let his uncle know that she would take an early leave of absence given the long-accumulated vacation she could not take for two years in the row. Gwendoly was extremely busy, monitoring the legal side of world strategic security standing for the Attorney General of the US. She did this relatively on a twenty-four seven basis. It was not a surprise that she was already gone by the end of November while the transition to the new administration barely began. Mr. O'Grady searched unsuccessfully for references for this counsel. He speculated that Vance M. Broadside must be part of the transition team from the departing team. These functions are usually filled by either light-way staff or very dependable cover people. Most departing administration staff members remember the fiasco that was left to Kennedy incoming administration to manage the Cuba Bay of Pigs invasion that was initiated by Eisenhower Administration. The operation was improperly transitioned to the new administration and resulting in a complete fiasco. It was a relief that Judge Alvaro Lopez rejected his request to monitor the court proceedings. That was just so unprofessional, Mr. O'Grady was not surprised that the counsel disappeared as soon as he showed up in Raleigh District Court. Mr. O'Grady also guessed, the counsel made such an egregious request, knowing that it would be quickly rejected by the judge. The rejection probably closed a case among perhaps hundreds of international cases he was asked to "monitor" at the end of the departing administration. A rather funny and empty exercise to cover international security concern tracks for the departing administration!

The review of indictments to be used in the sentencing became very difficult between the defense and the prosecution teams. The defense team first proposed a timeline of events, eliminating infractions that took place in the first five years after 1997, the year of the previous regime's downfall. That was the period Adamas was trying to impress the chain of command with wild infractions. The prosecution, with Reverend Stanislas's help and vigilance, rejected the proposal and any timeline proposal. The defense switched to mineral plundering functions: mines operations, minerals traffic logistics, mines expropriations. The prosecution rejected the proposal when violations would start in one function and would carry to two or three other functions. That was the case when minors were kidnapped to work in mines, evolving to minerals traffic logistics or becoming soldiers' experts in invading other mines for expropriation. The defense started ranking indictments by gravity of infractions; number of people killed, lost, or burned assets. The prosecution found the ranking not significantly or legally objective. It also rejected the proposal. The discussion went on for four days without a solution. The defense team asked the prosecution to develop proposals. But the prosecution would not submit a proposal. It maintained the full package of indictments and the defense team withheld any submission of goods to indict the upper echelons in the chain of command. That literally closed prospects to go beyond Adamas. DA O'Grady team went in circle back to the first stage of indicting nobody else but Adamas Kagita. The two teams requested Judge Alvaro Lopez's guidance.

Judge Alvaro Lopez begged the two teams to work from sentencing guidelines and facts.

"Counsels, I was hoping that you would come to an understanding to project a fair and equitable sentencing. The defense team had not disputed nor contested the bulk of indictments raised against the accused. The defense team wants to reduce the sentence time based on what the accused would do to assist the prosecution team in enlarging the basket of indictments including people higher in the chain of command in the commissions of infractions the accused had pleaded guilty for. In the meantime, the prosecution team is maintaining the full package of indictments for the purpose of sentencing, while the defense team is withholding all cooperation in advancing the prosecution goal. Did I correctly state the current standing of the sentencing negotiation?"

"Yes, your Honor, exactly!"

"Counsels, as far as I am concerned, there is a reservation I must raise in this give and take process. I submit that the defense team's assumption of enlarging the basket of indictments including people higher up in the chain of command is, well, just an assumption. There is no certainty that the defense team nor the accused will deliver for prosecution these people higher up in the chain of command, those people who supervised Adams in the execution of his share of infractions. As a matter of fact, what Adamas would provide in this context are statements accusing these people who supervised him in the commission of his crimes. Remember, in the court of law here in the US, that would be his word against the word of the new accused. That would need to be adjudicated as well, having Adamas' word against their."

. Are you following me?"

"Yes, your honor!"

"Counsels, if that is the case, the sentencing negotiating should be determined according to the probability of advancing toward the goal that the prosecution is pursuing, the probability of enlarging the basket of indictments. I am proposing that the length of sentencing should be determined depending on three factors: the ability of bringing these people to this court to face Adamas accusation, the ability of this court to prosecute these people and the ability of this court to gain the conviction of these people based on accusations leveled by Adamas against these people. Counsels, the way I see it, this undertaking would be a toll order for not just this court, it will be so for both the prosecution team and the defense team. Now, I must close my proposal by telling you that the undertaking would fall squarely on the prosecution, it would then all depend on the prosecution team to decide whichever way it wants to take this effort, whichever way it wants to go and to achieve its goal."

"May it please the court, I am relieved that you took time to think through the reservation the prosecution team was also struggling with around the topic. I really appreciate your analysis and proposal. Please give the prosecution enough time to get back to you and the defense team with a concrete response. Thank you so very much!"

"Counsel O'Grady, please, I would like to get a time frame for your response."

"Your honor, the prosecution team would get back to you by next week Thursday!"

"Thank you, counsels, this court is adjourned!"

CHAPTER 35
PROSECUTION'S INITIATIVE

DA O'Grady came out of the meeting that Judge Alvaro Lopez called a bit ambivalent. His long-term goal of prosecuting the drivers of the Eastern DRC civil war has now been entirely adopted by the court and surprisingly so by the defense. But the price to implement the goal was becoming prohibitive if not impossible to reach or match. The first step of bringing the drivers of the war was realistically impossible and it did not take a strategic analyst to state it.

First, the drivers residing in neighboring countries of DRC, Rwanda and Uganda were protected by the governments of these countries which have been raising the plundering of mineral resources of DRC to the level of national government sanctioned policies. These governments do not even try to hide it. The publicized statistics of their exported mineral resources shamelessly accounted for large quantities of plundered mineral quantities from Eastern DRC. Convoluted official statements justifying these export volumes were debunked by the fact that these countries did not have mines where the reported large quantities of coltan and gold could be extracted.

On top of raising the policy for plundering the mineral resources in Eastern DRC as a government policy, the same governments were ensuring that those who were sent in the areas to effectively conduct the plundering activities were protected at every phase of their activities from the time they entered DRC using fake identity to the time they were extracted from the fields of operations.and brought back to the neighboring original countries. This occurred whenever they were clearly identified and labeled as the main drivers and culprits by the international agencies which were trusted to conduct these surveys or international jurisdictions which have documented their involvement in various military campaigns which supported the plundering. These

313

war lords were welcome back to the neighboring countries as valiant national fighters deserving priority protection by the government.

The third grave obstacle resided right there with the central government in Kinshasa, which played a nebulous game of pretending to attempt to prosecute the drivers of the plundering by day while cooperating with the neighboring country governments at night in not just protecting the same culprits if they were still operating on DRC soil or simply appointing them to higher positions in the central government security infrastructure. The latest step would simply nullify any request to pursuit them in any shape or form while they would work day and night in getting rid of the proofs that have been compiled to incriminate them in their criminal plundering activities. Furthermore, the political leadership in Kinshasa, that was being pushed around by various international institutions and Occidental countries for trying to impose a third political mandate, was not going to provide any substantial cooperation with an American judicial court going after the drivers of Eastern DRC plundering. The political leadership considers the plundering of Eastern DRC as its own trump card, an undertaking it had tacitly supported, an undertaking that brought the regime closer with the neighboring governments which were the only ones providing unquestioned support to the regime.

DA O'Grady understood the depth of these three outstanding obstacles and wondered about how to overcome them at the current time. For whatever it was worthwhile, he realized that the Great Lakes governments appeared to work very closely together. For better or worse, their main support remains the United States of America. Therefore, DA O'Grady should use that fundamental factor to extract some judicial dividends from the trio. The DA prosecution may not get the top drivers of the plundering. But the exposure that Reverend Drago had left against the plundering community of the three governments in the Great Lakes region must and can be used to get the Reverend abandoned by the so-called "Enterprise", in the same manner Adamas was abandoned. That should be the first step to push to start the judicial ball rolling in the task of achieving the preliminary goal of prosecuting the main drivers of the plundering. It sounded farfetched to DA O'Grady, but he had no choice but to try it.

DA O'Grady convened his restrained staff dedicated to the Adamas Kagita case, including Pascal Bodavi, Ludmilla Garrov and Reverend

Stanislas Keregi. After exposing his preliminary goal pursuit against the three powerful obstacles he requested each team member to honestly share whatever he or she thought about it to shoot it down or to promote it.

Ludmilla started talking:

"I am no expert analyst around the politics of Greater Lakes region in Africa. But the three powerful obstacles you submitted look prohibitive to me to allow an effective judicial engagement in these three countries. It looks like the political leadership in these countries would do everything in their power to block any call for judgement of anybody involved in the plundering of natural resources in DRC. That is the case for a simple reason, they are engaged in the plundering business. It is extremely profitable to each of them on a financial and political level. There is no upside for them to get exposed. I read somewhere to what extent the profit motive had been animating these political leaderships in that region. Leaving aside the weak political leadership in Kinshasa, you need to remember how Rwandan and Uganda armies fought each in the so called Six Day War from 5 to 10 June 2000 in the town of Kisangani. That was the time when the two countries supported two different Congolese rebel groups against the central government of Kinshasa. Nobody could believe that these two countries which were closely allied in overthrowing the old Mobutu regime and implementing the plundering in Eastern Congo, would go on fiercely fighting against each other. In fact, after they managed getting the puppet president, they installed in Kinshasa, assassinated, and raised his son to take over the political leadership and to govern DRC with the blessing and the cover of the US. Furthermore, they came to a sort of common understanding sealing a sort of a political pact among themselves. Still, now the three political leaderships never stop to always watch each other to ensure that none of them is exposed to any international condemnation because of the endless calamity that the plundering of Eastern DRC caused in increasing the number of dead and displaced people. Currently, it is becoming obvious that Uganda and Rwanda are getting ready to abandon the weakest link in this murderous concert of plundering, in other words the current DRC political leadership. Rwanda and Uganda are ready to probably throw asunder the unreliable regime in Kinshasa which is being lambasted from every international side because of the stupid attempt to impose a third mandate with an accrued political repression on top of the complete neglect of leaving Eastern DRC people to face the murderous plundering of the region natural resources without any military campaign. You may have a good cynical probability to gain in pressuring Kinshasa to give up few actors in their chain of command if they are not of Rwandan affinity or origin. Through its intelligence services, the Kinshasa regime knows the key players in the plundering business. The regime also knows or has already established the ones to protect, to discard and or to sacrifice. The issue here would be whether the prosecution team would accept the bargain. At the end the prosecution would get some discarded unworthy war lords who have embarrassed publicly Uganda and Rwanda and are ready to be given up for the price of keeping and holding on to the international cover and protection from the US. That is my perspective."

"Woooah, Counsel Garrov, you have been listening to a bit too long to my cynical take of this case. I pray that the prosecution will not get to this end of bargain. But I appreciate your concise analysis. What do you say Pascal!"

"DA O'Grady, I lean toward Ludmilla's analysis minus the cynical twist. I also submit that I am no expert on the Greater Lakes region politics. Now I would not repeat the same analysis that Ludmilla has given us. I rather give the floor to the experts' expert, Reverend Stanislas who should with a concise historic take leading to a definitive approach to this difficult case."

"I am afraid that I did not find Ludmilla's analysis cynical but realist. In fact, that analysis is closer to what we have been living in the area for the past fifteen or more years in Eastern RDC. It goes back to the genocide that took place in Rwanda after the rebel invasion of Rwanda from Uganda. But before that it would be appropriate to provide a historical background over how we got to this tragedy. Back during the Belgian colonial administration of Rwanda, there was a net inclination of the colonial authority to raise the profile of one tribe against the other for the sake of the divide-to-conquer disposition to control the African population in these far away territories from Europe. That governance practice was widespread in all colonies in Africa. British, Portuguese, French and Belgian colonial authorities implemented it all over their colonies. Most selected one tribe over which they vested more education, administration, and police control to manage the other tribes in a colony. That always created a lot of resentment from the other tribes. In case of Rwanda, the colonial power vested a lot of administrative authority and education over the Tutsi tribe, a minority tribe, at the exclusion and expense of the Hutu tribe, a majority tribe. The Belgian colonial authority went even further entertaining the Tutsi kingdom that was found at almost the same level as the Belgian kingdom. It provided it with all the regal trappings reserved for a kingdom. Hutu were left to be consider as inferior below second-class citizens. However, the independence wave that liberated most African countries from 1960 found Rwanda in protracted civil war between the two tribes. When Rwanda acceded to political independence on July 2, 1962, the majority Hutu took over the governance of the country and directed a lot of political and economic repression against the Tutsi who were forced to leave the country going in exile to neighboring countries of Congo and Uganda or in many countries in Occident. The majority of Tutsi came to Uganda.as refugees, having lost practically all they had, starting all over their life in a foreign land, deprived of their royal status. The Tutsi refugees tried as best as they could to integrate in that foreign country which went to the post-independence instability from the administration of President Obote to be overthrown by Idi Amin. Afterwards, there was the civil war that Museveni and Obote waged from Tanzania first to overthrow Idi Amin. Later, Museveni managed to get rid of Milton Obote's regime. The later overthrow was accomplished with a great support of Rwandan refugees who felt no longer welcome during the last months of Obote's regime. For the first time after being forced out of Rwanda after about thirty years, these refugees started being targeted for active repression by Obote partisans and ethnic people. As usual, during times of economic hardship in most countries, foreigners and especially foreign refugees are usually blamed for the country failed economic management. For the first time, Rwanda refugees felt that they had overstayed their welcome and wanted to leave Uganda and to go back home in Rwanda and face those who had kick them out in the first place. There was that unspoken pact for Rwanda refugees to assist Museveni to gain power and to request to be armed and to go back home in Rwanda no matter what invasion included. That became possible when you can see that Museveni relied heavily on Rwandan refugees in his inner military and political circle when his rebel army waged war against Obote's army. Museveni was duty bound to help these warriors to go back to Rwanda to reconquer their prior political hegemony."

"After a few setbacks, the Rwanda refugees regained power in Kigali after the big blunder from the Hutu Rwandan government which unleashed the murderous genocide of more than 900,000 Tusti and moderate Hutu in 1994. The terrible massacre caught the Clinton Administration by surprise. The same administration went on to provide every military, political and economic support for the new Kigali government to ensure that it will vanquish the Hutu genocidaire regime by chasing its troops to the neighboring provinces of North and South Kivu in DRC along with more than two million Hutu refugees. This upset the military precarious balance in the area and broke the back of the armed forces of the dictator of DRC at the time, Marechal Mobutu. The same advance by Rwandan invading forces turned into a powerful rebellion movement uniting all armed rebellious forces against the central government of Kinshasa. All the way to Kinshasa which was taken over on May 17, 1997. It is debatable to what extent the American administration has assisted the invasion of DRC by the Rwandan invading forces to overthrow Mobutu's regime. The fact remains that the American administration has not stopped the furtive advance of these forces to accomplish what the administration has loudly proclaimed and wished since 1990 admonishing the dictator to leave power. Until today, DRC has continued to pay for the sins of the American administration for not being able to prevent the 1994 genocide and the unwillingness of Mobutu to leave power thirty years after he was put in power by the CIA twice, in 1960 and 1965. Everything that has happened in DRC from 1997 goes back to these two sins. It is amazing when you looked at everything that has transpired since then, you see how intractable the DRC issue had become. We are talking of six successive American administrations unable to advance the DRC quagmire: One Clinton Administration, two Bush Administrations, two Obama Administrations, a new Trump Administration; same issue and no solution. It has now evolved into a plundering sequence benefiting high technology corporations which have squarely decided to use Rwanda as staging warehouse from where to extract mineral resources plundered from Eastern DRC at the price of a mounting genocide of untold proportion of more than proven eight million dead and counting. Is it that the Kigali and Kampala regimes have been emboldened to the point of no longer listening to the very American administration that had protected them the same way that Mobutu was protected for … thirty years. I am afraid the price is now out of the reach of redemption when US is now confronting a genocide it cannot be left unaccountable of. And if DRC had persistently continued to pay that price, Rwanda had plunged from a majority tribe dictatorship to a minority tribe dictatorship postponing forever the advent of a true national reconciliation between these two belligerent tribes. As far as the US is concerned, it was dealt with the worst strategic cards and concerns in the Great Lakes region of Africa. The US has been left with an empty slate of managing and covering the growing genocide in DRC and the ethnic powder keg in Rwanda. The US must be wondering what in hell or heaven, why had it gotten itself in such a quagmire? And here in this court in Raleigh, we are left to cutting corners, to condemn Adamas for say twenty years and snatch along a few sacrificial war lords like Reverend Drago. But we are never going to reach higher up to claim that we have handed justice to the culprits. DA O'Grady, the culprits are higher up and we are never going to reach them. We are in the midst of an Administration change, the higher up culprits are going to disappear in the proclamation of the new Administration policy for Great Lakes region of Africa. I am here to get as little as I can to tell the world that at least one war lord is paying for the higher up culprits. I can live with that."

"Reverend Stanislas, I appreciate all that you shared. I hope that the younger counsels are appreciating as I am the long elaborate background you shared, and this country is facing in that part of the world. I entirely shared your frustration and dedication. I am not a fool when I was proposing to go higher up. I know very well that I would not reach that goal of getting the culprits in what you eloquently described as a quagmire. My goal, I pray that you have noted, is entirely political. I am trying to expose the endless pit these successive administrations had thrown the country into. It is not the only endless pits this country had been thrown into, dug itself and could not get out of it, there are quite a lot of these pits out there every time a politician stands out there and starts getting the country to dig another endless pit. I want to raise awareness about these arrogant politicians. In fact, and this is between us, in the process of getting the Reverend Drago's what I want to get is to find out what the government had negotiated to get that war lord, Adamas Kagita here among us and why? That is the bargain I want to extract from the government, and to get the government to publicize. In my mind that is the endless pit the government has started to dig when dealing with these recalcitrant governments overseas. If we don't stop it now, that pit will be thrown wide open in the future. If I can close it now, I can retire from a lifetime judicial quest in peace."

319

"My dear DA O'Grady, since I came here to Raleigh, I heard you talking a lot. I continue to underestimate your goals. I want to join you all the way! Ah, Ah, Ah!"

"So do I, Boss, you are amazing!" and "I concurred!"

"Pascal, thank you for your loud advice, you agreed with everything Ludmilla and Reverend Stanislas said!"

"Yes, Boss, they are much wiser than I am. I am still learning!"

"I see! What I heard from the team is that we will try to get a few sacrificial lambs that the current political leaderships in these three countries would offer us while we will force our government to publicize the deal that got Adamas here. Is that the prosecution strategy?"

"Yes, Sir!"

CHAPTER 36

IN KEREGI FAMILY'S GRACE

At the conclusion of the last meeting called by DA O'Grady, Reverend Stanislas realized that he did not see nor talk with his niece Charlotte for a time. He has been extremely busy and retained in a long series of reviews and discussions with the prosecution team after the unique court session when he had testified against Adamas Kagita. He had spent a great deal of time in Chapelle Hill office of Braxton and Associates assisting the two law students providing clinic support to the defense team. He was a bit reluctant to provide such a support. It took him a while to understand the predicaments of the American judicial system in terms of discover support. That support became a requirement for the reverend to assist expertly the two students in accessing the database features of African Studies Center in Uppsala, Sweden. As a major victim of heinous criminal retributions from the accused Adamas Kagita, it took both a leap of faith and his own religious background to reconcile himself to the task. Reverend Stanislas shared his misgivings with his niece Charlotte who was very upset to learn about this unaccustomed step imposed over his uncle who had lost his wife and children in the hands of Adamas. Charlotte felt guilty of having associated him with her own endless quest for justice. She could not believe that the prosecution of Adamas was going to turn into a family nightmare. She stopped reaching out to his uncle during that episode. There were days when the Reverend chose to stay in Chapelle Hill to reduce commuting expenses between Raleigh and Chapelle Hill. The Adamas delay lasted almost two months. The contacts between the uncle and the niece became a bit remote and rare. Charlotte became reluctant to call as long as possible not realizing that his uncle had completely reconciled with his role of assisting the defense team. In addition, Reverend Stanislas became thoroughly aware of the defense goals of Braxton & Associates, goals that were much closer to the prosecution. The uncle was not at liberty to share this turn of events with his niece Charlotte until he was certain of what he was witnessing. In the meantime, he had to attend a whole series of meetings between the Judge, the defense, and the prosecution teams. The last meeting that DA O'Grady called removed all reservations the uncle had. He called his niece.

"Hello Charlotte, don't you realize that I never went back to Sweden. I still have been retained here in Raleigh getting involved in all kinds of legal reviews.!"

"I am very sorry, Uncle Stanis, I was very upset to learn that you were forced to help Adamas defense team. That was not fair after all he did to you and the family. I just could not bear to call you. It was a real betrayal for me. I should not have dragged you into this situation. I felt ashamed and could not forgive myself."

"Charlotte, Charlotte, what are you talking about. First, you were not the only to bear this family burden we all share all these years. I came here to assist the prosecution not just to answer your call. It was a personal pursuit as well. Please, remove any doubt or guilt about what had happened. I am calling to share a lot of positive directions this judicial train is taking. Listen to me very carefully."

"Oh, really, my God, this or whatever you are calling judicial train or pursuit had so many heads I stopped counting from the beginning. I am all ears."

"But my niece Charlotte, before I shared what I wanted I got in my mind, I wanted to ask you what you think of the status of all that has been done so far in the case against Adamas?"

"Well, uncle Stanis, to tell the truth, I am at peace about what I wanted to see accomplished. I know that no matter what, Adamas would not see the light of freedom for a long time. He would stay where he is now for a long time. I am relieved that we have accomplished what we intended to do for our family and so many other people who have perished under the guns that Adamas had directed against them. I told you many times that I would rest only when Adamas has been locked up and he is."

"Indeed, he is! And you are right, Adamas would never walk as a free man in this country if he is here. He is done and it is only a matter of debate now about how long he would be incarcerated. From what

I am hearing it would not be below twenty years. I am calling you today to share what is happening about that sentencing. Adamas, for all practical purposes, had confessed to his crimes from the time he left Kisangani to the time he landed in Raleigh, NC. As usual in cases like his, he finally realized that those who enabled him to commit all these crimes in Eastern DRC, have abandoned him in that cell where he is. The same people have stopped paying for his legal defense fee, he had to hire a new defense team. So, what he got left, he is going to jail for a long time! Well, he had decided to negotiate a lower sentence in exchange for sharing all he knows about his murderous sponsors from his level to higher up. What is going on now is to establish a mechanism whereby the prosecution would be able to verify whether what he would share is true. That is what we are grappling with now with the Judge and the defense team."

"Hold on, my uncle, you and I know that this is impossible. We know that the current political leadership in Kinshasa would not dare deliver any culprit, war lord operating in Eastern DRC unless he gets an authorization from the political leaders in Rwanda and Uganda. The last two have imposed this one in DRC. He is a puppet doing the bidding of anything he is asked to do by his masters in Uganda and Rwanda. Maybe the Judge, the prosecution team and the defense team do not know it, I trust you to instruct these folks not to waste their time attempting to go higher up above Adamas. Uncle Stanis, I am a bit surprised that you are participating in that futile exercise when you have taught me time and again that it was a waste of time to expect any justice against Adamas from here in the US. You have convinced me that you have completely discounted any justice against the like of Adamas in the USA. You said it because you strongly believed that the US government was also a sponsor of all that Adamas had done in DRC. Remember how we have argued back and forth about the subject. Personally, I went in by faith and we got thus far. Of course, we could not have reached that stage without your tremendous documentation, thank God! But I resolved that this is as much as we would get, that is getting Adamas in jail. Whatever he is trying to negotiate is, in my uneducated humble opinion, trash, a distraction. Uncle Stanis, I must return the table for you, I must implore you, In Keregi Family's grace, to forget about going up that channel of death, that high command of evil to get those sponsors. I regretfully must remind you about who is sitting on top of that chain of command. You would find the chiefs of state of three countries from DRC, Rwanda, and Uganda! These people have been continually covered by the US government for very obscure reasons. And nobody else but you had told me that that this has been going on for the length of five successive administrations in the US. I wished the US had supported these people because they pushed for some form of democracy in the countries they govern. Absolutely not! They are no different from the other African political leaders we have seen all over Africa. They are no different from the one they imposed on DRC for thirty-two years only to come back and to get him deposed mercilessly through a savage civil war by these new leaders who are just as dictatorial as the one before. And what has happened in DRC, just worse than before. Carnage upon carnage, piles of dead people we stopped counted, a whole generation of young folks born and displaced from one refugee camp to another and with no end in sight. I gave up a long time ago trying to figure out their policy and the policy that the US is pursuing in our region. I wish sometime that these leaders and their sponsors in the US just come out and state clearly what do they want from the people of our region. I may sound crazy or foolish, but I would not be far to state as people who have be brutalized and displaced would tell them, "Take what you want, just leave us alone to raise our kids in peace". My God, this had gone forever with no end in sight, Uncle Stanis."

"I heard you, my dear niece Charlotte. Believe me I did not change in my resolve to see this tragedy end as I stand here. I concur on everything you say. I have cried as long as everyone for our people back there in Eastern DRC. But I am glad that you mentioned that this tragedy had gone forever with no end in sight. You may not believe me, but we need to invest our energy, from then on, to get the madness to stop. But guess what, we should not expect anything from Kinshasa, Kampala, or Kigali. I am sure that you have noticed that when Adamas was incarcerated there was nobody from Kinshasa, Kampala, and Kigali. You started the process not knowing nor expecting where it would go. I did not trust your effort, I even discouraged you, but guess what at the end thanks to your effort, we are thanking God that the blood of the lamb had closed the evil path of Adamas Kagita. I am still in disbelief that your effort worked. It happened outside the purview of the political pressures and entities that we, from outside the US, are quick to vet for solutions even when the political arena is just empty of purposes. That is a lesson I learned during the few days during my stay here. You see for many of us outside the US, we don't understand the drivers that move this country. When we analyze the political power plays in this country, we tend to give predominant spaces to the power of money in the conduct of social norms or politics. Of course, we should not discount it, that power of money. But the learned ones have determined that there are more drivers above the power of money to move this country. Outsiders don't understand nor appreciate that factor. The learned ones have also found that among so many other economic and social drivers, the power of money is neither static nor permanent. The power of money, like other social drivers that dictated the future of the country in 1950, are not the same as the ones that came in place in 1960, 1970, or 1990. In other words, what we believed were guiding the country in a particular period may no longer be valid in another period. The reason being that the owners of these economic or social drivers, from one period to another, are not necessarily the same. The mistake we make is to think that these drivers' owners are always the same people. That was the mistake I have made all along when I developed my analytical background of the Eastern DRC tragedy. I could not appreciate the changed format in prosecuting human rights abuses right here in the US. Nobody would tell me about the change until I came here to find it by myself. Most people from abroad, including yours truly, maintained that it was impossible to pursue a war lord in the US court system. Ignorance kept us in a permanent stage of paralysis. There were laws we could have taken advantage of a long time ago if we had just learned and entered the process. But we were afraid to try. Charlotte, I heard your complaint. I heard the same fear that had paralyzed me for so long. I am not claiming that I would break all the barriers that are in place against prosecuting the entire chain of command that had enabled Adamas Kagita. That chain of command is still well protected on both sides of the Atlantic, I know that. But every time an opportunity comes available to start breaking down that barrier against a link of that chain, by Almighty God, Charlotte, I would take advantage of that opportunity. I know it would be tedious, laborious, but I am coming to realize that that chain has been built for the past twenty years or so, it would take more than an overnight to bring it down. We must start somewhere. Charlotte, you started it. We cannot afford to sit back and pray that that chain would be broken by itself. We must test every means possible to do it."

"I see that you are in a new forceful tangent now, Uncle Stanis, I would only say, more power to you. If there is somebody, I must trust in the endeavor you explain to me, you must be the one. I have no basis to disclaim what you just said. I support you."

"I thank you. I must add that your friend Ludmilla and her boss DA O'Grady are good people bringing me up to embrace these new challenges. I would not bother you with these legal intricacies, but suffice to say they are going against each link of that chain of command. I must support that endeavor."

"Ludmilla came from an area of Europe that has experience what we are living in Eastern DRC. I am not surprised that she is dedicating a lot of energy and expertise in this step. She is a very great lady."

"Don't forget our brother Pascal Bodavi from Cameroun, his modesty hides a fierce legal engagement. I like him a lot."

"Well, you are well surrounded and supported. A gracious team you got! It is my turn to say sorry for my earlier reservation, Full God speed ahead, Uncle Stanis!"

CHAPTER 37

WHICH COURT?

One major stumbling block to advance DA O'Grady's goal of prosecuting the higher up in the chain command of the Eastern DRC plundering was in which court to conduct that prosecution. It was easy to prosecute Adams Kagita who violated the immigration laws of the US government. He was arrested while pretending to be someone he was not for and for a long time. Although he was no longer a fraudster to answer to American laws, he remained detained to answer for the human rights violations he committed, violations which opened him to the prosecution that the US government had signed up to do when it adhered to the conventions especially the 1948 Universal Declaration of Human Rights in its articles 1,2, 3, 4, 5, 9, 13, 14. There was no ambiguity in prosecution Adamas and, keeping incarcerated while deciding the length of his sentencing in the US.

It was not obvious to DA O'Grady how the higher up in the murderous chain command should be apprehended while not residing in the US. This condition was absent if any higher up in the chains was residing in territories forming the legal theater where Adamas had committed his crimes before coming to the US. The more the DA struggled with the prosecution issues, reviewing them with eminent academic experts in international law abiding by the 1948 Universal Declaration of Human Rights, the legal theater became distant, all the same. He was told that outside the US, the UN International Criminal Court, based in the Hague in Netherlands, founded by the Roman Statute in 2002, was the only court vested to conduct such a prosecution against people guilty of such human rights violations. The only problem was that the US is not a state party to the Rome Statute of the International Criminal Court and the US government opposes the work of the ICC in relation to its own citizens as Washington has still not signed the Rome Statute. The main reason is that the US military still fears that

327

the Court could be used to prosecute American soldiers abroad.

As far as the Adamas Kagita case was concerned, the prosecution of the higher up in the chain of command by the ICC would present a very serious diplomatic quandary. It was not only obvious that the chain of command went all the way through the political leadership in these three countries. This will require inviting them to testify at the Hague in Netherlands. There was no telling whether these three heads of state would or would not implicate the government political leaderships in the US, which have provided them military support and diplomatic cover all these twenty years while the Eastern DRC tragedy had lasted. As a matter of fact, the heads of state in these countries have cited that very diplomatic cover in the defense of their involvement in the Eastern DRC, in time raising it as a strong blackmail element they were ready to invoke anytime they will be called to testify. So much so that the US government would never dare try this venue.

Sadly, it looks more and more to DA O'Grady that the prosecution process he had in mind, above the Adamas Kagita of this world would, become and had always been political dead end. DA O'Grady was learning in explicit ways that the exercise of judicial process was completely inversed when you leave the US borders. It looks more and more that the only way to go up the chain of command and prosecute higher up would require that the top echelon of that chain be exempted and be forced to give up a few sacrificial lambs below them. This was exactly what her niece Gwendolyn understood and tried to share with him from the start in many unspoken and vague ways, pronouncements, and directives.

DA O'Grady can now imagine his niece Gwendolyn exchanging laconic laughs with her boyfriend, the Economics Expert, while resting on long chairs by the beachfront of Four Seasons Resort Bali at Jimbaran Bay in Indonesia. DA O'Grady can hear the conversation evolving in the direction of how much her niece tried in vain to get him to celebrate Adamas incarceration and to forget going further up that chain of command. Gwendolyn warned his uncle that it would be next to impossible. First, he would have to instruct the new legal team that was coming with the new administration. She mentioned that the new legal team would spend about the year to learn the tricky issues and not to rock the diplomatic boat except for the new big Boss urgent political promises which never included Eastern DRC. Gwendolyn insisted that since the big new Boss is all transactional, she doubted that he would sacrifice the three stooges in the Great Lakes region unless a higher financial campaign kick back is made. This would happen because the high technology corporations he had eagerly solicited during his unorthodox campaign would be eager now to return the perpetual campaign financial elevator. They would do that because they did not have established or replaced, to date, reliable sourcing alternatives for ... Coltan that they need desperately and remain tied to the murderous logistics of Eastern DRC. So, DA O'Grady initiative would go nowhere unless he is willing to play the new administration ball. And that ball would consist of getting culprits one step higher than Adamas Kagita and no higher and that is it! DA O'Grady agreed, he had other perspectives in mind to reach.

Resolving the judicial process under the new administration did not determine the court where the lower culprits would be prosecuted. The new team was not ready to determine the venue short of not bringing them to the American soil. Guantanamo military base was the only venue, the same way as it was opened for foreign 9/11 culprits. That was a bit unexpected for DA O'Grady. But he had no choice but to follow it. He decided to enlarge his net of lower culprits, he was going to increase the number of culprits higher up the chain of command that Adamas was going to list. He bargained with the new legal team to agree with the higher number of culprits. He convinced the new legal team that more intelligence about the top echelon would be extracted from a larger pool of lower culprits than with a few selected culprits. About thirty lower culprits were selected to the great surprise of the top echelon which had agreed initially to the new judicial process from the new legal team from the new administration. The top echelon was counting on this agreement as a testimony of its good faith effort to work with the new administration. It was evident that the new administration big Boss was always looking for deep secret diplomatic disasters that previous Democratic Administrations had manufactured. He was told that there were plenty of disasters to unearth in the Great Lakes region of Africa. He raised his antenna and made sur that he got few juicy compromising details from the area. At the same time, the top echelon of the political leadership from the same area shared its nervousness about this new administration with the high technology representatives, only to learn that the new administration was also very unhappy with the political leadership in DRC about the postponing of the planned election. That unfortunate initiative from Kinshasa was giving the new administration a lot of unwelcome headaches from many partners around the world. The new administration was very irritated and reacted appropriately. It even went further, it came out with a long list of first circle political, security and family individuals who were entered in the list of economic sanctions. This was a wake-up call that the other political leaderships in Rwanda and Uganda did not want and pulled back to defend their individual security and political interests. They started to abandon the Kinshasa political leadership to its own immature devices. There is no virtue in the den of thieves.

DA O'Grady took advantage of these openings and quickly set up the travel plan to collect as quickly as possible the lower thirty culprits wherever they were in DRC. To give it more imperium in DRC, the travel plan was going to be led by an FBI Counterintelligence Special Agent. The team included Ludmilla Garrov representing the DA, Pascal Bodavi representing the Immigration Services, Professor Julia Fama representing the defense Team, 3 Special Operations Military officers and 10 enlisted Special Operations from Marines Corps, two staff members from the Gwendolyn old office under Attorney General. Eighteen people all together were going to be part of the travel plan. It was going to take about four months to execute this plan from the time Adamas Kagita provided his list of about twenty-two culprits. Reverend Stanis added the remaining nine other culprits from his data from Uppsala. The list was quietly negotiated at the presidential level at Kigali and Kampala overriding Kinshasa indications and preferences as usual. The list comprised surprisingly of Reverend Drano over vehement objections from Kigali. Four Generals were included including three at the Kinshasa Chief Staff levels, fifteen Colonels, three Majors, two Captains, and six businessmen. Of the twenty-four military people selected, there were only three from Rwanda tribes, most were from the variety of autochthone tribes in Easter DRC. All had strong affinities with the political regimes in Uganda or Rwanda.

Like Adamas, most were involved in the plundering of the region for the incredible financial gain they earned in the execution of mining and logistics of coltan and gold resources from Eastern DRC to Uganda and Rwanda. The high-level officers were quickly promoted to top security posts in Kinshasa for one and only one reason, to monitor, guard and cover the profitable plundering business on behalf of the top echelon in the political leadership in Kinshasa, Kigali and Kampala. It was remarkable to notice that all of these military officers started their criminal enterprise in Eastern DRC, none attended any military academy, they evolved first as war lords, then magically self-promoted as Colonels or Generals, before the political leadership in Kinshasa confirmed them as high command officers, then keeping them in either mining operations or supervising the murderous logistics that evacuated the mineral resources to Uganda or Rwanda. After a few months or years, they were sent to Kinshasa for a high-level security rotation to protect the predation regime. Each of the generals had left behind major mining concessions which they continue to own and supervise from Kinshasa, sharing the untold gains higher up with the top echelon of the well-tuned enterprise. These hard-core officers had no other future or alternative but to serve the predation "Enterprise". Most of the lower-level officers were selected by the enterprise with no significant and noticeable plundering activities but only to confuse the American judicial appetite. Businessmen were listed as major go-between in the murderous logistics chain from mines operations to the warehouses located on the borders of DRC and Uganda and Rwanda. These businessmen provided the cash funding that oiled the entire predation enterprise including the mining equipment and the trucks to evacuate the mineral products to the borders. Reverend Stanis's selection was more reliable and solid. It included military officers and businessmen named in many reports registering long term violations of human rights. Their names and backgrounds were specifically identified in the United Nations report titled "DRC: Mapping Human Rights violations 1993-2003", publicized in 2009. Their listing was challenged by the "Enterprise" representatives in the US to no avail.

The thirty named culprits were informed, through the diplomatic services of the US Embassy, of the "invitation" extended to them by the American judicial court system to answer to statements made by Adamas Kagita accusing them of participating in violations of human rights in Eastern DRC during his own involvement in the said abuses. The "invitation" letter stated that "they were only accused of these violations and according to the American judicial process they were innocent until found guilty beyond reasonable doubt". However, the "invitation" letter also stated that "they could not refuse the "invitation" to come to the US "territory", as such a refusal will amount to nullifying their presumption of innocence until proven guilty and making liable to be found guilty". The culprits were assured that they would be provided with adequate legal defense during the interview, and they would be returned to DRC if the accusations were disproven.

The culprits were asked to sign the "invitation" letter accepting the invitation and the legal consequences of participating in the judicial process.

As far as the responsibility of DRC Justice Ministry was concerned in agreeing to and tolerating this unusual judicial process from a foreign government institution, it was obvious that the government had given up to the international community its sovereign legal supervision in prosecuting those who were consistently violating the human rights of its citizens for the longest time in country. A slew of war lords from Eastern DRC had already been sent to the ICC in the Hague for prosecution. At this time when the political leadership was trying to impose a third mandate through another hasty election, the government was facing multiple political pressures from international institutions and country partners. Scarifying thirty cumbersome people to the American Court system amounted to redirecting international unwelcome noise from the increasing dictatorial government posture to a forced cynical cleaning of its political standing. The government could care less about the thirty culprits.

By the time the judicial calvary reached Kinshasa to collect the culprit, about half of them had already surrendered including Reverend Drano who started feeling betrayed and abandoned by the enterprise he had served all his adult life. Two generals ran away to Nairobi, Kenya requesting exile, three Colonels committed suicide, a businessman took a flight to South Africa on medical leave only to be sent back to Kinshasa on military escort. The collection of culprits went on without fanfare for the remaining twenty-five who were guarded by enlisted Marines in a heavily protected compound strangely and surprisingly across the Congo River in a remote area of Brazzaville, the capital of the Republic of Congo. The compound was about twenty minutes from the international airport. When the collection process of the culprits was completed after about a week and half, the culprits were embarked in a C-141 Starlifter jet which was retrofitted to passenger seats arrangement with no windows for the long direct flight to Guantanamo Bay American military base, on the southwestern tip of the island of Cuba. The culprits were not told that they were headed to that military base camp after about ten hours of flight.

As soon as the Congolese arrived at the camp, they were settled in a motel looking building of about fifty individual rooms with bathroom.

The accommodation was more like a student dormitory in a big college campus. The rooms were not too spacious but comfortable. The culprits were not called prisoners or culprits but associate guests of the International Criminal Court in Guantanamo. Apparently, a middle course venue was found with the ICC organizational while they were being processed at their arrival at the Guantanamo base. The shocking surprise for the culprits was that this venue was never shared with them when they "accepted the invitation" at the beginning. The "guests" will be legally vetted and questioned, if the accusations against them stick, they will be sent to the Hague for definitive prosecution. Otherwise, they would be sent back home to DRC. This venue will save the new legal team face with advancing its hard-liner obligation to prosecute the culprits without moving them to US jails, the same way the previous government managed the judicial process of the 9/11 accused terrorists. This venue would remove any sentencing and jailing responsibility of the guests for the American government, they will be sent to jail in the Hague under the ICC supervision and DA O'Grady goal of extended prosecution would be somewhat achieved.

While the issue of "in which court the guests would be questioned" was settled, a logistic nightmare of moving the entire court system between the mainland and Guantanamo Bay was set in motion. Judge Alavarez Lopez, DA O'Grady and staff, Professor Fama and the defense team, the prisoner Adamas Kagita, and piles over piles of documentations must be shuttled back forth between Guantanamo Bay and Raleigh. Two associate lawyers from the old office of Gwendolyn in the Attorney General Staff had to be associated with the legal proceedings to adhere to ICC legal recommendations and to represent the US Government. All these expenses were to be shouldered by the US taxpayers. DA O'Grady was surprised by the largesse of the new legal team from the new administration. He underestimated the level of disdain and animosity the big Boss of the new administration had against the preceding administration and the extent to which he was ready to go to unearth and to dig out disasters it left in that region of Africa. This was a paramount objective for the Big Boss that DA O'Grady was surprised to learn and found unbelievably petty.Revenge was an understatement of the strategy executed in that region of Africa.

CHAPTER 38

COMMANDER MONO AT YOUR SERVICE

Commandant Mono's journey, from Likasi, a mining town in the Great Katanga province of DRC to the room H21 in the motel looking like building in the American military of Guantanamo, was extraordinary to say the least. Now a two-star General in the DRC Armed Forces, General Jado Mulengani, otherwise known as Commander "Mono", was born in the mining town of Moba/Likasi on March 12, 1977. His family was involved in artisanal mining of gold, copper and uranium in many mining concessions abandoned by the big state mining company name GECAMINES. His father was somewhat related to Laurent-Desire Kabila, a longtime opponent oof the former DRC President Mobutu Sesse Seko. He led the Rwandan and Ugandan sponsor rebel group that invaded DRC and overthrew Mobutu in 1997. Sometime before that overthrow, when Laurent Kabila autoproclaimed himself DRC President in Lubumbashi, Mono's father introduced his son to the rebel chief who asked him to join the rebellion march to Kinshasa. Unemployed with unfinished high school education, Mono accepted the offer to be a member of the close-knit rebel chief guard. When the rebel chief made it to Kinshasa as a new chief of state, Mono was quickly introduced to the son who kept him as a member of his own bodyguard team. Mono's military status grew as well, he was then designated as Commander Mono. He went to China along with Joseph Kabila when he went to get advanced military training. Joseph Kabila succeeded his father when he was assassinated and kept Commander Mono in his first security circle.

President Joseph Kabila, very young and inexperienced when suddenly elevated to presidency, was generally considered in the triumvirate political leadership of Great Lakes region as KD in Eastern DRC or "Kiungo Dhaifu" meaning Weak Link in Swahili when compared to his purported father Mze Kabila considered as "Kiungo Chenye

Nguvu" or Strong Link. President KD tried to consolidate his power seat in the plundering campaign led in Eastern RDC by the old wolves from Kampala and Kigali. He sent Commander Mono in the area as a close confident to monitor the big plundering that his Rwandan and Ugandan mentors and partners were conducting. President KD had already secured the mineral resources economic rent from his father 's Katanga province of origin. He did not have the same profitable coverage in the Eastern DRC over the coltan, gold and diamond mineral resources rent that his mentors insisted on confiscating for themselves and their countries. Commander Mono would join the dance very effectively. Commander Mono came in with a strong contingent of two local hands picked personally by President KD. Those hands asserted themselves as new Commanders prospecting their own mining concessions and supervising their own logistic routes. The major difference was the destination of mineral raw products which took a different destination but Uganda or Rwanda border warehouses. They were trucked to Kisangani to be airlifted to Mombassa for sea freight. Commander Mono kept challenging the chief mentors with the armed support of the two major local war lords. Commander Mono conducted the same plundering as the teams from Uganda and Rwanda, killing, brutalizing the same local population with the same intensity and wantonness. The challenge lasted a good year and half until such time the end beneficiaries, the high technology corporations mounted a huge protest when it was learned that there was a plan to set up refinery plants for the extracted coltan and gold in the port of Mombassa, Kenya with funds raised by and originated from Kinshasa. The high-tech corporations saw a losing bypass proposition to undercut their provision of the mineral resources, they were upset. President KD's mentors from Kampala and Kigali screamed betrayal and raised the specter of a new rebellion against Kinshasa. President KD backed down and abandoned the project. A new enterprise formula was quickly negotiated breaking the Kisangani logistic route and dividing objectively the plundering rent among the mentors and their puppet in Kinshasa. Commander Mono was quickly recalled to Kinshasa and promoted to a two-star General with his first military supervision of the lower DRC region, his two local war lords also made it back to Kinshasa with a promotion to two-stars General with also military supervision of DRC western large territories. All these promoted Generals kept the ownership of their artisanal mining concessions and continued receiving a generous rent from the extracted mineral resources. Everybody was, well, happy.

Everybody was happy until the enterprise faced major dislocation later, the mentors from Kigali and Kampala started exerting pressure on President KD political leadership or lack of thereof. The mentors insisted on recuperating the rent that was given to the troublesome generals. Furthermore, the mentors included the three generals in the list of sacrificial lambs. The other two generals, former war lords read the leaves correctly and ran away to request exile status in Kenya. They stated rightly that Kampala and Kigali have been after them for so long, they could not trust any deal that would come out of these two capitals. They communicated their strong reservation and discussed their plans with General Commander Mono who trusted his cousin, President KD, head of state in Kinshasa. The war lord's military assignment put them very close to the western borders. They did not wait to be asked to join the furtive interviews They flew to Nairobi. While Commander Mono was being reassured by the President KD telling him that he would see to it that he will conduct a safe interview wherever the American wanted to take him, and he will bring him back to Kinshasa very soon. He never found out what the interview was all about when he was asked to board the small army boat crossing Congo River to Brazzaville.

Commander Mono remained alone and quiet through the long flight to Guantanamo. He would not talk to anybody just whispering "At your service" in French to anybody who wanted to address. He took all the appearances of his cousin Boss, recognized to be the most silent leader in Central Africa. The American hosts became alarmed about his behavior. Commander Mono looked very depressed. The American hosts heard about the two Colonels who committed suicide when they received the invitation letter, and they did not want to take a chance to suffer a third suicide on their hand. They monitored Commander Mono very closely all the time. From the defense and prosecution teams from Raleigh, only one person understood the background of Commander Mone. From the beginning. That was the Reverend Stanislas. He had a full well documented dossier over the man. When he exchanged with the Commander Mono, he was shocked to hear a Swahili expression from the Great Kivu area. He became more relaxed. In no time he confessed that he had been betrayed by his Boss and he had no choice but to seek revenge against his former Boss in Kinshasa. He assured the Reverend that he was ready to share all he knew about the Great Lakes region plundering business led by President KD as well as the entire predation arrangement that was concluded between the three political leaders in the region. That was exactly what DA O'Grady was looking for. Commander Mono also added that he would do all that on one condition, gaining promise of exile status in Europe or Northern America. The strange thing about Commander Mono was the fact that he had no idea who Adamas Kagita was. He claimed that he had never heard of Adams. This became a puzzle for the teams from Raleigh to figure out why Commander Mono was put on the list. Was he a victim of a settlement of accounts between Kinshasa on the one hand and the combined set of Kigali and Kampala on the other hand. It did not really matter for the Raleigh teams if they would be getting more unexpected intelligence they did not plan to receive.

This happy turn of collaboration started to come to play with the remaining set of colonels. The colonels were the go-between the mining operations where the mineral resources were extracted and the warehouses at Uganda and Rwanda borders. They also were the ones exchanging with the paid masters who came from Kampala and Kigali. They were the sources of payment undercutting, double counting, and various additional frauds against political leadership masters in Kampala and Kigali. It was obvious that the predation business in Eastern DRC was full of intrigue, constant betrayal and all sorts of financial shenanigans which were settled most of time through death penalty. Given that dangerous environment, anyone should be prepared to assume that a legal invitation from a rule-of-law country like the US would provide a fair legal proceeding for those involved in the brutal murderous predation. It was therefore disturbing to see that two of these colonels decided to commit suicide when they received the invitation. They probably did not believe that they were going to be shipped to US territory. They probably suspected that they were going to be delivered to the gallows of one of the opposing predation partners.

Of the remaining four colonels, Adamas has worked closely with three. The three were engaged in more than twenty military campaigns that Adamas led or was a major party. Adamas had entertained them in his sexual slave's camp before it was closed. They were his drinking and carousing companions in many houses of pleasure in Goma, Beni and Butembo. Adamas mentioned them to be included in the list to extract them from probable death penalty which was coming sooner or later

337

if they stayed in Eastern DRC. At this stage, Adamas thought that he would and should do anything to save them, He would advise them to spill their guts against the three political leaderships which were going to abandon and betray them anyway. Adams did not know the last colonel. He intended to advise him to do the same thing as the other three colonels. It was obvious that anyone of these culprits returning to any of these three countries after Guantanamo, will be marked to be killed, so why not get a living deal in Guantanamo!!

As far as the Major and the Captain in the culprits list, they were explicitly mentioned by Adamas Kagita. They were part of his personal settlement of accounts. Adamas was playing his own game of getting back to people he hoped to punish for what they did to him back them. He was unable to get them killed back then before he finally realized what game they were playing in the mineral resource's logistics from Eastern DRC various coltan mines to Uganda and Rwanda borders warehouses. The two officers planned with UN contingents' officers to attack truck caravans in remote abandoned routes. They diverted the caravan's logistics, emptied the trucks of coltan bags into UN battle tanks or trucks. The UN officers managed either to resell these minerals shipments to financial go between businessmen or shipped them overseas through their own channels. They took these two officers as their intelligence informers and kept them under their permanent protection. Adamas Kagita learned about and resolved the deception and duplicity from these two Congolese officers very later when his own fate was set by the American Intelligence services to be evacuated to the US. Adamas was admonished not to reveal their identities to the enterprise. He did not but waited for the right time to disrupt the UN intelligence cover by including these two Congolese officers as culprits. The American Intelligence side did no longer hold them relevant to much value. In fact, it found them expandable one way or another. The fate of the Congolese Major and Captain would most likely be decided by the time they will be shipped to the UN ICC at the Hague in the Netherlands. Adamas wanted simply to enjoy a little bit of payback at the expense of the American. This personal manipulation completely escaped the prosecution and defense teams from Raleigh. Reverend Stanislaus did not have any reference of these Congolese officers. Adamas was not forthcoming about the reason why he included them in the list short of associating them vaguely and an unverifiable way with Reverend Drago. Adamas' manipulation of the culprits list demonstrated the dangerous multifaced terrain of the predation that people in the Eastern DRC had lived through for the past twenty or so years. It was a terrain where day was night, night was day, one can never tell right from wrong, every humanity value was turned asunder, and death triumphed daily.

It was a terrain where the go between businessmen thrived supreme. They were included in the culprits list thanks to the analysis done from the voluminous documentation accumulated by the non-profit African Studies center led by Reverend Stanislas. These businessmen were without faith, answering to no law but the mighty green dollar. They were the oil that engaged the predation machine on daily basis between the mining operations scattered all around the Eastern DRC from the mountain slopes and vast lakes which divide the three countries and the wild trails which provided the logistics for the spoils of war in addition for the cover for mass graves from the untold daily massacres of the local population. The businessmen were the crucial links in the provision of the mineral resources to their end users in faraway developed retreats in Northern America, Europe, and Asia. The businessmen were the actual representatives of the three political leaderships in the area. In exchange from the green cash they funneled in the murderous process, they were the main receivers of mineral resources at the three countries borders, moving them to warehouses after crossing of borders, ensuring that the raw mineral resources are promptly shipped by air, truck and or boat to the primary mineral resources end users. These last users refined them and brought them to an advanced stage of technological usage where they are transformed into the fundamental digital system component known as motherboard. This component known as the motherboard is the largest printed circuit board that distributes the electricity and facilitates communication between and to the central processing unit (CPU), the random-access memory (RAM) and all other devices and components that are necessary to make the digital system device works. In other words, without the mineral resource extracted from Eastern DRC, there won't be any top performing system mother board distributing safely high-level electricity and communication to all current advanced digital devices. There is therefore a direct connection between what is, has been and will happen in Eastern DRC and digital system advances and progress. Assuring the provision of the mineral resources from Eastern DRC by these businessmen provides a curious if not sad representation of their involvement in the tragedy of the region. Leaving them out would have made a mockery of scaling the chain of command of the enterprise predation in Eastern DRC.

CHAPTER 39

THE SACRIFICE OF REVEREND DRAGO

The listing of Reverend Drago among the culprits provided a distinct if not overwhelming step in the pursuit of prosecution of the chain of command in the plundering, in the predation of the mineral resources of Eastern DRC. It was plainly obvious that the listing of culprits had shown the limitation of that pursuit and there was no other way to qualify this. The listing of Reverend Drago was a victory in the revenge that Adamas Kagita was waging against those, he claimed, had thrown him in the gutter, abandoned him in a golden jail of permanent residency in the US until he was exposed by that lady after about nine years. In retrospect, Adamas had reconciled himself with the fact that he was going to be exposed soon or later. He had come to realize that with the growing number of victims he had left in his past, he was going to be exposed no matter what, when and where. This would have happened whether he stayed in DRC, secluded himself in Rwanda or Uganda, exiled himself in another country in Africa, America, Europe, or Asia. Changing political environments would have caught up with him for the simple reason that his protectors in the Eastern DRC predation would not survive forever, they would disappear along with their predation heinous crimes. That was a simple fact in the world that those engaged in such horrendous documented crimes would be made accountable for them sooner or later at all levels. His incarceration running three months in the Immigration jail had awakened him up to that reality. Even if it was a bit astonishing that the tragedy in Eastern DRC has lasted this long, there was going to be an end to it. While he was nursing his wounds in that small cell of immigration Services of the US, he was foreseeing the demise of the three political leaderships which, combined, make up the top echelon of the chain of command of the predation before the corporations which are the definitive end users of the same.

When Reverend Drago received his invitation, he quickly concluded that he was made expendable by the same top echelon, not for the long service he had rendered to the enterprise, but for his proximity to the troublesome Adamas Kagita. He knew that he was being punished for not having controlled his direct subordinate Adamas who was bringing a lot of negative exposure over the predation work. If Reverend Drago had read books about the organization scheme of the Maffia or had he watched the movies over the same, he would not have been surprised by his current fate. He was extremely proud to call the enterprise operated along the same principles as the Maffia. He realized also that he had enjoyed the political untouchable status for a long time. He also remembered how feared he was in Kinshasa for the simple fact that he seemed to have unlimited access to the US Embassy location. Access, he invented and nurtured for his own good. Access that was ignored when it came time for him to settle his long criminal accounts.

As far as Reverend Drago was concerned, his accrued involvement in the politics of Eastern DRC was not based on the obvious financial gain that all the other culprits wanted from the systematic predation over mineral resources of North Kivu. His first allegiance was never to the enterprise. It was the political philosophy that permeated his entire adult life after his college studies. Reverend Drago's allegiance was strictly to the setup of Hima Empire in the Great Lakes region. Everything else he did in his life was for that goal. It must be remembered that he came of age when the regime of Mobutu was going down and when people of Tutsi ethnic background, refugees in Uganda, were given the means by the President of Uganda to restore their political hegemony in Rwanda which they left around the Hutu Tutsi ethnic civil war over the independence political leadership of the country. The majority Hutu won and mercilessly chased out the Tutsi minority which had dominated the country administration through the ethnic Tutsi Kingdom under the perennial colonial guise of "Divide and Conquer strategy over the various tribes under colonial administration". Allegiance to the restoration of that kingdom as Hima Empire in the region was the priority for Reverend Drago. The genocide of Tutsi after the assassination of the Hutu president reinforced that priority. The combination of military campaign to track Hutu genocidaires and invading DRC were, for the reverend, means to accomplish the same thing. The retreat of Rwandan military contingents into the two DRC territories of Rutshuru and Masisi to foment endless rebellion against the central authority in Kinshasa and keep them was justified to put in place the Hima Empire. The Reverend was also the vanguard in establishing the Minembwe Tutsi enclave in the South Kivu. The goal of Hima Empire was Reverend Drago prime motivation even when he dedicated his entire adult life in furthering the murderous predation of mineral resources under the trio supervision of the enterprise. That motivation had permeated the life of Reverend Drago to a point where when he cited Revelations 12:11, the blood that is mentioned in that verse, according to the reverend, was exclusive to only one entity, the Tutsi entity, and the Hima Empire.

So, at the reception of the invitation, Reverend Drago tried to remember what he had done or not done on behalf of the enterprise: the fake lawyering he started out of university studies, the government positions he occupied to advance the predation goals, the churches he set up to cover the murderous predation undertaking, the diplomatic representations he fulfilled to defend the predation, the actual management of mining operations and logistics, the recruitment and supervision of Adamas Kagita and other war lords, the vast financial management cover provided over financial transactions with go between businessmen, money bagman for the top echelon of the enterprise, money laundering schemes, wire transfer frauds, tax evasion frauds, counterfeiting frauds, Ponzi scheme frauds, all to enable the financial flow of funds from the predation terrain to various bank accounts around the world. The Reverend had ensured that every transaction that benefits or enhanced the predation was fulfilled satisfactorily. For the first seven years, he acted as the Managing Director of the enterprise with three main clients residing in Kinshasa, Kigali, and Kampala. He was slowly demoted by younger vultures accountable directly to the three top member of the enterprise. Reverend Drago was in fact happy to be demoted as he would no longer be in service of the three bosses who were becoming routinely unsatisfied by the unequal sharing of the predation overall rent. He decided that those three bosses were far away from the realization of his prime motivation of setting up the Hima Empire. His supervision became untenable. He got himself disengaged, assuming the role of honorary Managing Director only in case there were major crises among the top echelon members. Reverend Drago got literally tired of the constant bickering at the top. Reverend Drago had a major drawback. He did not trust the intelligence service within the enterprise. He considered the intelligence service as self-serving political manipulation, not entirely focused on the realization of the Hima Empire. He found it not fact based and stayed away from it. He also had great suspicion of the American agents lurking around and had no respect for their work. The American agents were in fact, according to Reverend Drago, sabotaging the means and the goals of the Hima Empire. His constant access to the American agents was designed to monitor and to undermine their activities geared to sabotage his priority.

Two major supervision failures identified by the enterprise surprised him. The first was when President KD inserted his own folks to run parallel mining and logistic operations. These folks were supposedly under his supervision. Their disturbing undertaking that went as far as antagonizing the corporate end users was blamed on the Reverend Drago management style. The second failure came when Reverend Drago was surprised by the displacement of Adamas Kagita to the US. He never understood the reason why the enterprise top echelon agreed to his displacement. He was upset when he was told that Adamas Kagita was exceeding his authority under his supervision. He suspected that this was coming from the American side. Reverend Drago was in fact satisfied with Adamas' delivery. He appreciated his involvement in consolidating the mining operations and logistics. Hie ignored his sadistic trait, his wanton behavior, his sex slave camp, his razing of many villages antagonizing and displacing thousands of people, most from different ethnics irrelevant to establishing Hima Empire. He defended Adamas while the top echelon was looking for ways to get rid of him if not just to kill him when he was becoming largely unaccountable and unpredictable. However, when Adams was displaced to the US with a fake Ugandan identity, he blamed Reverend Drago. He became highly suspicious of Reverend Drago all the years he was in the US. Every time Reverend Drago showed up for a meeting in the US, Adamas really thought that he came to kill him. When he included Reverend Drago on top of the list of culprits, it was an act of revenge he was exercising when he was asked to go against all those, he believed, betrayed him. Adamas never thought that Reverend Drago was going to be sent in the package. He was shocked to learn that he was in Guantanamo. He confided to the law students, members of his defense team, that Reverend Drago was about to learn the betrayal from the top echelon the same way he learned his betrayal when he came to the US.

In the great circle of betrayal evolving in the enterprise, Reverend Drago assumed his. He decided that the enterprise was no longer an undertaking serving the pressing goals of the Hima Empire. The enterprise has becoming, according to Reverend Drago, a source of rapid enrichment for the top echelon members and their family members. The flagrant representation in Forbes magazine of the growing enrichment of DRC President KD and his family proved his point. President KD arrived in Kinshasa in 1997 wearing rebel yellow military boots, now his travels, however short, required the most expensive high technology private jets. President KD had never set feet in any alley in Kinshasa for a long time. He could not name any of the depressing slums of Kinshasa he never visited. Reverend Drago could no longer trust President KD in the drive to implement Hima Empire as he was expected to do. These ridiculous eccentricities may not be noticed in Kigali or Kampala, but at the same time and in the two cities the political leadership families were enjoying the highest forms of living luxury incompatible with the sacrifices needed to establish the Hima Empire. The enterprise money may be used in sprucing, cleaning, and raising few high-rise buildings in Kigali, the capital of Rwanda, but Reverend Drago did not recognize in these superficial steps as concrete steps to advance the setup of the Hima Empire in DRC territories. Because of that deep betrayal, Reverend Drago had to take steps to undo the enterprise profiteering scheme. He was going to open the big doors over many of the enterprise's major secrets he was privy to. He was going to blow over their international financial schemes to hoard huge amounts of money in remote banking accounts around the world, at least what he was supervising when he was the facto Managing Director of the enterprise about seven years ago. He knew that the top echelon must have managed to move their financial cards now, but a bit of financial forensics should help to trace their funds transfers and to determine the status of their money laundering schemes. Reverend Drago knew how difficult and time consuming it was to execute the transfers of their huge amounts of laundered money and above all the utmost secrecy that was needed to accomplish these transfers. Reverend Drago had maintained a huge database accounting for the top echelon family and contact names at the time. He brought that list with him, saved in a flash drive for the very purpose he knew he was ready to engage in. Just as the three Colonels in the list of culprits, he was going to throw himself at the mercy of the American court in exchange for these financial transactions.

CHAPTER 40

GUANTANAMO GLORIES

The judicial invitation that DA O'Grady had designed paid off behind all expectations entertained by the prosecution, defense teams, the US government legal, military, diplomatic and judicial support provided at all levels. With few exceptions, all the culprits in the preliminary conversations they had with a slew of interviewers, agreed that the events, facts, statements, and their involvement were concurred with what has been documented in various voluminous documentations, accumulated in various forms accusing them of an amazing array of human rights violations since 1997. In plain legal terms, with few exceptions, the culprits pleaded guilty for committing the violations that were leveled against them. Also, all expressed the same will to provide more incriminating events, facts, and statements against individuals higher up the chain of command in exchange for lighter sentence and promise at the end of their incarceration to be afforded exile opportunity in countries outside the Great Lakes region.

The collection of the interviews became a substantial intelligence gathering exercise for the three teams. The collection extended to another voluminous accumulation of incredible revelations of the enterprise engagement, well beyond what Reverend Stanislas had received for the last fifteen years or so. The collection clarified a lot of obscure events and facts that have puzzled those who spent their waking hours around what was going on in Eastern DRC. Langley agents, present in Guantanamo, busied themselves to vet most of these revelations. They were, at times, surprised by the depth, variety and change of what they assumed to be their current reading of Eastern DRC events. They were given the first crack to decipher the revelations before the other teams got engaged in interviewing the culprits. In some special cases, they sanitized the revelations into documents very quickly translated into classified information according to the precepts of Classified Information Procedure Act (CIPA), therefore preempting the members of prosecution and defense teams from touching these delicate subjects.

At the end of the preliminary collection and the Langley vetting, the government highest representative informed the prosecution and defense teams that the Statement department had started engaging the UN ICC contacts to initiate a process whereby some culprits would be transferred to the Hague in Netherlands where they would start in a modified court format to answer for the accusations, they have already pleaded guilty to. They culprits included Commander Mono and the two other generals who had antagonized the corporate end users as special agents of President KD operating parallel mining and logistic operations in the area. The American side had no longer need to hold them in Guantanamo, and they were bringing nothing of value in Adamas dossier, they did not know him.

The colonels will remain in Guantanamo a little longer. They knew Adamas very well back in the Eastern DRC during his involvement in mining and logistic operations and could add a few unknown events or facts in Adamas' dossier. The Major and Captain officers were quite a set of exceptions. Conversations with these officers had already revealed that Adamas was after them for a personal vendetta. Keeping them in Guantanamo was going to serve nobody purpose but Adamas'. The State Department was making arrangement to get them assigned into one of the UN peacekeeping forces around the world, preferably not in Africa where Kigali had spread its military contingents in many trouble areas. It was proposed that their intelligence service on behalf of UN forces in Eastern DRC will serve them well in the UN peacekeeping staging area on the island of Cyprus. They were no longer in the motel-looking building where the culprits were kept. Under the UN full honorable army officer rank, they disappeared and were relocated to the exclusive compound reserved for US military officers assigned for duty in the Guantanamo base. They were no longer invited prisoners. They stayed in a comfortable officer bungalow waiting for a coordinated flight to Cyprus. They were provided with all military base amenities reserved for visitor officers of their rank.

Likewise, the businessmen, also scheduled to go to be incarcerated in the Hague, were being kept in Guantanamo for much longer time DA O'Grady suspected that among all the culprits, the businessmen were holding even more critical intelligence over the top echelon of the enterprise. They assumed a very vague and frightened posture during the preliminary conversations from the time they arrived in Guantanamo. They seemed to communicate in an obscure language code among themselves as if comparing notes and advising each other what to say and how to say. It was becoming obvious to DA O'Grady a new strategy was required to get them to spill important beans about the higher up in the chain of command. Their conversations were generally muted with a few discretionary selective slips that never went anywhere, only to be reversed with a strong sense of denial. Langley agents advised that they were playing games holding up for the biggest and highest trade-off. They concurred that a new strategy to engage them was needed but not to their favor. They suggested that the prosecution threaten them with severe higher incarceration penalty. At the end, the Raleigh teams opted to play a wait and see scheme. They knew that Reverend Drago was resigned and ready to mount his revenge It will be more productive to get him spill the beans and to confront the go-between businessmen with his revelations.

The interview with Reverend Drago took on a full display of a court proceeding. Professor Juliana Fama, Adamas lead defense lawyer was going to lead the interview assisted by Ludmilla Garrov, the prosecution associate. In the conference room arranged for the circumstances, DA O'Grady was sitting on the same table as well as Pascal Bodari from the Immigration Services Investigation Unit and Reverend Stanislas. The Government representative from the Attorney General Staff of National Security Affairs was occupying another table with a young Associate counsel. Langley team occupied a table in the back and was invited to alert the assembly of any Classified Information intrusion.

Professor Fama introduced herself and gave the purpose of the interview. Reverend Drago directly raised a point of order:

"If I may, this assembly looks like a court proceeding. Is this a court interrogation or an interview as I was told I was going to submit myself. Ladies and Gentlemen, you should know that below this Reverend costume, I am a full-time lawyer and I participate in many court proceedings in DRC, Uganda, Kenya, Zimbabwe, Namibia and South Africa and I have been admitted at each of these countries bar associations. So, I must know at this time whether you are conducting a court proceeding or a conversation interview. You have prepared this setting as a court. Can you tell me who is the Presiding Judge here? I heard that the Judge presiding over Adamas case was Judge Alvaro Lopez. He did not introduce himself so far, is he here? What about my very good friend Adamas Kagita, where is he? Is he here as well?"

"Again, my name is Professor Juliana Fama, I am Adamas defense lawyer. I, I am sorry, all of us here in this conference room are very well acquainted with your background, your life background, your political background, your professional background and of course your legal background. You are not telling us here anything that we don't know. No, Sir! I want to remind you that you have signed a legal document before leaving Kinshasa inviting you to come to US territory and you accepted every provision included in that invitation and I repeated you signed willfully without any legal reservation of mind or thought. That document stipulated that you were invited to answer statements made against or for you regarding a chain of events, facts and statements concerning you and that were raised by a defendant named Adamas Kagita and or mentioned in many public and classified documents that were shared during the court proceeding in the legal case involving the same defendant Adamas Kagita. The invitation was clear in that if the statements collected during the interviews we are going to conduct concur or validated the precedent statements then you would be liable in the courts of law here in the US or abroad to answer to these statements which would amount then to accusations of grave violations of human rights in DRC. If these statements are neither concurred nor validated, then you would be free to return to where you were invited from or a third-party country of your choice. Every person invited in this package is answering to the same set of criteria which were attested and duly signed. It is very astonishing that in your case, being, I believe, the only invitee with extensive professional legal experience and exposure, you come here and started raising issues of your status and court venue at this time at this place. I would have gone to a great length to explain what I just say for any one of them but not for you. Not that I must or need to make an exception, but you know better. Unless you want to waste our time and we are very much disposed to stop these interviews and send you back to where you have obviously resolved not to want to go back when you signed the invitation documents. Reverend Drago, what is it going to be, interviews or return to DRC?"

"Interviews, Maam, I just wanted to refresh my mind around my presence here."

"I thought so! And I sincerely hope that this will be the last time we are going to go over your status here."

"Understood!"

"Just to be as comfortable as possible during this session, how do you want us to address you?"

"Reverend Drago would be fine."

"Thank you!"

"This interview would be a bit chronological, taking you from current time back to when you join this business of predation in Eastern DRC."

"Professor Fama, I must take exception to your qualification of my involvement. I never consider that I am involved in any business of predation whatsoever. I am involved in the restoration of an empire that predominated in the Great Lakes region of the region. And you know what I am talking about.it is the Hima Empire. I am not making this up. Check your own historical utility, I mean Wikipedia, you will see that this empire or kingdom had been in place since the fifteenth century. I am of the venerable opinion that all that has been going on in that part of the world had the unfortunate connotation of people fighting savagely for no reason. That is a big error, the fight is for one reason, as far as I am concerned, the restoration of that empire. That is a political engagement. I would not deny that there would be collateral victims along the way. But let not muddy the overall political engagement here."

"Don't worry we will get to that later. But I must strenuously object to your fallacious attempt to casually banalize the consequences of what you call political engagement. I cannot sit here, as a professor of Law specializing in violations of human rights anywhere in the world and listen to a flagrant relativization of victims of your involvement in a political engagement. We are here precisely talking about what you just designated collateral victims from, I must repeat myself, the consequences of the murderous predation of mineral resources that abound that part of the world. Collateral victims whose number is now more than ten million dead people. I don't need to beg your decency in bringing a neutral consideration, dear Reverend Drago, I don't need to invoke a religious consideration now, yes, a neutral consideration of the consequences of this murderous predation when more than ten millions of people have died. I am sorry that, ahead of myself, I must jump to moral considerations of this legal review."

"Professor Fama, I believe that I am entitled to my own evaluation of matters at hand."

"Yes, you do, just spare me, spare us any unnecessary provocation."

"Understood! And before we get far engaged in this interview, I must ask you a permission to pray citing Revelations 12:11 which had sustained me all my life:"

"Permission granted!"

"Thank you: "And they overcame him by the blood of the Lamb, and by the word of their testimony; and they loved not their lives unto the death." Amen, Amen, Amen!"

"As I was saying before being interrupted by the tangent observation. I must take you back to a recent event that occurred in Kwazimu mines concession area at the beginning of this year. There was a delegation of legal interviewers who came to the Kwazimu mines concession area. The legal purpose of the visit was to document as best as they could Adamas Kagita involvement in the mining operations of Kwazimu mines area. Unfortunately, there were no interviews as management of mining premises prevented the interviews. The report of the event is clear about what happened that day. It stated that a Reverend Drago made the decision to prevent the interviews and ordered armed guards to chase the interviewers in three or four armored vehicles not just from the mining premises but all the way to the western borders of North Kivu province with the Maniema province. The military chase took place within more than one hundred twenty-eight kilometers or about eighty miles. Can you validate this report statement? And please explain under what or whose authority have you decided to prevent the interviews which were legally authorized by the central government in Kinshasa, scheduled and duly notified by the US Embassy by letters and digital mail to the mines operations management team? Please explain under what and whose authority have you ordered a military chase and pursuit of a team of legal interviewers in the exercise of their legal functions from the mine's concession area to the eastern borders of North Kivu? The team of the interviewers were thankfully rescued by a UN military contingent in the province of Maniema."

"The Kwazimu mines operations team delegated me to prevent the interviews, upon receiving the Embassy note. The review of the note concluded that it was vague and a fishing expedition by the interviewers. It was the management view that Adamas Kagita never had any management function in the mining operations. Admas Kagita had provided consulting support to mining operations and was duly paid for these consulting tasks. Management responded to the Embassy note and was surprised to see a delegation of more than ten people showing up at the mining operations headquarters trying to interview management people. That was overdone and I was charged to legally share management displeasure. And I did that. I cannot speak of the interviewers being chased for eight miles to the province of Maniema. Our management is not a military operation. I never heard of such a military operation."

"Reverend Drago are you saying that the event report was inaccurate, and the UN rescue operation report was also inaccurate. Are you saying that the interviewers and the UN officers have decided to create inaccurate reports over an event that never occur?"

"I never saw the reports you are talking about, I have no idea of and never saw these reports reporting these events which I am saying did not occur the way these reports convey them. When I returned to Kinshasa, I never heard of any report about these events from the Embassy folks I talked with all the time. That was the extent of my involvement."

"I see, do you remember the US embassy folks or contacts you talked to all the time to ascertain whether or not these events occurred as reported?"

"I am not here to reveal my Embassy contacts nor the confidential conversations I had with them of daily basis."

"Of course not, as someone the same Embassy contacts have designated as a primary enabler of the Eastern DRC predation in their daily diplomatic cables from Kinshasa, do you want to verify these documented cables we have collected, and we have here by date and contacts? Reverend Drago, we are very much disposed to share them if you want to see them."

"I am not interested!"

"I thought you wouldn't! Just to remind you, we are very professional in our delegation and pursuit of legal matters. Every statement made, every event revealed is backed by detailed proof. Keep this in mind as we conduct this interview session. We are not here in fishing trip, we are above all fact based."

"Still, going back to your answer, are you saying that the management of mining operations does not include any military component?"

"I would say, military protection of the mining operations, yes, there was never military offensive operation outside the mines concession area."

"What about logistics of mineral products from mining operations. They needed to be protected from the mining areas in destination to clients outside the mining operations?"

"Well as I said, mining operations are protected by a small unit of guards within the concession, when mineral products leave the concession, they are no longer management property, they become the property of clients or end users who assumed their protection."

"That is very interesting. That is not our understanding of the predation business. Anyway, you are now saying that clients and end users assumed the logistics protection, right!"

"Exactly, that is also where people like Adamas Kagita come to play. They assume the protection of mineral products when they are moving to destination."

"So, this is what you called consultation function or protection that the Adamas Kagita of the world provide."

"That is correct!"

"So, the Adamas Kagita of the world must mount armed gangs or armed militias to protect the merchandise to destination."

"But how the Adamas Kagita of the world get funded to get arms and armed transportation to execute their mission."

"Professor Fama, tell me here the US, are logistics companies asked how do they organize themselves to transport product X from point A to point Z? They are not, the only thing they want them to do is to deliver the merchandize at point Z. That is not different in Eastern DRC."

"Please tell us if you may, where was going the merchandise, the mineral product extracted in the mines concession?"

"Well, to Uganda and Rwanda!"

"Where precisely in Uganda and Rwanda?"

"To the staging warehouses at the borders with DRC?"

"So, in your business model the mineral product was transported under the protection armed gangs or militias funded by the Adamas Kagita to the staging warehouses at the borders of Uganda and Rwanda. Is that right?"

"Yes, Maam!"

"So, what was the role of successive Uganda and Rwanda funded militias in the area?"

"Were there Rwanda and Uganda military forces protecting the same logistics?"

"I don't know, you should ask these governments?"

"Now let us go back to time, when did you start getting involve in mining operations?"

"Sometime in March 2009!"

"That timing is significant, isn't it? Is it not the same time when the Kwazimu mines concession was ceded to your military-political group CNDP by the central government of Kinshasa?"

"Yes!"

"Which country funded that militia?"

"Rwanda?"

"What was the governing leadership tribe of that group?"

"It was predominantly Tutsi?"

"But why?"

"It was made up of many military people from Rwanda who have pursued the genocidaire Hutu throughout the basin of Congo river all the way to overthrow Mobutu regime in Kinshasa. The same military people retreated to North Kivu rebelled against the new DRC President!"

"Is it not the beginning of the predation of mineral resources in the area?"

"That is your interpretation!"

"No, that is your logical flow. So, when did your restoration of the Hima Empire start in that logical flow?"

"From the start, what start!"

"From the start of the return of Tutsi refugees from Uganda to taking over Kigali after the genocide of Tutsi!"

"Reverend Drago, you are all over the place in your logical flow, if I could be kind enough to call it logical. Can you help me understand your involvement, your function in the chain of events from the takeover of Kigali by Tutsi refugees to preventing the legal interviewers who were conducting legal interview over Adamas Kagita in the management of Kwazimu mines operations? Somewhere in that time frame, you worked with Adams Kagita when he grew in power, stature providing what you have designated as consulting support to Kwazimu mines where you became also a very important key management person?"

"I am glad to clarify that flow. At the end of Mobutu regime, I was a student of law in one of the DRC state universities. I am from a Tutsi family which elected to come to DRC as refugees after Rwanda 1962 independence because our political standing was being repressed. I obviously welcome the return to power of Tutsi refugees from Uganda. I supported that military campaign by every means possible. It was also the time I graduated from the law studies, and I jumped into the military-political campaign that took place from the occurrence of Tutsi genocide, the chasing of Hutu genocidaire military contingents in refugees camps in Eastern DRC, to the chasing of the same through the western fronts to the overthrow of Mobutu regime in Kinshasa, to the brief transition power in Kinshasa, through the Rwanda military retreat to Eastern RDC to the RCD rebellion against the central government, through the assassination of President Mze Kabila and the advent of his son as a new president, through the Sun City gathering to set up the governing status of the third republic, the presidential election of 2006. Personally, as far as I was concerned, I was motivated throughout by the restoration of the Hima empire to have a Tutsi dominated nation. It was obvious the Tutsi have just suffered a genocide to lose close to a million people. I did not believe that this community could survive in any other independent country with other tribes but in a region for Tutsi only. In my view and opinion this required the restoration of the old Tutsi Kingdom including two Congolese territories Rutshuru and Masisi and three and four territories in Rwanda with majority Tutsi in the forest plains from Rwenzori Mountain. Everything I have done was to ensure that this setup of the Hima empire restoration comes to fruition. Whatever was going on in the Tutsi dominated government in Kigali must gear to make this happen. I was trusted to manage the mining operations to support that goal. You have seen me joining all kinds of operations in Kinshasa including the central government positions for that purpose and only that purpose. I was never interested in Kigali staging government because I am not interested in the Rwanda government where the Hutu would remain a majority. I have no interest in pretending to push for a peaceful coexistence governing Rwanda with Hutu, it won't going to happen in thirty, fifty or hundred years. Tutsi will never match democratically the Hutu majority. So, all prospects of coexistence and reconciliation in a democratic Rwanda are a mirage as far as I am concerned. That is just a simple mathematical reality. All that is going on today in Kigali is a political mirage. And the current Tutsi political leadership knows it. I rather take my chances in DRC with four hundred fifty tribes where they would never been any particular tribe hegemony."

"Your view, however honest, does not rest on honest practical grounding. You have executed every predation program delegated to you. I don't see any Hima empire priority executed when you have served the current three political leaderships in Kinshasa, Kigali, and Kampala more tuned to enjoy the rent from the brutal plundering of coltan and gold from North Kivu with the like of Adams Kagita. How can you explain it?'

"It looks like we are going in full circle about that predation business. I am afraid your reading of the events in North Kivu is most of the time biased and inaccurate. As you said it, you love to build your analysis from the present back to the past. I rather go from the past to the present. What do we have in 1994 after the genocide of Tutsi in Rwanda. Well, we had in North Kivu three major Congolese tribes, Nande, Hunde and Nyanga living with small ethnic tribes transplanted from Rwanda, Hutu, and Tutsi. We are talking about the last years of the Mobutu regime with very weak state authority. In 1994 we saw Hutu militias responsible for the genocide fleeing toward or being chased toward Eastern Congo with a very large Hutu refugee population. This is when the North Kivu conflict started. I have already shared where I stood during that drive. I stood with the invading Tutsi dominated military contingent all the way to Kinshasa. By the way you certainly heard of Congolese rebellious military contingent which came along. Those were people tired of Mobutu dictatorship and joined the Rwandan invaders to topple the dictatorship. They included the young rebels called "Kadogo" who were from various Congolese tribes in the area including the Nande, Hunde, and Nyanga in North Kivu. When the invading rebellious rag tag army won the war and there was regime change in Kinshasa, conflicts started between Rwandan Tutsi leadership and Congolese ethnic tribe leadership. The Rwandan military retreated to the Great Kivu area. Here again, ethnic tensions over resources flared up to the present. Remember the native Congolese ethnic groups lived of agricultural resources, planting and selling a slew of agricultural products and raising cattle. The large Hutu and Tutsi population arrival increased a fierce competition over land and other resources. This was also the time when on top of gold, North Kivu became a major source of coltan. Different armed groups and militias started fighting over the control of these resources, leading to extreme violence and population displacement."

"This is my version of the chain of events that took place, and you cannot deny it. I must take the opportunity at this time to rebut the lie that is constantly propagated as if the Tutsi entity was the only one-armed entity busy killing or displacing all other entities. That is far from the truth. The reality was that the political leadership in Kigali made its priority to protect the Tutsi entity in the area because it was a minority entity and it also wanted to set up the presence of Hima empire, however clumsily and not as efficiently as some of us expected. As far as protecting the Tutsi minority tribe in the area, I must confess that Kigali was firm in that goal. It extracted our military leaders back to Rwanda every time they were targeted for arrest as in case of Laurent Nkunda and many others. This is also the opportunity for me to state another fallacy around the predation business. It is alleged that only the Tutsi dominated government in Kigali was the sole beneficiary of the mineral resources rent from North Kivu. At the highest level, there is a trio supervision led by the political leaderships in Kinshasa, Kigali and Kampala which share the rent. Below this rank, you have the go-between businessmen who are generally people with non-African background. They are mostly from American, European, and Asian background. I guess Black African, owners of raw material cannot be trusted with the primary trade of their own resources. I did not make these rules, the top Bosses abide by them. I heard that you got few go-between businessmen invited. I did not recognize the ones I used to deal with on behalf of the top political echelon. That is another story. Below the businessmen you got the war lords and the mining operations management folks. Now the war lords come from all the belligerent tribes, some are Nande, Hunde, Nyanga, Hutu and of course Tutsi. These people are the ones controlling agricultural, mining, and logistic operations. They are the ones representing the tribe populations and making money out of agricultural plantations, cattle raising, artisanal mining operations. They are the ones who are protecting various natural resources caravans leaving North Kivu going through Uganda and Rwanda to far away markets. They are the ones with contacts with the political leaderships in Kinshasa, Kigali, and Kampala. Some of them are representing their tribes in the Parliament and Senate in Kinshasa, wheeling and dealing political transactions with the President. A lot of them have been bombarded into military high-level positions to precisely control the flow of the so-called predation business on location. I ran into them on daily basis in the fields, in Kinshasa, and in Goma and in other occasions when there major political and military flareups."

"My dear lady, I am sharing all this to let you understand the major dynamism that you underestimate in the so-called predation business equation, and that is Tribalism or Ethnicity. That is a major driver in politics in Africa and never forget this."

"I appreciated your long lecture about the North Kivu conflict. But I am getting the feeling that you are underreporting your prominent involvement in these events. And precisely how you met the likes of Adamas Kagita."

357

"I don't know how many times I must state the nature of functions that somebody like Adamas Kagita performed. He was the equivalent of war lord. Unfortunately, he had no tribal following. He became an enforcer for the mining and logistic operations. He was required to clear obstacles against our mining and logistic operations. Were there collateral victims in his functions, of course, how many, I cannot tell as he only reported the result that obstacles to mining and logistic operations were cleared. He was well compensated for that function. Whatever he was engaged in outside that function was of zero interest to me."

"Interesting, Reverend Drago, if you heard, for instance, that Adamas has raided two villages to make room for artisanal mining operations, killing say two hundred people in the process and displacing two thousand people, how would you react to, how should I call it, obstacles clearing execution?"

"Sheer speculation, your honorable Counsel, speculative! That observation should not be part of your interview. I know your legal limits!"

"Sorry, Reverend Drago, that was an event well documented in a UN report about the village named Hicazaragua, located about 37 miles from Kwazimu mines concession area, on April 24, 2009. You welcomed Adamas Kagita at the mine's headquarters office the next day. Do you remember the event?"

"I don't!"

"You cannot or you don't want to remember the event. You and Adamas became owners of the artisanal mining operations in the area after you cleared the two villages. Do you still not remember, Reverend Drago!?"

"No, I still don't remember!"

"I get the impression that you are never going to admit to any major transgression you have committed while executing a long variety and series of major human rights violations. And I also get the impression that you strongly believe that you will be protected by the political leaderships you served very well in Kinshasa which would not dare raise a finger over you as a well-protected Tutsi element in close contact with Kigali you have also served very well for so long and ready to extract you diplomatically as a Tutsi subject from any major human rights infraction. My question now is why did you accept the invitation to come here? Is this got anything to do with your resignation, your delusion around your Hima empire deception with Kigali for messing up your Hima empire priority"?

"Now you are getting to the core of me accepting the invitation to come here. You are right when you say that no Hima empire priority is being executed when I have been surrounded by three political leaderships keener to remain in power using every political deception in the books, and worse enriching themselves and their families. They are sacrificing the main goals of restoring the Hima empire. True, the political leadership in Kigali has no choice but to pretend to support the Hima empire goals but it must answer to external forces which have maintained its powers, the main beneficiary end users of what you call the predation business. I have repeatedly reminded the powers that be in Kigali that the main end users would run to Kinshasa and close the current financial vans if they can set up a reliable puppet ready to enhance the logistics of Coltan and Gold from North Kivu. The minute they would, there would be no need to stop over in Kigali or Kampala if they can negotiate profitably their provisioning from Kinshasa. And believe me, they also want to stop very quickly all that worldwide condemnation that is directly against them because of the murderous logistics they have been enjoying for the last twenty years now. The good reason I have accepted the invitation is simple, I have been resigned to not seeing much improvement in the current status quo for the Hima empire goals. I don't want to continue supporting a losing proposition. I am prepared to blow it up now."

"Woooooah, that is another honest statement I heard from you today.!"

"And I mean it!"

"And you want to do this, without any penalty for things you indulge in the past, for major grave human rights violations in the past!"

"Absolutely none!"

"And what make you think that you would not be held accountable and not to be penalized?"

"You still need to control these three current political leaderships in the Great Lakes region, and I am the only one to serve each one of them heads on gold platter and you know that?"

"Oh no, we don't"

"Oh yes, you do!"

"You sound very well prepared!"

"Try me!"

"As a lawyer, you know that we are not going to accept anything from you that would not have any significant impact in the judicial prosecution of Adamas case. I must also let you know that you will be severely punished if there is a slight indication that you are here under the false pretense to help your former political leadership or mentors, like a double agent. Do you understand where we are going here?"

"I do!"

"Let me repeat what I have just said; so far you are under various diplomatic protection, and we have said that we will grant you that. But the minute you start to cross that line, you will enter the other world of espionage where double talk can land you into American harsh judicial jurisdiction and where you would become our target liable to serious legal liability with zero reservation. Am I clear on this, do you understand what I am saying?"

"I do!"

"Before we proceed, I have few tests I must submit to you, and you must first agree to submit to this test."

"I agree!"

"What was the purpose of your last visit in the US?"

"I came to see Adamas Kagita to share with him the grave reservation the enterprise had about him going to a full-blown trial about his Ugandan identity. The collective political leadership wanted Adamas to quickly admit to a fraud and to accept whatever immigration penalty to get him expel from the US and be done with the stay in US."

"Was there a reason why the collective political leadership was so eager for Adamas to admit to an entry fraud into the US territory?"

"Yes, there was a very practical reason. The collective political leadership was very suspicious from the beginning when the US intelligence service insisted that Adamas Kagita changed his identity from Congolese to Ugandan to enter the US with a residency visa. The collective political leadership thought Adamas Kagita had such a long rapt sheet of human rights violations he could be exposed to a gross element of blackmail and most likely to reveal the enterprise inner core business."

"What kind of exposure Adamas can possibly present that the collective leadership was so bent out of shape?"

"To tell the truth, it was all speculation from the collective leadership. I was sent on fishing trip?"

"But you knew more than Adamas about the enterprise money business, why were you selected to go see him?"

"When I was asked to come see Adamas, I did not think much of it. But I was given a list of people to verify if Adamas had ever talked to them during his travels abroad or during his forays in Goma. That list raised a few eyebrows with me. I recognized few very lower-level contacts in the enterprise money laundering schemes spread all over the world banking. I knew that Adamas never had the expertise or skills set to get involved in these very sophisticated transactions. That is when I start suspecting that the collective leadership had sent me to the US to see how much exchange I would have with Adamas and his American handlers. When I saw Adamas in that house in Virginia I was also very alarmed. I can see that the house was entirely bugged with microphone listening devices. The worst thing came when I noticed that Adamas was also wearing a listening device under his jacket and was sweating profusely for no reason at all, not willing to touch his food. It was a bit ridiculous. I kept my cool throughout. But I left the house the first chance I got after a very tense conversation with Adamas when he proclaimed that he was going to go ahead with a vigorous legal defense. That was also the first time I heard Adamas stating unequivocally that he was abandoned by the enterprise after all the assurances I have given him all along. I knew that I was in the short betrayal list of the enterprise when I came back, I was asked if I knew anyone in the famous list. I had a very tense conversation with the main Kigali contacts. I was brusquely removed from the management of enterprise money laundering schemes. I bid my time keeping the same low loyal profile and executing the same activities until I accepted the invitation. By the way, for your information I was the first to cross the Malebo pool from Kinshasa to Brazzaville at around two in the morning under very dense fog."

"By the way, we also got the list from Adamas listening device. Are you saying that these contacts are not worth to be in the enterprise prime listing?"

"That is correct."

"Do you have a better list?"

"That is what I have been trying to tell you, but it comes with a price, of course."

"I see, you know and realize, the list, your list must be vetted as well to evaluate and to match your price."

"I think our friends from Langley team and the government representative will take it over at this time."

The exchange between Reverend Drago and Professor Fama was earth shaking to say the least. The prosecution and defense were very aggravated by the assurance that Reverend Drago projected in his answers of a politically and judicially untouchable beyond any penalty for his long legal series of human rights violations in Eastern DRC. Both teams were extremely annoyed to sit in the conference room and to listen to this man admitting to all kinds of crimes and going about them unpunished and worse making judicial demands about the final disposition of his standing. After the Langley team and the government representative cohort departed, there was deafening silence from the folks from Raleigh. It took DA O'Grady all his last grace to say something to both teams.

"Well, ladies and gentlemen, I take full responsibilities for having dragged you to this far away corner of US territories only to witness what I am assuming in your hearts and souls to be a terrible perversion of justice. I don't know about you, I have sat in court before when I saw a presumed guilty party walk out of the court because the jury had decided otherwise despite the prosecution vigorous legal presentation to incriminate the guilty party. I lived with that and went home to blame myself for having failed to convince the jury. But I lived with that lack of conviction because the judicial process took place from the beginning to the end under the supervision of a judge. Unfortunately, what we saw here is an example of what we tried not to witness back home, a stunted legal process in that a guilty party is confessing his crimes and he is not pronounced guilty, but he is not exacting a price for his freedom. That, ladies and gentlemen, hurts. But I will shock you today if I share one confidence after witnessing what I saw today. Let us not despair. We are marching toward a victory!"

"Let me explain, I worked with you the past two months to pursue the prosecution up the chain of command of the crimes the intrepid very courageous lady named Charlotte Keregi shared with my team and made the request to prosecute the guilty party of the crimes. We did it and Adamas Kagita is sitting in jail today waiting to hear the length of his sentence. After reviewing the voluminous testimony that his uncle Reverend Stanislas shared, I became agitated. I concluded that Adamas Kagita was not the only guilty party, there was a chain of command that we need to drag to court. I knew that I was shewing more than I could bite. I stood my ground. I pushed the issue to get here in Guantanamo. Today you saw why I persisted. When I said that I was shewing more than I could bite I meant it, and I knew that I had no way to set up a court venue to prosecute all those up the chain of command of the crimes we have already prosecuted. But we will be able to go back to where the prosecution should have started here in the US. Remember where it started, it started the minute Adamas Kagita set foot in the US. If Adamas has never set foot in the US, we would never have come here to Guantanamo, Adamas would not have been prosecuted for entering the US with fraudulent documents, Charlotte Keregi would never meet him in that wedding party. The trigger of this case has always been this "Adamas Kagita, a war lord criminal in that Eastern DRC, was given these fraudulent documents to come to the US". Well, ladies and gentlemen, when I exclaimed that we are marching toward the victory, I had a great premonition during the exchange we heard today, I believe that the exchange had opened venues to answer the paramount question that had animated the entire legal case about Adamas Kagita and the question is "Why the US Government provided these fraudulent documents to Adamas Kagita to come to the US?"

"Ladies and gentlemen, I sincerely believe we have started to see and to hear a bit of veil being lifted around that question and the response to that question today. No matter how you feel currently, please remember that we have pushed the issue as far as possible by our combined and persistent actions including all these legal interviews.

Maybe, just maybe we have also managed to lay the points of light to stop the horror we are witnessing in that part of the world. That will be a remarkable victory that we will cherish forever. However, the reality remains what it is, we still need to remove more veils over the cloud of mystery at hand. We still have more interviews to do, let's move our combine endeavor to more legal achievements and victories. What I shared with you is a heartfelt conviction that I wish to become a reality. I want you to take these reflections as a guide to form your own understanding and opinions of what we will see from then on. Keep your head high, you have accomplished a lot already. I want to also say, Thank you!"

The legal interviews of so-called go-between businessmen were generally disappointing. The six businessmen turned out to be in the far lower position than expected. They proved to be what Reverend Drago identified them to be, marginal and not significant as expected. They were essentially bag men posted at the border to hand deliver the crudely estimated cash proceeds in exchange for the raw material that the drivers of caravans have carried. The cash amounts were substantial, no doubt it, but they amount to below ten percent of what the go-between businessmen, sitting in quiet air-conditioned office rooms in Kigali, Kampala, Kinshasa, or Goma, in front of computer wide screens, were negotiating, in exclusive expert international trade language and format of selling and buying commodities. These go-between businessmen are never seen at the border crossings nor warehouses. Their function starts with a fax or expedition file receipt of the commodity received at the border, the commodity specification, the commodity quantity, and shipment. They take over from there and in the comfort of the same office room through their computer and communication devices using a variety of international trade applications, they determine the commodity price range, commodity rejections range and payment terms. They select and exchange with potential buyers who are also using the same devices and applications in faraway places to complete the sale. These go-between businessmen work strictly anonymously. They never carry guns.

The selected go-between businessmen did not know anything beyond the border crossing points, the border crossing time, the commodity quantity and shipment and the border warehouse where to drop the delivery. Any inquiry beyond these factors was met with a stunning silence. The reason was simple, they just did not know how and what to say. Furthermore, when they were asked whether they knew any of the people on the list that Reverend Drago checked with Adamas in his last visit in Virginia, none of them heard of these big shot players. The prosecution, defense and the government representative team were left with a grave decision, what to do with these unproductive witnesses. Under what guise to get them back to the area without any problem. Were they going to be retaliated against? They needed to get more intelligence to decide their fate. Another question that came to mind was to find out they were selected to make the list. Was the enterprise engaged to get them selected by various US agencies involved and why? Further investigation revealed that they were well known by most of the caravans' drivers and protectors who provided their names. There was obviously a mistaken assumption that they were significant enough to be selected as they were. Reverend Drago mocked that bad selection.

But the top-level go-between businessmen that were on the list that Reverend Drago mentioned to Adamas remained just as mysterious as expected. They could not be verified anywhere. Reverend Drago became convinced that they were invented by the enterprise to entrap both Reverend Drago and Adamas Kagita to confuse the US intelligence services. The genuine top-level go-between businessmen were so secretive in the service of the enterprise, they enjoyed top-level clearance to touch base with the political leaderships anytime and anyhow. They were trusted to manage large sums of money on behalf of these leaders, they prized their confidence and did all they could to cover it.

It was for the same reason that Langley team and the government team needed to take as much time and expertise to vet what Reverend Drago was proposing to deliver. It took him more than twenty years to accumulate its breath and depth. Reverend Drago knew that he was also signing his own death wish by delivering that prized intelligence. The price he expected to earn was rightful in proportion to what the US intelligence was getting. Reverend Drago knew that he was putting his family in danger. He quietly prepared his family members. First, he created a damning matrimonial circumstance to separate from his wife of twenty years through a very contentious and costly divorce that stripped him of his wealth built for more than twenty-five years. Second, he secured and established his three grown children in the US and UK with well-endowed financial assets portfolio to last them through two generations. Third, he progressively cut all contacts with acquaintances who could be adversely politically impacted by his planned evasion. He bid his time until he realized he was ready to jump into the dark side of betrayal. While the vetting of his delivery went on, Reverend Drago expressed the price in exchange as a new living identity and a peaceful life enjoying a secure lifetime financial retreat in a remote town along the Pacific coast of the republic of Costa Rica. The price was not extravagant and affordable by the standards of new secret identity. He added an alternative to that price as being established in Sao Paolo in Brazil enjoying the same secured financial retreat. The two alternatives were reviewed both as affordable.

The most interesting fact was the turnabout that Langley team and the government representative team took when they went on to vet whatever Reverend Drago started sharing in secret. They would not expose it to the legal teams. They insisted that they could not share the interview details until they were satisfied, they did not compromise the US Intelligence services. The legal teams decided to return to Raleigh to wait for the results from the vetting process. Unfortunately, weeks dragged on to a month and half. At that instant DA O'Grady suggested to Judge Lopez and Professor Fama that the government was going to come back not with the vetting process results but CIPA implications.

While DA O'Grady waited for the results from the vetting, he heard from his niece Gwendolyn who came back from the long vacation she took during the D.C. administration change. It turned out that Gwendolyn made major changes in her social and professional life. She married the economist from Brooking Institute in a private ceremony in Bali and took a very high strategic policy position with SIA, Semiconductor Industry Association in Washington D.C. Gwendolyn could not go too far from an industry she answered to daily in her previous job in the government. The US semiconductor industry was one of the world's most advanced manufacturing and R&D sectors The association represents in the capital locations where top Research and Development in semiconductor are conducted, intellectual property and chip design software providers, chip design, semiconductor manufacturing equipment and materials, and more precisely as far as Gwendolyn was concerned, semiconductor materials sourcing. The association included the big names in the industry including AMD, BROADCOM, IBM, INTEL, MICRON, NVIDIA, QUALCOMM, TEAXS INSTRUMENTS, WESTERN DIGITAL, SAMSUNG, TSMC, TOSHIBA, HONEYWELL, TRANE to say the least. Gwendolyn had prepared for this transition for a long time. She was sought after and quickly grabbed when a new administration was in place in Washington in the venerable musical chairs' routine between private and government positions only DC knows the secret of. Gwendolyn kept a steady set of eyes and ears over the legal issues portfolio surrounding the overall coltan and gold provisioning to the semiconductor industry from … Eastern DRC.

"So nice to hear from you, Uncle Timothy, my God, I heard that you won't let go of that Adamas case. I heard that you are pursuing it all the way to Guantanamo. "

"Yes, indeed, we will go wherever the truth will carry us. By the way, congratulations on your matrimonial extraordinary step with that economist from Brookings. I was disappointed not to walk you on for the wedding. That was not fair for you to prevent many relatives from attending that wedding. Could not make it to Bali. Too far really! I know we don't see eye to eye on many things politics, but that was no reason to keep me away, to keep many family members away."

"Uncle Timothy, I wanna a very simple wedding ceremony. Don't worry, I have been bombarded with many acrimonious reproaches. I am going to organize a wedding presentation as soon as the weather allows it in May. We are making the plan. You are top of my list. It will take place somewhere between Chapelle Hill and Durham, we have not decided, you will know. I am sorry for the letdown. This Grady family is just so big, my God, I learned my painful lesson. It won't happen again! Sorry! Now back to Guantanamo, I heard that you are clocking legal victory after legal victory. I also heard that the new team is cheering you on with folks from Langley. What a stupid idea! We would never allow this! You must be dealing with first year law school students from Kalamazoo State University masquerading as government legal counsels or what? I just could not believe it. I can assure you that before the big boys and ladies would get back in there and clean up the slate from the amateurs you are dealing with. They are screwing every CIPA procedure we have painful built for more than forty years! What a waste!"

"Gwendolyn, I am congratulating you on your matrimonial achievement, and all I am hearing is the downplaying of the noble engagement that the new legal team had provided us to reach the truth against the many obstructions you have built in that miserable coin of the world. I am very glad that the new legal team is not following your old obstruction way. I am all happy that the new legal team has not hidden behind the CIPA graveyard. Maybe they will get there but, in the meantime, we are getting more transparency that your old team was not able to provide. And I would dig more transparency I could get until I am stopped."

"Enjoy it as long as you can, it will be stopped very soon. Mark my word."

"I love it I don't have to hear your half-baked truth anymore, my dear niece. I still love you, Gwendolyn!"

"I still love you too, Uncle Timothy!"

The month and half prolonged vetting process was the sign that Gwendolyn was trying to convey. The dirty iceberg tip of the CIPA procedures was around the corner. The beautiful cooperation we have enjoyed with the new legal team was about to close. The SIA was about to unleash the usual legal double talks and torsions to awaken the new government to the legal business approach that its members prefer. After the talk with his niece, DA O'Grady realized that the legal teams needed to accelerate their legal engagement endeavor before the short-lived transparency door starts closing. He called up a meeting of the Raleigh entire legal staff team that was commuting back and forth between Raleigh and Guantanamo the past month. The prosecution and defense teams met in the neutral chambers of Judge Alvaro Lopez under his supervision. The DA led the meeting.

"Counsels, I urgently called this meeting because no so positive signals I have been getting around all the legal facilities the government had extended to our teams the last few weeks. I am afraid to tell you that we are about to lose these facilities. The end user corporate beneficiary of the predation had laid low for a time, not disturbing the big legal push we have exercised for a while. At the same time, the new legal team from the current administration had completed its learning curve and is getting ready to fall under the usual corporate line of scratching the business back on the international scene. For those of you wondering what I am talking about well the usual legal corporate line that every American administration takes is the one that was spelled out by the President Calvin Coolidge on January 17, 1925, when he said "The Business of America is business". President Coolidge said: "After all, the chief business of the American people is business. They are profoundly concerned with producing, buying, selling, investing, and prospering in the world." That prescription had determined most business activities conducted by American business enterprises overseas including what we have seen in Eastern DRC. While we are concerned about the human rights violations we witness there, the US government primary role and objective remains to reconcile the prosecution of these violations and the execution of business activities engaged by American business in this context. Unfortunately, corners are cut in this reconciliation and some at our distaste. That is why we have no choice but accelerate our prosecution side and close it with appropriate sentencing or referral we have developed. If we don't do it, we will be kicking ourselves for the delay we have exposed the legal prosecution we have conducted only to see the government new legal team nullify it under some unknown political pressures. What I am saying is this:

-We need to ramp up Adamas Kagita sentencing negotiations and determine what it should be and allow Judge Lopez to close the case with appropriate sentencing

-Document with the government the prosecution referrals for the culprits we are sending to the Hague ICC in Netherlands, this would be the case for the high-ranking officers, the Generals and Colonels in the culprits set.

-Assist the government in facilitating the reintegration of the Major and Captain officers in the UN Peace keeping assignments away from Africa,

-Assist the government in releasing the lower ranks go-between businessmen back to the predation theater terrain OF Eastern DRC

Counsels, those are my recommendations. If you want to update them please let me, Professor Fama or Judge Lopez know.

As you probably notice, I did not provide any recommendation about how Reverend Drago legal disposition need to take place. I must be frank and blunt with you. The government would decide his fate. The government had not seen it appropriate to appraise us of what it is planning to do. The government is in fact thanking us to have opened extraordinary venues in Reverend Drago case. Eventually it will get back to us whenever it has closed that chapter in its favor of course. I must advise you all not to wait for it. As I said above, to prevent any surprise from the government, we must speed up the implementation of these legal recommendations. The government would be reluctant to intervene in any legally binding decision that would carry the signature of Judge Alvaro Lopez. Thank you!"

CHAPTER 41
REVEREND STANISLAS FAREWELL

The urgence DA O'Grady raised in closing various legal undertakings connected with Adamas case in the court sent an urgent signal to Reverend Stanislas to return to the African Studies Center in Uppsala, Sweden. A leave that was planned to last three weeks has now dragged on to be more than three months. Reverend Stanislas shared his farewell ambivalence with the DA who was at loss to thank his crucial and expert contribution throughout the prosecution of the case. DA O'Grady also revealed that he would not have added the legal interviews process if he had not been motivated by his lecture of the voluminous testimony presented by the African Studies Center. He begged the Reverend to create redundant digital protection of his extensive data center to ensure that the crucial database saved in his center be archived in more than three distinct locations. DA O'Grady assured the Reverend that he had started to raise funds to accomplish the protection of that database to prevent any loss and to allow the timely recovery of the database anytime it will be needed. DA O'Grady told the Reverend that he was not going to say goodbye to him as he was certain that they will see each other before he had hanged his coat back home.

Reverend Stanislas shared his return plan with his niece Charlotte Keregi who surprised him with a different delighted news. She said that Reverend Patrick Chibere, "Papa Chi", Elder Pastor of the Raleigh Metropolitan Church of Our Savior, has been asked about him these last three weeks when he was commuting back and forth to Guantanamo. Charlotte did not want to reveal what he was engaged in. She was not sure whether she could reveal his whereabouts. She had him commuting to Washington D.C. Charlotte told his uncle that Papa "Chi" insisted that his uncle Reverend Stanislas could not leave Raleigh without a big thank you service from the church. Now that his uncle was returning to Sweden, she was going to talk to Papa "Chi" set up the date for the service.

Papa "Chi" and his wife made a quick reschedule of many other church services and decided to provide a big thank you service for Reverend Stanislas by the end of that week in late Friday evening ceremony. Charlotte invited Ludmilla Garrov from the DA staff office, Pascal Bodavi from the Immigration Service and the DA O'Grady who excused himself as he was scheduled to be later that end of the week in Guantanamo, with Professor Fama and the Judge Lopez, to sign off on the legal recommendations concerning the culprits from DRC. DA O'Grady had asked the teams to document these recommendations for implementation.

The farewell ceremony for Reverend Stanislas was pushed to eight thirty that evening, to give as many people as possible to return home from work and get ready for a full service at the church. To Charlotte Keregi's surprise, the church was packed. Charlotte thought that most people have grown a bit tired of the many legal churns that the legal proceedings have taken from the time she testified in the court. She underestimated the attention that these legal proceedings have raised in the community. People have followed these legal proceedings in the local papers, at least whatever was allowed to be shared publicly. In addition, Papa Chi took as a civic duty to share from time to time during his Sunday sermons the public available evolution of the same proceedings. The introvert Charlotte hardly raised this subject with anybody but Papa Chi and his wife. Her surprise was total when papa Chi, after giving the introduction prayer for the ceremony invited Charlotte to say a few words to her uncle.

"Brothers and sisters, I don't need to tell you tonight that my joy is immense. First, I want to invite you to give a standing ovation and greeting to two people who have carried this legal battle through to date. Ms. Ludmilla Garrov, Associate counsel for the DA Staff and Mr. Pascal Bodavi, also an associate counsel from Immigration Legal Services. The two lawyers have worked relentlessly with my uncle, Reverend Stanislas. I am very proud to welcome and to honor Ludmilla and Pascal to our humble church to express the full gratitude that every person you see today is extending to you two for the extraordinary contribution you brought in expediting this case. Thank you so very much!"

"Brothers and sisters, I would not lie if I say to you that this man we are honoring tonight, my dear uncle Revered Stanislas and I hardly saw eye to eye debating this legal case. My telephone exchanges every Saturday morning or so were very contentious and sometimes we hung it on each other. We were often far apart. Sometimes it looks as if I was going West from Mississippi while he was about to fly to Hawaii from Los Angeles. Sometimes I just did not want to talk to my dear uncle, thinking that he was not interested in what I wanted to accomplish. Well, let me confess in front of everyone here present, I was wrong. I was wrong because I did not know that he was the expert's expert about what I wanted to accomplish. It took two people I invited here today, Ludmilla and Paul to change my mind. These legal minds convinced me that they could not learn and advance their legal works without my uncle's contribution. And furthermore, Pascal decided to find out for himself, and he went to Sweden to discover the contribution treasure this legal team could not do without. In the process, it was also revealed to me that there was nobody in the Keregi family who had suffered more from the wanton background I wanted to get prosecute than my uncle Stanis. The funny thing, the most gracious thing I want you all to know is this, my dear uncle Reverend Stanislas Keregi never raised with me that he had suffered in the hands of the one I dare not name. My uncle never mentioned that he lost a still born baby, his wife, and his daughter in the savage hands of the one I was shocked to see that joyful wedding Saturday afternoon almost a year and half ago. Uncle Reverend Stanislas, I want you to forgive me for doubting your inner resolve, your grace in the pursuit of justice. You have elevated that pursuit to honor your family and the assembly of God-fearing brothers and sisters in this church, people who, today, have come to say thank you so very much for having renewed their faith in overcoming the devil in our land by the Blood of the Lamb. Amen, Amen, Amen!"

Papa Chi approached the lectern where Charlotte with flowing tears stood screaming "Hallelujah!". He guided her toward his uncle who embraced his niece tenderly while wiping her tears. Papa Chi returned to the lectern and proclaimed:

"Our sister Charlotte has said it all. Reverend Stanis, we are in pain to see you leave but we are forever thankful, our hearts are full of gratitude for the extraordinary contribution you extended in the never-ending fight for justice to sanctify the Blood of the Lamb, Amen!'

When Papa Chi was trying to close the thank you ceremony, Charlotte signaled to him that there were two new speech interventions that were raised: from Ludmilla Garrov and from the guest of honor, Reverend Stanislas. Ludmilla ran as quickly as she could to the lectern:

"Ladies and Gentlemen, my name is Ludmilla Garrov. Your devoted sister in Christ, Charlotte Keregi, a lady of incredible courage and who started the celebration we are enjoying today, my dear friend had already introduced me. What she forgot to mention is that we as associate counsels in the District Attorney staff have one primary obligation that is to prosecute griefs that the public brings, from the still born baby to the oldest person in town and irrespective of race, gender, or religion. We did the same for the griefs that Charlotte brought to our attention. Personally, I was skeptical about what Charlotte expected us to do and I told her so. Then I did not know, and I did not meet this lady. The more she shared her story, I was dragged without knowing it into a tale of grave injustice perpetrated against so many innocent people, and for more than ten years. That tale cannot be spun any way but to be a genocide. And I stand here to give a token of appreciation to the person who has educated all of us to call that tale nothing else but a genocide. The token of appreciation has been registered in the form of the certificate of appreciation for the awesome contribution that the Reverend Stanislas Keregi has extended to the prosecution of this case. The certificate is signed by Judge Alvaro Lopez and DA Timothy O'Grady on behalf of the District Court of Eastern North Carolina. Reverend Stanislas Keregi, thank you so very much."

Reverend Stanislas could not let this last recognition goes without an answer. He also joined the lectern.

"Brothers and sisters, my very dear niece Charlotte, Counsel Ludmilla, Counsel Pascal, Reverend Papa Chi, ladies, and gentlemen. Thank you, Ludmilla, for the certificate of appreciation from your august staff and management who have taught me a lot about the deep diversity in prosecution griefs in the US. Thank you so heartly to my niece Charlotte. As I go back to Sweden, I must find new topics we must disagree over to continue our family Saturday morning conversations. Please, do not stop calling, I always look forward to these contentious conversations during the long boring winter months in Sweden. Papa Chi and the assembly of the church, you have honored me beyond every expectation. I know that I would be coming home whenever I am asked to come back to Raleigh. I want in return to thank you all for making my stay among you the most enjoyable. I would not keep you much longer except to share what I got from my stay here in Raleigh. You know we are all guilty of judging people with our biases and prejudices. I had my significant share of them before coming to the US. From afar, we are all prisoners of what other people say about other people. I don't have to tell you that the views over America are well murky in Sweden. I brought them with me when I landed at your international airport. Charlotte had told you about our exchanges every Saturday morning. I did not give any inch in my reservations about how the cries of my niece will be received in the District Court of Law of Raleigh. She did not tell you that I saw her steps as a waste of time. I did this because of my own biases. I must confess that I was wrong. I learned very quickly that in America justice is delivered from the texts of law, not the feelings of this powerful person or that other significant person. If justice is driven by the texts of law, all of us can and would still have a prayer and a hope of seeing justice being delivered if those texts of law pursue just law. Brothers and sisters, I was not born yesterday to know that there are texts of law that are well, unjust. And I don't have to tell you that even where the texts of law are just and fair, if they are read or interpreted by a very biased judge, you will have a problem. Thankfully, I am not talking here about unjust texts of law or about the texts of law being read by a biased judge. I saw in this court here in Raleigh how the justice was delivered from objective texts of law, pushed by a prosecution team entirely driven by the spirit of justice and read and interpreted by an unbiased judge That was enlightening and gracious in my faith in justice. Going back to my previous statement of justice delivered by just texts of law, I also learned that that statement is not always obvious, because as we said it back home in Swahili, "the Truth arrives by slowly climbing the stairs while the Lie quickly flying up by the elevator". In other words, justice takes time, and that time could be long, as Paul said so divinely in Ecclesiastes 3:11 "He hath made everything beautiful in his time", justice always arrives in a shining armor, in his time. This is what I have seen in the prosecution of this case. I am carrying back that wisdom to my works in Sweden. This was true for me as a victim of wanton killings. I am now appealing to each one of you in this assembly of God in this church today. Do not give to despair because after a long wait, after a long God given time, I have seen how the truth and justice have renewed my faith in overcoming the devil in our country by the Blood of the Lamb, our Lord Jesus Christ! Amen, Amen, Amen!"

CHAPTER 42
GUATANAMO BITTER CLOSINGS

When DA O'Grady, Professor Fama and Judge Lopez met with the US government representative to deliberate over the format of indictments which were going to be forwarded to ICC in the Hague, Netherlands for prosecution of the invited culprits, they concurred over the same summary that were used for Adamas Kagita and where they applied:

A). Indictments over cases where culprits intimidated, brutalized, tortured, and killed workers and family members at odd with operating practices in coltan and gold mines he supervised,

B). Indictments over cases where culprits intimidated, brutalized, tortured, and killed workers and family members at odd with logistical practices he supervised to carry coltan and gold minerals to Uganda and Rwanda,

C). Indictments over cases where culprits led armed campaigns to raze entire villages suspected of hiding and providing shelter to self-defense militias opposed to unauthorized artisanal mining of coltan and gold in their areas.

D). Indictments over cases where culprits led kidnapping and holding in slavery bondage of minors to work in artisanal coltan and gold mines he supervised,

E). Indictments over cases where culprits led kidnapping and holding of young girls as sex workers in remote jungle camps,

F). Indictments over cases where culprits brutalized, tortured and killed recalcitrant minors and sex workers,

G). Indictments over cases where culprits led armed attacks and confiscation of dangerous caravans of coltan and gold minerals on their way to Uganda and Rwanda,

In addition, they also added indictments over cases where culprits engaged in money laundering from proceeds collected from the predation. The ICC representatives were more than pleased by the documentations that were provided to prosecute the Commander Mono and the other three Colonels and the three Generals. Their transfer was duly certified by Judge Alvaro Lopez.

In the same context the lower officers, the Major and Captain officers were also quickly transferred to the UN Peace Keeping contingent in Cyprus. There was a hold up over the return of the lower ranking go-between businessmen. They were not welcome back by the governments in DRC, Rwanda, and Uganda. They were being punished for spilling undetermined beans of the predation in Eastern DRC to the US judicial system. They would be kept in Guantanamo for a time.

Reverend Drago case remained taboo. The US government representative was adamant when answering a request by DA O'Grady. He stated that this case was being investigated and resolved at the highest level of the government strategic instances. In other words, Langley was still vetting Reverend Drago spilled beans against the enterprise top echelons. The case was being thoroughly instructed and would not be reverted to a Court legal public prosecution anywhere or any time soon.

It was noted that the vetting of spilled beans by Reverend Drago was slowing bearing fruits on the weakest link of the predation enterprise. The US government started directing its pressures over the President KD of DRC. It prevented him from running for a third term. Every other month it coordinated with the European Union in issuing a long list of economic sanctions first against the first circle of his government and army supporters, then enlarged the list including his family members and various members of his security and economic loyal members.

It was also observed that while the weakest link of the predation enterprise was being pummeled with all venues of sanctions, the other top echelons in Rwanda and Uganda were not touched. There were no sanctions directed against their closest loyal members in the army, various security instances, family or economic circles. None! It was clearly obvious that they were vigorously protected by end user beneficiaries of the predation enterprise. These end user beneficiaries always had a clear listening lobby path in the US government circle compared to the weakest link in Kinshasa who never entertained to build and feed it anyway. President KD was also convinced that the US government never forgave him when he turned East in 2008 and signed the so-called Chinese contract in the name of the DRC government and Chinese enterprises, the contract was geared to exchange DRC natural resources for the construction of development infrastructures in DRC. Unfortunately, the contract was never adequately stipulated, and President KD made the case worse when the contract had nothing to show for in terms of infrastructures development. It became obvious that the funding of infrastructures development never took place. The rent from minerals resources was confiscated to line up the pockets of President KD, his family, and cronies to the tune of billions leaving DRC as poorer as it was found in 1997 and later in 2001 when the new team took over. The absence of any visible development realization from the Chinese contract emboldened the US government to increase as much and many pressures as possible over the President KD and his administration by preventing him from running for a third term, closing all financial borrowing facilities from international western financial institutions from the like of IMF and World Bank, imposing all kinds of sanctions against the President KD, his family and cronies, imposing military arms embargoes, imposing all kinds of draconian sanctions overseeing for democratic reforms. All these restrictions over DRC pale in face of all anti-democratic steps that President KD partners in the predation of Eastern DRC, from Rwanda and Uganda, continued to lead and impose in their own countries. They were never significantly reproached or chastised over their dictatorial steps. The draconian imposition, over DRC compared to Rwanda and Uganda, from the US government of the policy of two standards and two measures regarding the Eastern DRC predation was at its highest glaring hypocritical display.

It was under that nebulous cover that the Raleigh team returned home with an aggravated sense of justice expended at piece meal with shameful gaps large enough to bury all the judicial inequities that have challenged the march toward justice for all from the birth of the republic of the United Staes of America. The team members returned quietly to their unfulfilled judicial functions for the next four months. They swallowed their pride during their now baptized regular four p.m. "Friday Bourbon Drain Club" waiting for the final government legal closure over the now intertwined cases of Reverend Drago and his disloyal lieutenant Adamas Kagita.

That wait was over when there was a note from the successor to Mrs. Gwendolyn O'Grady Mendelssohn's function on the staff of the US Attorney General. The note was addressed to Judge Alvaro Lopez and read:

Mr. Frank Dillon III
Associate Attorney General, National Security Division
Office of the Attorney General
Federal Government Office
Washington D.C USA.

Re: Legal Meeting Review

Honorable Judge Alvaro Lopez
Judge of the United States District Court for the Eastern District of North Carolina
Federal Courthouse
310 New Bern Avenue
Raleigh, N.C

Dear Honorable Judge,

This is to advise you that I will come to your office on Thursday of the following week to provide an important confidential government communication regarding the legal disposition of the legal cases we have reviewed at the U.S. Navy Base of Guantanamo during the past six months.

Please advise and invite only relevant Court Officers associated with these cases to attend this meeting review.

Sincerely,

Mr. Frank Dillon III, Associate Attorney General, National Security Division

Judge Alvaro Lopez promptly shared the note with DA O'Grady and Defense Attorney Professor Fama. Both agreed to attend the meeting review. As they arrived at the chambers of Judge Lopez, they were surprised to be welcomed by Judge Lopez who shared the government meeting review protocols. They must attend the meeting with no communication devices, no note taking instruments, devices, stripped of their attached cases guarded in the Judge's office. Two federal guard officers stripped them of these devices. Mr. Dillon II finally showed up to start the meeting.

"Honorable Judge Alvaro Lopez, honorable Counsels, I must apologize for the drastic protocols we have applied for this meeting review. As you will learn shortly, the protocols dictated for this meeting are a bit unusual but necessary for the disposition of the cases at hand. We have already disposed of most of the cases we have reviewed in Guantanamo. We have concurred with having disposed of these cases unless there is any objection at this time. I heard that there is no objection, I must assume that the dispositions registered at the time closed them for our purposes. There are two remaining cases we need to review today over Reverend Drago and Adamas Kagita. I know that the final disposition of Adamas Kagita is contingent to the disposition of the case regarding Reverend Drago. I am glad to tell you that the government is entirely satisfied with the provision that Adamas Kagita was supposed to fulfill in the Reverend Drago case. The government agreed to the fact that Adamas Kagita has fulfilled his bargain. The government is presently giving permission to the Raleigh judicial team to execute whatever was agreed regarding the sentencing of Adamas Kagita based on his fulfillment. That is essentially the bulk of the government confidential communication I intended to share with you. "

"Honorable Judge Alvaro Lopez and honorable Counsels as far as the disposition of the case of Reverend Drago the Government was restraint to communicate this to you under the stipulation of drastic protocols applied herein: Reverend Drago has been put under the Federal Witness Security Program (WITSEC). Its core element is the secret and permanent relocation with identity change offered to witness for providing key elements to the security of the nation. This is as much I was assigned to tell you at this time, Lady, and gentleman."

"Honorable Judge Alvaro Lopez and honorable Counsels, this concludes my government confidential communication. Do you have any question?"

There was a deafening silence in the conference room broken by DA O'Grady.

"Honorable Counsel Dillon III, there is one important question that has not been answered in this review by the government, the question remains for this Court, why Adams Kagita was brought here in the US by the Government of US?"

"Honorable DA, I believe that question has been answered by the Immigration Services. The Government never brought Adamas Kagita into the US, he entered the US territory fraudulently and he has been stripped of the official status that he had earned fraudulently. That was what the Immigration Court had decided. In addition to that this same court had found him guilty of major human rights violations and you are about to sentence him on that account. Am I missing something?"

"Honorable Counsel Dillon III, Adamas Kagita never requested to come to the US. Somewhere along the line he was convinced to come under the threats of being killed by the same people he had served in despicable human rights violations. His fate was sealed in Eastern DRC a long time ago before he heard of Raleigh, North Carolina. Honorable Dillon II, the prize was never Adamas Kagita, a worthless third string killer, the real prize was always Reverend Drago who told us clearly that he would never pay for the crimes of predation he led because he was going to rat for the top echelon of the criminal enterprise. "

"Honorable DA O'Grady, if we were in the court proceeding, I would have shout "Pure Speculation"! I would not do that because I have a lot of respect for the Honorable Judge Alvaro Lopez and this august gathering. By the way. I did not come here to debate the US government policy which I represent at this time. If you are not satisfied with the government review and Reverend Drago's entry into witness program, you know the process. You can appeal against the entire procedure we went through, and I wonder how and in what court! While you proceed with that venue, I must remind you that you made the request to conduct the legal interviews in Guantanamo Naval Base, you drove the interview procedure from the beginning to the end with the outstanding criminal references to the International Criminal Court to the Hague, Netherlands, do you remember that? Now you are raising speculatively requests over matters that have been classified by the Government of the US, you must realize, under CIPA procedures. You can also go the way of CIPA, yet I fail to see on what ground! I certainly would suggest that you would be free and allowed in about forty to fifty years to read the classified documents that motivated this government action about Reverend Drago. In the meantime, with Judge Alvaro Lopez's permission, I declare this meeting review closed.

Thank you, Honorable Judge Alvaro Lopez, and honorable Counsels.'

The next day on Friday, Judge Alvaro Lopez, DA O'Grady, and defense attorney Professor Fama met to decide on the final sentencing of Adamas Kagita who received fifteen years of jail time. Adamas was going to be reminded to Butner Federal Correction Institution Medium facilities in North Carolina. His defense lawyer Professor Fama provided Adamas with the news, insisting that the reduction in sentencing from twenty years to life was appropriate after what the government got from Reverend Drago. Professor Fama added that with good behavior, Adamas could be out in about seven years. At the time of his release, he would be expected to be sent back to DRC or another country of his choice. Adams requested to see his wife and kids for the last time before starting his jail time and to get his family expatriate back to Eastern DRC. The requests were granted by Judge Alvaro Lopez. DA O'Grady did not say a word and remained sullen throughout the case closing review.

EPILOGUE

Less than three months later, DA O'Grady submitted his retirement and resigned his District Attorney function after more than thirty-two years of continuous District Attorney leadership at the Eastern District Court of North Carolina. He signed up as Research Fellow Adjunct Professor at the University of North Carolina reporting to Professor Fama. He also joined Professor Fama in the law offices of Braxton Associates to be initiated in representing human rights violations clients.

About a year after his retirement, Counsel O'Grady took upon himself to send a very confidential letter to the members of the prosecution team in the case of Adamas Kagita. He included Counsel Ludmilla Garrov, Associate Pascal Bodavi, Reverend Stanislas Keregi, with copy to Judge Alvaro Lopez, and Professor Fama, as individual recipients.

The letter read as follows:

"Dear Prosecution Member,

I am deeply remorseful for having led the prosecution team in Case No. 56397, "US vs Jefferson Okito/Adamas Kagita" in the Eastern District Court of North Carolina, in Raleigh.

I am taking the time to share what has bothered me a lot regarding the prosecution of this case against Adamas Kagita. I don't have to repeat that my judicial goal was to reach the highest echelon members of the predation in Eastern DRC. The prosecution team knew who they were but were prevented from reaching them for purely political reasons. After extensive legal research, it has become evident that the painful legal redress sought by the prosecution team in the case was being manipulated, from the beginning, by the government of the US in that remote African region only to enforce another US convoluted strategic design. At the end, the prosecution team's failure to achieve the intended legal redress and my engagement in this failure had motivated my retirement and resignation from what I love above all, the delivery of equal and fair justice among our law-abiding people.

After further analysis, review and maybe speculation, I must submit to a final professional obligation to share with you my conclusion and answer to the crucial question that has driven the entire case from the beginning: "Why Adamas Kagita was brought here in the US by the Government of US?"

My answer and conclusion are for your own evaluation according to what I have determined to be the main driver of the US government objective in this case:

"Our government wanted to create a situation whereby the political leadership partners in the Great lakes region can be blackmailed any time collectively or individually whenever that political leadership did not tow the US government's line."

"When I reviewed the timeline of events surrounding Adamas coming to t the US, it was obvious that the US government did not know what and how it needed to start blackmailing its partners. The US government knew that the enterprise business of plundering mineral resources in Eastern DRC was growing, in sophistication, size, and money. It wanted to stop it because of the negative aspects of the rapidly growing number of dead people mounting into a de facto genocide of more than ten million people now. The US government would do anything not to be associated with this gruesome fiasco. The US government kept looking for ways to accomplish this without alienating the governments in Kigali, Kinshasa, and Kampala. It was becoming more than urgent to find an answer. Sadly, and unfortunately, the execution of the blackmail mounted by the government was successfully accomplished through the prosecution I personally led in the case against Adamas Kagita,"

"I am deeply remorseful for my actions and acknowledge the seriousness of my directives when you look at how the blackmail has evolved and how it was finally and effectively registered:

Adamas Kagita was brought to US under fraudulent documents using a Ugandan identity of Jefferson Okito. The US government told its partners that Adamas Kagita was getting too dangerous for their cover against human rights violations in addition to trying to set up a parallel logistic operation to evacuate mineral resources depriving the enterprise of major revenue.

The government knew that, given his impulsive behavior, Adamas

Kagita was bound to be exposed in an environment full of his prior human rights victims in Easter DRC, State of North Carolina

Adamas Kagita was finally exposed and lost his cover Ugandan identity in the US Immigration Court, and was found criminally liable of his prior extensive human rights violations in Eastern DRC,

Adamas Kagita felt abandoned by both the US Government and his support back home, vowed to carry a revenge denunciation of his former support in exchange for reduced sentence,

Adamas's revenge denunciation started producing cracks among former mentors and support back home. Prosecution used revenge denunciation to push for legal invitation along higher up chain of command back home,

Cracks started growing among mentors in the higher up chain of command of predation. The mentors are finally forced to give up sacrificial selected lambs.

Selected invited members, specifically the high target Reverend Drago, pleaded guilty in exchange for lighter sentences or better living dispositions away from the region of Great Lakes.

In the same exchange, the US Government finally got its most coveted list of the enterprise money laundering schemes most likely to be used for blackmailing the collective political leadership partnership of the predation in Eastern DRC."

"The vetting of the list that was provided was extraordinary. The extent of hidden wealth that the top echelon of the enterprise engaged in was staggering, in more than billions of dollars, in less than fifteen years, spread over thirty to fifty relatives in each of the three cases, in hundred offshore banking facilities of the world.

The US Government thanked Reverend Drago for providing the listing it needed to engage in permanent blackmail of the entire predation top echelon. Reverend Drago was awarded with access to Federal Witness Security Program. The lowly Adamas Kagita paid for his exposing Reverend Drago with a lesser sentence of fifteen years."

"The highest echelon members of the predation "Enterprise" in Eastern DRC, including the political leaderships in Kinshasa, Kigali, and Kampala, were never brought to Justice to account for the criminal atrocities they have perpetrated for more than twenty years in the area.

The ultimate worldwide corporate beneficiaries of the predation were never called to answer for the predation crimes that they have driven.

The Eastern DRC hidden genocide body count continues to climb.

My sincere apologies to Charlotte Keregi, My sincere apologies to the people of the Eastern DRC,,

My sincere apologies to the Prosecution Team Members.

Counsel Timothy O'Grady"